Advanced Strategic Management

A Multi-perspective Approach

Second Edition

Mark Jenkins
and
Véronique Ambrosini
with
Nardine Collier

First published 2007 by
PALGRAVE MACMILLAN
Houndmills, Basingstoke, Hampshire RG21 6XS and
175 Fifth Avenue, New York, N.Y. 10010
Companies and representatives throughout the world

PALGRAVE MACMILLAN is the global academic imprint of the Palgrave Macmillan division of St. Martin's Press, LLC and of Palgrave Macmillan Ltd. Macmillan® is a registered trademark in the United States, United Kingdom and other countries. Palgrave is a registered trademark in the European Union and other countries.

ISBN-13: 978–1–4039–8592–7 paperback
ISBN-10: 1–4039–8592–8 paperback

This book is printed on paper suitable for recycling and made from fully managed and sustained forest sources. Logging, pulping and manufacturing processes are expected to conform to the environmental regulations of the country of origin.

A catalogue record for this book is available from the British Library.

A catalog record for this book is available from the Library of Congress.

10   9   8   7   6   5   4   3   2
16   15   14   13   12   11   10   09   08

Printed in China

Contents

Part IV   Emerging and Integrating Perspectives

List of Figures and Tables

Figures

Tables

Foreword: Theoretical Pluralism and Multi-disciplinary Traditions

Howard Thomas

Introduction

The field of strategic management has advanced substantially in the past 40 years. From its beginnings as a capstone course in the business school curriculum and an applied area providing practical insights to strategic executives, the field has progressed significantly. There has also been a tremendous surge of research over the last 25 years and a substantial academic output as evidenced by the rapid growth of both the Strategic Management Society and, particularly, the Strategic Management Journal.[1]

Strategic management (Bowman, 1974) has three elements: its roots in practice, its methodology and its theoretical underpinnings. For academics working in this field, practice is typically captured in cases and business histories. The methodology, or applications, of strategic management is elaborated in the implementation of planning systems and associated tools for strategic analysis, and in the process of strategic decision-making. Theoretical roots come primarily from economics and/or the social and behavioural sciences. Indeed, it is quite clear that the growth of the strategy field has reflected a tradition of theoretical pluralism (Bowman, 1990) in its adoption of concepts from economics and the behavioural sciences, and the evolution of those concepts in strategic management terms is in parallel with the changing historical environmental conditions over the last 40 years. However, Bettis (1991) points out that research in strategic management has, so far, failed to produce enough useful results for managers to exploit. Thus, although the field has advanced, there are gaps between academic perspectives and practical guidelines, which provide a challenge for the field's future development.

The book reviews the main academic perspectives and lenses that have been evident in the field and illustrates them through a focused examination of research on competitive strategy, an area of my own expertise, from a multi-lectic perspective. It concludes by stressing the importance of theoretical pluralism and critical thinking to the future intellectual development of the strategy field.

Academic lenses in strategy

Following Bowman et al. (2002), we note that the field of strategy, as viewed from a historical perspective in the academic world, has nurtured at least three types of academics in the past few decades. While all three co-exist and thrive today, their relative significance and importance has changed.

The first set of strategy scholars can be described as field researchers, the institutionalists, whose influence was paramount in the middle 1960s and early 1970s. Though they varied in their approaches, they focused on a rich description of the elements of strategy and the strategy process from a top manager's perspective, both from within the firm and looking out at the environment. They supplied rich descriptions of strategy-related issues. They offered cases, histories and planning systems. These contributions were exemplified by authors like Chandler (1962), who provided a disciplinary base for studying the modern corporation exemplified by authors such as Mintzberg (1978) and Rumelt (1974, 1982).

A second influence came from economists in the late 1970s and 1980s, most notably by Porter (1980) in his seminal book on competitive strategy. Industrial organisation economics was the background on which they drew to analyse the problems of the firm but, especially, the industries in which they existed. A later generation of economists, whose interest in strategy has increased, are game theorists who have examined issues that surface in the competitive environment associated with industry competition and competitive rivalry (Dixit and Nalebuff, 1991; Saloner, 1991); evolutionary economists such as Nelson and Winter (1982) who have linked economics with organisational theory and resource-based theorists (Penrose, 1959; Wernerfelt, 1984; Barney, 1992) who examine the processes of building unique resources in competitive environments.

The third set of influences came from behavioural scientists, and gained increased momentum in the 1980s and the 1990s. These include the organisation psychologists, political scientists, sociologists (Granovetter, 1985; Scott, 1985; Burt, 1997), population ecologists (Hannan and Freeman, 1977, 1989) and cognitive scientists (Tversky and Kahnemann, 1986; Porac and Thomas, 1990). Their work has dealt with a broader spectrum, from the individual to firm, to the industry, to the population of industries. They focus not on the optimisation and equilibrium of the economists, but on the functioning and survival of the organisation and the behaviour of its people, and the intra- and inter-organisational networks they adopt. Cooperative networks, as distinct from competitive markets, start to inform this analysis.

It is clear that the relative impact of these three groups: Institutionalists, economists and behaviouralists has followed a historical progression; yet, over time, the views of these different groups have become much more integrated. In the following section, I use these multiple perspectives to show how competitive strategy research has evolved over the last 30 years.

The evolution of competitive strategy research

Over the past 30 years, one basic question which has occupied the attention of both strategy researchers and practitioners alike is 'With whom, and how, do firms compete and how do they sustain their competitive advantage over time?' The question of who competes with whom and how firms compete has been addressed from several different theoretical perspectives. How these perspectives are integrated and moulded to develop a multi-dimensional theoretical framework for understanding basic issues of competition and rivalry is important for the field of strategy. Economic, cognitive and social forces can all influence the ways firms define competitors, the strategies adopted by those firms in pursuing their interests and the outcomes of both their contests and collaborations.

Beginning with the earliest theories regarding spatial competition, competitive strategy research (McGee et al., 2005) gained its early inspiration largely from the literature on industrial organisational (I-O) economics (Bain, 1956) and from Porter's (1980) industry analysis, which questioned how the structural characteristics of industries constrain the strategies of firms competing in those industries. McGee and Thomas (1986) then examined how the economic characteristics of firms within an industry have been used to place firms within strategic groups. Drawing from the literature on managerial cognition, other researchers (Porac et al., 1989; Reger and Huff, 1993) have attempted to identify cognitive communities (akin to strategic groups) within an industry based upon the shared mental models and 'maps' that executives use to evaluate their environment and identify their rivals, as well as the dimensions along which they compete. As research has evolved, the methods and perspectives of social network analysis have also been used to examine issues of both inter-organisational rivalry and cooperation within industries. And, the more recent literature on the resource-based view of the firm (Penrose, 1959; Wernerfelt, 1984) and competence-based competition (Prahalad and Hamel, 1990) can provide a basis for integration of the economic, cognitive and social approaches to competition.

Notions of competitive space are discussed within competence-based competition. In their book *Competing for the Future*, Hamel and Prahalad (1994) suggest that, rather than behaving reactively by identifying how to compete within their existing competitive space, those firms which will be most successful in the future will strive, not only to reshape their existing competitive space, but to create new competitive spaces for themselves as well. The resource-based view encompasses elements of both the strategic groups and the management cognition literature. The resource configurations identified by strategic group researchers interact with the cognitive recipes or mental models which managers possess to shape the ways in which growth strategies are developed and implemented. Each can influence the other, and the degree to which management correctly identifies and leverages its resources impacts the firm's potential for developing a sustained competitive advantage. Firms do not develop these cognitive recipes (Spender, 1989) in isolation, however. As Porac et al. (1995), have shown, networks of relationships among competitors can help shape individual mental models and develop stable, commonly shared beliefs regarding firm capabilities and patterns of competition within an industry. Powell et al. (1996) have demonstrated that networks can be used for cooperative as well as competitive purposes, and that networks of relationships can be used to develop and leverage a firm's core competences. Further, the ability to develop and manage network relationships can be a core competence in itself.

The resource-based view and competence-based competition, thus, possess a number of qualities that can be used to direct competitive strategy research in the future. First, this theoretical perspective places substantial emphasis on performance, specifically the ability to develop and maintain sustainable competitive advantage. Questions regarding why some firms outperform others are the province of strategy researchers alone.

Second, this perspective is dynamic rather than static in nature. Much of the past research in strategy has attempted to answer the question 'What do firms do?' A more useful question is 'How do firms do what they do?'. The dynamic systems and routines through which competences or resources are developed and leveraged are then considered explicitly, rather than just assumed to occur.

Third, this perspective encourages a focus upon longitudinal evaluations of strategic activity. The temporal and path-dependent nature of longitudinal process examinations (Pettigrew, 1990) is significant in developing a greater understanding of firm strategy development and should be included in future research.

Finally, this perspective is process-, not just outcome-, oriented. Resources alone are not the key. The implementation of strategy is integral to the understanding of strategy itself; the two cannot be separated. Studying assets alone is not useful because tangible assets themselves become relatively insignificant in comparison to the ways in which they are deployed.

In summary, attempting to answer the question 'With whom and how do firms compete and how do they sustain their advantage?' has been at the centre of much of my research over the last 20 years. What started out as an analytical exercise has evolved into a much richer examination of competitive strategy from cognitive (CEO), firm (resource-based views), strategic group/cognitive community and industry perspectives. The insights have been much greater and the advice available to managers much more grounded and significant.

Conclusion

Theories from a number of disciplines (economics, sociology, psychology) have been used to understand phenomena in strategic management research. Each perspective provides a unique set of theoretical insights but there has not been sufficient success in putting the pieces of the puzzle together. The strategic management field can be conceptualised as one centred on problems relating to the creation and sustainability of competitive advantage, or the pursuit of rents. This problem-oriented approach has served the field well, but it has been important to bring in influences from multiple disciplines to address interesting research questions related to the creation of competitive advantage.

Indeed, many process-oriented pieces of research, on the process of strategy formation and on strategic decision-making, have also added richness to an understanding of how competitive strategy is developed.

While pluralism is a strength of the field, it has also generated some concerns, mostly about the lack of existence of a single unifying paradigm. The costs can often be a lack of rigour in research that is an application of theories and techniques developed in adjacent fields. Some of this concern is well-founded, although there have been some very thoughtful approaches recommended to deal with these concerns, namely that work done in the field should meet the highest standards of related disciplines (Camerer, 1991; Saloner, 1991). However, given the eclecticism of the field and its roots in multiple disciplines, a unifying paradigm is unlikely to emerge.

Early research in strategic management moved from field-based institutional research with little theory to research that drew rather heavily upon economics with an emphasis on high levels of rationality of decision-makers. More recently, with the rise of interest in firm-level capabilities and on the knowledge-based view of the firm, there has been an increase in the behavioural component of the field, with decision-making criteria based upon bounded rationality. Clearly, the next steps in research will develop insights from the tensions between these different views of decision-making, bridge complementary traditions and combine the best of each of these to provide academic insights and practical guidelines for managers. The process of looking for bridges across complementary research traditions, coupled with the increasing visibility and popularity of behavioural perspectives, has re-balanced the field from its earlier dependence on economics as a basis for theorising about firms, markets and performance.

Finally, the need for mapping and bridging multi-perspectives in the field must be enhanced by continued critical reflection of the type pioneered by Mintzberg (1978, 1990, 1994) in his sustained and effective critique of, and attack on, the view of strategy-making as intendedly rational thought. He argued that the process of strategising was not a rational, analytic, international process but, rather, an emergent process – a pattern in a series of decisions and actions. Mintzberg's critical contribution provided the impetus for the establishment of the field of strategy process research alongside analytical frameworks and de-emphasised the field's focus on the planning mode and the rational analytic view of strategy advanced by *inter alia* Ansoff (1965).

Postscript

Thanks are due to many colleagues including Avi Fiegenbaum, Taieb Hafsi, John McGee, Henry Mintzberg, Joe Porac, Andrew Pettigrew, Dan Schendel and David Wilson for conversations about this topic.

I commend the efforts of Véronique Ambrosini and Mark Jenkins in promoting both the field's multiple perspectives and a 1980 serious, and critical, mapping of the field's development.

Note

1. According to Hafsi and Thomas (2005), the *Strategic Management Journal's* list of topics for the 1990s shows a wide range of topics covered by many different authors. A closer look shows that the field is spread over all the traditional functions and disciplines. The field of economics alone represents the bulk of the disciplinary articles.

References

Ansoff, H. I., *Corporate Strategy: An Analytic Approach to Business Policy for Growth and Expansion* (New York: McGraw-Hill, 1965).

Bain, J. S., *Barriers to New Competition* (New York: John Wiley, 1956).

Barney, J. B., 'Firm Resources and Sustained Competitive Advantage', *Journal of Management*, 17, 1 (1992) 99–120.

Bettis, R. A., 'Strategic Management and the Straitjacket: An Editorial Essay', *Organisation Science*, 2, 3 (1991) 315–319.

Bowman, E. H., 'Epistemology, Corporate Strategy and Academe', *Sloan Management Review*, 5, 2 (1974) 35–50.

Bowman, E. H., 'Strategy Changes: Possible Worlds and Actual Minds'. In J. W. Frederickson (ed.) *Perspectives in Strategic Management* (New York: Harper and Row, 1990), pp. 9–37.

Bowman, E. H., H. Singh and H. Thomas, 'The Domain of Strategic Management: History and Evolution'. In A. Pettigrew, H. Thomas and R. Whittington (eds) *Handbook of Strategy and Management* (London: Sage, 2002), pp. 31–51.

Burt, R. S., 'The Contingent Value of Social Capital', *Administrative Science Quarterly*, 42, 2 (1997) 339–365.

Camerer, C., 'Does Strategy Research Need Game Theory', *Strategic Management Journal*, Special Issue, 12 (1991) 137–152.

Chandler, A. D., *Strategy and Structure: Chapters in the History of the American Industrial Enterprise* (Cambridge, MA: MIT Press, 1962).

Dixit, A. and B. J. Nalebuff, *Thinking Strategically: The Competitive Edge in Business, Politics and Everyday Life* (New York; London: Norton, 1991).

Granovetter, M., 'Economic Action and Social Structure: The Problem of Embeddedness', *American Journal of Sociology*, 91 (1985) 481–510.

Hafsi, T. and H. Thomas, 'The Field of Strategy: In Search of a Walking Stick', *European Management Journal*, 23, 5 (2005) 507–519.

Hamel, G. and C. K. Prahalad, *Competing for the Future* (Boston, MA: HBS Press, 1994).

Hannan, M. T. and J. H. Freeman, 'The Population Ecology of Organisations', *American Journal of Sociology*, 85, 5 (1977) 929–964.

Hannan, M. T. and J. H. Freeman, *Organisational Ecology* (Boston, MA: Harvard University Press, 1989).

McGee, J. and H. Thomas, 'Strategic Groups: Theory, Research and Taxonomy', *Strategic Management Journal*, 72 (1986) 141–160.

McGee, J., H. Thomas and D. Wilson, *Strategy: Analysis and Practice* (Maidenhead and New York: McGraw-Hill, 2005).

Mintzberg, H., 'Patterns in Strategy Formation', *Management Science*, 24 (1978) 934–948.

Mintzberg, H., 'The Design School: Reconsidering the Basic Premise of Strategic Management', *Strategic Management Journal*, 11 (1990) 171–196.

Mintzberg, H., *The Rise and Fall of Strategic Planning* (New York: Free Press, 1994).

Nelson, R. R. and S. G. Winter, *An Evolutionary Theory of Economic Change* (Cambridge, MA: Prentice Hall, 1982).

Penrose, E. T., *A Theory of the Growth of the Firm* (New York: Blackwell, 1959).

Pettigrew, A. M., 'Longitudinal Field Research on Change – Theory and Practice', *Organisation Science*, 1, 3 (1990) 267–292.

Porac, J. and H. Thomas, 'Taxonomic Mental Models in Competitor Definition', *Academy of Management Review*, 15, 2 (1990) 224–240.

Porac, J., H. Thomas and C. Baden-Fuller, 'Competitive Groups as Cognitive Communities: The Case of Scottish Knitwear Manufacturers', *Journal of Management Studies*, 26, 4 (1989) 397–416.

Porac, J., H. Thomas, F. Wilson, D. Paton and A. Kanfer, 'Rivalry and the Industry Model of Scottish Knitwear Producers', *Administrative Science Quarterly*, 40, 2 (1995) 203–227.

Porter, M. E., *Competitive Strategy: Techniques for Analysing Industries and Competitors* (New York: Free Press, 1980).

Powell, W. W., K. W. Koput and L. Smith-Doerr, 'Interorganizational Collaboration and the Locus of Innovation: Networks of Learning in Biotechnology', *Administrative Science Quarterly*, 31, 1 (1996) 116–145.

Prahalad, C. K. and G. Hamel, 'The Core Competence of the Corporation', *Harvard Business Review*, 68, 3 (1990) 79–91.

Reger, R. K. and A. S. Huff, 'Strategic Groups: A Cognitive Perspective', *Strategic Management Journal*, 14 (1993) 103–124.

Rumelt, R. P., *Strategy, Structure and Economic Performance* (Boston, MA: HBS Press, 1974).

Rumelt, R. P., 'Diversification Strategy and Profitability', *Strategic Management Journal*, 3, 4 (1982) 359–370.

Saloner, G., 'Modelling Game Theory and Strategy Management', *Strategic Management Journal*, Winter Special Issue, 123 (1991) 119–136.

Scott, R. W., *Institutions and Organisations* (Thousand Oaks, CA: Sage, 1985).

Spender, J. C., *Industry Recipes* (Oxford: Basil Blackwell, 1989).

Tversky, A., and D. Kahnemann, 'Rational Choice and the Framing of Decisions', *Journal of Business*, 59, 4 (1986) 251–278.

Wernerfelt, B., 'A Resource-Based View of the Firm', *Strategic Management Journal*, 5 (1984) 171–180.

Acknowledgements

We would like to acknowledge the contribution of a number of individuals that have supported us throughout this project. First of all, we would like to express our gratitude to Professor Cliff Bowman for his invaluable input in the early stages of this book. We would also like to thank all the authors for their cooperation, hard work and patience. Thanks are also due to the Directorate of Performance and Analysis at MoD for permissions for the figures in Chapter 8. Finally we are indebted to Margaret Hamer for all her efforts in helping us complete this volume.

Notes on Contributors

Peter Allen is Head of the Complex Systems Management Centre, which is involved in a wide range of research projects including working with the DTI and EABIS. Allen has also co-ordinated the ESRC priority network 'NEXSUS' over the past 5 years. He has a PhD in Theoretical Physics, was a Royal Society European Research Fellow 1969–1971 and Senior Research Fellow at the Universite Libre de Bruxelles from 1972 to 1987, where he worked with Nobel Prizewinner Ilya Prigogine. Since 1987 he has run two Research Centres at Cranfield University. For almost 30 years Professor Allen has been working on the mathematical modelling of change and innovation in social, economic, financial and ecological systems, and the development of integrated systems models linking the physical, ecological and socio-economic aspects of complex systems as a basis for improved decision support systems. Professor Allen has written and edited several books and published over 200 articles and has been a consultant to many organisations. He is Editor-in-Chief of the journal *Emergence: Complexity and Organization* (E:CO) and Director and Co-Founder of The Complexity Society.

José Luis Álvarez is Professor of Strategy Implementation at Instituto de Empresa Business School in Madrid and Visiting Professor at INSEAD, France. He has also been Visiting Professor at the Harvard Business School, where he got his PhD in Organizational Behaviour. His research interests centre around the political and social roles of top executives in complex organisations. Álvarez has published his work in journals such as *Organization Studies*, *Organisations* and *Corporate Governance*, and he has also written several books on Corporate Governance and the role of top executives, the latest (co-authored) being *Sharing Executive Power: Roles and Relationships at the Top* (2005).

Véronique Ambrosini is Senior Lecturer in Strategic Management at Cranfield School of Management. Véronique joined Cranfield in April 1994, prior to which she was an assistant manager working for McDonald's Restaurants. Her research is conducted essentially within the resource-based and dynamic capability view of the firm and the strategy-as-practice perspective. Véronique has had articles published in *Management Learning*, *Journal of Management Studies*, *British Journal of Management*, *European Management Journal* and the *Journal of General Management*. She is the author of *Tacit and Ambiguous Resources as Sources of Competitive Advantage* (2003). She is also co-editor of *Strategic Management: Multiple Perspectives* (2002) and *Exploring Techniques of Analysis and Evaluation in Strategic Management* (1998).

Duncan Angwin is Associate Professor in Strategic Management at Warwick Business School, University of Warwick. After graduating from Cambridge University, he spent 8 years in the City of London where he held a number of senior corporate finance positions in Merchant and Investment Banks. Duncan now holds Senior Visiting Appointments at leading Universities including Saïd Business School, Oxford; Georgetown University, United States; Ecole Nationale des Pont et Chaussees, Paris, France; Ecole Hassania Casablanca, Morocco.

Duncan is the author of many articles in leading academic journals, including the *Academy of Management Executive*, *European Management Journal*, *Journal of World Business*, *Long Range Planning*, and *Organization Studies*. He has also published widely in practitioner journals and national newspapers. He has authored with the *Financial Times* 'Implementing Successful Post Acquistion Integration' (2000), and published *The Strategy Pathfinder* (2006) with Stephen Cummings and Chris Smith. His latest work *Mergers and Acquisitions* is to be launched in June 2007.

Duncan's primary area of research is strategy-as-practice as an approach to mergers and acquisitions. He is currently Chair of the strategy and practice track at the Strategic Management Society.

Julia Balogun is Professor of Strategic Management at the Cass Business School, City University, London. Her research interests include strategy development and strategic change, with a focus on the managerial practice of strategy, and managerial sensemaking. In particular her research to date has focussed on how strategic activity is initiated and championed at multiple levels within organisations. Her current research is more concerned with investigating strategising as a distributed organisational activity, through a focus on activities such as strategic planning, strategic change and organisational restructuring. Julia has published in the *Academy of Management Journal, Organisation Studies, British Journal of Management* and *Journal of Management Studies*. She also seeks in inform practice through practitioner book and publications in journals such as *Long Range Planning*.

Suzanne M. Behr is Director of Engineering at Geophysical Research Company. She has undergraduate degrees in maths and chemistry, a master's degree in engineering and an MBA. Suzanne has over 20 years of engineering and management experience in the oil and gas and telecommunications industries. She holds several patents and has published articles in the engineering field. She has also successfully published in the management literature and co-authored a paper that was presented at the Strategic Management Society in 2005.

Jean Boulton is Visiting Fellow with the Complex Systems Management Centre at Cranfield School of Management; she is responsible for the MBA teaching of complexity thinking as applied to strategy and organisation development. She is also Managing Director of Claremont Management Consultants Ltd, established in 1994 (see www.embracingcomplexity.co.uk). Prior to that she was Practice Director of Organisation Change with Hay Management Consultants and prior to that Head of Engineering Operations with British Aerospace Regional Aircraft Ltd, responsible for 1,000 professional engineers. She has a PhD in quantum physics from the University of Cambridge, a first degree in physics from the University of Oxford and an MBA from Cranfield. She is Chair of Social Action for Health, a charity based in the East End of London and also a non-executive director for the Institute of Physics publishing company. She lectures on complexity in a range of settings including the University of Bath's MSc in Responsibility and Business Practice.

Nardine Collier is Research Officer in Strategic Management at Cranfield School of Management. In 2005 she was awarded a Master of Philosophy for her research on 'Clusters and the process and nature of innovation.' She has published an article in *International Journal of Management Reviews*, 'A contingency approach to resource-creation processes', with C. Bowman (2006) (4: 191–211), and a case study on Marks and Spencer in *Exploring Corporate Strategy* (G. Johnson, K. Scholes and R. Whittington) (2007).

Mahmoud Ezzamel is Cardiff Professorial Fellow, University of Cardiff, having held academic positions at the University of Manchester, UMIST, University of Wales (Aberystwyth), Southampton University and Queen's University (Canada). He has researched into the design and use of management accounting systems in organisations; contextualising the emergence and functioning of accounting practice; the statistical properties of accounting numbers and their predictive ability; the structure of the market for audit services; accounting and accountability in the public sector; corporate governance; accounting history; and the relationship between political ideology, accounting regulation and discourse analysis. He has published in many top journals including *Abacus, Accounting, Auditing and Accountability Journal (AAAJ), Academy of Management Journal, Accounting and Business Research, Accounting Historians Journal, Accounting, Organizations and Society, Administrative Science Quarterly, Critical Perspectives on Accounting, Journal of Business Finance and*

Accounting, Journal of management Studies, Organisational Studies and *Organization*. He has served as the Joint Editor of *ABR*, Associate Editor of the *International Journal of Management Reviews* and Member of the Editorial Board of *JBFA, AAAJ, Accounting and Finance, Financial Accountability and Management, Accounting, Accountability and Performance, International Journal of Accounting, The Review of Accounting and Finance* and *Organization*.

Royston Greenwood is Telus Chair of Strategic Management and the Associate Dean (Research) at the School of Business, University of Alberta. His research interests focus upon institutions, the professions and organisational change. Some of his works have appeared in the *Administrative Science Quarterly, the Academy of Management Journal, Strategic Management Journal, Organization Science* and *Organization Studies*. Much of this work examines changes in the institutional and professional context of professional service firms such as accounting and law firms. He serves on the editorial boards of *Academy of Management Journal, Organization Science, Organization Studies* and the *Journal of Management Studies*, and is a founding co-editor of *Strategic Organization*.

Gerard P. Hodgkinson is Professor of Organizational Behaviour and Strategic Management at Leeds University Business School, United Kingdom. He has authored or co-authored over 50 scholarly articles and chapters in edited volumes and two books. In recent years, his work on the psychology of strategic management and managerial and organisational cognition has been taken forward through the award of a senior fellowship of Advanced Institute of Management (AIM) Research, and will continue through the newly launched Centre for Organizational Strategy, Learning and Change (which he is the Director of) at the University of Leeds. From 1999 to 2006 he was the Editor-in-Chief of the *British Journal of Management* and currently serves on the Editorial Boards of the *Academy of Management Review, Journal of Organizational Behavior, Journal of Occupational and Organizational Psychology* and *Organization Science*. With J. Kevin Ford, he co-edits the *International Review of Industrial and Organizational Psychology*, and with W. H. Starbuck, he is co-editing the *Oxford Handbook of Organizational Decision Making*. A practising chartered occupational psychologist, he has conducted numerous consultancy assignments for leading organisations.

Sylvie Jackson joined Cranfield University as Senior Lecturer at the Defence Academy of the United Kingdom in 1999 after a period of consultancy work and a lengthy career in The Post Office where she started as a counter clerk and rose to Quality and Business Process Director for Purchasing and Logistics. Other roles included training counter clerks, sales, customer care and total quality management. Her qualifications include a PhD in Transformational Change, MBA and Postgraduate Diplomas in both Management Studies and Marketing, all achieved whilst working full-time. She has a range of publications which include journal articles and chapters in books and has spoken at more than fifty conferences. She has undertaken consultancy work with various departments in the MoD and with GCHQ. Sylvie teaches on a range of Master's Degrees and short courses and has developed a number of successful short courses.

Paula Jarzabkowski is Reader in Strategic Management at Aston Business School and an AIM Ghoshal Fellow. She teaches courses in strategic management and strategy as practice at undergraduate and postgraduate levels. Her research interests focus on the dynamics of strategising as a social practice, particularly in pluralistic contexts such as public sector organisations and regulated firms. She has published several refereed articles on this topic and in 2005 she published the first book in this field, *Strategy as Practice: An Activity-Based Approach*, with Sage. She also co-hosts the website www.strategy-as-practice.org, which has over 2,000 academic and practitioner members worldwide.

Mark Jenkins is Professor of Business Strategy and Director of Graduate Programmes at Cranfield School of Management. Prior to joining Cranfield he held positions at Nottingham University Business

School, Massey Ferguson Ltd and the Lex Service Group. His teaching and consulting activities focus on the areas of competitive strategy, knowledge management and innovation. He is the author of a number of books on strategic management issues, has published numerous journal articles and is on the editorial boards of *British Journal of Management*, *Long Range Planning*, *Organization Studies* and the *Journal of Management Studies*. He is currently researching the role of knowledge and innovation in the development of Formula 1 motorsport.

Gerry Johnson is the Sir Roland Smith Professor of Strategic Management at the University of Lancaster. He received a BA in Social and Physical Anthropology from University College London and his PhD from Aston University. He has worked as a marketing executive, as a management consultant and as an academic at Aston University, Manchester Business School, Cranfield School of Management and Strathclyde University Graduate School of Business. He was also Senior Fellow of the UK Advanced Institute of Management Research from 2003 to 2007.

His research interests are in the field of strategic management practice, in particular with processes of strategy development and change in organisations. He has published in the *Academy of Management Review*, the *Academy of Management Journal*, the *Journal of Management Studies*, the *Strategic Management Journal*, *Organization Studies*, the *British Journal of Management* and *Human Relations*. He serves on the editorial boards of the *Strategic Management Journal* and the *Journal of Management Studies*. He is also co-author of Europe's best-selling strategic management text *Exploring Corporate Strategy* (Prentice Hall).

Andy Lockett is Associate Professor and Reader in Strategy at Nottingham University Business School, United Kingdom. His primary research interests straddle the areas of technology, strategy and entrepreneurship. His research on these topics has been published in journals including *Journal of Management*, *Journal of Management Studies*, *Journal of Management Inquiry*, *Long Range Planning*, *Human Relations*, *Research Policy*, *Journal of Business Venturing*, *Entrepreneurship Theory and Practice*, *Managerial and Decision Economics*, *OMEGA* and *Small Business Economics*. He is on the editorial boards of the *Journal of Management Studies* and the *Journal of Technology Transfer*.

Stephen Regan is Lecturer in Managerial Economics at Cranfield School of Management. Prior to joining Cranfield he was Senior Lecturer in Economics at Anglia Polytechnic University and Visiting Lecturer at Birmingham University. His research interests are in the interaction between firm behaviour and regulation. He acts as a consultant in the public sector and in privatised utilities. He has published mostly in the area of international business and public policy. Stephen has a BA and an MBA from Warwick University.

Séan Rickard is a Senior Lecturer in Managerial Economics at Cranfield School of Management. He studied economics at the London School of Economics and Birkbeck College, London, and has an MBA from Cranfield School of Management. Prior to joining the Economics Group at Cranfield in 1994 he worked as a business economist and from 1987 was Chief Economist with the National Farmers' Union, Europe's largest trade association. As Chief Economist and Head of the NFU's European and Economics Department, Séan directed research into – and commented publicly on – a wide range of issues relating to the agricultural and food industries in the United Kingdom and the European Union. Séan has been a member of a number of prominent UK and EU committees and working parties, including the influential CBI's Economic Trends Committee.

Since joining Cranfield he has been a member of the Minister of Agriculture's Think Tank on future agricultural and rural policy and an employers' representative on the Agricultural Wages Board and wrote the present government's agricultural manifesto and is currently an academic adviser to the government. Sean appears regularly on radio and television and is a consultant to many organisations.

David Seidl is Assistant Professor of Organization and Strategy at the University of Munich. He studied Management and Sociology in Munich, London and Witten/Herdecke. He earned his PhD at the University of Cambridge. His current research focuses on sociological approaches to strategy and change. He is coordinator of the EGOS standing working group on 'Strategizing: Activity and Practice' and is guest editor of a special issue of *Human Relations* on 'Strategizing: The Challenges of a Practice Perspective' (both together with Julia Balogun and Paula Jarzabkowski) – see also www.strategy-as-practice.org. He has published in the *Journal of Management Studies, Organization* and *Human Relations*, and has (co-) produced three books, including *Niklas Luhmann and Organization Studies* (2005) and *Organizational Identity and Self-Transformation: An Autopoietic Perspective* (2005).

J. C. Spender served in experimental submarines in the Royal Navy, then studied engineering at Oxford (Balliol), worked as a nuclear submarine reactor engineer with Rolls-Royce & Associates, as a sales manager with IBM (United Kingdom), a consultant with Decision Technology International (Boston), a merchant banker with Slater-Walker Securities. His PhD thesis (Manchester Business School) won the Academy of Management's 1980 A. T. Kearney PhD Research Prize, later published as *Industry Recipes* (Blackwell, 1989). Served on the faculty at City University (London), York University (Toronto), UCLA and Rutgers. He became Dean of the School of Business and Technology at SUNY/FIT before retiring in 2003. Now researching, writing, and lecturing widely on knowledge management in United States, Canada and Europe, with Visiting Professor appointments at Cranfield, Leeds and Open Universities.

Silviya Svejenova holds a PhD in Management from IESE Business School, Spain. She taught Strategy across the MBA and Executive programmes, and Organization Theory across the PhD and DBA programmes of the Cranfield School of Management (United Kingdom). She has been a Research Associate of the Department of General Management at IESE, a lecturer in Strategy at ESCI-UPF and Assistant Professor in Management at Varna University of Economics (Bulgaria). She has been involved in management development assignments for organisations in the United Kingdom, Germany and Spain.

Her research has addressed issues of relationship management (from social networks to interorganisational arrangements), the career and work of top managers, and the role they play in the transformation and internationalisation of their companies. Her work has been presented at prestigious international conferences and published in books and journal articles. Silviya is a board member of EGOS (the European Group for Organizational Studies) and a co-chair (since 2001) of the Creative Industries' track at the EGOS Colloquia.

Stephen Tallman is the E. Claiborne Robins Distinguished Professor in Business at the University of Richmond's Robins School of Business. Tallman came to the university this year from the University of Utah where he was David Eccles Professor of Management and chair of the management and marketing department. He is a graduate of the US Military Academy at West Point and served as an officer in the US army for 6 years. He earned his PhD from UCLA in 1988 in international business and comparative management with a concentration in strategic management. Tallman has published numerous journal articles and chapters in several books and conference volumes. He is co-author of two books on alliance and joint venture strategies. He served as Chair of the International Management Division of the Academy of Management and Chair of the Global Strategy Interest Group of the Strategic Management Society. In 1999 he was named a Western Academy of Management Ascendant Scholar.

His current primary research interests include globalisation strategies, capabilities-based strategy, international diversification strategies, industry clusters and issues surrounding international business alliances and joint ventures.

Howard Thomas holds a BSc (London), MSc (London), MBA (Chicago), PhD (Edinburgh). He is Dean of Warwick Business School & Professor of Strategic Management. Howard has authored over 30 books and 200 articles in competitive strategy, risk analysis, strategic change, international management and strategic decision-making. From 1991 to 2000 he was Dean of the College of Commerce and Business Administration and James F. Towey Distinguished Professor of Strategic Management at the University of Illinois at Urbana-Champaign. Prior to this he held posts as Foundation Professor of Management at the Australian Graduate School of Management, Director of the Doctoral Programme at London Business School, and visiting and permanent posts at institutions such as the European Institute of Advanced Studies of Management in Brussels, the University of Southern California, the University of British Columbia, the Sloan School of Management, MIT and Kellogg School, Northwestern University. He is past President of the US Strategic Management Society, past Chair of the Board of the Graduate Management Admissions Council, a member of Beta Gamma Sigma, Fellow of the Academy of Management in both the United States and the United Kingdom, Fellow of the Strategic Management Society and the Sunningdale Institute of the Cabinet Office, Vice-President of EFMD and a board member of GFME, EFMD, ABS and State Farm Bank.

Steve Thompson has a BSc (Hull), an MA (Newcastle), a PhD (Newcastle) and a DPA. He is Professor of Strategic Management at the University of Nottingham. His research Interests include quantitative studies of merger activity, executive remuneration, firm performance and competition, and pricing in high-tech industries.

Margaret A. White is Associate Professor of Management at Oklahoma State University. She has a BS in mathematics and an MBA from Sam Houston State University and a PhD in management from Texas A&M University. She has been presented or published over 60 papers including articles in *Strategic Management Journal*, *Academy of Management Journal*, *Academy of Management Review* and *Organization Studies*, to name a few. Her primary research interests include organisational transformation processes and strategic management. She is the co-author (with Garry D. Bruton) of the book *The Management of Technology and Innovation: A Strategic Approach*.

Hugh Willmott is Research Professor, Cardiff Business School. He has previously held professorial appointments at the Universities of Cambridge and Manchester and visiting appointments at the Universities of Copenhagen, Lund and Cranfield. He has published 20 books including *Making Quality Critical*, *The Re-engineering Revolution*, *Managing Knowledge*, *Management Lives*, *Studying Management Critically*, *Fragmenting Work* and the textbook *Organizational Behaviour and Management*. He has a strong interest in the application of poststructuralist thinking, especially the work of Ernesto Laclau, to the field of management and business. He has published widely in social science and management journals, including *Academy of Management Review*, *Administrative Science Quarterly*, *Journal of Management Studies*, *Organization*, *Organization Studies* and *Organization Science*, and is currently a member of the editorial boards of the *Academy of Management Review*, *Organization Studies* and *Journal of Management Studies*. Further details can be found on his homepage http://dspace.dial.pipex.com/town/close/hr22/hcwhome.

CHAPTER 1

Advanced Strategic Management: Strategy as Multiple Perspectives

Mark Jenkins and Véronique Ambrosini with Nardine Collier

None of the authors of this book can claim to be dyed-in-the-wool 'strategists'; we have all arrived in this domain by following varied paths across other occupations, disciplines and functional areas. It is also fair to say that most of those who teach, research and practise strategic management have travelled through similarly eclectic paths. The variety of backgrounds to those working in the area of strategic management is indicative of a domain which is essentially driven by particular kinds of issues and problems rather than any specific doctrine. Strategy can therefore be seen not as a discipline or a function or even a tool-kit, but as an agenda: a series of fundamental questions and problems that concern organisations and their successful development. It can also be seen, as eloquently explained by Howard Thomas in the foreword of this book, as a field that has a rich history and that is constantly evolving.

Whether it be Barnard's (1938) treatise on the role of the individual executive in the strategy of the organisation, Ansoff's (1965) focus on strategic analysis for the purpose of decision-making, Mintzberg's (1994) energetic and eloquent critiques of the adoption of formal planning processes, Pettigrew's (1985) work on developing our understanding of strategic change, Eden and Ackermann's (1998) more contemporary view of strategy as a journey of organisational regeneration or Barney's (2003) proposal for an integrative framework necessary for understanding the rapidly evolving field of strategic management, they are all important contributions to the field of strategic management in that they are all concerned with addressing questions regarding the future performance of organisations.

If we define strategy as a particular kind of agenda then the imperative is to address these questions and problems by whatever means we have at our disposal. Organisations are some of the most complex phenomena studied in social sciences, while it may be convenient for academics to see strategy from unitary perspectives for the purposes of conducting research; the complexity and difficulty of the challenge means that we have to embrace any approach which can add to our ability to refine, develop and address some of these strategic questions. It also underlines the converse issue that if we restrict ourselves to unitary perspectives then we can never adequately explore such questions.

In addition to requiring a range of perspectives, the strategy agenda is concerned with a range of levels. Strategic management is concerned with the success of the 'organisation'; in order to address this, we have to consider the context or environment in which the organisation performs and the individuals whose actions help shape the performance of the organisation.

A review of organisational environment needs to consider competing firms or influential stakeholders, competing technologies or regulatory influence, all of which may impact on the nature of strategic issues. A consideration of individual organisations and how they operate deals with the ways in which resources and the know-how are combined to create performance. It is also about how distinctive such organisations are and the basis by which they are able to create advantage over others. The final level which strategic management needs to consider is the role of the individual. This role in developing, engaging and enacting strategy is central to the nature of the process. Each of these three levels interact and combine to create a dynamic set of ideas which form the basis of strategic management; neither is sufficient but each is necessary, and in our view each draws on differing perspectives in which to illuminate important aspects and qualities. The final point is that the strategy agenda requires us to move between these three levels, to understand the dynamics between them as well as exploring each level in depth. Clearly it requires a more sophisticated approach than simply applying the same lens to look at these different levels of analysis, and some emerging and alternative theories straddle and potentially integrate these levels.

In addition to recognising the importance of diverse perspectives, the need for multiple theoretical lenses and differing levels of analysis, there are also some important areas of commonality. To some extent many perspectives will cover strategic issues such as Context, Corporate, Competing, Change, Control, Competences and Culture. These are summarised in Figure 1.1. Some chapters will address many of these issues, while some will only be concerned with one or two. Each perspective offers different insights and addresses different aspects of the fundamental strategy questions.

While each chapter is unique and offers different interpretations, in what follows we briefly elaborate on how the strategy agenda is covered through the seven categories of Context, Competing, Corporate, Competences, Culture, Change and Control.

Context covers the issues concerned with an organisation's external environment: how the external environment is perceived, how it is scanned, what the organisation can do to control it and to change it. It also refers to industry and market structure, and strategic groups.

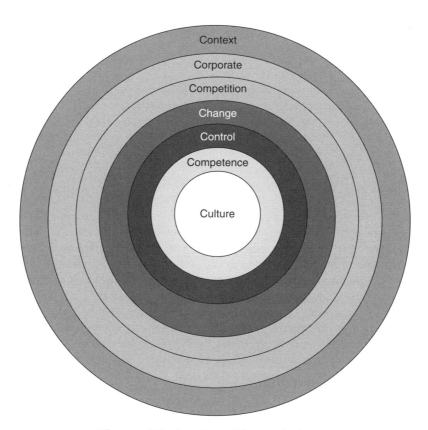

Figure 1.1 Strategy: The main issues

Competing deals with how organisations gain customers, how they identify their competitors and how they outperform them. It is also about the competitive strategies organisations can implement to achieve sustainable advantage and about co-operation and collaboration.

Corporate strategy typically addresses the multi-business context. So this heading deals with questions such as alliances, diversification, mergers, globalisation, corporate parenting, to cite just a few.

Competences deals with issues concerning the organisation's resources such as skills, know-how, organisational knowledge, routines, competences and capabilities. It deals with their role in the organisation and in generating competitive advantage. It also addresses issues such as the transferability and the immutability of resources.

Culture is about the organisation's internal environment. It includes the role of organisational culture, its importance and its influence on staff. It can also be about how culture is created or changed and how staff members perceive organisational culture.

Change concerns the types of change an organisation can implement and how change can take place or how change is constrained. It is concerned with the reasons for change, the change process and the possible outcomes of change programmes.

Control is about organisational structure, power relationships and the way managers control what is happening in their organisation. It is about the role of managers in the organisation, the extent to which managers can 'manage' what is happening inside organisations and the extent to which managers know what is happening around them.

At this stage it is worth remarking that if we consider these categories of strategic issues and apply these to six of the seminal teaching texts in the field of strategic management, we can account for most of the various chapters in this book (Table 1.1).

While these categories summarise the main issues, they are only one of many potential organising frames. As mentioned earlier, each perspective offers a distinctive view of strategic management and proposes a specific interpretation of what strategic issues are about and how they should be addressed.

Our argument therefore is that because strategic management is distinctive from other management fields in both its breadth and its complexity, it has to adopt a multiple-perspective approach in order to address the particular demands of the strategy agenda. This complexity is created by the need for questions that address different levels of analysis and different dynamics relating to organisations and their strategies. One of the real challenges in an undertaking of this kind is bringing differing and often irreconcilable perspectives together in ways which allow the reader to contrast and compare. We are therefore particularly grateful to those contributing to this book who have both endeavoured to restrict their creativity through, when possible, the use of a loose but common structure which covers the basic principles of the perspective, provides an illustrative case study designed to elaborate and illustrate the perspective, an overview of the perspective and how it links to strategy, finishing off with some reflections on the case study and a short summary. While we have this common format, the priorities of the differing perspectives often require different treatments, so there is some variability in the emphasis and even style of the different chapters. But all are intended to represent their perspective in a clear and effective manner.

We have attempted to structure the book in a way which makes it understandable and accessible to the reader. We have used, in part, the classification of the strategy literature suggested and described by Howard Thomas in his foreword. Parts I, II and III include chapters that essentially adopt an institutionalist, an economic and a behaviouralist perspective, respectively. Part IV covers emerging and integrative theories, those which have been attracting a lot of attention recently but which are yet to be considered mainstream and as a whole are not fully addressed in strategy textbooks. These theories by and large straddle many levels of analysis and offer a new perspective on the strategy issue. Naturally there are many different ways in which it could have been structured and we continue (probably at this very moment) to reflect on many more alternatives that we could have used. However, this is short of creating an interactive book in which you could design the sequence of chapters or indeed change the sequence of chapters to suit a particular agenda. We do not see these perspectives

Table 1.1 Strategic issues

	Exploring Corporate Strategy Johnson et al. (2005)	Strategic Management Hitt et al. (2005)	Strategy de Wit and Meyer (2004)	Strategic Management and Competitive Advantage Barney and Hesterly (2006)	Strategic Management Dess et al. (2005)	Contemporary Strategy Analysis Grant (2005)
Introduction to strategic management	What is strategy? Strategy context Strategic development Purpose of organisation	Strategic intent and fit Strategy development processes Purpose of organisation Mission	The nature of strategy Strategy processes Organisational purpose Synergy	What is strategy? Strategic management processes	What is strategic management? Strategic management process Organisational purpose	Strategic intent and fit
External environment	PESTEL framework, Porter's diamond Porter's five forces SWOT	External analysis, industry analysis, customer analysis Porter's five forces, strategic groups Competitor analysis	Industry context Porter's five forces	External environment, industry structure Porter's five forces	Environmental analysis, industry life cycle Porter's five forces, strategic groups SWOT	Environmental analysis, industry analysis Porter's five forces Competitive analysis
Internal environment	Resource-based view Value chain analysis	Resource-based view Value chain	Resource-based approach Value chain	Resource-based view Value chain	Resource-based view Value chain	Resource-based view Value chain

Core competences	Core competences	Core competences	Core competences	Core competences	Capabilities
Organisational knowledge	Knowledge	Learning organisation	Internal capabilities evaluation; Learning curve	Evaluation of firm performance; Identifying, evaluating and managing intellectual capital and learning, creating a learning organisation	Knowledge and learning
Cultural context	Organisational culture	Culture			Organisational culture
Leadership	Leadership	Leadership		Leadership	Modes of leadership
Types of competitive strategy	Types of competitive strategy; Strategic and tactical decisions	SBU and competitive strategy, Porter's generic strategies	Cost leadership strategies, product differentiation strategies	Porter's three generic strategies	Sources of competitive advantage, cost advantage, differentiation advantage
Game theory	Entrepreneurial strategies, innovation	Value innovation	Entrepreneurship	Entrepreneurship, managing innovation, new venture opportunities	Game theory; Innovation

Competitive strategy

Game theory

Table 1.1 Continued

	Exploring Corporate Strategy Johnson et al. (2005)	Strategic Management Hitt et al. (2005)	Strategy de Wit and Meyer (2004)	Strategic Management and Competitive Advantage Barney and Hesterly (2006)	Strategic Management Dess et al. (2005)	Contemporary Strategy Analysis Grant (2005)
Corporate strategy	Merger and acquisition, alliances, diversification International strategies Corporate governance	Merger and acquisition, strategic alliances, diversification International strategies Corporate governance Ethics Stakeholders	Corporate strategy, business portfolio, alliances International context Governance Stakeholders	Merger and acquisition, strategic alliances, vertical integration, diversification	Alliances and joint ventures, vertical integration, diversification International strategies Corporate governance Ethics	Diversification, managing diversified multi-business organisations Strategy in global industry
Others	Managing strategic change Structure Organisational configuration	Organisational structure Control	Kaizen Paths to change Control Networks	Organising structure	Structure and structure for global markets Strategic control E-business strategies	

as exhaustive, but indicative and hopefully reasonably complete. We are sure that there are many more contributions which could be included in a text on multiple perspectives on strategy, but this is our position at this point; we are sure that in potential future editions we will be able to introduce further perspectives to add to the breadth of this area.

This is not a book that can only be read from cover to cover in the sequence laid out. There are several ways of using it. The most straightforward approach is to use it as a source for understanding a particular perspective on strategy, but there are other routes around the material. You may be interested in exploring one strategic issue in particular and hence you might want to dip into several chapters and see how the various perspectives address it. Alternatively, you might take perspectives that appear to be contradictory and compare and contrast them. This tension between markedly different views of the world may provoke some new insights. Finally we would like to encourage you to explore the perspectives by using the integrative case study in the final chapter. By analysing Cosworth Engineering from the various contrasting perspectives contained in the book it will help you develop a deeper understanding of the context of Cosworth, but most importantly it will help to draw out the contrasting strengths and limitations of these differing perspectives and the real power of taking a multi-lens approach to a complex organisational situation.

We hope you find the book stimulating, and controversial! Strategy is an exciting domain of study dealing as it does with fundamental issues of organisation. We believe that by taking this advanced approach, by broadening the range of perspectives that can be brought to bear on strategy, we can generate stimulating thoughts and debates, but most importantly we can make real progress to answering some of the fundamental strategic questions about an organisation.

References

Ansoff, H. I., *Corporate Strategy: An Analytic Approach to Business Policy for Growth and Expansion* (New York: McGraw-Hill Book Company, 1965).

Barnard, C. I., *The Functions of the Executive* (Cambridge, MA: Harvard University Press, 1938).

Barney, J. B., *Gaining and Sustaining Competitive Advantage* (New Jersey: Prentice Hall, 2003).

Barney, J. and W. Hesterly, *Strategic Management and Competitive Advantage*, 6th edn (New Jersey: Pearson, 2006).

de Wit, B. and R. Meyer, *Strategy: Process, Content, Context*, 3rd edn (London: Thomson, 2004).

Dess, G., G. Lumpkin and M. Taylor, *Strategic Management: Creating Competitive Advantages*, 2nd edn (Boston: McGraw-Hill, 2005).

Eden, C. and F. Ackermann, *Making Strategy: The Journey of Strategic Management* (London: Sage Publications, 1998).

Grant, R., *Contemporary Strategy Analysis*, 5th edn (Oxford: Blackwell, 2005).

Hitt, M., R. Ireland and R. Hoskisson, *Strategic Management: Competitiveness and Globalization* (New Jersey: Pearson, 2005).

Johnson, G., K. Scholes and R. Whittington, *Exploring Corporate Strategy*, 7th edn (London: Prentice Hall, 2005).

Mintzberg, H., *The Rise and Fall of Strategic Planning* (New York: Prentice Hall International, 1994).

Pettigrew, A. M., *The Awakening Giant: Continuity and Change in ICI* (Oxford: Basil Blackwell, 1985).

Part I
Institutionalist Perspectives

CHAPTER 2
Institutional Theory Perspective

Gerry Johnson and Royston Greenwood

Basic principles

The arguments put forward in most books on strategic management are typically based on two core assumptions. The first is that the world of the manager – the external and internal environment of organisations – is an objective reality capable of examination and analysis. The second, and linked assumption, is that managers themselves behave in an essentially rational analytic way to make sense of that world. Institutional theory is not based on these assumptions but on the concept of *social construction*. The assumptions here are different. They are, first, that the external and internal world of organisations is that which is subjectively understood or perceived by people in those organisations, influenced by social norms and expectations; and, second, that when we perceive our world in a particular way, we then behave accordingly, and consequently help create a world in line with our perceptions.

The basic principles of institutional theory are now summarised and the rest of the chapter shows how these relate to some of the main issues in strategic management:

1. Organisations are not autonomous agents seeking to maximise economic opportunities but are set within a social web of norms and expectations that constrain and shape, often in subtle ways, managerial choice. The choice of strategies is not an unfettered act but is constrained by these social prescriptions.

2. Social prescriptions are transmitted to organisations through such agencies as the state, professional institutes and other carriers of ideas and beliefs about appropriate managerial conduct.

3. By conforming to social prescriptions, organisations secure approval, support and public endorsement, thus increasing their 'legitimacy'.

4. Social prescriptions may become 'taken for granted', that is institutionalised, and thus very difficult to change or resist.

5. Conformity to social prescriptions rather than attendance to the 'task environment' (e.g. markets) may adversely affect efficiency and other economic measures of performance, but may improve long-term chances of survival.

6. Because similar organisations experience similar social expectations, they will conform to the same prescriptions and thus adopt similar strategies and managerial arrangements. This is the process of 'isomorphism'.

CASE STUDY 2.1

THE SITUATION

Quill, Dipstick and Gold (QDG) is one of the larger accountancy firms in the world after the 'Big 4' (PricewaterhouseCoopers; KPMG; Ernst & Young; Deloitte Touche Tohmatsu). With its origins in the last century, stemming from auditing, it now offers many professional services including tax and financial advice, corporate recovery, management consultancy, information systems and so on.

Edward Gray, the senior partner of the UK practice of QDG, is having dinner with a number of his fellow partners in one of the private dining rooms of the firm's central London offices. Last week Edward attended a meeting of the QDG International Board where the topic was the increasing global development of accountancy firms. He has called this meeting to seek the views of three influential senior partners in the United Kingdom as to how he should respond to questions posed at last week's meeting.

Around the table are two long-established partners from the audit practice, Paul Madeley and Alan Clarke. Both joined the firm from university, one from Oxford and the other from Cambridge, both became partners in their early thirties and each has over 20-year experience as partners. They both have clients whose billings with QDG run into many millions of pounds. They are powerful men in the firm, not least because of the client business they control, but also because of their reputation in the wider accountancy profession, where they are both seen as leading authorities. Each has also represented the profession on government committees of inquiry. Also at the meeting is Michael Jones who is relatively new to QDG and, unlike the others, is not an accountant; he heads up the UK consultancy arm of QDG, having been recruited from a senior position in a specialist strategy consultancy firm.

Edward Gray explained the background to the meeting. At the International Board, the preceding week, the international chairman of QDG had argued strongly that the firm was at risk of being left behind in the global development of accountancy firms. Hitherto most accountancy firms had been content to organise themselves along national lines. There were the big national practices such as the United States, the United Kingdom, Germany and France; and there were the smaller countries. The larger practices, in particular, had a great deal of local autonomy and had developed their own services to a considerable extent according to local need. International co-operation did take place but it was largely down to the personal contacts of partners across the world. The Big 4 firms, in contrast, were much more integrated and claimed the ability to provide a 'seamless service' globally.

However, in the last few years a number of significant changes had taken place, one of the biggest being the increasing number of large, truly international clients demanding transnational business services.

The conversation

Edward Gray summarised the situation:

'The view being put forward last week was that unless we recognise the need to move towards a more global form of business, QDG could lose out on potential business in a big way and lose its position as one of the leading accountancy firms in the world. The fact is that our competitors are moving this way, so we have to. The implication is that we can't carry on doing things the way we have in the past. Last week's meeting came to this view pretty much unanimously. The discussion was then about how QDG might do this. That is the issue I would like us to discuss this evening.'

Paul Madeley was sympathetic. He also pointed out that many of their clients were not only becoming transnational but also looking at the previously underdeveloped economies such as China and India.

'There is no doubt at all of the huge need for the sort of services we can offer. There are increasing signs that governments there will insist on standards of practice that their own infrastructure cannot meet. But they have real difficulties; for example, in China there is often no real concept of what profit means, let alone how to measure it. If a market economy is to be developed, the need for the sort of services we can provide is high. We should also remember that our own clients will expect a consistent level of service from us as they move into these countries. It is, however, a major challenge. There are major problems, not least, the number of people that will be required, which is enormous. Where will we find experienced partners and senior personnel prepared to work in these countries? Moreover, there will be real challenges aligning the work of some of our colleagues in small counties. And if we have to acquire local firms, how will we ensure the same degree of accounting quality?'

Alan Clarke also raised a note of caution:

'I agree. Our professional standards simply have to be met. I hear what is said about our clients' needs; but we do have to be very careful that things are done properly. I have heard the suggestion that we crash train people. This just will not do. It is not possible to churn out accountants overnight; and standards would most certainly be compromised if we did try to do so. Presumably none of us would be happy to see the firm driven by a market opportunity at the expense of our standards. There is also another issue we should not forget. Our business is based on personal relationships and trust; this must not be compromised in the name of "global integration".'

This was an argument that Michael Jones had heard before. He recognised that QDG's reputation in the field of accountancy and financial advice was of a very high order and should not be jeopardised. He was also persuaded that personal relationships with clients often at a very senior level were indeed important to QDG. However, he suggested that the problem they faced was more challenging than had so far been expressed:

'You must forgive me if I do not have the same experience as some of you around this table. I approach this as something of an outsider. But it does seem to me that, whilst the imperative for global development is undeniable, there is a further challenge. All our competitors will be driving in the same direction. They will all be going global; they will all be pitching for business with the same sorts of potential clients; they will all be offering the same sort of services and promising the same high standard of service. They will all build their business by trying to cultivate the same sort of personal relationships at the same sort of level in these businesses and with governments as they have in the West. They will be exporting Western accountancy, building their firms around audit, accountancy and information services. Where is the difference? I suggest that to achieve any sort of advantage over competition we need to start thinking how we might do things differently from others. That suggests to me that we need to think beyond the obvious. I can see the way this discussion might go. We need to merge – another of the larger firms below the Big 4 perhaps – and then we need to pool resources to provide the same sort of services as the others will be doing. But that is the way everyone will be thinking. Can I suggest we might think about a different strategy? For example we might want to think about the constraints of a partnership. Why not move to a two-tier partnership, where smaller countries are non-equity partners. That would allow us to make decisions more quickly, allow us to enforce standards, and enable us to give formal authority to senior partners looking after our major international clients.'

Alan Clark had expected this line of argument from Michael Jones:

'I really do think we have to be careful about our responses to all this. We are not talking here about an opportunity to make money; we are talking here about fundamental change to an economic system. A number of colleagues from other firms – and from the legal profession – met with government representatives a month or so ago. They, like us, see as the main concern the development of an infrastructure to handle fundamental changes to the economies of previously closed countries. This is about the development of proper systems in such countries. It is also something we need to co-operate with others on, not least to make sure that there are compatible standards in accounting. I might also add it is important to ensure such standards from the point of view of our own clients. They will be operating there and will expect the same quality of service they receive elsewhere in the world. I do not see how any of this can be helped by changing the partnership structure. It is an arrangement that has served us well for almost a 100 years. In any case, even if we wished to, it is no easy matter: the partners are owners of the firm; why would they wish to change that? Apart from anything else partners have invested huge amounts of intellectual capital and time in becoming a partner; 12 or 15 years for most of them. Can I ask, Edward, what was being proposed last week?'

Edward Gray explained that the feeling the previous week was that the international partnership was overly dependent on national firms at the expense of international co-ordination; overly concerned with discipline-based organisation around audit, taxation and so on at the expense of co-ordination across discipline boundaries; and over-reliant on the personal relationships and contacts between partners, often based on years of working together, as distinct from finding ways of working with individuals and teams of the highest calibre from anywhere in the world. He went on:

'In short, what was being looked for is a more internationally co-ordinated firm, with less emphasis on national boundaries, more inter-disciplinarity, an effective client management system and a recognition that we need to be rather less reliant on who knows whom and rather more able to draw on the very best of our people when we need them. To do all that, we need to have a more concentrated authority structure. Some partners need to have more authority than others. We cannot remain with this "one-partner one-vote" system.'

Michael Jones: 'You seem to be saying Edward that what is needed is a more managed firm. By client management system I assume you mean we have to market ourselves effectively. I agree with that and, as you know, I have long argued that it makes sense to do so across boundaries.'

'It seems to me', argued Paul Madeley, 'that there is a risk here of jumping to an answer before we really discuss the problem. Structures can be fads. We may not have the right sort of structure, but jumping from what we have to a two-tier partnership may equally not be right. For example I could equally argue that we have an unparalleled network of personal relationships throughout the world which we have been building and nurturing for decades. This is the basis of the trust we have with our clients. What we have to do is strengthen this and we might well be able to use modern technology and modern communications.'

'Can I also repeat my previous comments', said Alan Clarke. 'The problem with these sorts of ideas is that, almost by definition, they weaken the nature of the partnership. What then is the role of the partner? If we are not very careful we end up with the situation where professional managers are managing the very people who own the firm. There is a real risk that we end up with diminished standards.'

Edward Gray acknowledged there were difficulties. 'We all recognise the problems of change, not least in a firm like ours. However there comes a time when the forces for change are so powerful that we may have to accept that incremental change is just not possible any longer; or at least, if it is, it may lead to our demise. This was the major concern raised in the discussion last week.'

At this point the meeting was interrupted. Edward Gray's personal assistant arrived carrying a telephone. He suggested that, bearing in mind the theme of the meeting, his boss might wish to take the call. Edward Gray listened with an expression rather more of resignation than surprise. It was a call from his counterpart in another country. Two major developments had happened in the last week. First, QDP had just lost one of its major clients because the client was unhappy with the weak service provided by QDP in the Far East. Second, the firm was being sued by shareholders of a company audited by QDP. It was alleged that QDP had failed to uncover financial improprieties.

Issues

In considering the issues arising from the case, it is worth asking to what extent the partners, in their discussion, seem to be conforming to 'orthodox' strategy principles such as the search for competitive advantage, the identification of profitable market opportunities and the identification of, and building on, core competencies. Or to what extent are the following issues, considered in the discussion in 'Linking institutional theory to strategic management', better explained by an understanding of institutional theory:

– What is the definition of success for an accountancy firm? Is this to do with financial performance and market share; or is it more to do with their 'standing' in the community; or both? What are the bases for such definitions?

– Do partnerships have particular competences? How similar are these to those in other firms?

– Is the idea of competitive advantage and competitive strategy appropriate to an accountancy firm?

– Why is entry to China so important to QDG? Is this because of external pressures, because of their own reputation and standing, because clients expect it or because other firms are doing it?

– How might QDG reconcile the potential conflict between maintaining standards and moving quickly? What do you think they will do?

– What are the problems of strategic change that might exist in a firm like QDG?

Key contributions

Origins of institutional theory

The starting point for the contemporary institutional theory was the 1977 publication of Meyer and Rowan's 'Institutionalised organizations: formal structure as myth and ceremony'. This paper had a significant impact upon the world of academia, but little apparent impact upon the world of practice. Strategic management theory has been dominated by perspectives in which organisational strategies and structures are deemed effective if deliberately aligned to the requirements and challenges of the task environment (by which institutional theorists mean the sources of inputs – supplies, labour and so on – and markets). The role of top management is conceptualised as understanding and ensuring that alignment. Meyer and Rowan's work, however, ran counter to this view of managers as essentially seizing market opportunities and outwitting potential competitive threats.

Meyer and Rowan argued two things. First, organisations are confronted with pressures emanating from arenas other than the task environment. Specifically, organisations use strategies, structures and practices that are socially *expected* of them. For example, accounting firms organise themselves as professional partnerships and are active in socially anticipated ways: they support university education, comment studiously and seriously upon government tax policies, and project accounting as a rigorous science with strong ethical underpinnings. Using such structures and practices meets with social approval (i.e. confers *legitimacy* upon the organisation) and increases the likelihood that external constituents will assist the organisation (e.g. by conferring grants and resources, and favourably appraising them publicly). Meyer and Rowan defined these pressures of social expectation as arising from the 'institutional environment'. In the case of accounting, the institutional environment would incorporate professional institutions, agencies of the state (e.g. the SEC), important interest groups and the media.

In one sense, Meyer and Rowan could be seen as merely raising a set of pressures through which managers have to navigate. In fact, Meyer and Rowan go further and suggest that these institutional pressures often come to be taken for granted, that is managers do not 'choose' whether to conform; they simply 'do' because alternatives are not recognised. Hence, accounting firms are organised as partnerships, perform certain services (large firms always provide assurance services), support certain community activities, and behave in accordance with prescriptions of how 'professionals' behave. They do so because that is how accounting firms are expected to behave. In the same way, it would be almost unthinkable for a business school *not* to have an MBA degree and *not* to teach accounting, strategy and marketing.

Social expectations may (but not necessarily) run counter to the pursuit of efficiency. That is, an organisation might be *less* efficient as a consequence of meeting institutional expectations. Giving financial support to universities or 'worthwhile' public causes, or simply spending time serving on community or government committees, increases costs, thus reducing efficiency. Meyer and Rowan's key point is that all organisations are embedded within an institutional, as well as a task, environment and that the model of managers as autonomous actors is simply not validated by empirical observation. On the contrary, managers are constrained by socially derived norms and expectations that contain assumptions about their organisational world and appropriate conduct.

Some industries are more tightly constrained by social expectations of appropriate organisational conduct. For example, in many societies, physicians are not expected to nakedly pursue efficiency and profit: there is an expectation of patient care. Similarly, law and accounting firms are expected to temper commercial pursuits with consideration for the public good. In other industries such as restaurants or the transport industry, economic factors appear more paramount. Nevertheless, institutionalists point out that (1) all organisations exist within a context of institutional rules – there is no such thing as 'the market': all markets are socially constructed (see below); (2) all organisations are set within a context of social expectations, which constrain 'acceptable' actions; and (3) all managers are socialised into seeing the world in certain ways, thus constraining their understanding of opportunities.

Meyer and Rowan's second point is that the possible contradiction between institutionalised expectations and organisational efficiency sometimes leads organisations to engage in the 'decoupling' of formal structures from actual work practices. That is, organisations adopt structures and practices that are aligned with institutional prescriptions but which are deliberately distanced from how work is actually performed. Conformity is thus 'ceremonial' rather than substantive. For example, accounting work is portrayed as a rigorous science, concealing the essential subjectivity that actually occurs; senior executives may debate the strategy of their organisation energetically in meetings without translating such rhetoric into action; and fads of management will be subscribed to as they come and go.

There is another important difference between Meyer and Rowan's focus and most other perspectives on strategic management. Strategy writers emphasise that organisations need to search for competitive advantage through building on uniquely different competencies. Meyer and Rowan, on the other hand, are intrigued by the *similarity* of organisational practices. Their focus is upon how social pressures that occur at the level of an industry (or organisational field[1] as the institutionalists prefer) apply equally, or roughly so, to all organisations within that industry/field and thus 'cause' organisations to converge upon similar strategies and structures. Instead of the rational-actor model, in which the manager dispassionately analyses the external world and makes competitive choices, Meyer and Rowan's world is comprised of actors who, wittingly or otherwise, acquiesce collectively to the expectations of the institutional setting. This homogenisation of organisational practices is known as *institutional isomorphism*, the process by which organisations facing similar pressures come to resemble one another in the pursuit of social legitimacy.

Meyer and Rowan's thesis draws heavily upon the social constructionist account of reality (Berger and Luckmann, 1967; Zucker, 1977, 1987). Collective beliefs are seen as emerging from processes of repeated interactions between organisations. Organisations develop categorisations (or typifications) of their exchanges, which achieve the status of objectification and thus constitute social reality. Organisations behave in accordance with this socially constructed reality because to do so reduces ambiguity and uncertainty. Reciprocally shared understandings of appropriate practice permit ordered exchanges. Over time, however, these shared understandings, or collective beliefs, become reinforced by regulatory processes involving state agencies and professional bodies, which normatively and/or coercively press conformity upon constituent communities. Regulatory processes thus both disseminate and reproduce the coded prescriptions of social reality. Deviations from such prescriptions cause discomfort and trigger attempts to justify (i.e. legitimise) specific departures from the social norm (Elsbach, 1994; Lamertz and Baum, 1998).

The notion that communities of organisations develop collective beliefs concerning both the dynamics of industry (or field) circumstances and the appropriate strategic responses for competing successfully within them is not unique to institutional thinking. Huff (1982) and Spender (1989) were early reporters of these phenomena, and Abrahamson and Fombrun (1994) and Porac et al. (1989) have discussed how organisational actors in the same industry develop similar understandings of the dynamics of their competitive circumstances and evolve shared views of basic strategies ('recipes' in Spender's terms) for coping.

Elaborations

Meyer and Rowan's work sparked considerable theoretical and empirical activity. Two works in particular were to exercise considerable influence: DiMaggio and Powell (1983) and Tolbert and Zucker (1983).

Tolbert and Zucker

Tolbert and Zucker examined the spread of personnel reforms in local government in the United States from 1880 to 1930. Their work uncovered possible stages in the *process* of institutionalisation not only in the public sector, but in the market sector. (This process was subsequently elaborated in Tolbert and Zucker, 1996.) According to Tolbert and Zucker, there is a pre-institutionalisation stage characterised by experimentation as organisations seek to align themselves to their task environment in such a way as to gain a competitive advantage. As the success of particular experiments (e.g. new strategies, new products, new technologies or new structures) becomes known, other organisations copy them. The motivation for doing so is to become more competitive. To this point, Tolbert and Zucker are entirely consistent with strategic choice theory. But, as more and more organisations adopt the same practices, mimicry occurs not because the new practices are calculated to give economic advantage, but because the practice has attained the status of being the 'appropriate' or 'right' way to do something. Adoption has become not the outcome of calculated intent, but the product of social beliefs and expectations. Importantly, organisations adopting the new practice in this semi-institutionalised stage are *knowingly* adopting the innovation. Other studies have found similar mimetic effects. For example Westphal et al. (1997) tracked the adoption of total quality management (TQM) practices across 2700 US hospitals and showed that *early* adopters customised TQM practices, whereas later adopters did not.

Full institutionalisation occurs (at least according to Tolbert and Zucker) only when a practice becomes taken for granted. That is, the practice (strategy, structure or whatever) becomes regarded as *the* way of doing things. The practice is uncritically adopted and taken for granted. Alternatives have become literally unthinkable. In Meyer and Rowan's (1977) terms, 'institutionalisation' has occurred because practices take on 'a rule like status'. For example, the way in which we talk of the functions of business – 'marketing', 'production', 'research and development' – is taken for granted. In Western businesses the concept of profit is taken for granted; and, as seen in the case study, it is very likely assumed that it should be similarly taken for granted elsewhere.

Tolbert and Zucker's contribution is particularly important because it fundamentally challenges the notion of unrestricted human agency in strategic decision-making. That is, in the full-institutional stage managers behave as they do *unwittingly*, with strategic 'choice' shaped and determined by taken-for-granted solutions. And even in the semi-institutional stage, in which managers take action knowingly, they are constrained by expectations of appropriate conduct. Strategic choice, to the institutionalist, is less a calculated act than a normatively constrained and often habitual effect.

The key point is that managers are not 'free' decision-makers. They *do* exercise choice, but not unfettered choice. Social pressures circumscribe available choices. Strategic choice is shaped by recipes and historically legitimated practices which inform the sector generally and individual organisations in particular. These socially coded prescriptions may be more intense in some decision areas than others and in some industries rather than others. But strategic choice *is* directed by institutional prescriptions.

DiMaggio and Powell

DiMaggio and Powell (1983) identified three mechanisms by which institutional isomorphism can occur: *coercive, mimetic* and *normative*. Coercive mechanisms occur as a result of actions by agencies such as the state or regulatory bodies, upon whom collectivities of organisations are dependent. For example, Slack and Hinings (1995) have shown how sports organisations transformed their governance arrangements in order to maximise opportunities for state funding. Normative mechanisms stem primarily from professionalisation. DiMaggio and Powell (1983) drew attention to the processes by which occupational groups socialise members into codes of conduct and behaviour, and sustain compliance, by career-long training, monitoring of behaviour and disciplinary action, and acts of ceremonial celebration. The professions such as accounting, law and medicine figure as exemplary sites of these processes. Professional firms and professionals behave in similar ways because of the essentially *normative* pressures promulgated by the profession and its constitutive agencies. Thus, accounting firms do what they do and organise themselves as they do because the professional community determines that they will do so.

Mimetic mechanisms occur primarily in circumstances of ambiguity and uncertainty. Under such conditions, managers copy organisations perceived to be more successful and more legitimate. Hence, for example, the spread of mega-mergers affecting each of the largest accounting firms.

DiMaggio and Powell's tripartite classification has sparked considerable empirical inquiry. But there are two other, albeit secondary, themes within their seminal contribution. First, they clarify the agencies that operate within the institutional context: the state, the professions and exemplary organisations that act as role models. By drawing attention to these agencies, DiMaggio and Powell sharpened the difference between the task and the institutional contexts and clarified how the two might be studied. As a consequence, later scholars have explicitly examined how state agencies and professional institutes are instrumental in monitoring and reinforcing institutional definitions of appropriate conduct.

The second sub-theme in the DiMaggio and Powell paper picks up the difficult notion of structuration, which refers to the process whereby institutionalised structures shape action and behaviour, but which are themselves recreated and reproduced by those actions and behaviours. That is, existing structures and relationships within an organisational field act to shape the behaviour of organisations within the field. Accounting firms are thus affected by the practices of the professional institute and the expectations of clients and other accountants. In this way the structure of the field shapes behaviour (action). But the very act of conforming serves to amplify those structures. Action thus drives structure, modifying its form. Accounting firms join in the actions of the professional institute, thus elaborating and supporting its role. Interaction amongst members of the field becomes more formalised. Relationships, roles and responsibilities become more sharply defined and thus more bound within the field's network. Hence, although the structure of the field shapes behaviour, that behaviour in turn clarifies the structure, reinforcing its constraining presence.

DiMaggio and Powell are thus emphasising the dynamic of reproduction. Institutional structures *arise from* social interaction, serve to *constrain* those interactions and are *reproduced by* those interactions. Institutionalists do not insist that all actors and organisations are equally or completely subjected to institutional expectations. Responses can, and do, vary. Nevertheless, in its early form-ations, institutional theory became associated with the idea of inertia and stability. Institutionalised practices, almost by definition, were seen as enduring. Change was treated as unusual. By uncovering the 'taken-for-granted' rules of conduct, institutional theorists emphasised the stability and resistance to change of much strategic behaviour.

Other works

In the more than two decades following Meyer and Rowan's 1977 classic paper, much empirical and theoretical work has appeared under the rubric of institutional theory. We comment on some of this in the next section but fuller reviews are provided elsewhere (e.g. Lawrence and Suddaby, 2006; Powell and DiMaggio, 1991; Scott, 1995). To date, most studies have been content to show the occurrence of institutional effects rather than their consequences. It is, however, worth commenting on two studies that have examined the link between institutional alignment and organisational performance, which is a relatively neglected part of institutional theory.

Baum and Oliver (1991) studied whether childcare service organisations had better survival chances if they had links to agencies with high social legitimacy. The argument is that organisations can obtain social support by reflected legitimacy: for example, a childcare agency licensed by the state, run in association with a church or as a not-for-profit body, would have greater legitimacy. Baum and Oliver found that institutional linkages of this form 'play a very significant role in reducing the likelihood of organisational mortality' (p. 213). Oliver (1997) also studied construction companies to establish if organisations with good relationships with institutional and/or task agencies were more successful (in terms of profits and control of construction costs). She found that institutional relationships were correlated with performance but much less so than task relationships, especially under conditions of tight market circumstances. However, profitability was significantly affected by the strength of institutional relationships under conditions of regulatory stringency.

Recent work has turned to understanding 'institutional entrepreneurship'. One of the central contri-butions of institutional work has been its focus upon the importance of *durable* social processes that shape how managers understand and respond to their worlds. Faced with pressures for social approval, they conform to institutionalised (i.e. taken-for-granted) expectations of appropriate conduct. As a consequence, organisations begin to resemble each other: only a limited array of organisational designs are used, similar strategies are used, similar practices are adopted. So where does novelty come from? If organisations are 'caught' within a web of social expectations, how does change occur? It is to these questions that institutional research has turned. One line of research is examining which organisations are more likely to deviate from existing practices: these organisations are referred to as 'institutional entrepreneurs'. Institutional entrepreneurs are often those on the margins of existing organisational fields and industry; they are motivated to introduce novelty because they are less privileged by existing routines; and they are more able to introduce change because they are less embedded within institu-tional networks and thus more alert to possible alternatives (Leblebici et al., 1991). Or institutional entrepreneurship might be accounted for by the more-or-less deliberate deviation from (or experi-mentation with) established ways of doing things (Feldman and Pentland, 2003; Johnson et al., 2000; Seo and Creed, 2002).

Another source of institutional change is central players within an industry or field. These organ-isations may become motivated to introduce change because they outgrow the scope of institutional constraints. Greenwood and Suddaby (2006), for example, show how the very largest accounting firms moved into consulting services and redefined themselves as 'business advisors' in part because their scale of operations took them beyond the regulatory processes of the accounting profession. Finally, change may be introduced from outside an organisational field. Thornton (2002) shows how mergers and acquisitions in the book-publishing industry led to the demise of traditional, 'craft' forms of organising, as large conglomerates introduced practices forged in other industries.

Complementing these studies of institutional entrepreneurs (with their focus on who they are), a second line of research examines *how* new ideas and practices become established as the new way of doing things. Here the focus is upon how relatively untested ideas become 'theorised' as widely appropriate and thus legitimated. Not all new ideas are successfully theorised: many are 'fads' or 'fashions' and have a short life span (Abrahamson, 1996). But some ideas do become successfully established and institutionalists are uncovering how this happens (Rao et al., 2003).

A very different line of institutional work that has important implications for the study of strategy is the examination of differences in the institutions of different countries. Much of this work arises from within political science and political economy and focuses upon how countries such as Japan, Germany and France have rather different institutions to those in, for example, the United Kingdom and the United States. This line of research (exemplified by Dobbin, 1994; Hall and Soskice, 2001; Thelen, 2004; Whitley, 1999) examines how differences in national institutions affect the structures of industries and the business strategies that tend to develop. Countries build upon their distinctive institutional arrangements to secure competitive advantages worldwide (e.g. Biggart and Guillén, 1999). National differences in institutional structures also affect how ideas and models about management do or do not diffuse across national boundaries. Some institutionalists show how the international organisations such as the WTO, IMF and even accreditation agencies enable the flow and diffusion of ideas globally, with the implication that organisations are converging upon similar practices and forms. Others, however, insist that idiosyncratic national institutions act as filters so that globally diffusing ideas are differentially received or translated to make them fit local institutions (e.g. Djelic, 1998; Guillen, 2001).

Linking institutional theory to strategic management

How, then, do the concepts of institutional theory help us understand issues to do with strategy and strategic management? In this section this is discussed, and the case study on QDG is used to illustrate the discussion.

It is, however, worth starting by re-emphasising the importance of the taken for granted and the concept of social construction as underpinning a good deal of what follows; this itself can be illustrated with regard to accountancy. A good deal of discussion in the case is about the need for excellence of service defined in terms of professional standards. This is taken for granted and indeed is the raison d'être of accountancy firms. In turn, the way in which the firms operate reinforces this. Established professional institutions lay down the norms and exert regulatory pressures to conform; there are university courses which educate people in the application of those norms and provide a supply of labour, and there are professional examinations which test the suitability of individuals to practice. An organisational field has developed within which the parties involved (universities, financial directors, partners in firms and so on) take all this as given and behave according to those norms. Moreover the clients of accountancy firms behave in ways which conform to and consolidate the system. It is, perhaps, no coincidence that many of the financial directors of large corporations are, themselves, chartered accountants who have worked or been partners in those firms. And we see from the case that the intention is now to export those norms, practices and standards to other areas of the world. This is all on the unquestioned assumption that those norms, standards and practices have a 'rightness' in themselves.

Context: The external environment

As has been explained, the traditional emphasis in the strategy literature has been on what was explained in 'Origins of institutional theory' above as the task environment. Institutionalists, on the other hand, have emphasised the institutionalised nature and regulatory role of the environment.

The environment is conceived of in terms of forces such as government or other regulatory bodies which impose rules and codes of practice with which organisations have to comply. These rules and regulations may be to do with how services are provided or what services are required. For example, an audit is required by law; similarly, businesses require advice on navigating taxation law. There are also other regulatory agencies. These include professional bodies that lay down standards and require conformity to particular practices; for example, the training and examination required to become a chartered accountant and the terms and conditions imposed on those who seek to practise within that profession. The institutional world for accountants is then an example of one which is highly regulated.

The case is also a good example of how the environment can be considered not only in terms of 'real' objective opportunities, but also as institutionally defined opportunities. Objectively, entry to China is important to QDG for several reasons. First, they have to serve their global clients wherever those clients go. Competitive (task) pressures are making accountancy firms nervous about losing clients if they cannot offer them the kind of service and breadth of geographical coverage that clients demand. But the case also raises strong institutional pressures for entering China. Accountancy firms are expected to play their part in 'exporting' Western economic institutions. The larger accountancy firms would find it uncomfortable to resist the expectations of the professional associations, their accounting colleagues and government agencies. Moreover, refusal to 'go' would receive adverse publicity. So there are good institutional reasons for their movement into these arenas. There is also the perceived need for the regulation of firms operating in such markets and the consequent real or assumed demand for services such as accountancy. The assumption in QDG is that the same sort of services is needed as is provided in the West by the same sort of firms. Very likely governments in economies such as China also believe that such services will provide the sort of institutionalised legitimacy of capitalism that they may or may not wish to convey: indeed if these economies want to do business with the West then they may have to conform to the institutionalised expectations of Western economies and governments regarding appropriate forms of accounting. It is of course quite likely that QDG and other accountancy firms are actively promoting this concept, not out of self interest so much, but because they genuinely believe it to be necessary.

Objectively, of course, it may be appropriate to question whether the sorts of rules, regulations and standards of the West in economic terms are necessarily appropriate to China. However, the important thing to stress here is that from an institutional point of view it should not be expected that such objective questioning would arise. To take one example in the case study, Paul Madeley points out that there is no concept of what profit means or how to measure it. Implied within this comment is that there is an objectively 'right' way of doing this and that this is laid down by the accountancy standards of the Western world.

There is another way in which institutional theorists conceive of the nature of the environment and which applies to a firm such as QDG. Institutionalists see the environment as consisting of a web of transactions within a network of participating organisations, all of whom have a common understanding of the form those transactions should take. This is the idea of the organisational field. It is taken for granted that accountancy firms work with banks and law firms, for example. Indeed they refer business from one to the other. It is taken for granted that business corporations need auditors and auditors carry out the work in particular ways.

In the case study, Alan Clarke, in particular, reflects this. He sees QDG as a professional service firm interacting with other such firms and, in many respects, acting as an agent of regulatory bodies such as the government to ensure that proper services are provided. In this sense the environment becomes bounded by the organisational field and the nature of the transactions in it. There are of course dangers here: there could be entrants who do not accept the orthodoxy of this; who seek to behave in different ways. For example, AMEX provides accountancy services in the United States; and their entry was not expected by the established firms when it happened.

It is important to stress, then, that whilst the strategic management literature tends to emphasise markets and competition, institutionalists emphasise institutional environments and the conformity to taken-for-granted norms and practices within those environments which endow organisations – in this case QDG – with legitimacy and standing. The main concern of Clark and Madeley, in particular, is with such legitimacy within their organisational field. To some extent all organisations are faced with these conflicting environments. In QDG the institutional environment is particularly important, but they are also faced with a market environment that they are finding increasingly intrusive. In other organisations the market environment might be especially significant, but there will still be institutional pressures to conform and behave in a legitimate fashion. So, for example, a manufacturing firm faced with significant market pressures also has to conform to the institutional environment represented by the accountancy profession, and also by that of the banks, financial institutions, government, society and so on.

Competences and competitive strategy

Much of the literature on strategic management emphasises the idea of competitive advantage under-pinned by core competences unique to an organisation. Institutional theorists, however, tend to emphasise the similarity between organisations rather than their distinctiveness. Accountancy firms are similar, banks are similar, universities are similar and so on. The extent to which this is so will, of course, vary. Some organisations are much more 'institutionalised' than others. How then, in this context, do we conceive of competences?

First, there is an overarching caveat: that the very idea of competences has become institutionalised. Managers in organisations, reinforced by academics, may talk as though competences are real and bestow competitive advantage when in fact there may be little evidence of this. In accountancy firms, to take an example, it may be very difficult indeed to pin down competences which really do achieve differentiation. For example, all accountancy firms claim to offer advantages to their clients through industry specialisation; and all are beginning to claim 'seamless global services'. But these are not distinctive differences. All firms are making the same claim. This does not mean that the partners in an accountancy firm (or any other firm) will not talk about competences as though they are real, especially as the language of competition starts to prevail. Talk of competences can, then, be seen as symbolic rhetoric bestowing social approval (legitimacy) upon those using it. However, as Meyer and Rowan (1977) argue, the rhetoric may be decoupled from what actually goes on.

There is, however, an institutional view that argues that competences lie within the very institu-tionalised nature of organisations. Competences are likely, in this sense, to exist within the taken-for-granted practices and structures of organisations. For example, it might be argued that some organisations are better able to legitimate themselves within their organisational field than others. They may, for example, have established a better reputation for whatever reason; they may have some figurehead who is especially recognised within the field or they may have developed ways of working which are regarded especially highly within that field. There is evidence in the case, at least from Alan Clark, that QDG is trying to position itself as influential in government circles. This could, conceiv-ably, be extended such that representatives of the firm sit on commissions of government bodies which are especially influential. Indeed, in the accountancy profession, representation on govern-ment and professional bodies is especially welcomed, as is sponsorship of charities and other 'good works'. There is, of course, a problem here. It could be that the organisation becomes over-reliant on activities that confer such legitimacy, which they may regard as competences, but which over time become counterproductive. It could be that QDG is facing this problem. It has prided itself on being a highly esteemed accountancy firm following rigorous professional codes of practice. What if the nature of accountancy changes in the face of global development? Might that mean that the inherited legitimacies/competences of QDG come to work against them?

Competing

Inherent in the notion of strategic management is the exercise of managerial choice over competitive strategy and the bases of competition. Institutional theorists argue differently. They suggest that the rules of competing are similar within organisational fields. For example, in case of professionals such as accountants and lawyers, solicitation of business from clients and advertising was not allowed until quite recently. Indeed in the past, many within professions would prefer not to see themselves as a business in a competitive sense at all; rather they would see themselves as offering a service of a high professional standard. Similarity, then, is more marked than difference: accountancy firms offer similar services, seek to enhance those services in similar ways, build relationships with clients in particular ways and so on. Competitive behaviour is constrained to conventions of acceptable professional conduct in the marketplace. Not conforming to these norms would be frowned upon even if competitive advantage might be achieved, hence the unease when Michael Jones raises the explicit notion of striving for competitive advantage through differentiation.

This is not to say that those involved in such firms might not employ the rhetoric of competition; and perhaps increasingly so. They might talk as though choice can be made about real differences which bestow real advantages. However, the tendency is to conform to the norms rather than seek for real advantages. The institutionalist's emphasis on mimicry seems more appropriate as a descriptor of what happens than the more usual portrayals of managers as autonomous 'captains' of their enterprise. Far from seeking to be different, organisations seek to be similar to others. This is especially the case where organisations face uncertainty and ambiguity – arguably as the accountancy profession does with regard to Eastern Europe. So, the partners in QDG feel 'obliged' to enter China, partly to service their clients (and avoid losing them) and partly to meet professional expectations. They also feel the need to become more integrated globally, again because of pressure from clients and also because other firms are doing so. These developments pose challenges to traditional conceptions of how a partnership format should be operated. The pressures of the market place and of the institutional context can thus coincide (over China, for example) or conflict (over the partnership format). The institutionalist might predict that in such circumstances QDG will indeed develop in China and more globally, but is likely to try to preserve the symbolic form of the partnership structure and relative independence of partners despite strategic and structural imperatives not to do so.

Institutional theorists also emphasise the faddish nature of much strategic behaviour. In the 1980s the emphasis, for example, was on competing on the basis of finding suitable markets in which to do so. This was the result of a marketing orthodoxy of the time and, more specifically, Porter's work on competitive forces at work in markets. In the 1990s the emphasis swung towards the importance of core competences, unique to the organisation upon which competitive advantage can be built. In the 1980s everyone was sure of the wisdom of the former; in the 1990s they became convinced of the wisdom of the latter. However, because at any one point of time everyone seems to have been convinced of the wisdom of one or the other, there was a general uniformity about the very bases of and questions being asked about competitive strategy. Again institutional theorists emphasise conformity for the purposes of creating legitimacy.

It should, of course, be observed that the very rules of competing differ by institutional context. For example, in the United States there is a much stronger emphasis on litigation than in many other parts of the world; in the Middle East and parts of Africa, what would be regarded in the West as bribery is common; co-operative behaviour rather than competition is emphasised a good deal more in the public sector; it would, therefore, be wrong to suggest that competition as discussed conventionally in the strategy literature is necessarily the norm.

Corporate strategy

For private sector organisations there are 'coercive rules' laying down that corporations are there for the purposes of meeting shareholder expectations. In fact, arguably, whilst there is ceremonial and rhetorical conformity to this, the evidence is that managers do not behave in this way. To take one example, managers in the United States and the United Kingdom will often argue that the evident short-termism of organisations is because investors take a short-term perspective. Actually there is at least much evidence that short termism results from organisations using (institutionalised) measures of performance which are short-term or historic in nature and encouraging managers to take a short-term view. Return on sales or return on capital employed is a typical measure used. Neither encourages a long-term shareholder benefit view of investment decisions.

The notion of institutionalisation at the corporate level has other dimensions. For example, the role of the corporate board is institutionalised and prescribed in law, as is the role of executive and non-executive directors. However, the form of boards is not determined solely in terms of regulation. There are strong normative pressures of conformity here, for example, in the networks of boards of directors in which one executive holds a non-executive position in another company. Arguably this is all about ensuring conformity of behaviour between such organisations. Certainly, there is considerable evidence that interlocking directorates are a key mechanism by which mimetic behaviour occurs.

It is also worth noting that the role of corporate executives, at the highest level in organisations, is explicitly about achieving legitimisation. Having 'respected' figures on a board provides the organisation with legitimacy. (This is particularly important for charities.) Such senior executives spend a good deal of time ensuring that their organisations are legitimate in the public eye, with government, and in the press.

A further aspect of corporate strategy is to do with 'parenting'. An important question is the extent to which the corporate parent actually understands and empathises with its business units. One of the implications here is the extent to which a corporate parent can operate *across* institutional boundaries. Arguably this might be one of the reasons why holding companies have problems. A holding company may have businesses as diverse as heavy goods manufacturing and retailing or financial services. These are very different sorts of organisations, arguably of different institutional forms. Questions have to be asked as to whether a corporate parent can relate to these different sorts of businesses. Corporations with a disparate mix of businesses do not perform well in terms of their share price. Arguably this is because financial analysts and investors operating within their own conventions and assumptions cannot make sense of them. It is worth noting here that economists would make the same observation about the difficulties faced by holding companies.

Mimicry is certainly evident at the corporate level. The 1970s was an era of diversification. The 1980s was an era of de-layering and cost-cutting and the 1990s was an era of de-merger and break-up as large corporates sought to get back to their 'core businesses'. Any one of these corporate moves may makes sense, but the institutionalist would make the point that all corporations seem to do the same at the same time. Haveman (1993) traced how organisations in the US savings and loans industry (equivalent to building societies in the United Kingdom) followed similar and successful organisations into new markets. The choice of new markets was affected by the number of successful firms already in those markets: firms entered those markets already occupied. That is, Haveman identified the occurrence of isomorphism within that industry via the mechanism of mimetic behaviour. Haunschild and Miner (1997) also observed mimetic behaviour in the investment banking industry, specifically in terms of how corporations chose investment bankers to advise on an acquisition. They found that under conditions of ambiguity and uncertainty, mimicry was particularly salient.

So the prediction with regard to QDG is that they will, indeed, develop into a more integrated global partnership. However, the explanation is just as much to do with mimicry as it is to do with debate in the boardroom. QDG will follow the behaviour of the Big 4 firms, which are already more integrated and which, as industry leaders, are 'exemplars'.

Strategy processes and strategic decision-making

Orthodox approaches in mainline strategy texts typically suggest or infer that strategic decisions are made and strategies come about through processes of rational analytic thinking, typically by top managers. Here in the case we have top managers – senior partners in QDG – deliberating on strategy. However, it is important to remember the institutional context and in particular the importance of their taken-for-granted assumptions, beliefs and practices. With the exception of Michael Jones, the partners have decades of experience in an accountancy profession where norms and beliefs are embedded through the ritualised 'indoctrination' of new firm recruits and via years of training to ensure compliance with expected behaviour in order to become partners, the position of partnership itself is also the form of governance structure recognised within their organisational field. Strategy deliberations are not, and cannot, be removed from this context within which there are such embedded taken-for-granted ways of seeing and doing things. So much is illustrated by the QDG case. It is likely that strategies will be developed that are compatible with the assumptions of Alan Clark and Paul Madeley. They are uneasy with the language and ideas of Michael Jones, who comes from a different institutional environment with different assumptions and ways of looking at the situation. It is also unlikely that decisions will be taken that build strategy on the basis of his advocated approach to building competitive advantage, or which fundamentally question the structure of the partnership and the way the firm works.

Of course, since these dominant assumptions and norms are to be found in accountancy firms generally, similar strategies will also be developed by other firms, hence the isomorphism that institutionalists have observed. Indeed researchers have identified 'industry recipes' (Porac et al., 1989; Spender, 1989) that are, in effect, institutionalised strategies which cross organisations within organisational fields. These are not just commonly followed broad strategies; they are quite detailed, quite specific strategic behaviours common across organisations within the field.

Moreover the way in which strategic decisions would be made might well be very common across such organisations. Indeed this is noted more widely than the accountancy profession. For example, strategic planning could be regarded as an institutionalised strategic process in that strategic planning processes tend to be common across organisations. Latterly researchers have noted other common strategic processes. For example, strategy workshops or away days tend to have common formats and purposes (Hodgkinson et al., 2006) using common strategy tools and techniques.

So institutional theorists would suggest that strategy processes and strategic decision-making are not so much rational analytic processes as institutionalised processes in which common approaches are adopted, common assumptions made and common practices followed. Indeed, arguably, the strategy tools and techniques advocated by strategy writers and consultants are employed in reality to post-rationalise and legitimise the relatively institutionalised strategies managers follow.

Change

Earlier we noted that fully institutionalised behaviours are literally taken for granted and operate with 'rule like status'. And there is no doubt that such institutionalised practices exist. But not all organisations comply with normative expectations, either fully or in part. This has led to an interest in understanding the extent to which, and how, organisations deviate from prevailing norms. There are several explanations from an institutional perspective.

One argument is that change is inevitable. The discussion above on strategy processes and decision-making makes the point that change tends to happen within the bounds of what is taken for granted; it therefore tends to occur incrementally. Faced with pressures for change, managers typically minimise the extent to which they are faced with ambiguity and uncertainty by looking for that which is familiar. However, here lies an explanation of more fundamental change too. Over time it is likely, perhaps inevitable, that such incremental change may not address the necessities of the task, not least the market environment. This can give rise to the sort of strategic drift shown in Figure 2.1. The organisation's strategy gradually, if imperceptibly, moves away from forces at work in its task environment. This may not be detectable for long periods of time; after all, the organisation may still be successful since it is doing what it knows to do well. Eventually, however, its performance will

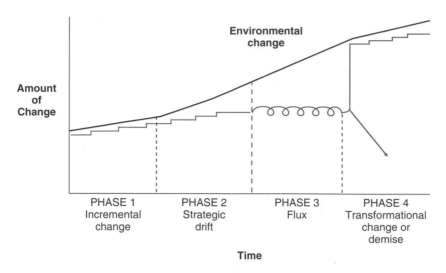

Figure 2.1 Patterns of strategy development

suffer in some way. It may eventually die of course, or it may go through some major transformational change. So much is intimated by Edward Gray in the case study. He is suggesting that there comes a time when such transformational change may be inevitable. He may, however, find it difficult to convince his colleagues that the time has yet to come.

Oliver (1992) has also argued that contrary to early statements of the enduring character of institutional rules, their power may dissipate over time if they are not actively reproduced and reinforced. This suggests that change can be understood in terms of the interplay, even contest, between prevailing institutional norms, reinforced by ritual and practice and the incursion of competing norms, ideas and expectations. There are also clues as to how such competing norms may develop.

Greenwood and Hinings (1996), for example, show how and why exogenous shifts in the task and/or institutional environment may trigger changes within organisations. They analyse how the incidence of radical change varies *across* institutional sectors, in particular the extent to which they are more or less insulated from ideas and practices in other sectors. Over time, organisations may become more 'permeable'; for example, many of the accountancy firms are becoming less focused on auditing and more multi-disciplined; they are also placing less emphasis on the primacy of partners themselves and more on conventional management with some of the partners playing more of a managerial role. Arguably, as this occurs they become more open to influences from outside the profession and therefore more likely to change. This may be increased as outsiders are brought into the organisation, as, for example, has happened with Michael Jones in the QDG case.

Change is not always exogenously driven even if that has been the focus of much institutional work. Seo and Creed (2002) theorise how 'contradictions' within organisational fields can lead to change. For example, an organisation within a field may be exposed to strong normative and mimetic pressures to behave in one way, yet increasingly become aware of market opportunities that those behaviours deny. Consequently, the organisation experiences the contradiction between legitimacy (attained through conformity) and efficiency (attained through deviation). Greenwood and Suddaby (2006) show how such contradictions affected the (then) Big 5 accounting firms. They also show that, as the Big 5 grew into transnational firms, they *internalised* training processes and effectively outgrew the normative and regulatory processes of the accounting profession, making them more open to change.

The incidence of radical change can vary *within* sectors because of variation in the *intra* organisational dynamics of particular organisations. Thus accounting firms vary in the relative development of tax and management consulting as structurally recognised practice areas and thus have different emphases upon the importance of ideas that appeal to these occupational communities. The greater the range of occupations and experiences inside a firm, the likelier that new ideas will emerge and prompt change. Firms that are homogeneous, on the other hand, are likely to interpret ideas in the same way, whereas firms containing diverse professional groups will generate debate because of multiple interpretations.

Change may, then, take place because of conflict between institutional norms within organisations. This seems to be what is happening in QDG, at least to some extent. Michael Jones is approaching the problem from one set of institutional norms and his colleagues from another. Arguably, Edward Gray is beginning to see the world rather more in Michael Jones's terms than his colleagues. This again emphasises the importance of 'outsiders' or people on the margins of organisations who benefit less from prevailing norms. Change is to do with the ability of an organisation to break outside prevailing institutional boundaries. New chief executives are sometimes appointed specifically for this purpose. It is argued that the role of the main board is to identify just when an organisation needs such an injection of new ideas. Institutionalists have observed, however, that when an organisation recognises the need for change, it often imports recipes from elsewhere, rather than building custom-made solutions.

A further explanation for change is to do with the 'bending of the rules'. For most of the time people in organisations conform to the 'rules of the game' generally accepted within institutional norms (Johnson et al., 2000). However, they may on occasions consciously or unconsciously bend, manipulate or defy the norms. Or it may be that someone, perhaps one of the outsiders mentioned above, might consciously seek to use the accepted rules of the game but to his or her own ends. An example in a partnership might be that someone like Michael Jones may seek to build up allies by trying to introduce new partners from commercial type organisations.

Institutionalists also point the way in which management consultants carry change within and across populations of organisations. They transfer practice from one organisation to another but imperfectly so. They are, in this respect, a basis of imperfect mimicry. As a consequence, minor changes may be instantly occurring within an institutional field: overall convergence around a given model might be the general trend, but imperfect mimicry can act as a dynamics of incremental variation.

Overall, institutionalists lay emphasis on the extent to which change is dependent on conformity to or challenge of institutional norms. They place less emphasis on the idea that change comes about because of the intellectual persuasion that might be exerted through some formal process. Indeed, they might argue that such processes are themselves rituals within institutions.

Control and structure

The wisdom in strategic management is that 'structure follows strategy'. In other words, organisations set their strategy and then determine the appropriate structure to implement the strategy. However, as we see within QDG, structure is often a manifestation of institutional norms. A partnership is not a partnership because of the strategy it is following. It is the structural form accepted in that professional arena as the way things are done.

Similarly the idea that organisational controls are formed in order to measure important aspects of strategy is the received wisdom in the strategy literature. But institutionalists argue that controls and measures are often manifestations of institutional norms. For example it is quite likely that in QDG, control systems emphasise the same sort of measures as other accountancy firms. Traditionally such firms have placed considerable emphasis, for example, on what is known as 'billable hours' – the amount of time individuals spend on fee-earning work for clients. This measure is not emphasised because of the strategy of the organisation; it is emphasised because an accepted sign of success is the fee-earning capacity of individuals and, arguably, because part of the ritual preparation for partnership is that more junior members of the organisation need to be 'kept busy'. The same point may be made about other types of organisation. A popular measure of control in considering performance in private sector organisations is return on capital employed; yet it is difficult to justify this objectively as a sound means of assessing the strategic health of a business since better returns must result from low-value assets (for example, depreciated plant) than from investment in more costly new assets. Such measures have, however, become institutionalised measures of control.

Again mimicry and isomorphism occur with regard to structures and control. There are many examples. The seminal study by Chandler (1962) showed how structural forms such as divisionalisation, once developed, became common across communities of firms. Palmer et al. (1993) have demonstrated the role of interlocking directorates in spreading the adoption of this organisational form. Other structural practices that have been found to spread across organisations without necessarily being connected to strategy include the use of TQM (see Westphal et al., 1997), matrix structures (Burns and Wholley, 1993) and accounting procedures. The whole field of HR systems is also highly institutionalised and regulated through professional institutions that lay down quite precise norms leading to conformity in such practices.

Note

1. Institutionalists use the term 'field' because it is broader than 'industry'. Industry usually covers a set or population of organisations producing similar products or services (e.g. accounting firms, car manufacturers). The 'field', however, would look not just at the producers, but at key suppliers, customers and, critically, *regulatory agencies*.

References

Abrahamson, E., 'Management fashion', *Academy of Management Review*, 21 (1996) 254–285.

Abrahamson, E. and C. J. Fombrun, 'Macro-cultures: Determinants and Consequences', *Academy of Management Review*, 19 (1994) 728–755.

Baum, J. A. and C. Oliver, 'Institutional Linkages and Organizational Mortality', *Administrative Science Quarterly*, 36 (1991) 187–218.

Berger, P. L. and T. Luckmann, *The Social Construction of Reality* (New York: Doubleday Anchor, 1967).

Biggart, N. W. and M. F. Guillén, 'Developing Difference: Social Organization and the Rise of the Auto Industries of South Korea, Taiwan, Spain and Argentina', *American Sociological Review*, 64, 5 (1999) 722–747.

Burns, L. R. and D. R. Wholley, 'Adoption and Abandonment of Matrix Management Programs: Effects of Organizational Characteristics and Inter-organizational Networks', *Academy of Management Journal*, 36 (1993) 106–138.

Chandler, A. D., *Strategy and Structure: Chapters in the History of the Industrial Enterprise* (Cambridge, MA: MIT Press, 1962).

DiMaggio, P. J. and W. W. Powell, 'The Iron Cage Revisited: Institutional Isomorphism and Collective Rationality in Organizational Fields', *American Sociological Review*, 48 (1983) 147–160.

Djelic, M.-L., *Exporting the American Model: The Postwar Transformation of European Business* (Oxford, UK: Oxford University Press, 1998).

Dobbin, F., *Forging Industrial Policy: The United States, Britain and France in the Railway Age* (Cambridge, MA: Cambridge University Press, 1994).

Elsbach, K. D., 'Managing Organizational Legitimacy in the California Cattle Industry: The Construction and Effectiveness of Verbal Accounts', *Administrative Science Quarterly*, 39 (1994) 57–88.

Feldman, M. S. and B. T. Pentland, 'Reconceptualizing Organizational Routines as a Source of Flexibility and Change', *Administrative Science Quarterly*, 48 (2003) 94–118.

Greenwood, R. and C. R. Hinings, 'Understanding Radical Organizational Change: Bringing Together the Old and the New Institutionalism', *Academy of Management Review*, 21, 4 (1996) 1022–1054.

Greenwood, R. and R. Suddaby, 'Institutional Entrepreneurship in Mature Fields: The Big Five Accounting Firms', *Academy of Management Journal*, 49, 1 (2006) 27–48.

Guillen, M. F., 'Is Globalization Civilizing, Destructive, or Feeble? A Critique of Five Key Debates in the Social-Science Literature', *Annual Review of Sociology*, 27 (2001) 235–260.

Hall, P. A. and D. W. Soskice, *Varieties of Capitalism: The Institutional Foundations of Comparative Advantage* (Oxford, UK: Oxford University Press, 2001).

Haunschild, P. R. and A. S. Miner, 'Modes of Interorganizational Imitation: The Effects of Outcome Salience and Uncertainty', *Administrative Science Quarterly*, 42 (1997) 472–500.

Haveman, H. A., 'Follow the Leader: Mimetic Isomorphism and Entry into New Markets', *Administrative Science Quarterly*, 38 (1993) 564–592.

Hodgkinson, G. P., R. Whittington, G. Johnson and M. Schwarz, 'The Role of Strategy Workshops in Strategy Development Processes: Formality, Communication, Co-ordination and Inclusion', *Long Range Planning*, 39 (2006) 479–496.

Huff, A. S., 'Industry Influences on Strategy Reformulation', *Strategic Management Journal*, 3 (1982) 119–131.

Johnson, G., S. Smith and B. Codling, 'Micro Processes of Institutional Change in the Context of Privatization', *Academy of Management Review, Special Topic Forum*, 25, 3 (2000) 572–580.

Lamertz, K. and J. A. C. Baum, 'The Legitimacy of Organizational Downsizing in Canada: An Analysis of Explanatory Media Accounts', *Canadian Journal of Administrative Sciences*, 15 (1998) 93–107.

Lawrence, T. and R. Suddaby, 'Institutions and Institutional Work', in S. R. Clegg, C. Hardy, T. B. Lawrence and W. R. Nord (eds) *The Sage Handbook of Organizational Studies*, 2nd edn (London, UK: Sage Publications, 2006).

Leblebici, H., G. R. Salancik, A. Copay and T. King, 'Institutional Change and the Transformation of the US Radio Broadcasting Industry', *Administrative Science Quarterly*, 36 (1991) 333–363.

Meyer, J. W. and B. Rowan, 'Institutionalized Organizations: Formal Structure as Myth and Ceremony', *American Journal of Sociology*, 83 (1977) 340–363.

Oliver, C., 'The Antecedents of Deinstitutionalization', *Organization Studies*, 13 (1992) 563–588.

Oliver, C., 'The Influence of Institutional and Task Environment Relationships on Organizational Performance: The Canadian Construction Industry', *Journal of Management Studies*, 34, 1 (1997) 99–124.

Palmer, D. A., P. D. Jennings and X. Zhou, 'Late Adoption of the Multidivisional Form by Large U.S. Corporations: Institutional, Political, and Economic Accounts', *Administrative Science Quarterly*, 38 (1993) 100–131.

Porac, J., H. Thomas and C. Baden-Fuller, 'Competitive Groups as Cognitive Communities: The Case of the Scottish Knitwear Manufacturers', *Journal of Management Studies*, 26 (1989) 397–415.

Powell, W. W. and P. DiMaggio (eds) *The New Institutionalism in Organizational Analysis* (Chicago: University of Chicago Press, 1991).

Rao, H., P. Morin and R. Durand, 'Institutional Change in Toqueville: Nouvelle Cuisine as an Identity Movement in French Gastronomy', *American Journal of Sociology*, 108 (2003) 795–843.

Scott, W. R., *Institutions and Organizations* (Thousand Oaks: Sage Publications, 1995).

Seo, M.-G. and W. E. D. Creed, 'Institutional Contradictions, Praxis and Institutional Change: A Dialectical Perspective', *Academy of Management Review*, 27 (2002) 222–247.

Slack, T. and C. R. Hinings, 'Isomorphism and Organizational Change', *Organization Studies*, 15 (1995) 803–828.

Spender, J. C., *Industry Recipes* (Oxford, UK: Basil Blackwell, 1989).

Thelen, K., *How Institutions Evolve: The Political Economy of Skills in Germany, Britain, The United States and Japan* (New York: Cambridge University Press, 2004).

Thornton, P., 'The Rise of the Corporation in a Craft Industry: Conflict and Conformity in Institutional Logics', *Academy of Management*, 45 (2002) 81–101.

Tolbert, P. S. and L. G. Zucker, 'Institutional Sources of Change in the Femoral Structure of Organizations. The Diffusion of Civil Service Reform, 1880–1935', *Administrative Science Quarterly*, 28 (1983) 22–39.

Tolbert, P. S. and L. G. Zucker, 'The Institutionalization of Institutional Theory', in S. Clegg, C. Hardy and W. R. Nord (eds) *Handbook of Organization Studies* (London: Sage Publications, 1996), pp. 175–190.

Westphal, J. D., R. Gulati and S. M. Shortell, 'Customization or Conformity? An Institutional and Network Perspective on the Content and Consequences of TQM Adoption', *Administrative Science Quarterly*, 42 (1997) 366–394.

Whitley, R., *Divergent Capitalisms: The Social Structuring and Change of Business Systems* (Oxford, UK: Oxford University Press, 1999).

Zucker, L. G., 'The Role of Institutionalization in Cultural Persistence', *American Sociological Review*, 42 (1977) 726–743.

Zucker, L. G., 'Institutional Theories of Organizations', *Annual Review of Sociology*, 13 (1987) 443–464.

CHAPTER 3

Military Strategy Perspective*

Sylvie Jackson

Basic principles

It could be considered that much of what we think of as strategy and indeed leadership today owe much to the military and military style. Military strategy continues to hold much interest judging by the 115 million results identified by a google.com search (search on military strategy).

'Military strategy' is a collective name for planning the conduct of war (www.wikipedia.org) and derives from the Greek '*strategos*' where strategy was seen as the 'art of the general'. As such it involves the planning and conduct of a campaign, the movement and disposition of forces and deception of the enemy – all of which will ring true to organisations operating in competitive environments. This chapter seeks to demonstrate the relevance of military strategy for strategic management and practice.

For the military, strategy and tactics are closely related as they both deal with distance, time and force. Strategy is large-scale and tactics are small-scale. Historically, strategy was understood to govern the prelude to a battle while tactics controlled its execution. However, the distinctions became blurred during the World Wars of the twentieth century. Historically, a king or political leader was the military leader but as professional armies developed the roles of politicians and the military became separated with some holding the view that there was a need for such a separation. Georges Clemenceu, French statesman, said (www.wikipedia.org), 'war is too important a business to be left to soldiers'. This led to the development of levels of war (discussed in detail later in the chapter).

An understanding of military strategy is relevant for strategic management scholars and business management students because of their common history and language. Business practitioners will use military metaphors and both military and business leaders share a common problem set: what to do under conditions of uncertainty and stress when the consequences of failure are unpleasant or viewed as unacceptable.

It would be easy for business management scholars to dismiss military experience as being of use, particularly if they cite the number of high-profile failures discussed in the history books or media such as the Battle of the Somme (1916) in the First World War or the US counter insurgency operations in Vietnam in the 1960s–1970s. Yet this is to discount all that has been learned, as military strategy has evolved in the face of changing environments and with the rise of a different style of threat.

Another argument might be that business organisations are not at war and do not seek to destroy each other but will act in co-operative ways as well as competitive ways for the common good. However, some organisations do seek to destroy their competitors, either through acquisition or price competition, such as Wal-mart in the United States, who aim to ensure that if there is only room for one store in a small town, it will be their store. When Komatsu entered the market, their mission was to 'kill Caterpillar' and this combative style allowed them to quickly pick up a considerable market share. The daily newspapers in the United Kingdom regularly engage in price wars in a bid

---

* This chapter is developed by Sylvie Jackson from Philip Davies' original chapter in *Strategic Management: A Multiple-Perspective Approach*.

to increase sufficient circulation over their rivals to make their longevity unsustainable. In grand strategy, enemies can become friends and vice versa. Germany has moved from being a friend of the United States prior to 1914, an enemy between 1914 and 1945 and a friend again since 1955 as a partner in NATO. The commercial sector sees similar trends within the commercial defence sector where organisations like BAE Systems will compete with or co-operate in a network of alliances with aerospace partners to ensure they gain lucrative contracts. Military and business strategies are both concerned with building and sustaining competitive advantage and organisational effectiveness under uncertain (maybe dangerous) conditions, where an unsuccessful outcome will have adverse consequences. Many countries in the world now have recent experience of warfare or compulsory military service. Former military personnel move into business and take what they have learned from their training with them to use for those requirements common to both business and the military, such as a need for cohesion, clear direction and division of labour. Case studies used in business schools are the equivalent of a campaign plan in a military academy. This commonality of purpose means that practitioners have an interest in learning from military examples and finding military metaphors useful when considering their own issues (Boar, 1995; Ramsey, 1987). The UK Defence Strategic Leadership Programme introduces generals, commodores and air commodores to their commercial counterparts in a specially designed day where a company brings their strategic issues to the military to get their viewpoint into how they might be solved and vice versa. Companies involved include LloydsTSB, Barclays Bank and the BBC. At least a dozen of these encounter days have been run to date with both sides finding them hugely informative and useful.

Overview of military strategy

Development of military strategy

The principles and ideas embraced within military strategy can be traced back to 500 BC in early Spartan thinking and writings of Sun Tzu in 400 BC (Sun, 1981). Strategic planning and movement were demonstrated in campaigns of Alexander the Great, Hannibal, Julius Caesar and Qin Shi Huang. Genghis Khan on the other hand did not use grand strategy but owed his success in conquering most of Eurasia to the manoeuvrist style approach and terror – he used the psychology of the opposing population. He achieved considerable rapidity of movement due to his armies' reliance on the horse-herds of Mongolia which not only provided transport but also horse milk and horse blood which were the staples of the Mongolian diet. Machiavelli (early 1600's) developed early insight on change (Machiavelli, 1962). However, military strategy did not become a subject of serious study until the eighteenth century. A 'strategy of exhaustion' was improvised by Frederick the Great during the Seven Years' War (1756–1763) to hold off the enemy and conserve his forces. By exploiting his central position, and moving along interior lines, he was able to concentrate on one opponent at a time and hold off defeat until a diplomatic solution was reached. The French Revolution and Napoleonic Wars revolutionised military strategy as the arrival of cheap small arms allowed for the growth of armies to become massed formations which could be divided into different levels of mobility and firepower. Napoleon as both leader and general dealt with grand strategy and operational strategy and achieved success through superior manoeuvre until his opponents adopted those same strategies. Carl von Clausewitz (1982) was a student of Napoleon's work, a Prussian with a background in philosophy whose *On War* has become a bible of strategy dealing with political and military leadership. Like Napoleon, he believed in the concept of victory through battle and destruction of the enemy at all cost although he did recognise 'the strategy of attrition' where the enemy would be worn down. Generals of the American Civil War (1861–1865), such as Lee, Grant and Sherman, were also influenced by Napoleon but the adherence to his principles in the face of the technological advances such as the long-range rifle often led to disastrous consequences. The time and space in which war was waged also changed with the advent of railroads and steam power which allowed for transportation of large forces and introduced combat at sea. Despite the introduction of the machine gun which had demonstrated its defensive capabilities in the Second Boer War (1899–1902) and Russo-Japanese War (1904–1905), the First World War strategy was dominated by the previous offensive thinking. The War saw armies on a larger scale than ever seen before but quickly developed into a strategy of attrition on the Western Front as the ability to manoeuvre was lost. This rapid expansion of forces outpaced the training of officers who would be able to handle strategic planning of such a large force. Technological advances also had a significant influence on strategy such as the automobile and the tank, telephones and radio telegraphy, poison gas, artillery techniques and aerial reconnaissance. More than any previous war, military strategy was directed by the Grand Strategy of a coalition of countries. Technological change has had a significant impact on strategy since, allowing for rapid movement of troops, used to great effect by the Germans in the Second World War and the development and deployment of strategic deception and sophisticated ruses led by British Intelligence to mislead German planners resulting in ineffective actions. The period following the Second World War, known as the Cold War was dominated by the threat of nuclear weapons and total world annihilation. The two most powerful nations, the United States and the Soviet Union, rather than overtly fight with each other used other countries as proxies. With improved communication and command technologies, the difference between the strategic and the tactical levels became more confused. Strategy since the Cold War has been defined and dominated by the superpower status of the United States. Technology's role is now viewed as a way to minimise casualties and improve efficiency. In the same way that organisations change in line with their environment, so the role of the military in many countries today has changed. Whilst there is still a need to defend the country and its interests, the perceived increased threat of terrorism post 9/11 has led to many security reviews and the introduction of joint working of the armed forces with security services to provide 'homeland security'. In addition, peacekeeping and humanitarian aid support have become new roles for some countries with the rise of what is known as the 'three block war' – which embraces the idea that within a small area, armed forces may be responsible for warfighting, peacekeeping and offering humanitarian aid. These are clearly very different roles and require considerable flexibility. Coupled with this is the new idea of 'effects-based war', where the actual 'war' itself is part of a much wider strategy; an example of this is Iraq, where removal of Saddam Hussein and defeat of his troops could be seen as part of a wider strategy of bringing democracy to the country. Conflict and warfare continue in many parts of the world often remaining unresolved and resulting in human suffering. As long as there are independent states, disagreements over territories and resources and minorities whose political or religious aspirations are being denied, there will be conflicts.

Principles of war

Military strategists analyse actual campaigns and aim to deduce from practice the essential principles of war and construct a clear doctrine on the basis of which commanders can plan and fight battles. This is a highly pragmatic and theory-building process. New technologies are tested in simulations and exercises test their impact. Defeat in campaigns allows for many lessons to be learned and innovations in military strategy. There continues to be considerable intellectual investment in military strategy not only in military staff colleges and headquarters but also in academic departments and specialist professional journals.

Doctrine is the best estimation of the way the country's armed forces and those who command them should go about their military business. According to British Defence Doctrine (BDD, 2001, p. 3-1), doctrine is not merely a record of past practice, it is an assessment of the best approach based on a sound understanding of current imperatives and lessons learned from past experience – both the good and the bad. As far as the British are concerned, doctrine is flexible to allow commanders to seize the initiative and adopt unorthodox or imaginative courses of action as the opportunities arise; doctrine is about a way of thinking, not about what one must think.

Doctrine states that in planning for war and in executing that plan, commanders and their staffs at all levels need to take certain principles into consideration. These are not rigid laws but provide guidance. The 10 principles of war (BDD, 3-2–3-3) are addressed below. These are similar to those of NATO and the US Army.

1. *Selection and maintenance of aim.* It is essential to select and clearly define the overall aim (the Master Principle). Each phase of the war and each separate operation is directed towards this supreme aim, but it will have its own limited aim which must be clearly defined, simple and direct. Once the aim is defined, all efforts are directed to its attainment unless/until the situation changes and a new aim is required.

2. *Maintenance of morale.* Morale is often the key to success, rather than physical qualities. Good morale provides courage, energy, determination, skill and a bold offensive spirit which cannot be compensated for by numbers of forces, armament and resources. Development and maintenance of morale are therefore essential.

3. *Offensive action.* Until the initiative is seized and the offensive taken, success cannot be achieved. The attacker will gain the initiative as the enemy has to react to the attacker's movements. Whilst offensive action involves risk, it does improve the morale of its forces.

4. *Security.* This entails adequate defence of high value assets (such as bases, platforms, weapons systems and men) and information to preserve a commander's freedom of action. It should not imply undue caution and avoidance of risks, as it is bold action which leads to success.

5. *Surprise.* Surprise is a most effective and powerful influence because it can achieve results out of all proportion to the efforts expended. The elements of surprise are secrecy, concealment, deception, originality, audacity and speed.

6. *Concentration of force.* Military success goes to the side which can concentrate superior force (moral and material) at the decisive time and place. It is not about numbers but about being able to deliver the decisive blow when and where required.

7. *Economy of effort.* A balanced employment of forces coupled with judicious expenditure of all resources provides economy of effort in achieving an effective concentration at the decisive time and place.

8. *Flexibility.* A high degree of flexibility allows pre-arranged plans to be altered to meet changing situations and unexpected developments. It entails good training, organisation, discipline and staff work along with rapidity of decision-making by the commander.

9. *Co-operation.* All military operations require co-operation to be successful. The increased inter-dependence of the individual armed services and increasing mutual dependence of armed forces of allies and coalition partners has made co-operation vital. Goodwill and the desire to co-operate are essential at all levels. With the increased humanitarian role, it is also necessary to co-operate with non-governmental agencies, many of whom will have aims and objectives which seem at variance to those in the military plan.

10. *Sustainability.* This covers the logistics and administrative arrangements which allow the force to maintain the necessary of combat power for the time required to meet its objectives.

The above principles of war need to be adapted to context, so their relative importance will vary according to circumstance. Historical perspectives and experience are likely to creat[e] on importance in different countries. For example, Australia's involvement in the Vietnam the 1960s has made it very wary of mission creep – where a small initial commitment b[ecomes] major involvement. The United States is in a similar situation with Iraq, where what they would be a short-term commitment is likely to continue to be a lengthy commitment of large numbers of troops. The United States is also conscious of the need to minimise casualties to maintain civilian morale and support for the conflict which dates back to its own involvement in the Vietnam War.

Linking military strategy to strategic management

Whilst these are the principles of war, a parallel can be seen with organisations operating in highly competitive environments. They also need to identify a key aim with all operations supporting the key aim. They need to maintain the morale of their staff to foster the will to win and secure their assets and information which is likely to be their competitive advantage. Surprise and offensive action are key to the introduction of new products and services, whilst maintaining economy of effort and flexibility in their planning and execution of strategy. Finally co-operation is increasingly important with suppliers and partners in alliances and, like the military, sustainability must be built in to ensure the overall objective is gained and not just the quick wins. Essentially, the military approach does fit well into the classic business strategy framework of analysis, choice and implementation. Using the framework of our seven Cs model – context, competences, culture, competing, corporate, change and control, let us look at some of these areas in more detail.

Context

Context is the environment in which the military campaign is to take place. According to British Doctrine (BDD, 2001, p. 1-2), military activities are conducted at different levels involving different people, from the senior political leadership of the state to the armed forces at the forefront of military operations. Within NATO there are four levels currently accepted as providing a framework for command and analysis: the grand strategic, the military strategic, the operational and tactical. Grand strategy covers the full range of issues associated with the maintenance of political independence and territorial integrity and the pursuit of wider national interests. The difficulties in Iraq which have been seen since the defeat of Saddam Hussein have stemmed from a lack of consensus about the policy objectives in the region – the Grand Strategy! Similar difficulties have occurred in the Balkans and reflect a poor strategy process in NATO. The lack of a defined end state has led to a lack of agreement over military strategy. Military strategy is the component part of the grand strategy. The operational level is where campaigns are planned and the tactical level is where war fighting actually takes place. The levels of war provide a framework for the command and control of operations and a useful tool for the analysis of politico-military activity before, during and after the conduct of military operations. According to British Doctrine (ibid., 1–3), this essence of planning at each level is to identify the desired *end*, the *ways* in which it is to be achieved and adequate *means* of achieving it. If this cannot be achieved at any level, the issue needs to be balanced at the level above.

Military strategy recognises that the strategic environment is complex and uses an analysis very similar to PEST (Greiss, 1985). This covers political, economic, physical, scientific and technical, social and cultural and legal, ethical and moral perspectives. Assessment of these areas is subjective just as it is with business, but the military also have to consider the idea of national interests within it. Whilst there may be general consensus of essential interests, there is also the idea of vital interests and marginal interests where there is considerable scope for interpretation. The strategic doctrine needs to be flexible enough to cope with shifts in perception of national interest reflected in policy.

With the changed environment and war on terror, there has been a need to develop counterinsurgency operations which do not fit readily into the different levels described above. This has led to the manoeuvrist approach. The aim is to shatter the enemy's overall cohesion and will to fight rather than his material. It aims to apply strength against identified vulnerabilities and covers the three concepts of *deep, close* and *rear* (Bulloch, 1996, pp. 4–16). Deep operations tend to be political, diplomatic and psychological in nature. Military involvement may be through covert and clandestine action such as cross-border co-operation and surveillance of areas. Close operations take place at the tactical level and involve reassuring the public and fostering improved community relations or they will be reactive to insurgent group's activities. Rear operations cover not only physical protection of the force, but also secure political and public support from which all government freedom of action follows. The military commander may identify government vulnerabilities such as important people or economic assets and use these as decisive points in their campaign. With deep, close and rear operations, Bulloch (ibid.) suggests there is a discrete and undefined balance among reassurance, the application of deterrence and military action. To achieve victory, British Doctrine (BDD, 2001, p. 3-6) states that those commanding at all levels of warfare need to comprehend the ways in which the enemy's military force is structured and deployed, and what are its inherent strengths and weaknesses. Emphasis is on defeat and disruption of the enemy by taking the initiative and applying constant and unacceptable pressure at the times and places the enemy least suspects. A key characteristic is the attacking of the enemy commander's decision-making process by attempting to get inside his decision-making cycle and presenting them with the need to make decisions at a faster rate than that with which they can cope, thus taking inappropriate or no action and paralysing their capability to react. Colonel John Boyd, a US Air Force pilot and military strategist of the late twentieth century, is credited with the concept that the decision cycle or OODA loop (see Figure 3.1) reacts to an event and the key to victory is to be able to create situations wherein the commander can make more appropriate decisions more quickly than the enemy. This manoeuvrist approach is one which could be considered and used by business organisations more. We do see some use of the approach with the discrediting of competitors – Nat West banking offering what other banks have stopped offering (branches, personal contact, etc.) and the campaign between Proctor and Gamble and Lever Brothers over the new washing powder which the competitor said disintegrated clothes.

Competences

Competences fall into two areas for the military – the attributes, skills and competences of individuals and military competence which is referred to as capability. A capability will allow the military to achieve a defined purpose at various levels – strategic, operational or tactical and take into account anything

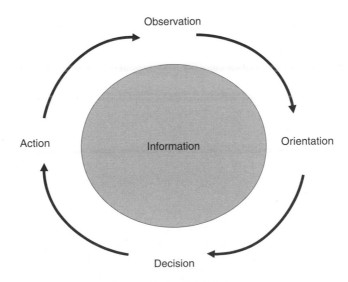

Figure 3.1 OODA loop

the enemy might do to prevent the action. Tactical capabilities will generally only influence the actual battlefield as they have a shorter range. Strategic capability could, for example, cover considerable distance and destroy the enemy's strategic assets, such as a cruise missile. Maritime capability could prevent the enemy from using a sea area and might entail the use of aircraft or even space-based surveillance, which might mean that ships were not used at all. Hinge (2000) (www.defence.gov.au) in his book *Preparedness* suggests that when defining the military capability required for a future force, the capability will not be built in response to a single context nor a single point in time, rather future capability decisions are based on being able to meet the challenges of a range of possible futures.

For the military, strategic capability can take considerable time to build up. An additional challenge is that the capability must be relevant to requirements for both the present and the future (www.ameinfo.com, 25 August 2006). This challenge is made more difficult by the cost and long lead times for acquisition and the length of time that capital equipment will remain in service (in some cases 30–50 years). Capability like competences is not just about equipment but needs to be understood as a number of areas which contribute. These include organisation, equipment, personnel, training, doctrine, facilities and support. By adopting this wide view, armed forces can ensure that investment is made in all the appropriate areas. For example introducing new technologies will not give capability if forces are not trained in their use. The Australian Defence Forces have engaged Noetic Solutions (ibid.) to assist in the development of tools that will assist in capability decision-making. The tools are concepts of operations for a range of illustrative planning scenarios that identify potential military responses to crisis events. The possible responses are able to employ a range of military capabilities that can then be tested against one another for their cost-effectiveness. Whilst capability takes time to build up, it can be lost relatively quickly either because of changes in structure or because of not keeping up with technology developments; for example, the extensive reduction of British troops in Germany during the last couple of years means that the capability shown during Exercise Lionheart in 1984, where 131,000 troops carried out a field training exercise in West Germany, is no longer in place and would be difficult to rebuild. At the same time, other capabilities have been deemed too important to be lost. In 2006 the British Government revealed that it had agreed to the continuance of nuclear deterrent capability despite the huge costs involved, the non-proliferation agreements in place and without consultation with Parliament.

The long decline of Canadian Defence Forces through lack of investment has led to loss of considerable capability and a difficulty in fulfilling their NATO and peacekeeping obligations for the UN. General Rick Hillier, Chief of Defence Forces, reported (Hobson, 2006) the government had announced CAD 17.1 billion worth of new projects: 3 Joint Support Ships, 4 strategic transport aircraft, 17 tactical transport aircraft, 16 medium-to-heavy lift helicopters and 2300 medium-sized logistics trucks to plug the capability gap.

The military and business perspectives on competences are very similar. Force planners in defence policy use resource-based theory (Chapter 9) to argue for capabilities implicitly, while business strategists have applied resource-based theory to help explain Britain's defeat of the Franco-Spanish fleet at Trafalgar in 1805 (Pringle and Kroll, 1997) in terms of the superior resources that the British had in respect of tactical ability. They argue that the Royal Navy had developed superior competences in terms of skill with weapons, acceptance of casualties and a more aggressive tactical doctrine. These competences were inimitable because the Royal Navy had, by means of its naval blockade, prevented French and Spanish naval units from acquiring the necessary experience.

For military the key capability is 'fighting power' and this is made up of three inter-related components: conceptual, moral and physical. The conceptual component provides the thought processes needed to develop the ability to fight. It comprises lessons from the past and also thinking about how the Armed Forces can best operate in the present and in the future. It includes not only doctrine and the principles of war but also conceptual thinking to ensure the development of fighting power into the future. The defence capabilities (BDD, 2001, p. 4-2) to deliver fighting power are a robust and responsive means of command; a process to inform; a means to prepare; measures and resources to project; the means to protect; the ability to sustain, all of which are necessary to operate. The moral component is about persuading people to fight. Napoleon (ibid., p. 4-1) is supposed to have remarked 'the moral is to the material as three to one'. The moral component is dependent on good morale and the conviction that the purpose is morally and ethically sound. Contributors include training, confidence in equipment, fair and firm discipline, self-respect and a clear understanding of what is happening and what is required. Morale in the British Forces in Iraq during the current conflict has been dented by lack of equipment (body armour) and by the prosecution of individual soldiers for ill treatment of Iraqi soldiers and civilians. The physical component is the means to fight and covers five elements: manpower, equipment, collective performance, readiness and sustainability. These clearly defined components make it relatively easy to determine whether 'fighting power' capability is in place. How many businesses have clearly defined their required competences and how they can measure their performance against them?

Culture

Despite the fact that each of the services, regiments, ships and air bases has its own unique traditions, stories and rituals, culture is the glue that holds the military forces together. To the outsider it might seem that there is but one common culture but in reality it is not the case. However, the military recognise the need to co-operate at all levels and increasingly with other organisations, be they allies, through NATO, in joint peacekeeping forces with other nations or in more and more joint working within their own armed forces. There is often much good-natured joking between the different services. In the United Kingdom, the army always comment that the RAF when away from home base must first search out the nearest five star hotels to stay in. The Australian military describes its separate service cultures as the Three Ds: dumb (army), devious (air force) and defiant (navy). The fact that this terminology is actually approved of by the services themselves is perhaps indicative of their self-confidence.

Research has shown (Marshall, 1978) that culture is important because people do not ultimately fight or die for their country alone but also for their friends – the members of their team. This has been demonstrated by soldiers like Wilfred Owen, the poet and infantry company commander, who despite hating the war, after recuperating from concussion and trench fever, returned to the battlefield to be with his troops. He died in action in 1918.

The military world is a very different one to that of the civilian and it is the culture that makes it so. The 'soldier' is marked out by the different style of his uniform, his lifestyle, rank and what is expected of him – to kill or be killed. The military world is self-contained and provides everything; at the same time, it asks everything of its members. Only recently, with the entry of women into a wider role in the military, has the culture begun to change. For some countries, this is not the case, as women have always had an equivalent role to men, for example Israel. The self-contained world is sustained with much socialising for both the military and their families, thus creating inclusiveness. Former military wives complain that wives and families are regarded as appendages of the soldier and say they grew tired of being 'the wife of . . . '. Officers and soldiers go through a type of rite of passage when they join which is rigorous and provides a clear set of values – this creates a feeling of being elite. The life of the soldier is very structured and whilst this makes it difficult for long career soldiers to fit back into the wider choices of society when they leave; it is also becoming clear that the structure and values are a draw for many young people whose lives lack them.

Organisations such as the management consultant McKinsey have used similar techniques with candidates passing a series of tough interviews and taking on new codes and values. Like the military, there is a sense of belonging, even after you leave the organisation. Professions such as the law and medicine also have strong cultures and a sense of belonging.

There is a divide between operations and staff jobs in the military: only those who in the infantry, armour or cavalry will attain the top-ranking jobs, as it is felt that to send other people to war you must have experienced combat yourself. Staff jobs are increasingly complex and there is recognition that more professionalism is required in areas such as logistics, procurement, human resources, finance and project management, although the notion of military staff becoming functional specialists in staff jobs is still facing resistance. With the civilianisation of an increasing number of staff jobs, the cultural difference between military staff and civil servants is a wide gulf according to many military staff who do not understand the clock watching, but are quick to praise the political skills of their civilian colleagues. Health services have similar problems with medical staff regarding themselves as the elite against an army of pen-pushing management, who do not add value. Any large organisation can learn from the military that although a common culture is ideal, the common values and co-operation are the components of success and a coherent organisation.

Competing

The idea of choosing how, when and where to compete and for what purpose is different for the military. The choice to compete is made generally at political level which will determine some sort of end state. This should allow the military to devise a suitable mission with a set of objectives. The mission is broken down into a set of activities for each component of the force. This is known as mission analysis. An important part of mission analysis is to always keep in mind the reason for the operation (Master principle), so that if circumstances alter, changes can be made to the plan. The concept of Mission Command was adopted by the British in relatively recent years but the need for decentralised command, freedom and speed of action and initiative which is responsive to superior direction can be traced back to the loss of British troops on the beaches at Gallipoli. Officers were told to take the beaches, which they achieved relatively easily, but as they had no further orders or knowledge of the superior commander's intention to continue further inland and defeat the enemy, they stayed on the beaches, becoming easy targets. Had they known of the intent, they could have pressed on inland and fewer lives would have been lost.

Mission Command has the following key elements (BDD, 2001, p. 3-7):

1. A commander ensures that his subordinates understand his intentions, their own missions, and the strategic, operational and tactical context.
2. Subordinates are told what effect they are to achieve and the reason why it is necessary.
3. Subordinates are allocated sufficient resources to carry out their missions.
4. A commander uses the minimum of control so as not to limit unnecessarily his subordinate's freedom of action.
5. Subordinates decide for themselves how best to achieve their missions.

Another contribution by military strategy to competitive strategy is the idea of offensive action and the use of surprise. Offensive action, particularly where forces may be widely dispersed, whilst risky, is usually more successful than remaining locked in a defensive enclave. Lawrence (1962) describes how the Arab forces in the Middle East gained the initiative over the Turks by means of such tactics. Businesses may find this a useful strategy when operating in new markets where there are no established competitors, or when developing new technologies.

Corporate

As identified earlier the role of defence in many countries has changed, particularly in the last 10 to 20 years. A number of countries such as Chile and Jordan have always used their armed forces for a number of roles above and beyond that of defence, for example the development of infrastructure such as roads and for supporting medical services or even running hospitals. The wider remit than defending 'hearth and home' has led to new vision statements – the UK Ministry of Defence, for example, 'Defending the United Kingdom and its interests; acting as force for good in the world.'

This changed role arose in response to the Strategic Defence Review of 1998 which recognised the changing environment. The UK had also seen more deployment of its armed forces (and continues to do so) in the last 10 years than since the Second World War. Indeed there is a view within the UK MoD that they are operating in permanent 'overstretch' and are having to call on a higher level of reservists than ever before and are also in danger of regularly breaching the agreed targets for number of days per year on deployment.

In 1999 in response to calls from the UK Cabinet Office and Treasury to demonstrate value for money, the Balanced Scorecard was introduced as a strategy and performance review tool. This tool developed by Kaplan and Norton (Kaplan and Norton, 1992) is widely known and used by tens of thousands of organisations. Its development in the United States meant that early interest and adopters have been in the United States and Europe but interest is spreading to defence in other countries through teaching and discussion at courses at the Defence Academy of the United Kingdom.

In response to the suggestion by Kaplan and Norton that the scorecard be adapted and tailored to suit the organisation (an unusual aspect to most management models), both the US Department of Defense and the UK MoD have adapted the original scorecard discussed in a number of books and articles by Kaplan and Norton (Kaplan and Norton, 1992). The original scorecard populated by the author but as suggested by Kaplan and Norton is shown in Figure 3.2. As can be seen, there are four perspectives: Financial, Customer, Internal Business, and Innovation and Learning. The latter being an area often neglected by most organisations.

Realistically these perspectives work well for 'business' type organisations but are less applicable to the public sector. Some organisations have made minor amendments but stuck largely to the original format. Others have felt the need to identify a specific 'people' perspective either in addition or instead of one of the other perspectives. The US DoD is one such organisation, but keeping four perspectives. We see in Figure 3.3 that the Customer perspective has widened to embrace Operational Goals (essentially the role of the organisation as defined by government – the customer); the innovation and learning perspective has become 'future challenges'; financial and internal business perspectives have become institutional goals and the people perspective is called force management goals. Interestingly,

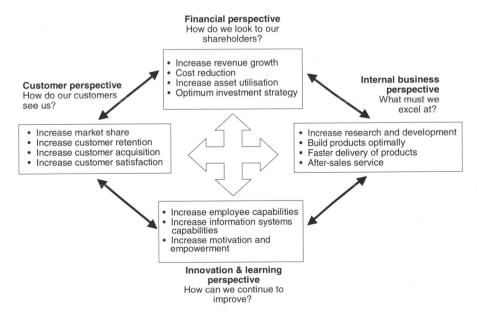

Figure 3.2 Completed Balanced Scorecard as suggested by Kaplan and Norton

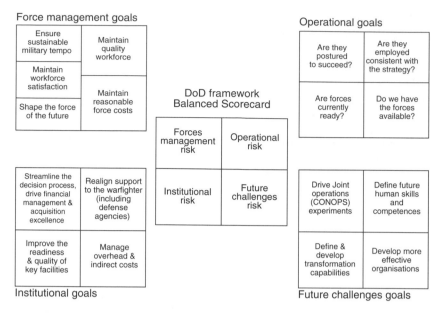

Figure 3.3 US Department of Defense Balanced Scorecard

the central box covering the headings of the perspectives refers to these as risks, which reminds the organisation that there are risks to be considered and taken into account before the goals will be achieved.

The UK MoD has also identified the importance of risk in achieving its strategic goals and has adapted the 3 × 3 matrix, showing likelihood and impact (high, medium and low), to the Balanced Scorecard, to show the key potential problems facing the goal realisation of the four perspectives (Figure 3.4). Like the US DoD example, the four perspectives have also been adapted to suit the organisation. An alternative is to show each of the strategies for each perspective separately on the risk grid but this would not identify the specific risks. As expected, taking into account the current 'overstretch' situation, operations success and sustainability are the key risks identified on the current scorecard.

The UK MoD Balanced Scorecard was introduced in 1999 and has seen a series of changes, with the current scorecard shown in Figure 3.5 being the first one to be in place for more than a 1-year period. As use of the scorecard has matured, the scorecard becomes a better management tool. The Defence Management Board has stated,

> The Defence Balanced Scorecard is for managing, not just for reporting performance. It should allow the Defence Management Board to make sensible, informed assessments of how the department is doing, in order to decide where particular efforts have to be made.

The UK Defence Balanced Scorecard now forms the basis of the Departmental Plan as it encapsulates the Board's key objectives and priorities, including the Public Service Agreement targets (from the government) which cover the full range of MoD business.

Like the US DoD scorecard there are four perspectives, although in this case they are laid out in the same style format as the original Kaplan and Norton scorecard. In the same way that the United States has used operational goals instead of customer, the United Kingdom has identified 'Purpose' as its customer perspective, again picking up the idea of its role. Future Capabilities (similar to that of the United States) covers the innovation and learning. The financial perspective has been broadened to cover all resources including manpower, and enabling processes covers the internal

Key:

1. Operations 2. Finance 3. Manning levels 4. Equipment availability 5. Sustainability 6. Infrastructure

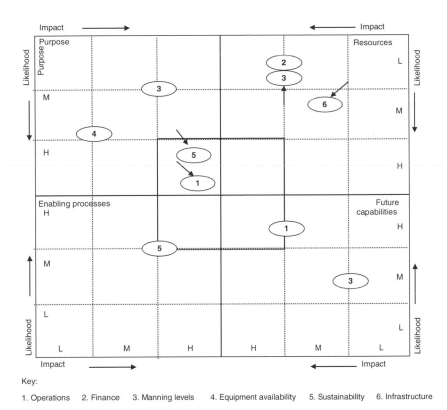

Figure 3.4 Illustrative example of risk picture for UK MoD
This figure is used with permission of UK MoD; however the views expressed are those of the author and not the UK MoD

Purpose
A Current operations: To succeed in Operations and Military Tasks today.
B Future operations: Be ready for the tasks of tomorrow.
C Policy: Work with Allies, other governments and multilateral institutions to provide a security framework that matches new threats and instabilities.
D Wider government: Contribute to the Government's wider domestic reform agenda, and achieve our PSA and PPA targets.

Are we fit for today's challenges and ready for tomorrow's tasks?

Are we making the best use of our resources?

Resources
E Finance: Maximise our outputs within allocated financial resources.
F Manpower: Ensure we have the people we need.
G Estate: Maintain an estate of the right size and quality in a sustainable manner, to achieve defence objectives.
H Reputation: Enhance our reputation amongst our own people and externally.

Defending the UK and its interests: acting as a force for good in the world

Are we a high performing organisation?

Enabling processes
I Personnel management: Manage and invest in our people to give of their best.
J Health and safety: A safe environment for our staff, contractors and visitors.
K Logistics: Support and sustain our Armed Forces.
L Business management: Deliver improved ways of working.

Are we building for future success?

Future Capabilities
M Future effects: More flexible Armed Forces to deliver greater effect.
N Efficiency and change: More flexible and efficient organisations and processes to support the Armed Forces.
O Future capabilities and infrastructure: Progress future equipment and capital infrastructure projects to time, quality and cost estimates.
P Future personnel plans: Develop the skills and professional expertise we need for tomorrow.
Q Science, innovation and technology: Exploit new technologies.

Figure 3.5 UK Defence Balanced Scorecard 2005–2007

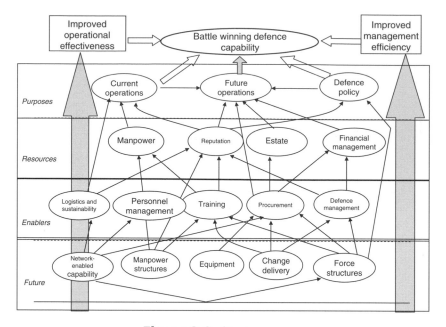

Figure 3.6 Strategy map

This figure is used with permission of UK MoD; however the views expressed are those of the author and not the UK MoD

business perspective which identifies those activities which will allow achievement of the purpose. With the development of the Balanced Scorecard by Kaplan and Norton into a strategy tool came the development of strategy maps which show how the strategies feed into the overarching goals or vision for the organisation. The UK MoD developed their strategy map (shown in Figure 3.6) in retrospect, thus it tends to suggest that all strategies feed into each of the strategies in the above perspective. However, what has been interesting is the revised strategy map which shows it illustrated

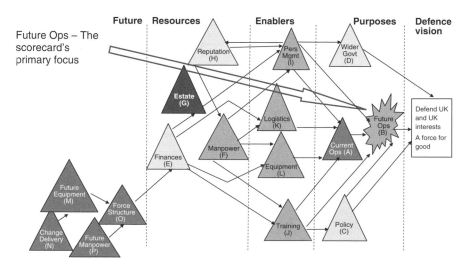

Figure 3.7 Strategy map as campaign plan

This figure is used with permission of UK MoD; however the views expressed are those of the author and not the UK MoD

as a campaign plan (Figure 3.7). Management tools and techniques have not always been received well in the military as there is often a view that business has nothing to do with them – indeed while teaching the Balanced Scorecard to a group on the Advanced Command and Staff Course at the Joint Services Command and Staff College at the Defence Academy of the United Kingdom, the author encountered some hostility from military historian staff and foreign military students, whose view was 'we are warriors, what is the relevance of this to us . . . ?' The adaptation of the tool to meet organisation needs, culture and language is a useful lesson for all organisations.

The adoption of business strategy has been useful for the military in many countries, but it can also be useful to us because they have often adapted it to suit their needs and in some cases added value to the original models, tools and techniques. One such area is the UK MoD adaptation of the Balanced Scorecard. By changing the perspective titles, they have created a simple model to explain strategic management.

The model shown in Figure 3.8 was developed by the author to explain the concept of strategic management to the newly appointed majors on the Intermediate Command and Staff Course (Land) run at the Defence Academy of the United Kingdom. The explanation begins by asking them if the organisation is still the same as the one they joined about 10 years ago. When they respond in the negative it allows the author to explain that all organisations undertake some sort of environmental scanning and analysis to see if the world is changing. As the world changes, so too does the role of the organisation. If the organisation changes, then the resources required to achieve the purpose change too; as do the activities to achieve the purpose. Finally we need to consider potential future challenges and prepare for change to ensure future capability and capacity. The model shows this in a simple way and allows an easier explanation of the MoD Balanced Scorecard as a useful one-page business plan.

This model has been received well by military students both inland and overseas and has now been adopted by the Directorate of Performance and Analysis who compile the Balanced Scorecard on behalf of the Defence Management Board. Figure 3.9 shows the same diagram with the key activities and tools and techniques mapped against each area.

The model also forms a useful basis for any organisational business plan as it reminds us to consider resources and activities. Most strategic plans consider the products and services of the organisation and their future linked with their markets. Often the resources and activities play a much smaller part if they even warrant a mention. Since organisations seldom follow the logical steps to strategic choices and implementation which takes into full account competences and resources, this is a useful reminder.

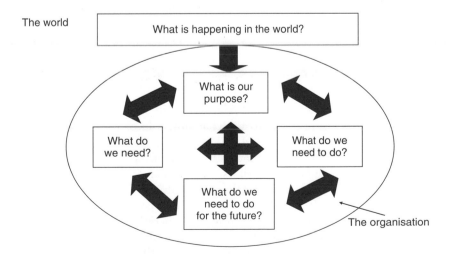

Figure 3.8 Strategic management

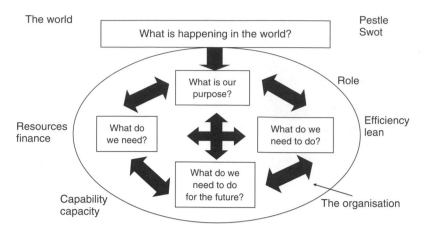

Figure 3.9 Strategic management with management tools and techniques

Change

Change within the existing paradigm has worked well for many years within the military. Historically, the military has always had to embrace new weaponry – although the tank was fiercely resisted by the cavalry in 1916. However, even today, the British Army is not convinced of the demise of the tank, citing its deployment in Iraq – Operation Telic – as vital. The idea of changing roles every 2–3 years is all part of the job and is welcomed by most. Whilst it keeps people fresh, there is little doubt that the military loses out with people in new posts having to go through a steep learning curve (particularly in staff jobs), doing the job well for 12–18 months, then taking their eye off the ball as they become interested in what their next posting will be. In terms of knowledge management, there are a lot of generalists in the military but few specialists, and knowledge is often lost as due to staff shortages, posts are 'gaped' with no opportunity for proper handovers. In addition, since recognition in most armed forces is by promotion, officers openly acknowledge that they will engage in change for change sake to prove they achieved something during their posting for their assessments by senior staff.

Changes outside the paradigm also present problems. Much major change is regarded as being imposed by government and unnecessary. In the United Kingdom, the Strategic Defence Review in 1998 led to significant changes to role, resources and activities, creating a Russian doll nesting effect for change which was clear and logical. Unfortunately this was sideswiped by demands from government to reduce costs further which led to the introduction of an efficiency programme and later the introduction of business process management. However, coupled with the major change programme leading from the Strategic Defence Review and the individual changes, it becomes clear that change in the UK MoD is confusing and in danger of sub-optimisation as different areas search for quick wins.

Furthermore, whilst army regiments merged relatively easily in the past, this was not a regular or significant occurrence. Today, in response to the changing role of the Armed Forces, the need to merge or even disband regiments (Northern Ireland) has led to major change particularly for front-line troops with, for example, all six Scottish Regiments merging into one. This had been felt very keenly in the Army where you join a regiment with all its traditions and culture; whereas in both the Navy and the Air Force you join the organisation and therefore reduction in staffing is less immediately felt.

However, the military approach is one of command, leadership and management and therefore once a decision is made and an order given (even in non-operational work), open opposition is not allowed and people are expected to get on with the implementation of change. The army style of 'can do' even if they are short of resources and focus on task means that a great deal can be achieved. This positive attitude is one which many organisations could learn from.

Control

Control is of vital importance to military strategy. Loss of control leads to mutiny and is something to be feared. Control is exercised through command which is supported by orders, culture and norms of behaviour. To reinforce this, the military use their own police and separate legal system. During operations, obeying orders is vital and in the past included extreme measures such as shooting deserters – in the First World War, 360 British soldiers were shot for desertion, which has caused some controversy since. In August 2006, the British Government announced that all 360 soldiers would be pardoned, much to the relief of their families who have fought to clear their names, declaring that most were suffering from shell shock. The announcement has brought further controversy, with suggestions that this is sanitising history, as shooting deserters was a common response in the military in the past. Indeed, in 1942, when the German Army was advancing on Moscow, Stalin issued a no retreat order and enforced the order by deploying squads of secret police to execute those who did not obey it. This action saved the Red Army. There is considerable concern even today in the military, where there have been refusals by some to be deployed to Iraq on the grounds that this is an 'unlawful war' and which has led to court cases at the highest levels in the United Kingdom.

Command is different from Leadership and Management, all of which are recognised in the military. The UK Defence Leadership and Management Centre (set up as a result of the Strategic Defence Review) has offered the following definition:

> Command is a position of authority and responsibility to which military men and women are legally appointed. Leadership and management are the key components to the successful exercise of Command. Successful management is readily measured against objective criteria but commanders are not leaders until their position has been ratified in the hearts and minds of those they command.

The DLMC have depicted this in the diagram in Figure 3.10, although they acknowledge that leadership is not just about the power of authority. Military officers are used to having command in operational settings where their subordinates will operate 24/7 as required. The move to staff postings where they may be working with large numbers of civilians in the purchasing, logistics, finance and human resources areas causes problems for some, as civil servants have very different expectations at work and do not respond to command. However, most military officers continue to function in their operational style and exercise control through use of deadlines and orders. The requirement for such a flexible style from officers has meant that many Armed Forces have resisted the civilianisation of their defence departments, even though it saves a considerable amount of money.

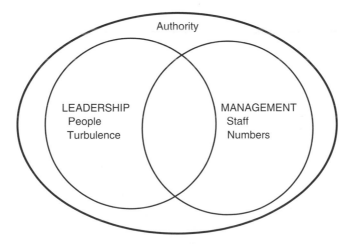

Figure 3.10 Military command and its relationship with leadership and management

Operationally, control over strategy is exercised through the use of maps and concerns how much land has been gained or lost – this can be clearly seen by everyone involved on both sides of the conflict.

The use of visual communication like these maps, rather than a lot of text, is a useful way of conveying progress towards strategic goals and is an area of use which can be transferred to business. The traffic light systems of the Balanced Scorecard and Tableau du Bord are used for non-operational reporting of performance in the military.

Summary

Like business strategy, military strategy has evolved but due to its resource-based approach, it has largely evolved in response to technology in providing capability or competence. The role of military, as one that defends the nation and its interests, has not changed, nor its key capability. The changing operating environment has meant that the old way of running military campaigns using the levels of war is no longer applicable but needs to take into account a grand strategy of coalitions of nations such as through NATO or the UN Security Council or alternatively be much more flexible using strategies like the manoeuvrist approach. The military show us that they are clear about their key capability 'fighting power' and its components and have a way to measure whether this capability is in place. At a lower level, some sub-components of capability have been lost but new ones gained in line with changes in technology and the perception of a changed 'enemy' in the form of terrorism.

Many military commanders now feel that their biggest battle is with government over allocation of funds and pressure for efficiency in delivering capability. Business is not and never will be war. We do not actually kill competitors, although sometimes we are happy to put them out of business. Like the military we can learn from the practices and wisdom of other contexts. The main lesson to be learnt from this reflection on military practice is the importance of human factors in the strategy process (the moral component). Clausewitz, who took part in the Napoleonic War, reminds us that the General lives in a realm of emotion, fear and intellectual turmoil. He has to take decisions based on inadequate data while physically tired and afraid. His mistakes could result in national defeat. Even victory is painful. Wellington, as he inspected the battlefield of Waterloo in 1815 after the French had been defeated, said that there was only one thing worse than a battle won – and that was a battle lost. Under such conditions of extreme fear the individual strategist cannot rely merely on a sound analytical technique. Strategists need to understand and deal with emotions.

The military have begun to learn from business as they begin to understand that if they get the business space right (human resources, finance, procurement and logistics) through the adoption of best business practice then the battle space will end up with better resources and the commander has more chance of success. As the military become more confident and mature in their use of business strategy and practices, their adaptation of them to fit their different set of circumstances can offer business a benchmark in understanding the need to tailor models, tools and techniques to fit differing organisations.

References

Boar, B., 'Sun Tzu and Machiavelli on Strategy', *Journal of Business Strategy*, xxvi, 1 (1995) 16–18.

British Defence Doctrine (*BBD*) (2001) Joint Warfare Publication, 0–01.

Bulloch, G., 'Military Doctrine and Counterinsurgency: A British Perspective', *Parameters*, XXVI, 2 (1996) 4–16.

Greiss, T. E., *Definitions and Doctrine of the Military Art* (Wayne, NJ: Avery, 1985).

Hinge, A., *Preparedness* (Canberra: Australian Defence Studies Centre, 2000).

Hobson, S., Interview General Rick Hillier, *Janes Defence Weekly* (9 August 2006).

Kaplan, R. and D. Norton, 'The Balanced Scorecard – Measures That Drive Performance', *Harvard Business Review*, 70, 1 (1992) 71–79.

Lawrence, T. E., *The Seven Pillars of Wisdom* (London: Penguin, 1962).

Machiavelli, N., *The Prince* (London: Penguin, 1962).

Marshall, S. L. A., *Men Against Fire* (Gloucester, Mass.: Peter Smith, 1978).

Pringle, C. D. and M. J. Kroll, 'Why Trafalgar Was Won: Lessons from Resource-Based Theory', *Academy of Management Executive*, 11, 4 (1997) 73–89.

Ramsey, D., *The Corporate Warriors* (London: Grafton, 1987).

Sun, T., *The Art of War* (London: Hodder and Stoughton, 1981).

von Clausewitz, C., *On War* (London: Penguin, 1982).

CHAPTER 4

A Spatial Perspective on Strategy

Stephen Tallman and Mark Jenkins

Basic principles

While most strategy theory and empirical testing of that theory give little consideration to location in space, the practice of strategy is much more aware of place, and the sub-field of international strategy concerns itself specifically with the intersection of strategic management and international business. This chapter will argue that in today's information-age, globalised world of business, the role of place in providing competitive advantage is becoming ever more critical to ever more firms – even those that do not particularly see themselves as multinational companies. A spatial perspective has several critical aspects for today's firms, particularly for those in the most technologically advanced industries. First, as *New York Times* columnist Friedman (2005) has it, 'the world is becoming flat'. That is, information technology, rapidly growing markets and new business processes are driving firms to look to customers, resources, suppliers, information workers and ideas on a global scale. If some companies do not supply demand in China, others will – and will return to compete in traditional markets from a position of strength. Activities that do not involve the idiosyncratic, rent-generating core of knowledge of the firm must be outsourced, often to emerging markets with large numbers of highly educated but underpaid workers – or at least this option must be considered. Even core value-adding activities may need to be sited outside the home market in order to access the best available ideas and skills. Firms without the global perspective to seek access to the best and most efficient factors of production, no matter where they might be located, are struggling.

Second, companies must understand where, really, these factors are located. World-class capabilities may be spatially distributed more widely than ever, but they are not evenly spread. Indeed, even as the world is becoming flat, in Friedman's terms, it is becoming more 'spiky', in the phrase of Florida (2005). That is, the assets and capabilities needed to face global competition may be in many places, and these places may be moving rapidly towards equal accessibility to the global market, but at the same time these places are becoming ever more tightly delimited – they are regions or cities, not countries. Inter *national* business is becoming more anachronistic even as inter*spatial* business is becoming ever more critical to strategic success. That is, the United States does not have human capital advantages in biotechnology; rather, the San Francisco Bay area, Austin, Texas, Los Angeles, the Washington DC region, and a number of other closely defined regional clusters do. India as a whole does not have an advantage in supplying commodity IT services (indeed, much of the country barely has electricity), but Bangalore and a couple of other cities do. China has 750 million people struggling to survive in the countryside, but the high-tech centers around Beijing, Shanghai and Guangzhou (and other key cities, mostly on the coastal plain) offer modern, world-class manufacturing and increasing intellectual capital. Thus a global perspective must be supplemented by knowledge of where – *exactly* where – world-class suppliers and collaborators may be located, and the acumen or contacts to know just who those individual companies might be. And, from the perspective of the many location-tied firms that may become parts of the global networks focused on the biggest multinationals, it is important to understand what skills and abilities can be built effectively from local competencies and also to have the global perspective to know how and with whom these capabilities can best be expanded and exploited. On both sides of the value-adding transaction, firms must have a sense of the local and the global to build the strategies that will succeed in the information-intensive, high-tech world.

CASE STUDY 4.1

In 1993 the name Mercedes-Benz appeared on a grand prix car, the first time for over 50 years since the 'silver arrows' had dominated grand prix racing in the 1930s. It was on a Sauber, a new Formula 1 team run by Peter Sauber, an enigmatic motorsport entrepreneur who had previously run the Mercedes-Benz sports car team. The partnership between Mercedes and Sauber was a logical one, both in terms of their past relationship and also also in terms of the physical and cultural proximity between Mercedes operations in Stuttgart in Southern Germany and Sauber's base at Hinwil near Zurich in northern Switzerland, a distance of just over 200 km by road. However, the engines would not be designed or manufactured by Mercedes in Stuttgart, but by Ilmor Engineering, a small specialist operation based just north of Northampton in the United Kingdom, 1000 km from Stuttgart. Mercedes had signed a 5-year contract with Ilmor to design and build engines for their Formula 1 programme.

Ilmor was founded on 1 January 1984 by two former employees of Formula 1 engine manufacturer Cosworth (Cosworth were based in Northampton, 11 km south of Brixworth and 100 km north of London), Mario Ilien and Paul Morgan (hence Il–mor). Ilien was an engine designer, and Morgan, also an engineer, took on the role of managing director. They were also able to attract a number of former Cosworth employees who had the expertise they needed to set up and run such a specialist operation. Having been based at Cosworth they all lived in the locality; this made the choice of location fairly straightforward, as explained by Paul Morgan: 'I live in Brixworth, and as racing involves long hours of work, it has always been handy for me to be able to pop home for a bite of supper, then come back afterwards!'[1]

Ilmor was founded in January 1984 with the objective to build an engine for the North American Indy car series. They were able to secure backing from Roger Penske, a US racing team owner who Paul had met while working for Cosworth. Penske's Indy racing headquarters was based in Reading, Philadelphia, United States of America, but they also had a chassis-building operation based in Poole, Dorset, United Kingdom. Penske put up the initial capital for the project and in return received half of the shares in the business; he was then able to secure further funding from General Motors to badge the engine as a Chevrolet and to whom he sold half of his stake, splitting the equity equally between Ilien, Morgan, Penske and General Motors. Ilmor proved able to create a very effective engine, and while Chevrolet got the credit, Ilmor created a very strong reputation in the motorsport industry. Between 1986 and 1999 they won 116 races, including 7 wins at the legendary Indianapolis 500, their engines finished first, second and third on no less than 56 occasions.

However, Ilmor also had ambitions to enter Formula 1 (which Cosworth had dominated in the early 1970s); this they did with the Leyton House team in 1991. Although they finished last in the constructors world championship, they did manage to gain their first world championship point. In 1992 they supplied both the March (formerly Leyton House) and the Tyrrell teams finishing ninth and sixth in the world championship, respectively.

Mercedes initially avoided putting their name on the engines, which were badged as Ilmor for the first year of competition (1993) with the statement 'concept by Mercedes-Benz' on the side of the car. The team produced an encouraging performance in the first year finishing sixth in the constructors championship out of 12 teams. As the success of the team grew, this was then modified to 'power by Mercedes-Benz' in 1994 with the engine now badged as a Mercedes-Benz, although it was still designed and manufactured at Brixworth. At the end of 1993 Ilmor strengthened their relationship with Mercedes-Benz by agreeing to build engines for the Indy racing programme in the United States; again these were badged as Mercedes-Benz and involved another collaboration with Roger Penske. Furthermore owners of Mercedes-Benz; DaimlerChrysler, took over the General Motors shareholding in Ilmor giving it a 25 per cent stake in the company. These engines were designed and built in only 23 weeks, underlining Ilmor's incredibly fast design and manufacturing process, a characteristic of many of the small British specialists operating in a region known as Motorsport Valley.

However, Sauber were not a front-running F1 team and towards the end of 1994 Mercedes announced that they would supply engines to the McLaren F1 team in 1995. McLaren were based in Woking, Surrey, and had previously used their engine partnership with Honda to great effect, winning 15 out of 16 grand prix in 1988. This relationship led to a highly successful period with Mercedes-badged Ilmor engines winning the F1 constructors world championship with McLaren in 1998 and the drivers championship for Mika Hakkinen in 1998 and 1999. The reason why Mercedes-Benz used Ilmor was summarised by board member Jürgen Hubbert in 1996: 'We could build an engine that would be powerful and strong. But the trouble would come when it took three hours to change the engine in the car! Because of our inexperience at that time, we had no understanding of what was really needed. It's not just about power. It's how to build the engine, the dimensions, the weight, having the centre of gravity in the right place, and making it so an engine can be changed in forty-five minutes. Ilmor had the knowledge to bring these things together and we had no doubt that this was the way forward for us.'

In the space of 15 years up to 1999 Ilmor had grown from 13 employees in their first year to 500 people with annual sales of over US$140 million and profits of US$7 million. In May 2001 Paul Morgan was tragically killed in an accident in his vintage aeroplane; Morgan was 52 years old at the time of his death. This created something of a crisis in Ilmor as Morgan had been so pivotal in the organisation. Mercedes-Benz responded by extending their shareholding in 2002 to 55 per cent and renaming the company Mercedes-Ilmor. They also agreed to purchase a further 15 per cent per annum over 3 years until 2005. On 1 July 2005 the company was wholly owned by DaimlerChrysler and was renamed Mercedes-Benz High Performance Engines Ltd, but while the name had changed, the address remained Brixworth, Northamptonshire.

Consider the following questions relating to the case while reviewing the content of this chapter:

1. Who are the key players in the Ilmor case?

2. What are the spatial aspects in their relationship?

3. Why did both General Motors and Mercedes-Benz use Ilmor to design and manufacture their engines?

4. What evidence do you see of competence-generating and competence-applying strategies in this case?

Overview of the spatial perspective on strategy

To understand a spatial perspective on strategy, it is essential to understand the basics of international strategy, foreign direct investment and the multinational firm (MNF), the key aspects of the role of location in strategy. Studies of international business derive from neo-classical trade theory. The critical driver of this foundational theory of international business is the concept of comparative advantage. As originated by Ricardo in 1817 (Ricardo, 1948) and extended by Heckscher (1949) and Ohlin (1933), the theory of comparative advantage suggests that different countries have relative advantages in producing different goods because of their natural endowments of factors of production. The most efficient use of resources comes about when countries specialise in producing the goods for which they have a comparative advantage and trade with each other to distribute all goods to consumers in all countries as required. In these models, more goods are produced by the system and consumers pay lower prices and have greater choice in all markets by separating domestic production from consumption. Foreign direct investment, in this model, occurs when capital, rather than capital-intensive goods, is exported to countries where it is in short supply (and has higher return), to be combined with less-mobile production factors such as land or labour. The character of any location determines what is best produced there and what may be demanded in that place, and strategy would consist of matching up the two at the lowest cost.

As spatial analysis becomes more specific, the comparative advantage construct can be applied to more defined locations than countries. For locations that are tied in with the global marketplace, for instance Bangalore in a variety of information technology-based service sectors, key inputs are priced globally – Indian software engineers are rapidly moving to pay based on their productivity in the world market for intellectual capital (Farrell et al., 2005). India as a whole has no apparent advantage in intellectual capital, nor is it closely tied to world IT markets, but Bangalore (and a few other cities in India and China) are part of a worldwide production effort for IT services, and quality inputs are priced in a way that suggests these locations have a surplus of talent at the moment – though rapidly rising wages suggest that demand is rapidly approaching supply, and that India cannot quickly increase its supply of trained engineers.

The study of the MNF emerged from international trade theory, according to most analysis, with Hymer (1976). His work observed that the patterns of international trade and investment proposed in macroeconomic models, primarily between countries with very different factor endowments, did not actually dominate real international markets, which were largely based on trade among industrial nations, and proposed what has been called the strategic behaviour model of foreign investment (Kogut, 1988). This model bridged the gap between neo-classical price theory and the sort of grounded observational case research that characterised early business strategy, and its influence on the emergence of international strategy is apparent in the work of Vernon (1966), Stopford and Wells (1972), Doz (1976), Prahalad (1975), and the dominance of the Integration – Responsiveness (I–R) model. This model of international strategy is based on the idea that industries can be characterised by how intensively they require Global Integration to gain economies of scale and how much they are influenced by National Responsiveness or adaptation of products to local demands in each national market. Doz (1986) describes firm strategies as responses to these interacting demands, with responsiveness driven by governmental requirements and local tastes, and integration driven by industrial concerns for efficiency and cost control. This work peaked with the 'transnational model' of Bartlett and Ghoshal (1989), who introduced the concept of learning or knowledge exchange across borders to the I–R model of the MNF, bringing a new theoretical dimension to a model dominated by concerns for matching firm actions to industry demands in the search for product differentiation and/or cost minimisation. Location is as critical to production as to markets. Again, in order to access the most productive sources of intellectual property today, firms must be willing to access locations around the globe, whether through wholly owned subsidiaries, formal alliances or development contracts. The role of MNFs has become one of identifying the most productive sites for intellectual capital, connecting local capabilities to a larger production apparatus and providing access to worldwide markets for consequent goods and services. Issues of local adaptation, asset control, integration into larger organisations and market power are as relevant today as they were 30 years ago, if in a somewhat different guise.

The transaction cost model of the firm introduced by Coase in 1937 began to make inroads into international business after books by Buckley and Casson (1976) and Rugman (1981) described MNFs as efficient solutions to international market failure. The 'internalisation theory' of the MNF shifted the focus away from the act of foreign direct investment to the MNF's decision to govern international transactions internally, by investing in foreign subsidiaries, rather than through external market mechanisms. Where internalisation theory essentially assumed the existence of international markets, Dunning's (1977, 1988) Eclectic Model explicitly addressed why, as well as how, MNFs might develop. In this model, firms possess some 'ownership assets', typically derived from their experiences in their home domestic market, but that can be exploited through goods or services sold in foreign markets. If it turns out that such goods are more efficiently produced in the foreign market due to factor cost advantages, then productive activities will be set up in the target markets, and if it is further apparent that internalised transactions are more appropriate, the company will extend its corporate boundaries across national boundaries and become an MNF. We see that Dunning explicitly identifies home location as the source of competitive advantage for MNFs and foreign location characteristics (factor costs) as the determining factors of international production. Even the internalisation decision is influenced by tariffs, shipping costs, availability of trustworthy partners and other factors related to locational specifics. The MNF can internalise the market for intellectual property as this knowledge moves into the international realm, but the availability of constant and instantaneous communication is changing the transaction cost characteristics of foreign locations. The risks and opportunity costs of market, or market-like, relationships even for the development or management of key intellectual properties are lower than ever, with the consequence that full ownership of such assets is giving way to alliance relationships, development contracts, service agreements and contract manufacturing.

An important step in the application of spatial dimensions other than national boundaries to strategic management was the recognition that the comparative advantage of a location may not be tied to fixed natural endowments of resources. Porter (1990) developed his diamond model of 'constructed comparative advantage', in which the character of competition in a region would drive local firms to develop particular know-how that could be used to compete in wider international markets. This model was quickly applied at the regional level as the importance of knowledge-based competition was combined with work in economic geography (Saxenian, 1994) that pointed to specialised knowledge development in industrial districts or regional clusters. Markusen's (1999) phrase 'sticky places in slippery space' has become popular in describing knowledge-based advantage and spatial strategies. It means that know-how tends to develop in particular, rather small and well-defined, places and is largely tied to these places. Firms can only tap into this knowledge by setting up operations in the right place, but will then pursue strategies of applying the know-how more widely by adapting it to their own knowledge systems, processes and products aimed at world markets. MNFs become arbitrageurs of knowledge, rather than of more concrete resources and inputs.

The application of the concept of regional clusters has continued to develop in strategic management. Tallman et al. (2004) constructed a model of knowledge development and exchange to explain how firms in a cluster could develop common knowledge and demonstrate similar performance, despite competition from other regions, while simultaneously maintaining some degree of private know-how and show differential levels of performance even within a region. Consideration of regionally tied competitive advantage has extended international business theory, in that apparent anomalies, such as the rise of India and China as major suppliers of high-technology services and goods to world markets while remaining very poor, can now be addressed. At the same time, recognition that different regions of any one country might have very different strengths (Porter, 1998) has begun to show non-international strategy scholars that spatial dimensions of strategy could well play important roles in determining sustained competitive advantage.

Linking the spatial perspective on strategy to strategic management

Several ties between the traditions of international business strategy and strategic management are apparent in the previous section. First, all of the major theoretical perspectives that have advanced business strategy have had analogs in the international strategy literature – location and strategy have never been far removed. Second, both areas of study are shifting focus to knowledge and organisational learning as the key source of competitive advantage in the present and the future. Third, as international business studies are shifting their locational focus to smaller regional clusters, strategic management is coming to recognise the importance of a spatial component to any good business strategy, whether international or domestic.

The strategic behaviour model and subsequent developments such as the I–R model are grounded in the same industrial organisation ideas as the structure–conduct–performance model of business strategy that drives Porter's work in strategy (Porter, 1980). The focus of these two lines of inquiry, which emerged from Harvard Business School at the same time, is on the role of industry characteristics in determining performance success, thereby relegating strategy to the process of identifying and moving the firm to competitive conditions favored by the industry. The link between space (or location) and strategy is in the determination of international reach (how many national markets the firm can enter) which ties to concerns for market power, economies of scale and so forth, and to worldwide or region-wide integration (whether activities in different markets are interdependent), with implications for efficient scale, economies of scope, lower factor costs and disconnecting production from consumption to turn comparative advantage of markets into competitive advantage for MNFs (Porter, 1986; Tallman and Fladmoe-Lindquist, 2002).

Internalisation theory is closely related to the transaction cost economics (TCE) theory of Williamson (1975), as both are driven by concerns for bounded rationality, transactional investment and opportunistic human nature, and both are derived from Coasian theory. Indeed, internalisation theorists have largely agreed that they offer a particular case (albeit a very successful one) for TCE (Teece, 1985). In both cases the intellectual rigor of transactional analysis, combined with the observation that industry membership did not fully explain performance differences, led to these models of the firm (or MNF) partially (in strategic management) or largely (international business) supplanting IO models in business research (Dunning, 1988; Rugman, 1981; Teece, 1985). The emergence of organisational economics coincided with developing interest by strategy researchers in organisation theory models from other social science disciplines to re-focus the emerging discipline on the firm and its activities (transactions), rather than the industry, as the key to strategy analysis.

The combination of industry-level studies of sustained imperfect competition and firm-level foci on transactional efficiency and organisational theory led to yet another theory of business strategy that has resonated with the international perspective. Resource-based strategy (Barney, 1991; Wernerfelt, 1984) and its progeny (capabilities or competency-based strategy, knowledge-based strategy) continue to focus on the firm, but look to the unique assets, skills and know-how of the individual firm to explain differential economic success rather than focusing solely on exchange efficiency. This model has come to dominate strategic management theory. It has likewise been applied to the analysis of the MNF and its strategic roles by various authors working at the boundaries of international business and strategic management (Collis, 1991; Hitt et al., 1997; Tallman, 1992; Tallman and Li, 1996). While not as dominant in the international strategy realm, the resource-based view has been applied successfully to studies of international diversification, alliances and joint ventures, and the emerging role of sub-national locations in providing competitive advantage to MNFs.

Spatial strategies are particularly relevant to the resource-based view of strategy and its related perspectives. The idea that unique, firm-specific, inimitable and non-substitutable resources can generate quasi-rents (Peteraf, 1993) for the firms that own or control them is well established in strategic management. The more difficult question has proved to be 'Where do resources (capabilities, unique knowledge) come from?' Establishing that rent-generating resources are anything other than idiosyncratic embedded routines or unsuspecting but lucky investments has proved to be somewhat more difficult than would appear to be the case. Among other possible sources, strategic resources come from certain places. The theory of comparative advantage makes the case that natural resource endowments are not evenly distributed in space, but are tied to specific locations. Firms that intend to use such resources to conduct business and gain advantage must access these resources in some manner and will need to pursue a spatially aware strategy whether through trade, direct investment or alliance. As we saw in the previous section, technologies and other knowledge-based resources are also typically tied to place (Porter, 1998; Tallman et al., 2004), if a bit less obviously than iron ore or coffee plantations. The competitive and cooperative conditions, market focus and exogenous conditions (research universities, venture capitalists, suppliers, etc.) in a particular location make it more or less effective in generating knowledge with rent-generating potential.

Understanding how location is part of generating unique resources and capabilities and of how these resources are exploited through spatially oriented strategies provides both conceptual and practical answers to this fundamental strategic question and is at the core of current issues in a spatial focus. The intense interest in strategy on regional clusters is based on their apparent value for generating unique knowledge resources. Silicon Valley, the Research Triangle or Hollywood offers know-how with no specific cost to firms in these places. The firms must determine how to gather the knowledge that is available in these locations, how to incorporate it into the firm – both moving it out of the original location and adapting it to the specifics of the firm – and how to apply or exploit this knowledge in multiple markets, foreign and domestic. If rent-generating skills and assets can be derived from participation in the communities of practice in a tightly defined location (Brown and Duguid, 2001), firms can be given direction towards at least one way to develop such resources, and researchers have a metric for defining such resources that escapes the tautology of pure internal generation. Likewise, firms that have developed capabilities for identifying and entering such clusters successfully and then for extracting 'sticky' knowledge from its original home for application in locations around the world are apparently those with both theoretical and practical advantages in the modern marketplace.

This is generally the model offered for the Diversified MNC or Metanational (Doz et al., 2001) firm in international markets, but it applies as well to the domestic company seeking an alliance with a biotech start-up in Austin, Texas, in order to gain technology that can be exploited in New Jersey for sale in the US domestic market. If the relevant knowledge to produce the exact technology needed exists only in the Austin bio-tech cluster, then firms that need this technology must tap that cluster. Likewise, if the large-scale production of the resultant drug requires skills that are highly specific, it is probable that the manufacturer is likely to have limited locations to investigate for production facilities. Presuming the drug proves safe and effective, today's permissive climate with regard to marketing of pharmaceuticals, means that the skills needed to launch it as a product are likely to be concentrated in certain locations (New York, Los Angeles, London, etc.). Thus, as specialisation increases along the value-adding chain, the cross-fertilisation and knowledge spillovers associated with local knowledge clusters increase the likelihood that the needed skills and capabilities will be found in small geographical centers of activity. Only a strong spatial awareness will allow the focal firm to tap into excellence in all its necessary operations.

Thus we see that both competence-generating (or asset-seeking) and competence-applying (or market-seeking) strategies have strong attachments to a spatial perspective. International business theory and applications provide a large and developed body of knowledge about the ties between location and strategy, but in today's flat (but spiky) world of widespread knowledge, information technology and fast-changing demand, strategists cannot settle for the international solution. They must understand space and location at many levels, and know both when the nation is relevant and when it is not. What they must see is that ideas – knowledge, know-how, technology and the rest – are not evenly distributed in space any more than is copper ore or petroleum, and that they are not often best applied where they happen to originate. With this understanding, firms, both multinational and domestic, open tremendous opportunities for competitive advantage as movers of ideas across space and time – not a bad strategy!

Case study revisited

In order to conclude the chapter we revisit the key issues in the short case on Ilmor Engineering Ltd:

1. Who are the key players in the Ilmor case?

The central players have to be Mario Ilien and Paul Morgan; it was their decision to leave Cosworth and set up Ilmor. However, it is unlikely that the operation would have been a success without other players who brought different assets and resources to the firm, some of which were spatially constrained and some were not. These would include Cosworth Engineering (who were also a competitor), who provided the founders with the knowledge and network necessary to develop the business, Roger Penske, whose identification of the potential of the Ilmor operation to support his racing activities in the United States was key and encouraged him to provide both finance and contacts to the emerging firm. The other key players are the customers of the business: General Motors and Mercedes-Benz, both of which provided the basis for the firm's growth and long-term success.

2. What are the spatial aspects in their relationship?

The spatial aspects of their strategy are most strongly illustrated in the relationship with Cosworth Engineering. As both the founders originally worked at Cosworth they had established homes and social networks close by. Cosworth also provided a potential source of labour for the growing Ilmor and would have linkages with local suppliers which Ilmor could also exploit. In contrast to the proximity of Cosworth many of the other key players were distant from the location in Brixworth. Roger Penske was based in the United States, as were, over many years, the key markets for Ilmor using both the Chevrolet and the Mercedes-Benz brands. Similarly, in working with Sauber and Mercedes-Benz these were relatively distant relationships.

3. Why did both General Motors and Mercedes-Benz use Ilmor to design and manufacture their engines?

Both General Motors and Mercedes-Benz have immense knowledge and technology related to the design and manufacture of engines. The issue here is that building engines that work well in race cars has some important differences to building engines that work well in mass-produced cars and trucks. The quote by Jürgen Hubbert provides a clear statement of the distinction. Areas such as weight distribution – keeping the engine as light as possible with the centre of gravity as low as possible – are critical. This in addition to designing the facility to rapidly remove and change engines in a matter of minutes rather than hours provides the race teams with the opportunity to quickly change and repair engines thereby improving their race results. The focus of engine design in both Chevrolet and Mercedes-Benz would be to optimise the production process and thereby the cost of the engine; for Ilmor the focus is to build the most effective race engine within the regulations for a particular series such as Indy car or Formula 1. A further issue is specialisation. While both GM and Mercedes-Benz could potentially have developed the capability to do this over time, it was far more efficient to sub-contract the expertise from someone who already had the expertise and to which they could be a large-enough customer to guarantee exclusivity.

4. What evidence do you see of competence-generating and competence-applying strategies in this case?

In the story of the development of Mercedes-Benz High Performance Engines we can see how Ilmor embarked on a competence-generating process to develop the firm by building up local assets and expertise and then focused on ways to apply these assets. This came opportunistically through the relationship with Roger Penske and applying their competence to create a championship-winning engine for Chevrolet and then repeating the exercise for Mercedes-Benz both in the United States and then in the global shop window of Formula 1. In such a specialist area as this the emphasis is strongly on competence application. In this case competence-generation processes are spatially constrained due to the specialist nature of the competence, but competence-application processes are global with the firm seeking opportunities to exploit these competencies anywhere in the world.

Note

1. The two quotations used in this case study have been taken from 'Ilmor: Creating Racing Engines' published by Ilmor Ltd.

References

Barney, J. B., 'Firm Resources and Sustained Competitive Advantage', *Journal of Management*, 17 (1991) 99–120.

Bartlett, C. A. and S. Ghoshal, *Managing Across Borders: The Transnational Solution* (Boston, MA: Harvard Business School Press, 1989).

Brown, J. S. and P. Duguid, 'Knowledge and Organization: A Social-Practice Perspective', *Organization Science*, 12, 2 (2001) 198–213.

Buckley, P. J. and M. C. Casson, *The Future of the Multinational Enterprise* (London: Macmillan, 1976).

Coase, R. H., 'The Nature of the Firm', *Economica*, 4 (1937) 386–405.

Collis, D. J., 'A Resource-Based Analysis of Global Competition: The Case of the Bearings Industry', *Strategic Management Journal*, 12 (1991) 49–68.

Doz, Y. L., 'National policies and multinational management', DBA Dissertation, Graduate School of Business Administration, Harvard University, 1976.

Doz, Y. L., 'Government Policies and Global Industries', in M. E. Porter (ed.) *Competition in Global Industries* (Boston, MA: Harvard Business School Press, 1986).

Doz, Y. L., P. Williamson and J. Santos, *The Metanational* (Boston, MA: Harvard Business School Press, 2001).

Dunning, J. H., 'Trade, Location of Economic Activity, and the MNE: A Search for an Eclectic Approach', in B. P. Ohlin, O. Hesselborn and P. M. Wijkman (eds) *The International Allocation of Economic Activity* (London: Macmillan, 1977), pp. 395–418.

Dunning, J. H., *Explaining International Production* (London: Unwin Hyman, 1988).

Farrell, D., N. Kaka and S. Sturze, 'Ensuring India's Offshoring Future', *McKinsey Quarterly* (2005). http://www.mckinseyquarterly.com/article_page.aspx?ar=1660

Florida, R., 'The World Is Spiky', *The Atlantic Monthly*, October (2005) 48–51.

Friedman, T., *The World Is Flat: A Brief History of the Twenty-First Century* (New York: Farrar, Straus and Giroux, 2005).

Heckscher, E., 'The Effects of Foreign Trade on the Distribution of Income', Reprinted in H. Ellis and L. Metzler (eds) *Readings in the Theory of International Trade* (Homewood, IL: Irwin, 1949).

Hitt, M. A., R. E. Hokisson and H. Kim, 'International Diversification: Effects on Innovation and Firm Performance in Product-Diversified Firms', *Academy of Management Journal*, 31 (1997) 771–801.

Hymer, S. H., *The International Operations of National Firms: A Study of Direct Foreign Investment* (Cambridge, MA: MIT Press, 1976). Originally published in 1960.

Kogut, B., 'Joint Ventures: Theoretical and Empirical Perspectives', *Journal of International Business Studies*, 9 (1988) 319–332.

Markusen, A., 'Sticky Places in Slippery Space', in T. J. Barnes and M. S. Gertler (eds) *The New Industrial Geography* (London: Routledge, 1999), pp. 98–126.

Ohlin, B., *International and Interregional Trade* (Cambridge, MA: Harvard Economic Studies, 1933).

Peteraf, M. A., 'The Cornerstones of Competitive Advantage: A Resource-Based View', *Strategic Management Journal*, 14, 3 (1993) 179–191.

Porter, M. E., *Competitive Strategy: Techniques for Analyzing Industries and Competitors* (New York: The Free Press, 1980).

Porter, M. E., 'Competition in Global Industries: A Conceptual Framework', in M. E. Porter (ed.) *Competition in Global Industries* (Boston, MA: Harvard Business School Press, 1986), pp. 15–60.

Porter, M. E., *The Competitive Advantage of Nations* (New York: MacMillian, 1990).

Porter, M. E., 'Clusters and the Now Economics of Competition', *Harvard Business Review*, 76, 6 (1998) 77–90.

Prahalad, C. K., *The Strategic Process in a Multinational Corporation* (DBA dissertation, Harvard Business School, 1975).

Ricardo, D., *On the Principles of Political Economy* (New York: Dutton, 1948).

Rugman, A. M., *Inside the Multinationals* (New York: Columbia Press, 1981).

Saxenian, A., *Regional Advantage: Culture and Competition in Silicon Valley and Route 128* (Cambridge, MA: Harvard University Press, 1994).

Stopford, J. and L. Wells, *Managing the Multinational Organization of the Firm and Overlap of Subsidiaries* (New York: Basic Books, 1972).

Tallman, S. B., 'A Strategic Management Perspective on Host Country Structure of Multinational Enterprises', *Journal of Management*, 18, 3 (1992) 455–472.

Tallman, S. B. and K. Fladmoe-Lindquist, 'Internationalization, Globalization, and Capability-Based Strategy', *California Management Review*, 45, 1 (2002) 116–135.

Tallman, S. B. and J. T. Li, 'The Effects of International Diversity and Product Diversity on the Performance of Multinational Firms', *Academy of Management Journal*, 39, 1 (1996) 179–196.

Tallman, S., M. Jenkins, N. Henry and S. Pinch, 'Knowledge Clusters and Competitive Advantage', *Academy of Management Review*, 29 (2004) 258–271.

Teece, D., 'Multinational Enterprise, Internal Governance and Economic Organization', *American Economic Review*, 75 (1985) 233–238.

Vernon, R., 'International Investment and International Trade in the Product Cycle', *Quarterly Journal of Economics*, 80, 2 (1966) 190–207.

Wernerfelt, B., 'A Resource-Based View of the Firm', *Strategic Management Journal*, 5 (1984) 171–180.

Williamson, O. E., *Markets and Hierarchies* (New York: Free Press, 1975).

Part II
Economic Perspectives

CHAPTER 5

Industrial Organisation Economics Perspective

Séan Rickard

Basic principles

The economics of industrial organisations or, as it is more widely referred to, industrial organisation (IO) economics, is a branch of microeconomics that seeks to theorise and explain the economic behaviour of firms, as individual entities, within market structures and in reaction to public policies. To describe IO as a branch of microeconomics is to risk seriously under-valuing the role IO plays within applied microeconomics. The theory of the firm and the theory of consumer behaviour form the twin foundations of microeconomics, and IO is central to an understanding of the economic behaviour of firms. It provides economic theories to explain and predict behaviour, ranging from the internal organisation of the firm through relationships with customers and suppliers to dynamic, strategic interactions with rival groups of firms. In essence, IO seeks to explain how individual firms achieve productive efficiency, develop competitive advantage and grow their scale and scope: as such it provides the microeconomic foundations of strategic management. IO is highly relevant to contemporary industrial policy. Takeovers and mergers, deregulation and privatisation, the increasing globalisation of competition and political concerns regarding national competitors are issues that sit squarely within the domain of IO.

CASE STUDY 5.1

THE SITUATION

A private breakfast meeting on 23 June 1994 between two senior UK newspaper executives operating in the broadsheet sector: a classic differentiated oligopoly where a small number of rivals compete on the quality of their interpretation and analysis of world events. The defining characteristic of an oligopoly is that the success of a strategic move by one of the firms depends to a large extent on subsequent decisions taken by commercial rivals in response. In September 1993, Rupert Murdoch, the multi-millionaire owner of News International, reduced the cover price of *The Times* from 45 to 30p. For a paper that was probably already making loss this was a bold strategic move. By his action, Mr Murdoch was risking a price war. The extract of conversation that follows is based on a fictional discussion between two senior News International executives, Andy McFee and Dale Wildgoose Jr, at their breakfast meeting – some 10 months after the cut in *The Times* cover price. They had agreed to meet at short notice following the decision, the day before, by *The Daily Telegraph* to slash its cover price from 48 to 30p.

Andy: I don't know what Conrad (the owner of *The Daily Telegraph*) is up to. Doesn't he realise the Boss (i.e. Rupert Murdoch) means business? This will spark a real price war.

Dale: Hey, just calm down Andy. There was always a risk of this response once *The Telegraph*'s sales fell below a million and Conrad reduced his shareholding. The Boss was right when he concluded that Conrad would be constrained by the impact of a price war on *The Telegraph*'s stockmarket valuation, but he took nothing for granted.

Andy: I suppose we should be thankful Conrad waited 10 months. His sitting on the fence has enabled our daily sales to rise 22 per cent and in the process the addition of 80,000 daily sales has done wonders for our unit costs by more fully utilising our presses.

Dale: Yeah, and don't forget the benefit of those extra sales for advertising revenue. The Boss's action has resulted in *The Times* breaking even, and that's a big improvement on the losses we were making.

Andy: Well, I'm worried. We have succeeded so far by taking sales from the other broadsheets. But how can we hold on to our market share with *The Telegraph* costing 30p? This is all going pear-shaped.

Dale: Relax will you. The Boss seems to know what he's doing. By closing *Today* and utilising the spare productive resources we are a much more efficient organisation with much lower unit production costs. You know he has ordered that we cut *The Times* cover price to 20p tomorrow?

Andy: Oh no! Then it really is a fight to the death. We'll be making losses from tomorrow.

Dale: There you go again. That's the trouble with you Brits. Always looking on the dark side. Yeah, it's going to be a rough for a few weeks, maybe months, but look at it from our point of view. We have first mover advantage. We have gained market share, and we have reorganised our business. Conrad now has the additional handicap of having to win back readers who have switched and, you know, price isn't everything. Look at the way we've revamped *The Times* – more sport, more features – all the result of careful selection and development of editorial staff. *The Times* is less stuffy and more appealing. We altered the product to make it more attractive to a wider range of you Brits.

Andy: When push comes to shove its all on the price. And we can't make money on daily sales of 450,000 and a cover price of 20p. You're just not facing up to the implications of a price war, and you're overlooking . . .

Dale: For god's sake Andy cool it. Yeah, price is important, but its not the only consideration. *The Guardian*'s cover price is still 50p and their daily sales are more or less unchanged. That shows the value of a clearly differentiated product and a loyal readership.

Andy: I was going to say that you're overlooking the cost of newsprint. Our suppliers say costs are going to rise massively in the coming months. Up 50 per cent is their estimate. This price war could not have come at a worse time. We are bound to lose sales and despite the Boss's deep pocket he won't fund a cover price of 20p for long if newsprint costs rise 50 per cent. You know him. If he isn't winning he'll cut and run.

Dale: I don't think you know the Boss. In fact, at times you seem out of step with the aggressive competitive culture he has built in News International. He's a gambler, but he's also a tactician who seems to have an intuitive grasp of the economics of business and strategic rivalry. You've spent the last fifteen minutes worrying about costs. Yeah sure, in this business volume lowers unit costs but its demand, not unit costs that will get our profits up. With daily sales of almost one million, the economics of Conrad's operation are more impressive than our 450,000 daily sales. But the Boss has a target of one million daily sales and I think he'll get there.

Andy: What one million daily sales! Are you mad? You know it that the UK market is about 3 million – ignoring *The Scotsman* – and even if we drive *The Independent* out of business we can only realistically expect to pick-up a proportion of its 300,000 sales. In my view the Boss was lucky that Carsberg (Sir Bryan Carsberg, Office of Fair Trading Director) threw out *The Independent*'s claim that we were engaged in predatory pricing.

Dale: Predatory pricing: no one can make that stick. No one in their right mind could conclude that that was our game. The Boss knows as well as anyone that there will always be some rich guy prepared to buy a newspaper so that they have a vehicle for pushing their views to government. No Andy, the world has changed, people are more price conscious, success now depends on being able to offer both a distinctive product and a low price.

Andy: Are you telling me that the Boss is indifferent to the presence of say *The Independent*?

Dale: Yep. He has his sights set on another market. He knows, like you, that the traditional broadsheet market is probably limited to 3 million and declining, but unlike you Brits he doesn't have any of the class hang-ups. As a true entrepreneur he is always looking for new profit opportunities. It was his reading of the downward trend in broadsheet sales and the competition from alternative news sources that prompted him to act. The name of his game is to find that price at which *The Times* becomes an alternative to middle class tabloids; in fact, becomes the flagship tabloid. Not so much the top people's paper as 'the people's' paper. If he can get a hold on that market we are talking sales of a million a day.

Issues

This meeting raised a number of issues that are the subject matter of IO. By the end of this chapter we will have shown how over the past 70 years IO has developed a body of theory to help explain the economics of Rupert Murdoch's strategic behaviour. The following issues arise from the mini-case.

■ Only firms with market power, for example that have a significant market share and/or produce a differentiated product, have the ability to alter their prices.

■ If the market is in decline then firms must seek a strategy to offset the loss of profits; they must either take market share from their rivals or find new sources of demand.

■ If the market is supplied by a small number of players, that is an oligopoly, a price-cutting strategy would be an aggressive response, but success – in terms of revenue and profits – will depend critically on the reactions of rivals.

■ The influence of industry structure, for example oligopoly on the nature of the competitive rivalry within an industry is not decisive. Other factors, in particular the entrepreneurial judgement of its senior managers and its organisation capabilities, are arguably of greater importance.

■ Development of IO economics since the 1930s has moved from a dominant focus on the relationship between industry structure and behaviour to a more balanced emphasis, including the organisation and motivation of individual firm's resources.

■ Modern IO economics views firms as populated by principals and agents. The way in which relationships between these parties are structured will influence how efficiently a firm accumulates and utilises knowledge to create and capture value.

Key contributions

The origin of industrial economics

The school of IO is a relative newcomer to the science of economics. As a discipline in its own right it can be traced back to the 1930s and the publication of a number of seminal papers intended to address deficiencies in the traditional or, more correctly, neo-classical microeconomic approach to the firm. The neo-classical school was preceded by the classical school, most commonly associated with

Smith (1776), who was primarily concerned to identify the 'laws' governing the relationship between production and value rather than the behaviour of individual firms. He set down the foundations including the productive benefits of specialisation and the central role of profits in bringing the factors of production – labour, land and capital – together. It was, however, left to Say (1803) to provide an explanation as to how these factors of production were to be organised or managed with his concept of the entrepreneur: the so-called 'fourth' factor of production.

Towards the end of the nineteenth century the views of Smith and his 'classical' successors were superseded by the emergence of the neo-classical school who identified markets, rather than production methods, as the determinant of value. Most importantly, they recognised that market efficiency was driven by individuals' demand arising from the exercise of free choice. However, this insight into individual behaviour did not spread to the supply side. Following Smith, economists throughout the nineteenth century were concerned to explain what firms 'should do' rather than what they actually 'did do'. At the turn of the century, one of the giants of the neo-classical school, Marshall (1890), was writing of the 'representative firm' rather than the behaviour of the individual firm.

Defining competition

Neo-classical economists were not blind to the fact that in practice individual firms had distinctive characteristics but this empirical fact was viewed as no more than a stage on the path to the ideal of 'perfect competition'. The deductive theory of perfect competition had many contributors but was finally refined by Knight (1921) in the early years of the twentieth century. Under perfect competition, industries are characterised by an atomistic structure, homogenous products and perfect information. That is, industries should consist of a very large number of relatively small firms each of whose output is perfectly substitutable for another's. Perfect information implies all firms rapidly adopt the most efficient technology and working practices. These conditions ensure that no one firm can influence the market price by altering its level of output. The theory also requires that firms should be able to freely enter and exit the industry and that new entrants have access to the same knowledge and technology, that is in a world of imperfect information there are no exploitable learning economies. One consequence of these highly restrictive conditions is that the demand by these firms for resources, for example labour, would result in the equalisation of costs across the industry.

A good theory is one that can explain observed behaviour and provide testable predictions. The fact that restrictive assumptions are used in its construction is not the point. It is its ability to accurately predict behaviour that has allowed the model of the firm under perfect competition (summarised in Figure 5.1) to stand the test of time. The analysis is static in the sense that it relates to one production period, say 1 month. The horizontal price line P_0, reflects the individual firm as price taker, that is unable to influence the market price by changing its level of output. Within a production period the firm's choice of inputs is restricted – for example the capital inputs such as buildings, plants and machines are fixed – and consequently any change in the level of output alters the ratio of variable to fixed costs, causing unit production costs to vary. This is the justification for the law of diminishing returns and its associated U-shaped, short-run average cost curve (SRAC). The U-shaped curve reflects the marginal cost (MC) of production, namely the addition to total costs of producing an additional unit of output. The rising section of the SRAC reflects the fact that as output rises beyond some point the increase in MC causes the rate of increase in average variable costs to exceed falling unit fixed costs. Most importantly, the costs of capital inputs, and hence average costs, are defined to include 'normal' profits. That is, that level of profit just sufficient to offset the opportunity cost of capital and therefore to provide the incentive for an entrepreneur to invest capital in the enterprise.

In Figure 5.1, market demand is such that it yields a market price of P_0. Under perfect competition the addition to revenue from selling another unit of output, the marginal revenue (MR), is equal to price. In effect the horizontal line P_0 represents the firm's demand curve, visually demonstrating that the firm lacks the power to alter its market price. One of the perfect competition model's most

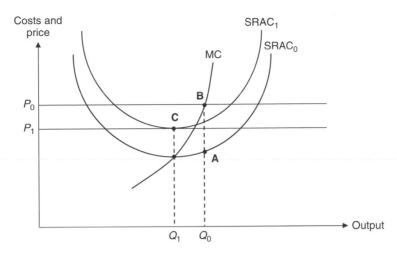

Figure 5.1 Perfect competition model

important conclusion is that profits will be maximised at the output level where MC = MR and for firms operating under perfect competition this implies that profits are maximised where P_0 = MC. At output Q_0 the market price is above the firm's average costs generating an economic rent, that is a profit in excess of the normal profit, represented on a per unit basis by the vertical distance AB. For the neo-classical school this is not a stable equilibrium. As entrepreneurs are assumed to be profit maximisers, a price in excess of average costs will attract new entrants to the industry. Consequently, in successive production periods the number of firms in the industry will rise. These new entrants will increase the market supply, which in turn will depress the market price. And the new entrants' additional demand for productive resources will also raise the costs of production for all firms in the industry represented by the vertical upward shift in the average cost curve from $SRAC_0$ to $SRAC_1$.

Although not shown to reduce congestion, the increase in SRAC reflects an upward shift in the MC curve through point C and it is at this point where firms in the industry reach an equilibrium. At this point P_1 the market price is equal to the lowest point on $SRAC_1$. Thus Figure 5.1 incorporates two production periods. In the first period firms were earning economic rents – AB – and in the second production period where the price has fallen to equal unit costs our representative firm's rent has been reduced to zero and market entry is no longer an attractive proposition for entrepreneurs. Thus, point C becomes the neo-classical ideal of economic efficiency: the exercise of consumer choice, that is demand, has attracted resources into the industry causing supply to rise and the market price fall to a point where unit production costs for this level of output are at their lowest possible level; and profits are reduced to the minimum necessary to produce Q_1.

The importance of scale

The theoretical elegance of the neo-classical theory of the firm, the emphasis on correct logical deductions from precise assumptions in order to determine conclusions, ensures that it remains one of the most powerful models of economic behaviour. However whatever its merits the theory suffered a number of major failings. Its ability to explain differences between firms operating in the same market, in particular a firm's vertical and horizontal boundaries, was severely limited. Taking a one product, one plant firm, the nearest the neo-classical model came to explaining horizontal boundaries was in distinguishing between the short- and the long-run. The situation outlined above represented the short-run because the U-shaped, average cost curve reflects the fact that at least one of the firm's resources is fixed. The long-run is defined as a sufficient period of time over which the firm's choice of resources is unrestricted and therefore a scale and associated combination of resources that will deliver the lowest unit costs can be chosen.

Of particular relevance for strategy is the inverse relationship between an increasing scale of operation and unit production costs. The reason for the inverse relationship are many: construction costs generally rise at a slower rate than the increase in productive capacity; indivisibilities in buildings, plant and machines can be accommodated at large scale; specialised resources can be more efficiently utilised at large scale; and scale also increases bargaining power with suppliers. The relationship between technology, unit production costs and the scale, that is horizontal boundaries, is generally known as returns to scale (Viner, 1952) and is illustrated in Figure 5.2.

Figure 5.2 shows increasing returns to scale, more generally described as economies of scale. This concept augments the neo-classical theory of the firm by providing an explanation for the horizontal expansion of a firm's boundaries, namely the desire to lower unit production costs as shown in Figure 5.2. In the first production period the firm has planned to produce output Q_0 and at this level of output it minimises unit costs at A. But if demand rises in subsequent periods, it will find itself producing a higher output, say Q_1, at a higher unit cost represented by point B. If the firm believes this higher level of demand to be permanent it can invest in a larger scale of production with the effect that it achieves scale economies, point C, in the production of output Q_1. We could repeat this exercise a number of times and the curve that is drawn to envelop the short-run cost curves associated with each short-run period is defined as the long-run average cost curve (LRAC). The LRAC shows the theoretical minimum unit costs for different scales of production and essentially it reflects the prevailing knowledge, for example technology. The benefits of scale for a single plant, single product firm increase at a diminishing rate and at some point, known as the minimum efficient scale (MES), economies of scale are exhausted and the LRAC becomes horizontal, generating constant returns to scale. However, the neo-classical school was forced to argue that at some scale of production beyond the MES diseconomies set in causing the LRAC to start rising. Thus, the LRAC was also assumed to be U-shaped because without this assumption, in the neo-classical paradigm there were no limits to the horizontal boundaries of firms.

It is obvious from the foregoing that the perfect competition model could not explain why, within an industry, different firms display different scales of production. Armed with perfect information and hyperrationality, senior managers in each industry would guide their single product, single plant firms to the same MES. This would remain an equilibrium until it was disturbed by some external shock, for example a fall in demand. The theory owed nothing to empiricism; it was a triumph of theory over empirical fact and, as we have seen, relied on a long list of restrictive assumptions.

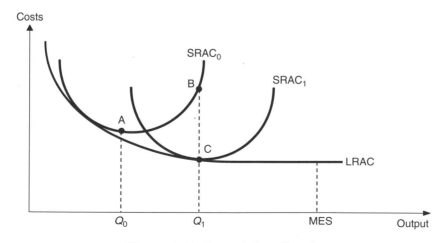

Figure 5.2 Economies of scale

The purpose was not to explain the many examples that deviated from the model but rather to use correct, logical deduction from precise assumptions to determine absolute rules or laws. The approach could be justified on the grounds that it demonstrated how, within an industry, unfettered competition and the dissemination of knowledge concerning the most efficient technology could, in principle, bring about an allocation of resources such that consumer demands were satisfied at the lowest possible price. The essence of the neo-classical economists' approach to the firm was to set out the conditions for achieving this ideal. Deviations from this ideal were recognised as possible – indeed, the neo-classical school developed a profit-maximising model for pure monopoly – but viewed as temporary exceptions as all firms had the same information on prevailing technologies and the prices of inputs. Real-world factors such as advertising, product differentiation and multi-product diversification had no place in the neo-classical model of the firm. Under the neo-classical model of perfect competition, the only strategy open to a firm was to minimise its costs of production.

Linking industrial organisation economics to strategic management

The first major challenge to the neo-classical, perfect competition, approach to the firm was the seminal paper by Staffa (1926). He noted that in practice firms generally refrained from further expansion not because it would cause unit costs to rise, that is diseconomies of scale, but because it would require an unacceptable fall in price. This was completely at odds, not only with the idea of the firm being a price taker, but also with the reliance on a rising LRAC to limit firm size. Staffa argued that firms generally faced downward sloping demand curves as a result of producing a differentiated product; that is, customers viewed individual firms' products as being in some respect, for example quality, different than offerings by industry rivals. As a result individual firms have some degree of market power, the more so if there are a small number of producers, and are therefore in a position to influence the prices they charge. Staffa's contribution is summarised in Figure 5.3. The diagram combines a downward sloping demand curve with a firm's cost curves. He pointed out that a firm operating at point A – charging price P_0 and selling quantity Q_0 – would have to lower the price of its product in order to increase output. In the short run it could not go beyond B without making a loss, and in the long run it could not go beyond point C unless it engineered a rise in demand; represented by a rightward shift in the demand curve. Thus, demand limits the size of a firm even if it benefited from economies to scale.

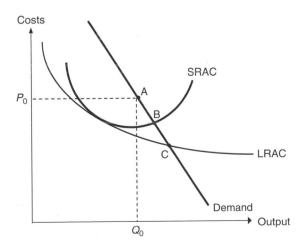

Figure 5.3 Demand and firm size

Staffa's short article, just 15 pages, paved the way for two of the most important antecedents of IO, namely the theories of oligopolistic competition and monopolistic competition. Both theories were developed in the 1930s and both represented attempts to acknowledge the influence of a downward-sloping demand curve on the behaviour of firms. Although the monopolistic competition model preceded the oligopolistic model we will start with the latter as it provides a more straightforward explanation of the impact of demand on strategic behaviour.

A market that is supplied by a small number of sellers is described as an oligopoly. The sellers may produce a homogenous product, for example oil, or a differentiated product, for example newspapers. In such markets each seller is likely to have a degree of market power and therefore the power to influence sales by altering price. Even in markets with larger numbers of sellers, product differentiation can mean that a firm faces strong competition from only a limited number of competitors. Such 'local' oligopoly will tend to generate the same competitive interdependence as in an industry compromising only a few firms.

Figure 5.4 illustrates perhaps the best-known, if elementary textbooks are any guide, attempt to explain oligopolistic competition within a neo-classical paradigm; the so-called 'kinked demand curve' (Sweezy, 1939). The motivation for Sweezy's model was the empirical evidence that oligopolists rarely seemed to compete on price despite their ability to alter price. He set out to demonstrate, summarised in Figure 5.4, why 'competition amongst the few' was unlikely to involve price competition. The firm's costs are represented in the short run by SRAC and in the long run by LRAC. As illustrated the firm is earning an economic rent at price P_0 since price is above unit production costs. Starting at point A, suppose our firm contemplates raising its price to P_1 – say, in the mistaken belief that rivals will follow. However, according to Sweezy, the behavioural response of the firm's rivals is that they are likely to leave their prices unchanged and consequently our firm will suffer a fall in demand as its customers switch to rivals with cheaper products. This is represented by the leftward shift in demand from D_0 to D_1, bringing the firm to point B.

Alternatively, the firm may contemplate reducing its price to say P_2 in the expectation of attracting some of its rivals' customers, that is increasing demand (represented by D_2). But the reasoning underlying the kinked demand curve is that the firm's rivals are likely to respond in kind and match the price cut in order to protect their market shares. Hence, for our oligopolist the increase in sales resulting from a price cut to P_2 is likely to be point D not point C. Thus, the line d_0d_0 shows the *ceteris paribus* demand curve facing the firm at point A, that is the curve *if no other competing firm*

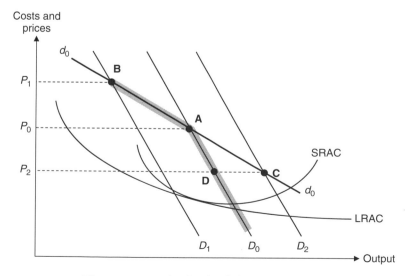

Figure 5.4 The kinked demand curve

changes its price. D_0 shows the demand curve facing the firm if competing firms change their prices in proportion; that is, the *market response* curve. Because the model determines that the firm's rivals will respond differently depending on whether the price is raised or lowered the oligopolist faces a kinked demand curve: arrived at by joining points BAD. The kinked demand curve illustrates an important point: the strategic advantage of reducing price depends on achieving a rise in demand. As the likelihood of a rise in demand is minimised by the high probability that rivals will match a price-cutting strategy, the kinked demand curve model served to provide an explanation for the empirical rarity of price competition between oligopolists. In fact the kinked demand curve is the first attempt to model tacit collusion, an area of strategic rivalry now more commonly analysed using game theory (see Chapter 6).

The motivation for Chamberlin's monopolistic competition model was the empirical evidence of a world in which firms competed with brands, that is differentiated products (Chamberlin, 1933). The theory allowed individual firms discretion over their products' characteristics and as no two firms' products were perfect substitutes this implied the ability to alter the price charged, within margins, without either losing or gaining large numbers of customers. The essence of the monopolist competition model is set out in Figure 5.5. Because Chamberlin's model assumed a large number of firms competing for market share, for example the London hotel market, each firm behaves as though it faces the *ceteris paribus* demand curve $d_0 d_0$, that is it assumes its rivals will not respond (see Figure 5.4 for its derivation). If all firms lower their prices together each firm moves down $D_0 D_0$. With free entry and a price above SRAC firms will enter the market attracted by the prospect of earning an economic rent. As the number of producers rises so the demand for an individual firm's differentiated product will decline – consumers will have more alternatives to choose from – and this is represented by the leftward shift in both $D_0 D_0$ and $d_0 d_0$.

The limit of this leftward shift is represented by $D_1 D_1$ that passes through point A, where the $P_1 Q_1$ combination generates only normal profits. Once economic rents have been competed to zero new entry ceases and therefore point A appears to be the point of equilibrium for a firm operating under conditions of monopolistic competition. To the delight of the neo-classical school, Chamberlin's model implied an equilibrium with excess capacity – it seemed to confirm the neo-classical *dictum* that any departure from perfect competition resulted in inefficiency. Chamberlin's 'famous' conclusion of excess capacity is derived from the fact that at equilibrium unit production costs are being held above

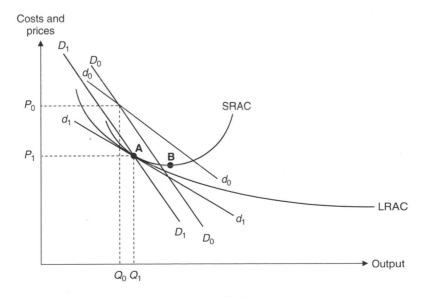

Figure 5.5 Monopolistic competition

their minimum short-run – represented by point B – and long-run levels. In the absence of product differentiation higher output could be achieved at lower cost. Note also that as more firms enter the market and consumers are offered greater choice, so the scope for substitution increases reflected in a flatter *ceteris paribus* demand curve $d_1 d_1$.

Context

Both the monopolistic competition and the oligopolistic models were rapidly absorbed into the economics literature, possibly reflecting the unease of the profession's reliance on an ideal model of perfect competition that did not appear to have much in common with the environment within which most senior managers operated. The importance of the models from the perspective of strategy is that they necessarily focused attention on the market environment facing the firm. These theories provided a way of thinking about strategic behaviour and its anti-competitive implications. By placing the firm in context it opened the door to the empirics of competitive behaviour and in so doing it raised a host of contextual issues, which are now the substance of IO.

By recognising that most firms attempt to produce differentiated products, Chamberlin was forced to introduce the concept of the 'competing group' (now more generally known as the strategic group); that is, firms within the group produce products that are close, but not identical, substitutes for each other. But the recognition of a strategic group raises a host of difficulties. Products within the group might be physically very dissimilar, for example hot water bottles and electric blankets, and therefore a firm's key competitors may not all be within the same industry. Some competing products might, in the eyes of customers, be viewed as very close substitutes, the so-called 'near—neighbours', implying an almost flat demand curve facing the firm. In short, the competitive group is not easily defined: substitutability between products is not capable of a clear definition and the limits of the strategic group becomes an empirical matter.

The introduction of product heterogeneity and a failure to define the limits of strategic groups seriously compromised Chamberlin's model. In such a model cost curves must include selling costs, for example advertising expenditure, and as the units of output are physically dissimilar unit costs will vary. The logic of these assumptions is that competing firms do not face the same LRAC curves. The failure to define the limits to substitutability allows for the possibility that the firm faces the same flat demand curve faced by firms under perfect competition. Figure 5.5 is therefore seriously flawed – a point that seems to have escaped the authors of many economic text books. In short, Chamberlin's bold attempt to establish a more empirically based economic model of the firm is compromised by the logical inconsistency of combining a downward-sloping demand curve – derived from product heterogeneity – with free entry and the assumption of uniformity of costs when both product characteristics and selling costs are likely to vary from firm to firm.

The kinked demand curve model has also attracted criticism. First, many oligopolists produce differentiated products, thus the points raised above on costs are equally applicable. Second, like the monopolistic competition model it is a static analysis in the neo-classical tradition; neither model provides an explanation as to how the starting price was arrived at – any price between unit costs (SRAC) and the monopoly price can be the starting point. Third, there is no allowance for a possible relationship between the starting price and costs, both the oligopolist and the monopolist competition models failed in the very area they were designed to address, namely empirical relevance. Both models lack predictive power. It has been shown that virtually no predictions emerge from these models (Archibald, 1961). They are incapable of providing even qualitative – let alone quantitative – predictions regarding the firm's price, output and capacity utilisation following a change in market demand and/or a change in costs.

The significance of both Sweezy's and Chamberlin's models to the development of IO are the issues they raised rather than their attempted solutions. Both models had raised the contextual issue of proximate market structure – for example the number of sellers, strategic groups – as the determinant of performance in terms of prices, selling costs and profits. Most importantly both models switched attention from the 'representative' to the individual firm. In so doing they opened up strategic issues such as, what products to produce, how to differentiate products, the price to charge and the scale of production. Multi-product diversification and scale are directly relevant to the strategically important issue of a firm's boundaries. This contribution of both models to business strategy was not, however, immediately perceived. It was their focus on industry structure that seized the interest of economists and formed the platform upon which one of the major developments of IO was built, namely the structure–conduct–performance (SCP) paradigm (Bain, 1956; see also Mason, 1949). The focus of the SCP model is emphatically the industry, not the firm. It postulates crucial relationships between the number and size distribution of firms in a market and their competitive behaviour and consequential performance. The famous SCP paradigm marked the shift from the deductive theoretical reasoning of the neo-classical school, in which both Chamberlin's and Sweezy's models were founded, to the empirical approach of the IO school.

According to the SCP paradigm, rivalry can take many forms including pricing, product design and promotional strategies, plant investment, R & D, innovation and legal tactics. This conduct delivers market performance, which is manifested in productivity, allocative efficiency, product variety, innovation and profits. Thus the SCP paradigm emphasised the causal flow from the context of industry structure to conduct and strategic behaviour to the individual performance of firms (see Figure 5.6). Most importantly the policy issues of interest to the IO school were those of public policy, not business strategy.

Competences

The SCP paradigm gave rise to a decade or more of cross-sectional empirical analysis to test the model's many propositions. But by the 1970s there was growing dissatisfaction with the premise, inherent in the SCP model, that market structure was exogenously determined by the scope for economies of scale, which in turn is determined by current technology (Viner, 1952). The SCP school's unwillingness to probe the influence of behaviour within the firm on its boundaries was increasingly at odds with research indicating that market structure could also be endogenous; that is, the conduct and performance of firms in the industry was also an important influence on structure. For example, mergers directly affect the size and distribution of firms, advertising and innovation could raise post-entry costs and limit or predatory pricing might constrain or reduce, respectively, the number of competitors – in essence, behaviour that directly or indirectly raised the costs of entry into a market also influenced structure. The idea that resources controlled by established firms could form the basis of entry barriers and that therefore market structure could be the result of deliberate measures (i.e. conduct) taken by established firms was alien to the SCP paradigm.

Economists in the field began to draw a distinction between innocent and strategic entry barriers. Innocent entry barriers arise where the prevailing technology requires entry on a very large scale in order to achieve unit production costs that would make the new entrant's selling price competitive, for example oil refining. In contrast, strategic entry barriers are created by the strategic behaviour of established firms who, through their accumulated knowledge and control of industry resources sought to place new entrants at a competitive disadvantage. For example, they may have established their products in their customers' preferences, forcing a new entrant to incur very costly promotion costs in order to overcome the advantage of the established firm. Once incurred such costs are sunk – that

Figure 5.6 The structure-conduct-performance paradigm

is unrecoverable – thereby forcing the new entrant to contemplate the exit costs if the entry proves unsuccessful. Study of strategic entry barriers has resulted in an appreciation of the interdependence between sunk costs and strategic rivalry (Sutton, 1992).

The inability to explain the boundaries of a firm, and hence market structure, was only one of the causes of dissatisfaction with the SCP paradigm. Like Chamberlin's and Sweezy's models the model rested firmly on the neo-classical approach to the firm; namely, non-cooperative behaviour by firms was typically assumed, producers and consumers all had the same information, and preferences and current technology were taken as being exogenous, that is uninfluenced by the behaviour of the firms. These assumptions are a serious weakness when it comes to analysing business strategy. As most clearly articulated by Richardson (1960), if opportunities are equally available to all they are available to no one in particular. In short, the SCP model ignored the wealth of empirical evidence showing that individual firms were very heterogeneous in their competences.

The growing recognition that individual firms, or rather their senior managers, could influence both market structure and the nature of competitive rivalry inevitably began to focus attention on the competences or capabilities of individual firms. The IO school was coming to realise that the resource endowments of individual firms, for example the accumulated skills of its workforce, its routines and systems created within the firm and the ability of managers to develop and motivate the firm's resources, were of crucial importance. If competitive behaviour was to be explained, a much sharper focus on individual firms would be necessary. The idea that each firm is unique can be traced back to Penrose's resource-based approach to the firm (Penrose, 1959) and arguably to Schumpeter (1942). Penrose and her influence in the area of strategy rests on her being considered the founding matriarch of what has come to be known as the competency or resource-based approach (see Chapter 9 for a more detailed discussion). This approach acknowledges that firms have similar physical resources – such as labour, machines and so on – but the services they generate from these resources depend on accumulated experience and learning, that is knowledge, as well as the ability to identify and effectively exploit new, profitable opportunities. In other words, the way in which a firm's senior managers perceive and take advantages of business opportunities are path dependent and will therefore vary from firm to firm.

Culture

We may have got a little ahead of ourselves with talk of individual firm competencies. It would be wrong to argue that a focus on the individual firm and its boundaries, or rather the behaviour of its managers and workforce arose solely from dissatisfaction with the SCP paradigm. As early as the 1930s, descriptive studies of firms, particularly the giant ones, showed that senior managers exercised discretion over prices, output and advertising (Chandler, 1962). This led to greater scepticism amongst empirical economists regarding the neo-classical assumption that the pursuit of profit maximisation alone explained the behaviour of firms and it also encouraged the development of alternative theories of the firm. These alternative models of the firm represented an attempt to understand the process of decision-making within firms. The nature of decision-making within firms is of a different kind than individual choice in markets. A firm's senior managers are likely to be agents for the firm's owners and the firm's workforce act as agents for their superiors. In the aggregate the internal environment within which decisions are made is the result of a complex joint decision process within a network of agency relationships. If we define culture as 'a complex set of values, belief assumptions and symbols that define the way in which a firm conducts its business' (Barney, 1986) then these new IO theories were directly concerned with explaining a firm's culture and predicting behaviour.

These alternative theoretical approaches to the firm can be divided into two schools: management theories and behavioural theories. Much of the subsequent research into these alternative approaches to the firm would strictly fall outside the scope of IO and would more properly be located within managerial and/or organisational economics, but the links between these schools and IO have become increasingly blurred. The IO literature has developed the *transaction cost* economics, which adopts a contractual approach to the study of economic organisations. Transaction cost economics traces its origin to a seminal paper by Coase (1937) who observed that in a world where agents exhibit both perfect information and hyper-rationality there was no reason for firms to exist. Transaction cost economics is explored in more detail in Chapter 7, but in essence it is distinguished from the neo-classical conception of hyper-rationality and profit maximisation by the acceptance that *homo economicus* is boundedly rational and subject to contract. According to a leading exponent of this approach (Williamson, 1998), contracting man, like homo economicus, is given to self-interest but in a way that makes allowance for guile. Specifically, economic agents are viewed as disclosing information in a selective and distorted manner. Calculated efforts to mislead, disguise, obfuscate and confuse are thus admitted.

One of the early notions developed by the management school developed from the belief that the separation of ownership and the control of day-to-day operations by salaried managers gave rise to non-profit maximising behaviour (Beale and Means, 1932). According to this view a firm's behaviour depends on the objectives of senior managers whose motives result from a desire for income, status and power, subject to constraints, for example profits on managerial discretion. Good examples are Baumol's sales maximisation model (Baumol, 1958) and Williamson's (1964) expense preference model. But in both cases the models are not easy to test empirically and as demonstrated by Williamson's (1966) detailed analysis of Baumol's model firm growth implies something very close to profit maximisation of both shareholders, and the resource costs of expansion are to be satisfied.

Building on Coasion foundations the behavioural approach to decision-making within the firm is a direct attempt to integrate economic and organisational theory. The seminal description of this theory is credited to Cyert and March (1963), who argued that the firm is a coalition of individuals, some organised into groups. These individuals and groups have their own objectives and this gives rise to goal conflicts. Senior managers lacking perfect information and being boundedly rational must devote some of the firm's resources to meeting the demands of these groups; for example, production managers want long production runs in order to lower unit costs even if this means a build-up of stocks. That is, the behavioural approach to the firm gives rise to the concept of organisational slack and the assumption that firms do not maximise anything; instead people normally *satisfice* – managers aspire to a satisfactory rather than the maximum level of performance that is achievable. This concept of satisficing can be traced back to Simon (1959).

These alternative approaches to the inner workings of firms have in common with transaction cost economics the objective of attempting to explain decision-making in organisations characterised by asymmetric information and opportunism. It is the insights imparted by transaction cost economics in explaining the boundaries of the firm that makes it a serious candidate for playing a synthesising role in the discipline of strategy management (Volbeda and Elfriny, 2001). This perceived role arises from Williamson's work over three decades on transaction cost theories of the boundaries of firms and the continuation of the work through the study of contractual relationships; see for example Alchian and Demsetz (1972), Grossman and Hart (1986) and Jensen and Meckling (1976). By the early 1980s Oliver Williamson's attempts at providing the theoretical underpinnings of transaction costs had done much to elevate the influence of imperfect information, bounded rationality, opportunistic behaviour and asset specificity in determining the boundaries of a firm. The significance of these elements is their contribution to an understanding as to why a firm's vertical boundaries might embrace more than one production stage or, having vertically integrated, find it economic to downsize. Moreover, transaction costs provide an explanation for the frequent resort by firms to inter-organisational vertical relationships to produce a good or service within virtual boundaries by forming close, longer-term trusting relationships with suppliers and customers.

The transaction costs approach, or as it is now more generally known, the governance approach to the firm, has done much to open up the issue of imperfect and asymmetric information in exchange relationships – both within the firm and between firms as buyers and sellers. But its contribution to strategy is primarily in the area of the determination of a firm's vertical boundaries; it has less to offer when it comes to horizontal boundaries and the issue of diversification and it does not address competitive strategic behaviour. We will deal with this issue and the issue of contracting, in particular principal–agent relationships below, but first, keeping to the historical development of IO, we need to return to the issue of strategic interaction. One of the first economists to directly deal with the subject of strategy was Ansoff (1965). Ansoff was explicit that his work was motivated by deficiencies in the neo-classical approach to the firm, though in this he was foreshadowed by Chandler's (1962) study of large corporations. But Ansoff's attempts to address the deficiencies of neo-classical microeconomics cannot be said to have developed into a rival theory of the firm. The main tools of the strategic management school – for example the learning curve and portfolio matrix – are drawn from economic concepts and owe more to exhortation than theories that yield statistically robust predications. Arguably one of the most important contributions to the development of a theory of business strategy is Porter's (1980) Five Forces Model, which, together with the PIMS database (Buzzell and Gale, 1987) – one of the largest bodies of empirical studies that might fairly be located under the heading of strategy – derives from the SCP paradigm.

Competing

Porter's model (Figure 5.7) is essentially structuralist, attributing the nature of competition to five key forces: rivalry, entry barriers, substitute products, relationships with suppliers and relationships with customers. The genesis of Porter's model is the SCP paradigm; in Porter's own words, '. . . competition in an industry is rooted in its underlying economic structure' (Porter, 1980). Nevertheless, it adds a dynamic dimension and is considerably more complex in recognising that competitive strategies will vary according to whether the industry is emerging, mature or declining. But there is no theory of the organisation in his model, and hence no guidance on the competitive contribution of a firm's boundaries – both horizontal and vertical – on diversified strategies. Porter's Five Forces Model was developed from the SCP, industry perspective and it is therefore not surprising that the model is less successful when applied at the firm level (Porter, 1985).

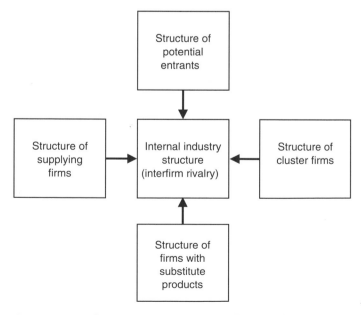

Figure 5.7 Forces driving competition. Adapted from Porter (1980)

This lack of an organisational perspective necessarily limits Porter's Five Forces. In his attempt to apply his model to the firm Porter argues that the firm or business unit of a corporation attains sustainable competitive advantage – that is a sustained rent-earning capability – from a superior market position such as highly differentiated products or the ability to produce at unit costs lower than rivals. But on the organisational structures and resources necessary to achieve these superior positions Porter is silent.

At about the same time as business leaders and business schools were embracing Michael Porter's Five Forces model the description of IO was embarking on significant developments in its approach to the firm and, by implication, strategy. In the early 1980s, Baumol's (1982) concept of *contestable markets* was casting doubt on the idea that structure could shed as much light on competitive rivalry as previously supposed. Baumol argued that markets are contestable if a potential entrant has access to the same technology, knowledge and resources as incumbents and is able to salvage the capital costs of entry upon exit (i.e. there are no sunk costs). In such a situation there is the constant threat of entry and forcing incumbents to seek productive and allocative efficiencies and to resist the temptation to use market power to raise prices to achieve economic rents. Thus, conduct in contestable markets is not determined by market structure but by the need to deter entry. Baumol's theory of contestable markets was just one of a number of significant developments in the field of IO, at the start of the 1980s, that attempted to explain industrial structure endogenously. Other seminal contributions showed how innovation (Dasgupta and Stiglitz, 1980) and product improvement (Shaked and Sutton, 1983), that is differentiation, could influence market structure.

Another significant IO development during the 1980s, in part a reaction to the strongly empirical traditions of the SCP paradigm, is commonly referred to as the strategic conflict approach. This approach is generally traced back to a seminal paper by Shapiro (1989) and is founded upon game theoretical studies of behaviour and performance in imperfectly competitive markets (see also Saloner, 1994; Tirole, 1993). The strategic conflict approach uses the tools of non-cooperative game theory (explanation is given below) and thus implicitly views competitive outcomes as the result of engaging in strategic behaviour designed to influence rivals' expectations as to a firm's future behaviour. According to Shapiro, non-cooperative game theory can virtually be identified with the theory of business strategy. Indeed, he asserted that *game theory provides the only coherent way of logically analysing strategic behaviour* (Shapiro, 1989, p. 125).

Game theory can be traced back to the 1940s (von Neumann and Morgenstein, 1944), but despite Carl Shapiro's bold claim few books on strategy deal with the subject and those that do only provide a superficial account possibly reflecting the fact that game theory requires more mathematics than is generally found in strategy text books. In non-cooperative games players are unable or unwilling to enter into binding contracts and as applied by IO game theory has two basic themes: reputation and commitment strategies. Both describe beliefs about the future behaviour of a firm. One of game theory's major contributions to strategy is the insight that if strategic actions are to work they must influence the beliefs of those whose behaviour it is designed to influence. The strategic move, if it is to influence the actions of rivals, must be credible and have a lasting effect on cost or demand conditions such as investment in capacity, R & D, advertising or product development. Strategic moves of this kind require irreversible commitment and these considerations have led to a greater appreciation of the importance of sunk costs (as opposed to fixed costs) (Sutton, 1992). In many settings what matters is the degree to which costs are irrecoverable, that is sunk, rather than the relationship between unit costs and output, that is economies to scale.

Game theory sheds light on the interactions between oligopolistic rivals. Paradoxically, Chamberlin (1929) was one of the first economists to draw attention to the interdependence of oligopolist markets. We saw in the kinked demand curve model that for the individual firm, the profitability of changing price depended on rivals' reactions. The essence of such interdependence is that it gives rise to the incentive for various types of co-operative behaviour – including tacit collusion – between corporate decision-makers. In the absence of a binding agreement between two firms not to reduce prices, both will be tempted to engage in 'tacit' collusions subject to their management culture (Tirole, 1993).

Corporate

We observed above that the origins of Porter's Five Forces Model were clearly in the Bain–Mason SCP paradigm. But it would be incorrect to give the impression that SCP theories were the hallmark of IO economists. An influential group of IO economists, commonly referred to as the Chicago school, was very critical of the SCP approach. In the Chicago view, entry barriers are based on asymmetric information and both concentration and profits are the result of efficiency rather than stemming from anti-competitive behaviour by oligopolists. The Chicago influence can clearly be seen in the resource-based approach to the firm, which as noted above is generally traced back to Penrose (1959). The firm according to Penrose is '. . . a collection of productive resources, the disposal of which between different uses and over time, is determined by administrative decision' (Penrose, 1959, p. 24). According to this view resources represent a capability or competency: when in excess and subject to their fungibility, they provide the means of diversification into new markets. We noted above Staffa's insight that demand was the limiting factor for the growth of a single product firm, but it was Penrose's notion of firms deploying their excess capabilities to new markets that represented a seminal attempt to develop a theory of a firm's horizontal boundaries from the supply side. According to Montgomery (1994), Penrose's view of the firm, combined with transaction cost considerations, provides the dominant mode of explanation for diversification (Montgomery, 1994).

Resources that are both surplus and fungible can yield a multi-product firm with cost savings if they have the nature of a public good. Formally a resource that yields cost savings if deployed in the production of more than one product is said to achieve economies of scope (Panzar and Willig, 1981). But Penrose was adding a dynamic, learning element. In essence as firms carry out their normal business they accumulate excess knowledge resources, for example the managerial knowledge to launch a new product. Because transaction costs rule out market exchange, in-house use is more efficient and the firm will accordingly apply the excess resources in new markets. This insight tied together the concepts of competency and horizontal boundaries. Penrose's argument has been embraced and developed by strategic management scholars (see Chapter 9) but from an IO perspective her arguments sit within the IO tradition of a critique of neo-classical theory. In her words, within the neo-classical theory of the firm there is '. . . no notion of an internal process of development leading to cumulative movements' (Penrose, 1959, p. 1).

A number of mainstream IO economists took an interest in Penrose's work (Baumol, 1962; Marris, 1964) but with the effect that it became subordinated under more general theories of adjustment costs and investment (Treadway, 1970). From a mainstream IO perspective, Penrose's ideas point to the existence of a constraint on the development of firms, stemming from the difficulties of expanding the management team. It also points to the development and experience of management as a prime source of heterogeneity revealed by competitive advantage. From an economic viewpoint, this suggests a dynamic control theory approach to investment whereby the profit-maximising firm determines and follows its optimal time profile of outputs. Indeed, IO scholars have demonstrated that a steady-state, diversified growth pattern exists in which firm size and management capability grow at the same rate (Gander, 1991; Marris, 1964). Thus, from a mainstream IO perspective, the issues raised by Penrose are in danger of being relegated to no more than a detail in the modern theory of optimal investment.

Change

From a strategic management perspective, this attempt to relegate Penrose to a detail of optimal investment theory merely represents evidence of the failings of IO in the area of strategy. By definition investment is a dynamic analysis, but for Penrose it was 'history' that mattered. The growth of a firm for Penrose is an evolutionary process based on the cumulative growth of collective knowledge. Whereas the neo-classical approach is to compare positions of equilibrium, for Penrose firms never achieve a point of equilibrium, they are constantly changing. In this Penrose had much in common with the Austrian school. The Austrian approach to competition ignored structural issues, for example oligopoly, and concentrated instead on dynamic progress. For the Austrians the major issue was the competitive process itself a '... voyage of exploration into the unknown, an attempt to discover new ways of doing things better than they have been done before' (Hayek, 1945). The Austrian view of competition clashes head on with the neo-classical view of profits. For the neo-classical tradition, economic rent is evidence of the exploitation of market power – consumers are being forced to pay a price higher than the costs of production – and as such represents a loss of efficiency. For the Austrians economic rents operate to encourage entrepreneurs to seek out new ideas, to be innovative and hence to progress welfare. The difference between the two schools was highlighted by Schumpeter as early as the 1940s, when he observed that the competition that mattered was '... the competition from the new commodity, the new technology, the new source of supply, the new type of organisation ... competition which commands a decisive cost or quality advantage' (Schumpeter, 1942). For Schumpeter, the process of change involved invention, innovation and diffusion. The neo-classical model's assumption of perfect information cannot explain the processes of invention and innovation, or indeed change in general.

Following Schumpeter and Penrose, it was not until the 1980s that IO utilised the concept of evolution to help identify the characteristics of firms and markets likely to generate invention, innovation and growth. Research in this area has generally concentrated on attempting to integrate concepts such as organisational knowledge and routines to Schumpeter's concept of dynamic competition (Nelson and Winter, 1982). As a branch, or sub-set of IO, evolutionary economics emphasises the inevitability of mistaken decisions in an uncertain world where there is no agreement on the way forward. The relevance of this to business strategy is a concern with technological change and its implications for firms and their managers who are exposed to such change. Evolutionary economics has brought to the fore a framework in which firms compete primarily through a struggle to improve or innovate. In this process, the knowledge possessed by a firm's managers is path dependent and in a world of uncertainty they have only a partial understanding of the opportunity set. As the opportunity set is itself largely determined by a firm's capabilities, this and the fact that managers will take different views of an uncertain future is sufficient to demonstrate heterogeneity. Organisational capabilities are based on routines and accumulated knowledge which are not explicitly comprehended and therefore cannot be easily replicated even when observed. In this respect, evolutionary economics has brought IO back to one of its founding principles, namely an emphasis on empiricism rather than hypothetical sets of alternative theories.

The IO models to explicitly deal with change have tended to focus on the growth of firms. One of the first was Baumol's (1962) model of sales revenue maximisation. Over the years models to explain the growth of firms have become numerous in the IO literature. Most owe something to Marris (1963) whose theory integrates both supply, that is resources, and demand, that is diversification. This basic model produced a stream of subsequent research covering areas such as firm growth and profit maximisation (Williamson, 1966); growth through vertical integration (Williamson, 1971); and the influence of finance on growth performance (Heal and Silberston, 1972). Central to much of this work on the growth-maximising firm is the threat of takeover. Takeovers, however, are also a means by which firms can grow. Empirical studies suggest that up to a third of growth for UK firms was achieved through acquisition (Aaronovitch and Sawyer, 1975). A continuing debate concerns the impact of market structure on the incentive to innovate. The traditional view was that only firms with a degree of market power had the incentive and resources to exploit innovation. But this viewpoint has been challenged, at least to the extent that a competitive market structure can provide an incentive to innovate given a robust patent system (Arrow, 1962).

Control

We noted above that since the launch of Porter's Five Force model, IO has done much to provide a well-ordered body of knowledge that seeks to explain strategic behaviour both within and without the firm. We explained above how dissatisfaction with the SCP paradigm caused economists working in the IO field to research the way in which firms set about controlling their external environment. Using game theoretic models, researchers focused on oligopolistic interdependence and the implications for competition given the incentive to cooperate, even in the absence of formal collusion, to exploit the profit opportunities afforded by barriers to entry (Hay and Morris, 1991; Nalebuff and Brandenburger, 1996). The issues generally addressed by game theory are of direct relevance to competitive strategy, the branch of strategic management concerned with a firm's proximate external environment. But it is perhaps in the area of internal control that new developments in IO hold out the prospect of a theory of the firm that will embrace relationships within and between firms. This area of study involves issues concerned with asymmetric information, principals and agents, the nature of contracts and ownership, and it is an area of study that is rapidly developing (Holmstrom and Tirole, 1989).

In practice there is a separation of ownership and control with the effect that firms are mostly controlled by managers. This begs the question, how will managers and therefore the firm actually behave? We noted above the managerial school's attempt to provide theories to answer this question, but principal-agent models appear to offer a more theoretical paradigm within which management behaviour, indeed incentive issues in general, can be studied. Principal-agent models are focused on the design of incentive schemes that keep opportunism under control and constrain unproductive rent-seeking behaviour by agents. Such models are concerned with the alignment of objectives, for example owners and managers, and in a world characterised by asymmetric information, such alignments carry costs. Agents, for example managers, have their own objectives, will hold private information and engage in hidden practices. If, as is generally assumed in such models, the agent is risk adverse, the principal-agent problem is one of finding the optimal balance of risk sharing and incentives. Principal-agent models are not confined to the relationships between owners and senior managers, they are also applied to relationships between managers and subordinates, and their form varies according to market and organisational structures.

The principal-agent approach is closely allied to Alchian and Demsetz's (1972) theory of the firm which is contractual. Contracts are central to incentive problems, but in a world where individuals suffer imperfect information and are boundedly rational, contracts are inevitably incomplete. In practice, contracts are not independent of the organisational setting and Williamson (1985) has argued that an incomplete contract's perspective is essential for explaining different organisational forms. For Williamson, bringing transactions within a firm's boundaries reduces the risk of opportunistic behaviour arising from incomplete contracts. Grossman and Hart (1986) have developed this argument by suggesting that the crucial difference between governance structures resides with their implied residual decision rights, that is the right to control what has not been explicitly contracted for. Owners delegate these rights to managers, and once this is appreciated it is but a short step to conclude that organisational form, contracts and incentives influence behaviour and performance.

The developments within IO over the past 30 years have resulted in the individual firm emerging as the central player. Individual firms can no longer be viewed as passive units, rather they emerge as active players in a world of imperfect and asymmetric information taking strategic decisions with the purpose of influencing their competitive business environment and aligning and motivating their strategic resources. The elevation of the individual firm to centre stage has necessarily focused attention on the discretion afforded to senior managers to formulate and carry out strategic objectives. Organisational structures and managerial compensation systems offer a degree of control but there is little reason or evidence to suggest that these constraints can do more than place limits on the extent to which managers pursue their strategic objectives. The relationships involved are very complicated and involve an integration of economics and organisational theory; the more they are explored the more complex these models become, reducing their generality and the provision of testable predictions.

Another area of control concerns public policy. Through explicit regulatory intervention, government agencies can exercise a great deal of control over the behaviour of firms. The array of possible policy instruments is large and, not surprisingly, a substantial area of IO is devoted to identifying appropriate policies. Cost, investment, prices and output can all be influenced by taxes and subsidies. The government might act to increase the amount of information available to firms and use legislation to keep market structures conducive to competition. This area of public control has encouraged an integration of IO and law and a vast empirical literature on antitrust actions (Scherer and Ross, 1990).

Tools and techniques

We noted above that the introduction of the SCP paradigm gave rise to a decade or more of empirical analysis to test the model's many predictions. The reason for this was only partly the perspective opened up by the SCP model; arguably of equal importance was the fact that the introduction of the SCP model coincided with the arrival of computers. Computers made the complex calculations inherent in multiple regression considerably easier. Thus, suddenly economists in the field could use the power of multiple regression techniques to statistically test relationships between market structure, conduct and performance. Such techniques allowed, in principle, for the influence of explanatory factors – seller concentration, entry barriers, the growth of demand and so on – to be separately identified and their impact on, say, profits measured. Armed with such a powerful tool, it is perhaps not surprising that the SCP paradigm held sway for so long. With the benefit of hindsight, it appears that the opportunities for empirical analysis provided by the computer outweighed the development of rigorous theoretical support.

The next significant tool was game theory and in particular multi-period game theory. It is only with the development of multi-period game theory that IO has been equipped with a tool to analyse the dynamics of competitive behaviour (Shapiro, 1986). Multi-period game theory models have shed light on 'tacit' collusion demonstrating that any cheating by a firm in one period can, if detected, be punished in subsequent periods by non-cooperative behaviour by the rest of the oligopolist group. This work suggests that 'tacit' collusion will normally cause profits (i.e. performance) to rise above the non-cooperative level, which supports the neo-classical analysis of oligopolistic markets. But with game theory the outcome is the result of rigorous analysis of the interactions involved (i.e. the process) rather than interpolation between fully competitive and monopolistic behaviour. Repeated games bring a dynamic aspect to the static approach of traditional IO models. Indeed the successes of game theory in the area of IO have arisen largely because game theory provides a language and techniques for modelling dynamic, competitive interactions (Kreps, 1990). This chapter sets out in more detail how game theory as a tool has allowed a focus on the process of rivalrous behaviour rather than just the outcome. And in the process it explicitly allows for uncertainty and the transaction costs associated with a lack of, or asymmetric, information.

Ironically, given that empirical relevance was such a driving force for the founding fathers of IO, game theory is a highly theoretical tool and has taken IO to new highs of mathematical elegance and obscurity. The pendulum is now swinging back; many of the hypotheses arising from the theoretical contributions of the 1980s are now the subject of empirical analysis. Statistical and, in particular, regression analysis has a key role to play but increasingly applied researchers are augmenting statistical studies with detailed case studies, the running of controlled experiments in laboratories, particularly appropriate for testing theoretical game theory developments, and evidence from antitrust cases (Scherer, 1988).

The firm as a nexus of contracts with an internal organisation consisting of a set of contractual relationships between principals and agents is viewed as engaged in non-cooperative games with rivals, suppliers and customers. All these are areas which are at the centre of IO research and the race is on to derive robust general predictions which can then be tested by empirical studies. In this respect the wheel has turned full circle. As in the 1930s economists are turning to empirics to resolve the many questions raised by game theoretic and principal-agent models that are multi-period and utilise limited information. Thanks to the burst of theorising in the 1980s, researchers now have an incomparably richer understanding of 'behaviour' within markets and within firms. Over the coming years we are likely to see the emergence of a number of robust predictions that will elevate the IO branch of microeconomics to the same role in relation to business and corporate strategy that macroeconomics currently has for political issues.

Case study revisited

Armed with the foregoing we can now return to Andy and Dale. Andy was expressing the classic IO stance, namely for an oligopolist to engage in price cutting is to invite retaliation from rivals. The effect according to the traditional view would be a general reduction in prices with only a small increase in sales and hence a fall in revenue and profits (see Figure 5.4). But the classic conclusion may not always hold. Dale was reflecting an appreciation of the fact that Rupert Murdoch's price-cutting strategy was less a move in a game of strategic conflict, and more an attempt to widen *The Times'* opportunity set in a way that would utilise surplus tangible and intangible resources.

Demand is crucially important to profits and longer-term growth. From a game theoretic, strategic conflict perspective, if *The Times'* rivals found it difficult to match the price cut then *The Times* would enjoy an increase in demand – in terms of Figure 5.4, sales would go from A to C. And there were good reasons why *The Times* might conclude there was a high probability that its rivals would find it difficult to respond in kind. The market for broadsheet newspapers – after something of a renaissance in the 1980s – was declining. As sales fell, so each publisher was being pushed up his cost curve – see Figure 5.2. Falling sales also reduces advertising revenue so the inevitable result is the pincer action of falling revenue and rising per unit costs on profits – or, one suspects in the case of *The Times* in 1993, growing losses. In this situation, unless action is taken, it can only be a matter of time before *The Times* would have to exit the market or be taken over by a new owner who was either prepared to subsidise further losses or had confidence in reviving *The Times'* flagging performance.

Even so, to cut price is to risk a price war and at this point the culture and management style of *The Times* would have been a crucial influence on the decision. News International's experiences in Australia, and particularly New York, would have provided learning and guidance, which together with Rupert Murdoch's willingness to take risks and to compete aggressively would have been decisive. Oligopolistic interdependence and game theory suggests that as rational individuals *The Times'* senior managers would have done their best to anticipate their rivals' response and this would have been weighed against News International's accumulated knowledge and capability to withstand an aggressive response. No doubt one of their considerations was the fortuitous timing. *The Telegraph* was a publicly quoted company and its share price would have plummeted if investors believed a price war was looming. *The Independent* was already in financial difficulties and *The Guardian* had just taken over *The Observer* and was therefore financially stretched. In such a situation Murdoch appeared to judge that if he engaged in aggressive behaviour rivals may not respond. He gambled, correctly, and *The Times* enjoyed an undisputed first mover advantage.

As *The Times* was believed to be making loss – its accounts were lost inside News International – it was perhaps inevitable that Murdoch would be accused of predatory pricing – taking a profit sacrifice to drive a rival out of the market. But, falling sales meant that he had to take action and the competition authorities would always prefer a price cut and competition to non-cooperative 'tacit' collusion between rivals. An important conclusion of game theory is that strategic actions must be credible. After 10 months of falling sales *The Telegraph* was forced to respond. When Conrad Black reduced the price of *The Telegraph*, Murdoch's immediate reaction was to cut the price of *The Times*. Although this worried Andy it was the correct response. It sent a signal to Conrad that Murdoch meant business and was prepared to engage in a price war if necessary. Within 3 months the price of *The Times* and *The Telegraph* were raised: the price war was over. By that time, almost certainly by design, Murdoch had reaped a real benefit from his aggressive behaviour.

A quarter of a century ago Murdoch's audacious move would have been analysed using some variant of the SCP paradigm and strategic conflict approaches. Today IO economists would also enquire as to what happened inside News International. Following the work of Schumpeter and Penrose, IO scholars now recognise the contribution of organisational capabilities and entrepreneurial judgement to the creation and capture of value. Entrepreneurial judgement refers to the Schumpetarian characterisation of a search for higher profits and in this realm the economic activity that creates new sources of value-adding endeavours by disturbing the established norms, a process that Schumpeter (1942) termed *creative destruction*. Murdoch's entrepreneurial judgement suggested he could create a new field of value-adding activity by lowering the price of *The Times*, not to spark a price war with rival broadsheets, but to attract large numbers of tabloid readers into the broadsheet market. Murdoch's action had the effect of not only disturbing the broadsheet market, but also substantially increasing the demand for *The Times*, by taking sales from rivals and also widening the market.

Organisational capability follows the work of Penrose and refers to the managerial reorganisation that accompanies the entrepreneurial judgement and through which the new opportunity is created. Composed of human actors who are necessarily boundedly rational, the process is embedded, as argued by Nelson and Winter (1982), in the routines of the organisation and must to some degree rely on trial and error. For both Schumpeter and Penrose the new organisational form that accompanies the new creative opportunity involves not only the skills and efforts of individuals, but also the efficiency of the working relationships between individuals. It is the interplay of entrepreneurial judgement and organisational capabilities that determine the opportunities, the effectiveness and the speed at which they are carried out.

References

Aaronovitch, S. and M. C. Sawyer, 'Mergers, Growth and Concentration', *Oxford Economic Papers*, 27 (1975) 136–55.

Alchian, A. and H. Demsetz, 'Production, Information Costs and Economic Organisation', *American Economic Review*, 62, 5 (1972) 772–795.

Ansoff, I., *Corporate Strategy* (London: Penguin Books, 1965).

Archibald, G. C., 'Chamberlin versus Chicago', *Review of Economic Studies*, 24 (1961) 9–28.

Arrow, K., 'Economic Welfare and the Allocation of Resources for Invention' in *Rate and Direction of Inventive Activity* (NBER, 1962).

Bain, J., *Barriers to New Competition* (Cambridge, MA: Harvard University Press, 1956).

Barney, J. B., 'Organisation Culture: Can it be a Source of Sustained Competitive Advantage?' *Academy of Management Review*, 11 (1986) 656–665.

Baumol, W., 'On the Theory of Oligopoly', *Economica* 25 (1958) 87–98.

Baumol, W., 'On the Theory of Expansion of the Firm', *American Economic Review*, 52 (1962) 1078–1087.

Baumol, W., 'Contestable Markets: An Uprising in the Theory of Industrial Structure', *American Economic Review*, 72 (1982) 1–15.

Beale, A. and G. Means, *The Modern Corporation and Private Property* (New York: Macmillan, 1932).

Buzzel, R. and B. Gale, *The PIMS Principles: Linking Strategy to Performance* (New York: The Free Press, 1987).

Chamberlin, E. H., 'Duopoly v Value Where Sellers Are Few', *Quarterly Journal of Economics*, 43 (1929) 63–100.

Chamberlin, E. H., *The Theory of Monopolistic Competition* (Cambridge: Harvard University Press, 1933).

Chandler, A. D., *Strategy and Structure* (Cambridge, MA: MIT Press, 1962).

Coase, R. H., 'The Nature of the Firm', *Economica*, 4 (1937) 386–405.

Cyert, R. and J. March, *Behavioural Theory of the Firm* (Englewood Cliffs: Prentice Hall, 1963).

Dasgupta, P. and J. Stiglitz, 'Industrial Structure and the Nature of Innovative Activity', *Economic Journal*, 90 (1980) 266–293.

Gander, J., 'Managerial Intensity, Firm Size and Growth', *Managerial and Decision Economics*, 2 (1991) 261–266.

Grossman, S. and O. Hart, 'The Costs and Benefits of Ownership: A Theory of Lateral and Vertical Integration', *Journal of Political Economy*, 94 (1986) 691–719.

Hay, D. A. and D. J. Morris, *Industrial Economics and Organisation* (Oxford: Oxford University Press, 1991).

Hayek, F., 'The Use of Knowledge in Society', *American Economic Review* 35, 4 (1945) 519–530.

Heal, G. and A. Silberston, 'Alternative Managerial Objectives: An Explanatory Note', *Oxford Economic Papers*, 24 (1972) 137–150.

Holmstrom, B. and J. Tirole, 'The Theory of the Firm' in R. Schmalensee and R. Willig (eds) *Handbook of Industrial Organisation*, 5th edn (Amsterdam: North Holland, 1989).

Jensen, M. and W. Meckling, 'Theory of the Firm: Managerial Behaviour, Agency Costs and Ownership Structure', *Journal of Financial Economics*, 3, 4 (1976) 305–360.

Knight, F., *Risk, Uncertainty and Profit* (New York: Kelley, 1921).

Kreps, D. M., *Game Theory and Economic Modelling* (Oxford: Oxford University Press, 1990).

Marris, R., 'A Model of the Managerial Enterprise', *Quarterly Journal of Economics*, 77 (1963) 185–209.

Marris, R., *The Economic Theory of Managerial Capitalism* (London: Macmillan, 1964).

Marshall, A., *Principles of Economics* (London: Macmillian, 1890).

Mason, E., 'The Current State of the Monopoly Problem in the US', *Harvard Law Review*, 62 (1949) 1265–1285.

Montgomery, C., 'Corporate Diversification', *Journal of Economic Perspectives*, 8 (1994) 163–178.

Nalebuff, B. and A. Brandenburger, *Co-Opetition* (London: Profile Books, 1996).

Nelson, R. and S. Winter, *An Evolutionary Theory of Economic Change* (Cambridge, MA: Belknap Press, 1982).

Panzar, J. and R. Willig, 'Economies of Scope', *American Economic Review*, 71, 2 (1981) 268–272.

Penrose, E., *The Theory of the Growth of the Firm* (Oxford: Oxford University Press, 1959).

Porter, M. E., *Competitive Strategy: Techniques for Analysing Industry and Competitors* (New York: The Free Press, 1980).

Porter, M. E., *Competitive Advantage: Creating and Sustaining Superior Performance* (New York: The Free Press, 1985).

Richardson, G. B., *Information and Investment* (Oxford: Oxford University Press, 1960).

Saloner, G., 'Game Theory and Strategic Management: Contributions, Applications and Limitations' in R. Rumelt, D. Schendel and D. Teece (eds) *Fundamental Issues in Strategy: A Research Agenda* (Boston: Harvard Business School Press, 1994).

Say, J. B., *Traité d'Economie Politique* cited in Alexander Gary, *The Development of Economic Doctrine* (*1948*) (London: Longmans, Green, 1803).

Scherer, F. M., 'Review of The Economics of Market Dominance', *International Journal of Industrial Organisation*, 6 (1988) 517–518.

Scherer, F. M. and D. Ross, *Industrial Market Structure and Economic Performance* (Boston: Houghton Mifflin, 1990).

Schumpeter, J., *Capitalism, Socialism and Democracy* (New York: Harper and Row, 1942).

Shaked, A. and J. Sutton, 'Natural Oligopolies', *Econometrica*, 51 (1983) 1469–1483.

Shapiro, C., 'Theories of Oligopolistic Behaviour' in R. Schmalensee and R. Willig (eds) *Handbook of Industrial Organisation* (Amsterdam: North Holland, 1986).

Shapiro, C., 'The Theory of Business Strategy', *RAND Journal of Economics*, 20 (1989) 125–137.

Simon, H. A., 'Theories of Decision Making in Economics and Behavioural Science', *American Economic Review* (1959).

Smith, A., *An Inquiry Into the Nature and Causes of the Wealth of Nations* (London, 1776).

Staffa, P., 'The Laws of Return Under Competitive Conditions', *Economic Journal*, 36 (1926) 535–550.

Sutton, J., *Sunk Costs and Market Structure* (Cambridge, MA: MIT Press, 1992).

Sweezy, P., 'Demand Under Conditions of Oligopoly', *Journal of Political Economy*, 47 (1939) 568–573.

Tirole, J., *The Theory of Industrial Organisations* (Cambridge, MA: MIT Press, 1993).

Treadway, A., 'Adjustment Costs and Variable Inputs in the Theory of the Competitive Firm', *Journal of Economic Theory*, 2 (1970) 329–347.

Viner, J., 'Cost Curves and Supply Curves' in *Readings in Price Theory* (Chicago: Irwin, 1952).

Volbeda, H. and T. Elfriny, *Rethinking Strategy* (London: Sage, 2001).

von Neumann, J. and O. Morgenstein, *Theory of Games and Economic Behaviour* (Princeton, NJ: Princeton University Press, 1944).

Williamson, J., 'Profit, Growth and Sales Maximisation', *Economica*, 33 (1966) 1–66.

Williamson, O. E., *The Economics of Discretionary Behaviour* (Englewood Cliffs: Prentice Hall, 1964).

Williamson, O. E., 'The Vertical Integration of Production: Market Failure Considerations', *American Economic Review*, 51 (1971) 112–123.

Williamson, O. E., *The Economic Institutions of Capitalism* (New York: The Free Press, 1985).

Williamson, O. E., 'Transaction Cost Economics' in R. Schmalensee and R. Willig (eds) *Handbook of Industrial Organisation*, 5th edn (Amsterdam: North Holland, 1998).

CHAPTER 6
Game Theory Perspective

Stephen Regan

Basic principles

Game theory is a set of tools for answering questions about how economic agents will react when what they do affects the actions of others. For instance, in an industry where there are a few firms, all of whom can observe each other's behaviour, how will these firms take each other's reactions into account in formulating their strategies? Questions such as 'Can we use pricing to increase our sales without causing a price war?' or 'Can we commit to defend our market from a potential new entrant?' are the sorts of questions game theory seeks to address.

Game theory is thus the theory of how firms (and others) *interact* rather than act. There are a great many models of such interactive choices in game theory and many interesting theories about how *firms* in particular solve such problems.

CASE STUDY 6.1

THE SITUATION

The Board of Directors of Sheffield Readymix Ltd are considering whether to reduce their capacity for the production of ready mixed concrete. The date is October 1997, and the local market has two principal producers: Sheffield Readymix and Rotherham Concrete. Rotherham Concrete have roughly twice the market share of Sheffield Readymix. Prices are falling due to declining demand – more and more builders are able to mix their own concrete on site using portable mixing machines. This gives them lower costs and higher control over when the mix is made, which greatly improves the cost-effectiveness of mixing on site.

Current projections are that demand for readymix will fall by 5 per cent per year, on average, for the foreseeable future. As this happens, both Sheffield Readymix and Rotherham Concrete will find it difficult to maintain the same level of capacity without cutting prices. They both know this, and they both know each other knows it.

Conversation

Laurence Anthony is the Sales Director of Sheffield Readymix. He is concerned about maintaining sales in the declining market. He has asked for a meeting with the Finance Director *Annabel Grace*, who is concerned about the profitability of aggressive price cutting to gain market share in a declining market. *Derek Anderson* is the MD of the company, and is present.

Laurence: For the last eight quarters our sales have declined steadily at about 11/2 % quarter on quarter, and yet we have maintained price. As a result our unit costs are rising since we are spreading our fixed overheads over reduced volumes. What I want to know is, why doesn't it make sense to cut prices, and get the volume we need to keep costs down? A 1 % cut in price will bring about a 2 % increase in demand for our products in this market, which will lead to reductions in unit costs, and an improvement in margins.

Annabel: That would be true if we could be sure that Rotherham Concrete won't react. If they do, then we will just have started a price war, and we will effectively be slitting our own throats. With their volume they could flood the market and force us out of business very quickly.

Derek: So what's your strategy, Annabel?

Annabel: I think the name of the game here is to stay in the market as long as possible, and that means both us and Rotherham Concrete cooperating to keep margins as high as possible, for as long as possible.

Laurence: But our costs are rising, our volumes are falling, and we are just not reacting. It seems irresponsible not to try to be competitive. At the moment we are just allowing our business to run itself into the ground. If you want to keep us in business as long as possible, surely we have to find a way of forcing Rotherham Concrete out of the market.

Derek: Laurence has got a very strong point – surely there has to come a time where we try to force Rotherham out, and wouldn't it be better to do it sooner, rather than later? If we cut price now, we have the reserves to sustain losses for a while, and we also have the chance of forcing out our main rival sooner. This would give us longer to run the industry after their exit if we were to win the price war. The longer we have the industry to ourselves, the more money we make.

Laurence: I completely agree with Derek. I think we have to take a long-term, strategic view and manage our own contraction. We could have several years of profitable monopoly if we force Rotherham out now, or a couple of years of bleeding to death jointly if we don't. I don't see the logic of trying to maximise short-term gains. If we start a price war, we make short-term losses, but long-term, more profits.

Annabel: I hear what you both say, but I still think we shouldn't forget the likely reactions of Rotherham to our actions. It is not immediately obvious that we would gain from a price war, so there is a risk. I don't like taking risks I don't have to. I've prepared a spreadsheet, which I'd like you to look at.

[*Annabel clicks open the Excel File on her PC and turns the screen so that her two colleagues are able to see the display below*]

Net profits per cubic metre (% return on sales)

Date		Sheffield alone (%)	Rotherham alone (%)	Rotherham and Sheffield together (%)
2001	January	9	6	2
	July	8	5	1
2002	January	7	4	0
	July	6	3	−1
2003	January	5	2	−2
	July	4	1	−3
2004	January	3	0	−4
	July	2	−1	−5
2005	January	1	−2	−6
	July	0	−3	−7
2006	January	−1	−4	−8
	July	−2	−5	−9

Laurence: So what's your point, Annabel?

Annabel: We don't have to start a price war to force Rotherham out – we can wait them out. They'll have gone by January 2002 anyway. If I know this, then they do too. We don't have to do anything. A price war would just waste both our and their resources.

Derek: I don't see why they *have* to leave in January 2002. Surely if they start a price war, and force us out, they can make profits right through to January 2004.

Annabel: Quite right. Rotherham *have* to leave by January 2004 – even if they force us out before then. That means they know we can make profits of 6 % on sales, cumulatively, that is an average of 2 % per half year from January 2004 to July 2006, after they have left, if we hang on.

Derek: Which means they know we know we can cover any losses we make by sharing the market with them right back to July 2002.

Annabel: So if we *are* still there in July 2002, they know they can't force us out after that, so they would do better to leave. In fact, they may leave in January 2002 because they'll just be covering costs for the first half of next year.

Derek: So we can expect to treble our return on sales, starting sometime in 2002, if we keep our capacity as it is.

Laurence: Doesn't this make a price war even more certain? Won't they have to force us out before they start to make a loss in July 2002?

Annabel: I don't think that makes sense. They should be able to see that the value of the industry is greater to us than it is to them. Thus if they start a price war they don't change our relative positions – they just turn the industry into a loss-making one quicker. This just forces their own exit faster than we would force them out without a price war. They know we won't want to start a price war – since it reduces our overall profits – neither we, nor they, can benefit by making a single penny of losses here, and neither of us has to. They know that, we know that, and we have to believe they'll play the game in the way we see it.

Laurence: I think I'll phone their sales director for a round of golf this week.

Annabel: You do that. I hear he plays a good game. Maybe you should let him win!

Issues

This conversation reveals the importance of certain key ideas from game theory, applied to a business problem. They are as follows:

(a) Understanding the game

Annabel is able to calculate various *moves* or strategies available in the game, to each of the two players. She has identified the *payoffs* in each of the potential strategy profiles in each time period from now to the end of the game, for each of the players.

(b) Reasoning strategically

Effectively this means designing your strategies based upon your assessment of your opponent's best responses to each of your potential strategies. Your best response to their best response is the correct strategy for both of you. In the language of game theory, it is the *equilibrium*[1] of the game. One of the main insights from game theory is that there is always *at least one* equilibrium strategy.

Key contributions

Origins of game theory

Game theory was first developed by John von Neumann and Oskar Morgenstern who published a path-breaking book (in 1944) called *Theory of Games and Economic Behaviour*. Von Neumann was a 'mathematician', though the term does not begin to cover the immense contribution he made to modern thought in a great many areas. He was a pure mathematician, but worked in the field of theoretical physics with the community at Princeton University that included the greatest concentration of scientists in the twentieth century, including Einstein, Nils Bohr, Richard Feynman and others. He built computers, he designed logistics systems for the Pacific War and in game theory he produced the first successful attempt to develop a mathematical theory for human behaviour. Basically von Neumann and Morgenstern's[2] idea was that in many areas of human activity (including business) people solve problems that are rather like the problems they solve when they play games – they decide what to do on the basis of what they think others will do, including making decisions that try to influence what others do. If mathematics can solve these game-type problems, then it will have gone a long way towards illuminating human behaviour. This is what game theory has been doing ever since 1944.

The initial applications of game theory were in military strategy, where it was used to design optimal battlefield strategies. For instance to predict the best strategies for anti-submarine surveillance it is important to get inside the mind of your rival. This is exactly what game theory does, and hence its popularity during the Cold War.

The greatest uptake of game theory since the 1950s has been in economics, where it has revolutionised the way economists model oligopoly, which is the study of rivalry between large firms. Game theory is also popular with biologists, who use it to study the interaction between animals and have developed successful models of everything from optimal foraging behaviour for baboons to the distribution of tongue length in bees.[3]

Game theory is beginning to make inroads into strategic management, as economists develop more insight into the practical applications of their previously rather theoretical models. We shall now look at the key principles of game theory as it has been applied to strategic management.

Key principles of games

Conflict and cooperation

A central insight from game theory, of great value to managers, is that there are always two sides to every game. In one dimension, all the players have come together to achieve some shared goal (in business, to create value). For instance, even in warfare, there is often a subtle cooperative agenda underneath the most bloody encounter, without which the two sides would not be able to structure their interactions.

However, as well as cooperation, there is also in every game a degree of competition. Once the shared objective of the game is achieved, there is then a tremendous pressure for each contributor to that objective to make certain they walk away with the biggest possible share of whatever is created. Thus games which appear to be highly cooperative (such as family interactions) are often highly competitive; games which appear purely competitive (such as warfare or business competition) often are played in subtly cooperative ways.

In business both parts of the game have to be played as well as possible. You have to cooperate *and* compete to succeed in business. This has been captured by two game theorists leading the way in applying the subject to business: Brandenberger and Nalebuff, using a strategy tool they have termed the value net (this is developed below in the 'value net' section).

This chapter defines game theory as the economic theory of strategic *behaviour* and the economic theory of strategic *rationality*. Implicit in this is an economic definition of what a *strategy* is: *choice in an interdependent context*. It is about how to act and how to think about your rival's actions. Game theory is about getting inside the mind of your rivals. What could be more powerful in business strategy than this? Thus game theory is the theory of interdependent choice behaviour *and* the theory of what is rational in such a context. The reason for this insistence on the twin meaning of game theory is that solution concepts in games depend crucially on equilibria in both beliefs (rationality) and actions (behaviour). (As can be seen in the Sheffield example, Annabel does not just act strategically, she thinks strategically.)

The economic theory of strategic behaviour

The remit of game theory as the theory of strategic behaviour in business is not narrowly defined (for instance, as inter-firm rivalry), but extends widely. For instance it includes managerial behaviour inside firms, regulation by government and industrial relations bargaining between employers and employees to name but a few of the more common strategic problems where game theory has been useful. Since many of these problems involve choices made by an individual within an organisation, or actions by institutions outside the organisation, game theory includes more than *corporate* strategy: it might be described as a general theory of strategy, including competitive, corporate and cooperative strategy.

Also the methodology of game theory is mathematically based and thus forces the strategist to be more explicit about the nature of the relationships which are being modelled and then to abide by those relationships. Informal conjecture about how one rival *may* respond to another is not what game theory does; game theory quite rigorously reduces the possible sets of actions the players may reasonably be expected to demonstrate. In the immense complexity of business, game theory provides a useful simplicity.

What is a game?

There are two ways to represent a game: the strategic form and the extensive form. The strategic form is a simpler, reduced form, which shows the players, their strategies and their payoffs, with each player taking one side of a matrix.

A game in extensive form is a richer representation and makes use of a device called a game tree. This shows not only the players, the strategies and the payoffs, but also the order of the moves in the game and the information each player has about the game at each point in time. It is also able to represent the game as a sequence of smaller games (sub-games). The game in extensive form (the game tree) should be the preferred tool for business strategists due to its greater detail (Figure 6.1).

Firm 1 and firm 2 are producers of watermelons. Each has three strategies (choices) – a low-output strategy (180 melons supplied), medium (240 melons) and high volume (360 melons). There are two players, each with three choices, and thus $3 \times 3 = 9$ potential outcomes, represented by the branches of the (game) tree on the extreme right-hand side. The numbers at the ends of each of the nine branches are the payoffs to each player from that combination of strategies. The first number is firm 1's payoff and the second is firm 2's payoff. These payoffs represent dollars of profit resulting from that particular outcome. The numbers *on* the branches leading to the right are the strategies of each player. Thus if firm 1 produces 180 melons and firm 2 produces 180 melons, then these firms get $64.80 of profits each. In this game firm 1 gets to move first, and firm 2 moves second. What game theory allows us to do is given below:

1. Model the strategic situation in the way we have just done. We have identified the players, their strategies, their move orders and their payoffs. Already we have evolved a useful way of structuring the strategic problem.
2. Solve the game. This means we can predict which is the rational way to play the game, which could be very useful.

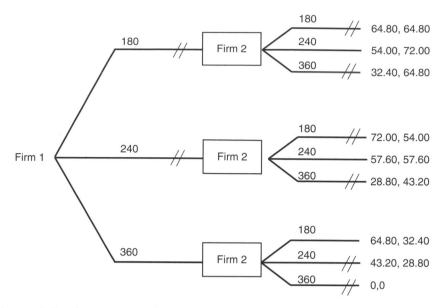

Figure 6.1 The water melon game: An example of extensive form games

To see how good you are at strategy, *before* we work out the answer using game theory, answer the following question:

(a) Is firm 1 better off to move first, or does firm 2 gain by being able to watch for what firm 1 does?
(b) Who will walk away from this game with the highest payoff?

Now let us see if you were right. We solve this sort of (extensive) game by a method known as fold back. We work out what player 2 will do first and then work back to player 1's best strategy after that.

If firm 2 is faced with the three choices at the top of the tree, that is the three strategies which are a response to firm 1 producing 180, then firm 2 will produce 240, since this gives them a profit of 72.00, which is higher than the 64.80 they get by producing either 180 or 360. We show this by blocking off (≠) the two strategies they would not choose.

If firm 2 is put into the middle node, they will choose 240, for the same reason (though they get less profit, since in this case firm 1 produces more, and this extra volume suppresses market prices and thus profits).

If firm 1 chooses 360, then firm 2 will maximise profits by producing low volume of 180.

We then '*fold back*' to consider which strategy firm 1 and firm 2 will actually take. We assume that firm 1 has correctly drawn the game tree (or that intuitively they understand the game tree as we have drawn it). So firm 1 knows that only three outcomes matter.

So they have to choose between profits of $54.00 (along the track (180, 240)). Or they can have $57.6 (240, 240) or $64.8 (360,180). This means they will choose 360, which gives them the highest payoff of 64.80; firm 2 will choose 180, and payoffs will be $64.80 profit to firm 1 and $32.40 to firm 2.

Thus in answer to the question set above: (a) firm 1 is better off by moving first: there are first mover advantages in this game; (b) firm 1 makes twice as much profit as firm 2.

You may be upset by this logic. You may imagine you are firm 2, why don't you just tell firm 1 that unless they produce no more than 240, you will produce 360? If they agree and produce 240, you will produce 240. Total payoffs will be higher, and you may even promise that you will reimburse them back up to $64.80 from $57.60 – this still leaves you with $50.40,[4] which is significantly more than the $32.40 you get without such a deal.

If this is the way you have been thinking then you are to be commended. First, because this is exactly the way many firms try to react strategically in such a situation. For instance this is the way OPEC have run the world oil industry since 1973: restricting output and sharing the higher profits amongst the players. Second, because this sort of cooperative behaviour between players is where state-of-the-art game theory has been working for some time. Third, because the next game we look at, prisoner's dilemma, shows exactly how such agreements (known as cartels) tend to break up (Figure 6.2).[5]

The story behind the game is as follows. Two spies are caught behind enemy lines and given the opportunity to turn each other in (defect on each other) or to stick to their previous agreement not to do this (cooperate with each other). Their payoffs reflect these moves.

If player A cooperates and B defects, player A is shot (payoff zero) and B is released to spy for their captor. If A cooperates and B cooperates they are both treated as civilians and given a light prison sentence. B's payoffs are symmetrical to A's. If they both defect, they are tortured for further evidence. The payoffs here are in utilities, which are numerical representations for happiness. Often in business applications we assume the payoffs are in terms of profit, but the principles are the same; the number games we look at represent the satisfaction each player has with that outcome. By convention, the first number in a cell represents the payoff to the player on the left (player A in this case) and the second number represents the player on top (player B).

Here the best strategy for B is to defect (whatever A does), and thus defect is the *dominant* strategy for B. This is only the case if B is unable to make a deal with A (rather like a cartel in the previous game), in which case he may prefer to choose to cooperate if he can be sure A will cooperate. This deal-making type of game theory is known as cooperative game theory, and it includes an extra dimension to non-cooperative game theory, since it makes B's strategy dependent not only on what A does, but on B's beliefs about A (A's type). This means that solution concepts (equilibria) become much more uncertain in cooperative game theory, but such cooperative behaviour, and the modelling of beliefs, is fundamental to corporate strategy problems, such as entry deterrence or structuring a joint venture.

Here the grim logic of the game is that to cooperate is *never* chosen, it is *irrational* to cooperate for reasons outlined above. This gives a particularly gloomy view of the value of rationality (so defined) since, clearly, human beings cooperate at least as much as they defect. Most biologists suggest that a combination of large brain and intense cooperation is what is most unique about human beings

		Player B	
		Co-op	Defect
Player A	Co-op	3, 3	0, 4
	Defect	4, 0	1, 1

Figure 6.2 Game 2 – prisoner's dilemma

and the basis of our success as a species. Many readers would probably play cooperate in prisoner's dilemma and believe that your fellow player would do so.

Solutions to games

A game in strategic form: matching pennies. Players A and B choose independently of each other whether to turn a coin heads up or tails up. If the outcome is heads–heads or tails–tails, player A gets player B's coin. The entries in the cells of the payoff matrix represent this. If the outcome is heads–heads or tails–tails, then player A gets $+1$ and player B gets -1; this makes these outcomes zero sum (since $-1 + 1 = 0$).

The game is symmetrical, meaning that heads–tails or tails–heads give player B $+1$ and player A -1. The first entry in each cell is player A's payoff from that strategy profile and the second is B's payoff (Figure 6.3).

This game is a zero sum game since the players' payoffs sum to zero for each of the outcomes. In other words, the game itself does not add value. In corporate strategy we may be interested in value-adding games (positive sum) and value-destroying games (negative sums).

You may like to conjecture what you *should* do in a game of this type if you were player A. Your preferred outcome is heads–heads or tails–tails. Actually, the best you can do is flip the coin and play whichever face lands up. Anything else will let B beat you if he adopts the head-flipping strategy. Can you see why? Note here that the rational strategy is to leave it to chance – there are many (more realistic and complex) games, in business, where leaving it to chance works well. The example below is a game in extensive form, which relates to a business situation.

For instance if A cooperates, then B gets a payoff of 4 if he defects, but only 3 if he cooperates. So he maximises his payoffs if we defect whenever A cooperates. What makes this a dominant strategy is that B should defect even if A does not cooperate since he gets a payoff of zero when he cooperates if A defects, and a payoff of 1 if he defects when A defects. So he will defect. In this sense to defect is better than to cooperate for B, in all cases, and is thus dominant. Whatever the equilibrium of this game, B will play his dominant strategy, and thus we have an outcome where at least one player defects. The other player knows this, and this knowledge greatly simplifies the game for him. (It may not greatly please him, but it sure does simplify it.)

The game's solution thus unfolds as rational sets of calculations between players about their best response to the other's possible actions. At a deeper level, we have seen that notions like dominance also allow you to understand how the other player *should* play the game, rather than just how he

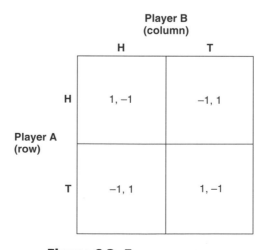

Figure 6.3 Zero sum game

might. This is quite deep reasoning and helpful since this allows you to calculate how you must play the game. It is a theory of strategy (if strategy means choice).

In many cases the players will wish to hide their future intentions from each other, and game theory gains much as a methodology if it is able to model such behaviour in a systematic way. When a player chooses a given strategy with certainty, say because it is a dominant strategy, then the agent is said to have a *pure* strategy. However, when the probability of a strategy is less than 1, then the agent is said to have a mixed strategy, since there is a more than zero chance that he/she will play another strategy. This adds an extra problem for the other player(s). Matching pennies (see above) is an example of a game where each player's best strategy is mixed: to play heads and tails randomly, with a 50 per cent chance of each.[6] Game theory is beginning to find how to apply such models to highly uncertain business problems, in order to solve risk management problems, for instance.

Conclusions

This section has attempted to show some of the main features of game theory as it exists today in economics. Its conclusions are that game theory is a new and disciplined language for a range of strategy problems. This language allows the strategist a range of modelling options when confronted with the facts of a particular industry; for instance, zero or variable sum games; one shot or repeated games; pure or mixed strategy games. This classification system gives access to sets of tools which have been developed to specifically solve these problems. We explore these in the next section.

The second major conclusion of this section is that game theory is beginning to shed light on what is rational. The analysis of *strategic rationality* is finally beginning to bridge the gap between the ideal 'rational economic man' and the actual boundedly rational corporate men and women who populate the real world. This project has hardly begun, but it is a promising one for the role of game theory in understanding business problems.

Linking game theory to strategic management

Game theory is a very general tool, with wide applicability in many areas. It has entered the language of strategic management through the application of economic theory to the problems managers face. In particular game theory is widely used, being applied to analyse not only the behaviour of managers within firms, but also the structures of firms themselves and the nature of relationships between firms (such things as the types of contracts or alliances firms might agree with each other). Beyond this, game theory has made significant contributions to how we understand a very wide range of problems, such as in biology, political science, military strategy and psychology, to name just the main ones. Given the wide range of fields where game theory has been applied it would be surprising if game theory was absent from the range of tools we use to understand strategic management. We now apply game theory to a number of real problems strategic managers face.

Context: Game theory's application to the competitive structure of the US auto industry in the early 1980s

Game theory has been employed as a device to analyse the business environment from a strategic group perspective. The role of game theory is its ability to show what forces are able to determine the number and size of strategic groups. Also, out of the whole range of possible strategic groups, which ones would be viable and which not, and for which firms, and for how long the strategic groups would last.

The implication from this research is that this sort of analysis will identify strategies which are likely to have long-run viability. For instance, the reorientation of the US auto manufacturers in the 1980s, in response to the entry of Japanese producers, can be analysed via game theory. Broadly the strategic variables on which the firm competed in this context were cost, quality and innovation. Ford were average in quality, high cost and average in innovation. GM had chosen/evolved average cost. The development of the industry is as follows:

1. The strategic group Ford were in was not feasible (efficient in the game theoretic sense), in that the strategy they were playing was *dominated* by other strategies. This was evidenced by the fact that their performance was declining in relation to GM. However, it is not obvious that they should seek to reduce costs, since another 'strategy move' may be preferred in a game theory context (e.g. raise quality and hold cost or raise innovation and reduce cost).

2. The arrival of Japanese producers was characterised as the opening up of a new strategic group (low cost, average innovation, high quality).

3. Ford responded with a high-cost, high-innovation, high-quality strategy. GM went for low cost, high quality and low innovation (i.e. their previously average innovation was now below average, due to the strategy moves of both the Japanese and Ford).

The result was that GM's new strategy was no longer the efficient one, but Ford's was, in that their performance began to improve in terms of profits. The Japanese strategy was also dominant.

Thus, what game theory could do for a firm such as Sheffield Readymix, in dealing with analysing their market context, would be to identify potentially viable long-run positions, by allowing them to predict with more confidence the likely responses of their rivals to any strategy they adopt. This is pretty well exactly what Annabel manages to do in the discussion at the start of this chapter. The approach could be taken further, for instance if they chose to expand into home insulation, game theory would indicate to them the likely response of the incumbent firms whose market they enter.

Culture: Game theory and human behaviour

Rationality has a central place in economics in the sense that explanations of phenomena are regarded as part of mainstream economics if they make contact with some version of the theory of rational choice. One of the complaints often made about game theory by strategists is that it idealises perfectly rational behaviour.

Managers want practical tools, which are based on realistic assumptions about the way the world works, and if game theory asserts that every decision is made by ideally rational individuals, most managers with experience of how decisions are actually made would question the extent of its potential contribution. So we have to ask, what can game theory, or economics for that matter, add to our understanding of a boundedly rational world? To put it at its most extreme, can game theory help us to understand the emotional and passionate nature of real people and real decisions. The answer is a very emphatic yes!

For instance, one variant of game theory is known as Drama Theory, and it suggests that in many contexts the best thing you can do is to indicate that you will not act in your own best interests. For example there is a famous game called 'Chicken', which is depicted in the James Dean film 'Rebel without a Cause'. In this film two young men agree to get in their cars and drive towards a cliff, the first person to swerve away from the cliff is a chicken and the other player is the winner. These games are an important part of display behaviour amongst young men. When we analyse these games, the result is usually that the two men never actually meet, and the game never takes place. The real game occurs over the weeks before the car race takes place, when the players play out roles towards each other designed to intimidate the other into not turning up. Much modern military strategy is of this type, deriving from Cold War experience, where the occurrence of an actual battle would be seen as failure.

Thus game theory can be seen as an important way of understanding all sorts of interactions between players which are designed to influence the emotions of the other players. The emotional element is not always as negative as this; for instance, game theory has been used to model the dynamics of relations between lovers as they establish trust with each other (deterrence models on the other hand are very good for modelling divorce). In the Sheffield Readymix example, think about the script and the drama of these interactions, think about what game is really being played here between the players. In the game within the game, is it not the case that Annabel wins and Laurence loses? Could Laurence have lost the argument and still won the game? What if Laurence had provoked Annabel into losing her temper, deliberately? How could he have done this?

One of the outcomes of this concern with the interaction between games and the emotions of the players is a definition of what is strategically rational. For instance, when we assume that players are all equally rational we might use a concept known as the *transparency of reason*, which is the notion that any player who arrives at a conclusion about a game has arrived at the same conclusions as all the other players and they know this and he knows they know. However, this kind of outcome is very close to a deterministic notion of rationality: it excludes players from arriving at different conclusions and even from believing in the possibility of different conclusions being formed by others. This is clearly nonsense! So where do we go with *this* notion of rationality?

Whether or not this transparency of reason is empirically true is not the key question: it is certainly very strong. Some weaker versions which suggest themselves (two amongst many) are as follows:

(a) All players are rational, but not all believe others to be rational.

(b) Not all players are rational, but they believe they are and that others are.

The point is that these *non-transparent* notions of rationality may be closer to the actual nature of rationality than the idealised common knowledge version above and may thus attract the interest of the corporate strategy community. Game theory is the ideal tool for exploring the logical possibilities for these different notions of strategic reason, and this would seem to be a project which parallels some of the interest in the cognitive aspects of strategy. All we are saying here is that if you are going to play a game you have to make assumptions about the degree of rationality and emotion your other players are bringing into the game, and play accordingly.

Competing

Signalling, which we would broadly define as communication between players, is an important concept in game theory. The nature of a signal is not entirely a new concept; for instance, there are strong similarities between signalling and what Porter describes as building a competitor profile (Porter, 1985). But the analysis in game theory is slightly different: here a player has private information about his own preferences (the player is assumed to know his own preferences), but makes public information available to other players by the signals he makes. The value to the agents of information about the other agents' true type is immense, since it allows them to choose their own actions better, and thus agents are strongly incentivised to form beliefs about each other.

There are models which consider what this concept means for organisations in terms of reputation building within and between them. For instance, if I believe that firm A is unaggressive then I will exclude from my beliefs any potentially aggressive strategies (i.e. I will assign a low probability to their likely occurrence and act accordingly). However, firm A may be much better off if I do not believe this, since their best strategy may be to threaten aggression, since it will cause me to act in a way favourable to them. For instance, they want to keep me out of their market by threatening aggression. The result is that firm A will attempt to develop a reputation for aggressiveness, and the best way to do this is by signalling.

Signalling comes in three types. The least sophisticated is called 'cheap talk', which is just what it says: you make promises and threats that you have no desire nor intention of keeping. For instance, cheap talk in the Sheffield Readymix case might occur if Rotherham Concrete phoned up their rivals and said they intended to stay in the market for at least five more years. It is a threat and the assumption is that when faced with having to carry out the threat (i.e. lose money) they will back off. Cheap talk generally, therefore, means promising to do things which you are not likely to carry out later.

Two other types of signalling are reputation and commitment. The difference between reputation and cheap talk could be summed up in the phrase 'actions speak louder than words'. You signal via reputation by repeatedly acting in a certain way. For instance, in supply chain relationships both parties have a lot to gain by acting cooperatively with each other, and they signal that they are like this to *other* potential contractors by refusing to damage their existing relationships (even though there may be a short-term gain).

Commitment involves making your signal irrevocable. For instance, if you want to commit to defend your market share, you might sign contracts with all your customers which guarantee you will match any other price they receive. If these are legally binding, an automatic, so you have no choice but to honour them, then you have made a commitment. Commitment is a very deep signal, since it involves taking away your own freedom to choose further actions in the event that something happens to trigger the commitment.

This can be applied to the problem of entry deterrence, modelled as a game, as follows (Figure 6.4).

In this game, with a finite number of potential entrants, *share* strictly dominates *prey* when there is incomplete information. The entrants know this and will thus enter (if there are no other barriers). However, the incumbent knows this and will thus act to affect the entrants' beliefs, perhaps by cutting price in response to other threatening behaviours; the only thing which will convince the entrants not to enter is a belief that the incumbent is irrational: that is that he does not know (what is common knowledge) that he should not cut prices. A nice variant of this is that the entrant may look at the reputation-building behaviour as a sign of weakness and thus interpret it as a sign they should enter the industry and compete against the very firm which is acting aggressively.

This has led to a Dr Strangelove[7] version of the entry deterrence game. Where reputation is not enough to deter entry, a higher level of signalling is to make an irrevocable commitment to act in a certain way if the entrant comes into the market. The Dr Strangelove deterrent is the construction of a Doomsday Machine – a machine which automatically detonates the industry from the moment a competitor enters. Such a strategy, tying one's hands in advance, is referred to as commitment – a

		Entrant	
		Enter	No entry
Incumbent	Share	2, 2	5, 1
Incumbent	Prey	0, 0	5, 1

Figure 6.4 Entry deterrence game. 'Prey' means predatory price to drive the rival out, and 'share' means to accommodate entry and share the market with the new rival

promise to act in certain ways in future. In the case referred to, a common version of the doomsday machine is limit pricing. This involves committing to supply a quantity of output from now to far into the future, the result of which is a commitment to drive price down whenever the entrant comes into the market. This effectively means the incumbent committing to destroy profits for both himself and the entrant, and thus the entrant will be deterred in so far as he believes in the commitment of the incumbent. The incumbent's only problem is to establish the irrevocable nature of the commitment. This might be done by signing contracts with suppliers (e.g. take or pay contracts) or by building a new plant with heavy fixed costs which establishes the capacity to produce output at very low marginal cost if the entrant comes in. It is risky, but it happens; for instance, large steel producers sign such contracts with their major automobile customers.

Cooperative strategy

Perhaps the highest profile contribution of game theory to corporate strategy has been in the area of cooperative strategy (Brandenburger and Nalebuff, 1995). There is a branch of game theory known as cooperative game theory which deals with situations where the players are able to communicate with each other (this is sometimes known as bargaining theory which better describes the behaviour it models).

It is important to note that not all bargaining is cooperative – thus bargaining theory could be used to analyse highly competitive games (zero sum) as well as less hostile ones. Cooperative strategy is best thought of as looking at positive sum games or turning zero sum games into positive ones, using the techniques of game theory.

One area where game theory is particularly useful is in vertical relationships along the supply chain. For instance, in the following typical supply chain, 'games' are being played all the time and there are games where the benefits of cooperation are very high, but the incentives to be competitive at the level of the individual lead to a less-than-optimal solution for the players as a whole, just as in prisoner's dilemma.

Grocery supply chain

Along this value chain the assembler and the manufacturer may find that their margins are squeezed both by rising raw material costs (due to high global demand driven by China) and reduced price from the retailer (i.e. having to give retailers bigger discounts) (Figure 6.5). The overall price to the consumer need not be falling at all; what is causing the problem for the manufacturer is the shifting balance of power within the supply chain towards the retailer.

The retailer knows that this category (say, 'male' deodorants) is a growth category, and that there are a number of other, well-supported (by advertising) brands, which globally might be the brand they would like to position as the leading brand in their stores. Increasingly retailers will tend to make

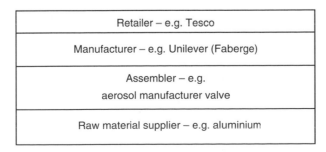

Figure 6.5 Grocery supply chain

these decisions at a regional (e.g. European), rather than a national level, and they will choose the brand which looks best across the entire region. The best margin will be given to the premium brand, the retailer will expect heavy support and/or strong discounts for stocking sub-premium brands. The issue for the national managers within Unilever (say) is how to create cooperative strategies with the retailer. It is not enough to be purely competitive (e.g. heavily advertise *their* brand) since L'Oreal or P&G can – and will – match this spending dollar for dollar. The issue is *strategic* – that is how can they spend their marketing dollars in a way which changes the game between themselves and the retailers, such as Tesco, into a cooperative one and (if it is a zero sum game) to turn the game between Tesco and the other consumer brand businesses into a competitive one.

One approach is to be allocentric, which means to look at the game from others' perspective. The best way to do this would be to draw value nets up and down the supply chain. A value net for Tesco (in Europe) might look like this (Figure 6.6).

Unilever's approach should then be to design a strategy which (a) maximises value for Tesco and (b) makes sure that the share of that pie which goes to Unilever (as opposed to any other player) is greater than under existing arrangements.

Change and control

Information asymmetries involve limits to the information set of one player vis-à-vis another. These limits are of two kinds: incomplete information and imperfect information. *Incomplete information* is where one player does not know what the preferences of the other player are (but he does know his own). Another player's preference function defines her *type*, and lack of knowledge about what type of player the other is will involve lack of knowledge about what her payoffs are to any given outcome. *Imperfect information* is where one of the players (at least) is unable to observe all of the actions of the other players. Information asymmetries are central to problems of agency and thus control.

Within this informational architecture a great deal of modelling of the effects of information asymmetries can be done. For instance, it is possible to model situations where players forget their own past decisions, which opens some interesting possibilities for strategy theorists; for instance, if the player is a senior management team which loses one or more of its key members during the game.

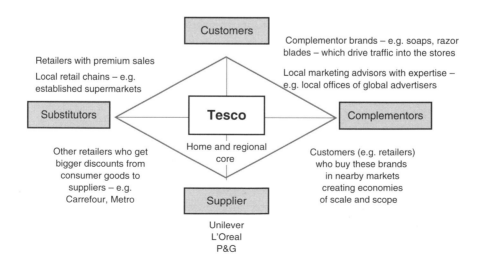

Figure 6.6 Tesco's value net

One important group of incomplete information games are those concerned with signalling. In such games players form beliefs about other players, and they update these after each round of the game. Signalling is where one player acts to affect the beliefs of the other.

This kind of thinking agrees with a lot of ideas on bounded rationality which permeates the strategy literature. With bounded information, even complete rationality produces indeterminate choices. Does this not admit the possibility that the adoption of rules of thumb may be as good as any choice rule?

Where information is imperfect rather than incomplete, the principal can observe the outcomes of the agents' actions (such as profits) but not the actions themselves (such as effort or skill). The agency problem is one of avoiding over- or under-rewarding agents for their actions. Game theory is well suited to this analysis, since the agent is inclined to signal (bluff) to the poorly informed principal, and this behaviour is well modelled within games of asymmetric information. Mechanism design is a branch of information economics which uses game theory to force agents to reveal this information and thus to restore principals' control over the agent, for example control over the worker by the manager or over the manager by the shareholder.

Tools and techniques derived from game theory

Several well-known game theorists have attempted to produce strategic tools for business managers which are practically relevant. These have often had limited success, largely because business problems are often much more complex than the stylised situations economists analyse using games. For instance, business games are free-wheeling entities which do not really have a clear start or a clear ending point, where the strategies are often very difficult to describe (because they are so numerous) and where players are able to enter or leave the game at will. However, one way of capturing this approach has been via the value net, a tool developed by Adam Brandenburger and Barry Nalebuff.[8] Their basic idea is that strategic behaviour is an attempt to change the nature of the game, so that you are more likely to win. Their idea is that players should choose the right game, rather than the right strategies in a game.

The value net

The value net is a way of identifying the players in a game (Figure 6.7). The horizontal axis represents players who are interactors, but not transactors. Thus, they influence the outcomes for everybody in the game, but no money changes hands. These interactors are of two types: those who sell outputs or buy inputs in competition with you (competitors), and those who sell outputs and buy inputs in a way which adds value to your selling and buying activities (complementors). For instance, two airline

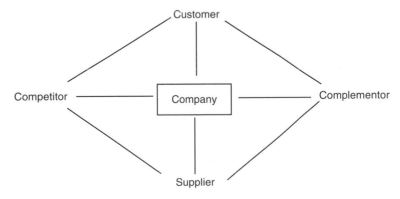

Figure 6.7 Value net: Identifying the players

companies who buy aircraft from Boeing complement each other's purchases – since they both get the possibility of lower costs via the economies of scale they generate. An airline and a hotel company are complementary in relation to customers, since each product enhances the value of the other. Two airlines may be complementors in the market for aviation fuel, and competitors in the market for business air travel.

The vertical dimension represents transactors. The value net thus gives the game some structure by identifying who are the players, and what are the relationships between them.

The game is defined first as being a set of relationships between players. The idea behind the value net is that players come together to create value as well as to divide it up. The first of these is cooperative and the second is competitive – these players thus have to both cooperate and compete with each other all the time. And this works in all the dimensions of the game – competitors have to cooperate with each other as well as compete. Excessive competition, as in the prisoner's dilemma, may be destructive for both parties. The name of the game is to structure these relationships in a way that you walk away with the maximum value you can, even if that means taking away less than your other players do. In this type of analysis you are as likely to be competitive with your customers as cooperative with them and as cooperative with your competitor as you are with your suppliers.

The way to use game theory is to follow the following steps:

1. Draw the value net – identify each of the players in each of the categories; for example, for a university (Figure 6.8).
2. Identify values.

The next step is to identify the value of each player in the game, in terms of economic value added. This means adding up the total value of all the players in the game. Draw the game without yourself as part of the value net and add up the payoffs here. The difference between these two is your value in the game – it is your value to the other players. If you are actually receiving less value than this, then you are playing the game too cooperatively, and you should be able to structure the game better to achieve higher payoffs for yourself.

One way to use the value net is to make decisions about games before you start to play them, to see if there is enough value in the game. Here again you draw the value net with and then without your involvement; the difference is the maximum value you can get from the game, and if this is not

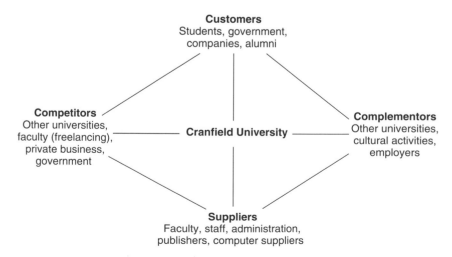

Figure 6.8 A university's value net

as high as you like, either you should not enter the game or you should attempt to restructure the value net before you get in.

3. Change the game

If you do not like the look of the game you are in, or might soon be in, what can you do to improve the situation? One approach here is a tool called PARTS, an acronym which stands for *p*layers, *a*dded values, *r*ules, *t*actics and *s*cope. You can reshape the game by changing any of these five constituents of the game.

Players

If we draw the value net for Sheffield Readymix, we can see how they might have played the game (Figure 6.9).

Sheffield Readymix can bring in extra players and thus increase their value in the game. The most obvious benefit is to be found by bringing in more customers – this increases the value of the pie and increases the size of the slice which is owed to Readymix.[9] The only problem is it is difficult to do. However, there may be certain things Sheffield Readymix have overlooked, which are outside the non-game-theoretic approach. These potential customers have a value in the value net, and one way to induce them to enter is to pay them their full value; in fact to pay them to play.

Added values and rules

If Sheffield Readymix want to attract Do It Yourself customers to use small amounts of Readymix, then they may find it worthwhile to offer an aggressively low price, which reflects their true value to the game. Thus they bring into their own value net the customers of their own customers, and this increases their own value and reduces the value of their customers. In this way the value net leads to market development strategies, and the usefulness of game theory is that it shows the logic of paying someone to play, by rewarding them with their share of their value to you. One outcome of this could be forward integration – so you end up rewarding yourself – effectively this would mean

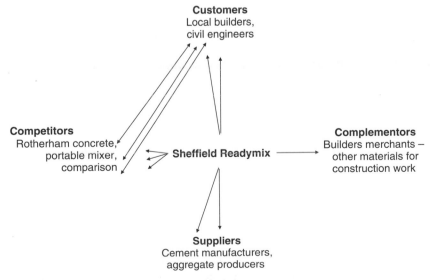

Figure 6.9 Sheffield Readymix's value net

Sheffield Readymix becoming their own customers and setting up a civil engineering and/or building subsidiary to buy its own products at very low prices.

Sheffield Readymix could also bring in more suppliers. One way to do this would be to form a buying club with Rotherham Concrete to negotiate lower prices than the smaller, less-organised builders merchants. Combined purchasing would generate more competition for their business amongst their suppliers, and lower prices. This might make all the difference in competing for customers against the builders.

Bringing in a complementor may also work. For instance, Sheffield Readymix might be able to negotiate lower prices for the non-concrete materials which builders use, and these complementary services may be passed on to their customers at reduced costs when tied in with the purchase of their Readymix products. This works very well if your complementor can not respond.

Tactics and scope

It may even be beneficial bringing in another competitor, which changes the scope of the game. Actually we have already seen how Sheffield Readymix and Rotherham Concrete could both cooperate to bring in more suppliers and more complementors. The more competitors who join the buying club, the better. Tactics involves signalling (e.g. to be cooperative) and scope involves increasing or reducing the size of the game.

Evaluation of the potential rule of game theory in strategy

Strengths: Game theory as a potential unifying language

The idea that game theory has unifying properties, and hence may act as a paradigm for corporate strategy, is supported by the fact that it unified certain aspects of economics and is still doing so.

Areas which have been generalised and integrated into game theory paradigm include the following:

- A more unified theory of horizontal mergers, allowing for advances at both public policy and business policy level in that it enables both the value and the allocation of value in pre–post merger scenarios to be determined. Until now this type of prediction was rather unsystematic.

- Investment in physical capital, which is now modelled as a commitment to compete vigorously as well as merely a cost shifter.

- Investment in intangible assets has been analysed and has developed new theory in the area of patent races, using tournament models. Game theory is able to analyse R&D strategies where there are spillovers and also to theorise in a systematic way about joint ventures.

- Strategic control of information is analysed via learning models within repeated games.

- Network competition and product standardisation now have a more unified theoretical language, as does the theory of contracting as an entry deterrent which in turn examines the implications of large firms being unambiguously at a disadvantage in declining industries.

Weaknesses

Rasmussen (1991) puts forward (with tongue perhaps half in cheek) an interesting technique for operationalising game theoretic concepts in a corporate strategy context, which he describes as the 'no fat' approach. It involves the following:

1. Observe and stylise some facts about the industry. These stylised facts are empirical regularities, which are more or less known or which may be discovered by a casual empiricist process, for example correlating trends.

2. Select a set of premises, which are consistent with it.
3. Explain the causality of the process which runs from 2 to 1 (i.e. think backwards).

The appeal of game theory is that it can explain almost anything and thus can be used as part of this no fat process of modelling. In this sense game theory has the potential to act as an engine of theory, as it has done in economics, where it is not without its critics since its very facility may produce facile theory.

Notes

1. Equilibrium means neither player has an incentive to change their strategies, and thus the game is in a position of stability.
2. Morgenstern was an economist at Princeton. His contribution was to take game theory on the road, attending conferences and loudly proclaiming that all other economists could not do maths. This meant he was not especially popular.
3. One criticism of game theory applied to business problems is that you have to be a mathematician to be good at it. Clearly this is only true in the sense that you have to be as good at maths as a baboon. Most MBAs are at least this good.
4. 57.60–(64.80–57.60).
5. Unfortunately, except when pursued by sovereign governments or explicitly allowed by them, cartels are illegal.
6. Note that this does not mean playing HTHT: this eventually means being certain of playing heads in odd-numbered plays of the game, which is not truly random.
7. Named after the Stanley Kubrik film about nuclear deference.
8. See 'Co-opetition', B. Nalebuff and A. Brandenburger (London: Harper Collins, 1996).
9. Here we mean bringing more customers into the game, not to attract existing customers from your competitors. This does not add value, merely captures it.

References

Brandenburger, A. and B. Nalebuff, 'The Right Game: Use Game Theory to Shape Strategy', *Harvard Business Review*, 73 (1995) 57–71.

Porter, M., *Competitive Advantage: Creating and Sustaining Superior Performance* (New York: Free Press, 1985).

Rasmussen, R., 'A Communication Model based on the Conduit Metaphor: What do we Know and What do we take for Granted', *Management Communication Quarterly*, 4 (1991) 363–374.

CHAPTER 7

Transaction Cost Economics Perspective

Andy Lockett and Steve Thompson

Basic principles

Transaction cost economics (TCE) is based on the simple principle that efficient economic organisation requires that firms minimise the sum of production costs and transaction costs. Production costs here means merely the costs of inputs (labour, raw materials, machinery, etc.) used in the production process. Transaction costs, on the other hand, are less transparent. These are the costs of using markets. Even relatively simple purchases may involve costs in searching out buyers or sellers, negotiating deals, monitoring deliveries, metering payments, and so on. In part, these costs result from a universal and benign condition that market participants must engage in the expensive business of acquiring and processing information. They also reflect the reality that transacting parties may behave opportunistically with the intention of exploiting situations to their own advantage. Opportunistic behaviour can have both a direct influence on costs and an indirect effect if its threat causes market users to require costly safeguards in their transacting.

It is immediately apparent that costs vary enormously across transactions. For example, compare the resource costs of buying today's newspaper in its city of publication (approximately zero) with those of locating and buying a part for an antique clock (high search costs) or those incurred by a management consultant when hiring a new MBA (search and interview costs, etc.) to a career position. More importantly, these costs also vary substantially across alternative organisational forms. For example, a long-term supply contract can save a car assembler the transaction costs of renegotiating component procurement batch by batch. Thus alternative organisational arrangements can be compared according to their levels of transaction costs. Furthermore, transactions may be internalised within a firm (or hierarchy). If we assume that production costs are invariant to transactional arrangements, TCE collapses to the even simpler proposition that an efficient set of organisational arrangements is one that minimises transaction costs.

Managers usually face a choice among alternative organisational arrangements. For example, the familiar 'make versus buy' decision involves deciding whether to produce some component, required activity or business service in-house or purchase it from outside, that is via a market transaction of one form or other. TCE suggests that in the absence of production cost differences the solution hinges on the relative costs of using the market or internalising the transaction. Where the costs of using the market are high, the make – or vertical integration – option will generally be preferred. Where the costs of using the market are low it will usually be cheaper to use the buy option. Of course, there are costs in managing in-house production that will need to be considered and these are discussed later.

Thus far all the argument has required is a simple statement of the obvious that efficiency requires managers to minimise costs. However, beginning with the work of Oliver Williamson, a number of economists have developed an analysis of the determinants of transaction costs. This has sought to identify those features of supply relationships that are likely to encourage the types of behaviour – costly haggling, misrepresentation, carelessness, cheating, holding up supply, and so on – that inflate transaction costs, either directly or indirectly.

Economists had long known that markets worked best where there were many buyers and sellers interacting in an environment of full information. Williamson recognised that very often transacting parties face informational problems – if only because of limits to their capacity for processing information – and some will behave opportunistically. In the presence of small numbers bargaining (buyers or suppliers), and/or where information is asymmetrically distributed between the parties, the difficulties may become acute. Subsequent work suggested that in reality the small numbers problem generally results where a transaction requires some asset with a highly specific use. Where relevant assets are non-specific (i.e. have multiple uses) there are typically many suppliers. Conversely, where assets are completely specific to one use the number of suppliers tends to be low and the risks of ownership high.

These insights have received support in a series of empirical tests across a wide variety of industries. Several other factors, including frequency of repetition of the transaction, its underlying uncertainty and the complexity of the product/service, also turn out to influence the level of transaction costs. However, these results do suggest that asset specificity usually plays a key role in determining whether market transacting is preferred to an internal administrative solution and, if so, what form of market exchange is optimal.

While the academic studies may validate the TCE approach and indicate broad generalisations about preferable arrangements they do not downgrade the key strategic role for managers in making organisational choices. First, to the extent that transaction costs are technologically determined the preferred set of arrangements will change as technology, including organisational and contractual forms, changes. Transactional arrangements may be equally subject to innovation as is physical production. Second, research on business suggests strongly that there is rarely only one viable solution. Industry rivals frequently employ different organisational forms over substantial periods, sometimes without either experiencing obvious difficulties. Finally, there is the converse possibility that transactional arrangements may be a major route to sustainable competitive advantage. Firms such as Toyota that develop a trust relationship with suppliers or customers, that cuts the costs of market dealing, may enjoy significant advantages over less favoured rivals. Moreover, this advantage may be hard to replicate and hence the resulting competitive advantage may be sustainable over an extended period.

CASE STUDY 7.1

Ramsbottom's Brewery Company is a medium-sized, family-run brewer and pub chain north of England. It currently operates 120 public houses in Greater Manchester and West Yorkshire, almost all of which are wholly owned outlets. It also owns and operates a brewery in a distinctive Victorian building on the edge of central Manchester, with a bottling plant attached and a nearby distribution depot. The company's turnover has increased from £50m to £70m over the past 3 years, but its profits have remained anchored around £3m. This reflects pressure on margins in the industry. Some 90 per cent of the firm's revenues are generated in its pubs, with most of the remainder coming from sales of bottled *Rampart* to a supermarket chain. Sales volume through the latter deal has been increasing but the associated profit margin is invariably small and sometimes eliminated through enforced discount schemes. A downward drift in the share price has accompanied Ramsbottom's trading difficulties. Rumours have begun to circulate that the company could become a takeover target for a national brewer.

The company was founded by Eli Ramsbottom in 1874 and five generations of the family have served on the board. The current non-executive chairman is Roger Ramsbottom, and his son Roger junior is marketing director, while his sister Chastity Dingle-Ramsbottom is a non-executive director. The firm's flagship product is its award-winning *Rampart* bitter ('A delightful, hoppy yet fruity ale', Good Beer Guide, 2005) and it also produces a dark mild (*Ramshackle*) and a strong winter brew (*Rampage*). The company was slow to respond to the demand for lager and its initial product (*Ramraid*) was over-strength and soon withdrawn after some negative publicity attaching to binge-drinking reports. It now produces *Hunbrau*, a weaker but more heavily promoted lager, under licence from a national brewer.

A recent consultant's report evaluated the strengths and weaknesses of the company's tied estate. While the overall geographic concentration is seen as strength in assisting the promotion of the company's reputation and products, Ramsbottom is significantly under-represented in the growth markets of Manchester and Leeds city centres. Conversely, it is over-represented in older industrial districts where competition from supermarket sales has eroded weekday trade. However, the company does have a number of highly lucrative suburban and rural 'gastropubs', whose reputations are reflected in leading food and drink guides.

Periodic share issues for expansion have diluted the family holding which now amounts to 35 per cent of the equity. Of this, the chair and Mrs Dingle-Ramsbottom control about 20 per cent, while 15 per cent are owned by cousins who are not involved in company management and who are rumoured to want to sell up. Fund managers hold 50 per cent, while the remaining 15 per cent is owned by a large number of small investors, many of them living in the Greater Manchester area.

The proposal

A board meeting was called to discuss the CEO's proposal to close and sell for redevelopment the company's brewery and bottling plant and to switch to the outside sourcing of beer for its pubs. An agreement has been reached with Bogson, another Manchester brewer, under which the latter would brew *Rampart* to the current recipe and supply its own mild *Bogoff* under the *Ramshackle* badge. Bogson would supply the lager *Hunbrau*, which they also brew under licence, and other beers would be discontinued or replaced with Bogson's own products. Under the deal, which would run for 1 year initially, the average delivered cost of beer to Ramsbottom pubs would be 80p a pint, compared to a current estimated cost of 85p per delivered pint. Alternatively, the beer could be delivered to the depot for 70p a pint, and Ramsbottom, retaining control over distribution, would then deliver, as required, at a projected inclusive cost of 85p a pint.

The CEO, together with Roger junior and the finance officer, argued that the cost savings were necessary to ensure the company remains competitive. Beer, he argued, is increasingly a commodity while consumers are ever more concerned with pub ambience. Moreover, most breweries have under-utilised capacity and are pleased to produce other beers under contract. The £4m net proceeds from the disposals (£5m if the distribution depot is sold as well) would be used to purchase pubs in suburban locations and to rent and equip city centre bars in Manchester and Leeds. He concluded his opening remarks with a summary of his strategic aims:

> 'We have the opportunity to shed Ramsbottom's low value-added manufacturing past and embrace the future as a high value-added service provider. We are too small and too peripheral to remain as beer producers. Outsourcing beer supply will allow us to benefit from our larger rivals' economies of scale rather than struggle against them. We must make hospitality management, not the production and distribution of ale our core competence'.

The proposal was vigorously opposed by both the chairman and the other non-executive directors on the board. The opponents argued the company would lose control over the quality and distribution of the products that define its distinctive identity. Furthermore, they argued that the company would be in a particularly weak position when renegotiating the deal, since any loss of familiar beers would alienate its consumers. They opposed the redundancies involved in the closures, on both ethical grounds and concerns that they would damage the company's local reputation and so hit its sales. Roger Ramsbottom proposed an alternative strategy. The company would make a £5m share issue, the proceeds of which would be used to acquire pubs being divested by national chains. The additional tied estate would help to raise utilisation of brewery capacity, and make Ramsbottom one of the largest regional brewers in the United Kingdom. The chairman concluded,

> Ramsbottom is known above all for just one thing: good beer! Our beer wins prizes. It has kept our customers coming back for 130 years. This has been achieved by the highest standards of quality management in production and delivery. If we surrender this to outsiders we lose control of our own destiny. If we are too small then let us expand, but in a way that plays to our traditional strength.

Issues

The central proposal of the CEO is of course the idea that the company should divest itself of production and distribution facilities and contract out the supply of its own beer brands. The CEO is able to point to operating cost savings:

- Brewing is characterised by substantial economies of scale and economies of utilisation.
- If the outcome of contracting out is one brewery, one bottling plant and one distribution system working at or near full capacity instead of two running at a fraction of full capacity, the operational cost savings should be substantial and can be shared between the parties as agreed in an appropriate contract.

And gains from re-deploying assets:

- The net proceeds from the asset sales will finance the development of the company's pub chain, particularly in areas where it is currently under-represented (e.g. Manchester and Leeds city centres).

The brewery closure and outsourcing route, however, does raise several potential risks:

- Can the supply agreement with Bogson be trusted to guarantee the quality of product and the reliability of delivery?
- If the agreement proved unsatisfactory, what would be the fallback position once the brewery had closed?
- Before the end of 1 year the agreement needs renegotiating. If Bogson seek a substantial rise in beer prices, are there alternative sources of supply?
- Will the negative publicity surrounding brewery job losses and product outsourcing damage sales?

Overview of transaction cost economics

The first to draw attention to the role of transaction costs in shaping economic organisation was a British-born economist Ronald Coase as early as 1937. Coase wanted to explain the existence of firms as ongoing social institutions. Why, he asked, did producers not merely hire inputs, particularly labour, on a casual basis as required? (After all we do still observe some purely temporary arrangements, such as casual workers taken on for specific events such as (cricket) test matches or Wimbledon, and casual employment was very much greater in Coase's day.) His answer was that repeating the hiring process day by day involves incurring repeated hiring costs. These could be eliminated if both parties had the expectation of a continuing contractual relationship. Amongst other things, Coase's insight helped to explain why labour contracts tend to be general, rather than specific, giving the employer some discretion in setting tasks in exchange for giving the employee some continuity of work. Thus university lecturers' contracts typically require the performance of ' . . . such duties as the head of department might require', thus allowing adaptation as circumstances develop in an uncertain world.

Fashion applies in the world of ideas as much as anywhere else, and economists were soon more concerned with the potential of Keynesian theories to provide a basis for macroeconomic management and the avoidance of business slumps. As a result, Coase's insight was largely ignored until the 1970s when concerns to analyse the behaviour of large firms re-entered the agenda. The stimulus was a realisation that most large quoted companies had developed highly dispersed shareholdings, leaving effective control in the hands of salaried managers with little direct financial interest in their firms. This had led to a reassessment of corporate objectives. A series of models of the firm resulted in which economists explored the consequences of managers departing from profit maximisation in favour of the pursuit of preferred goals such as sales revenue or employment. Among the foremost of these managerial theories was that of Oliver Williamson who explored how the firms would look if managers were able to exercise discretionary spending in privately preferred directions. As he immersed himself in the details of corporate development, especially as described in the work of a Harvard business historian Chandler (1962), he became convinced that large firms were evolving to counter the very type of managerialist problems that he had analysed.

Chandler had described how the functional form of organisation, what Williamson (1975) later termed the Unitary or U-form (see Figure 7.1), became overstretched as very large corporations emerged in the twentieth century. He went on to describe the emergence of the Multi-divisional or M-form structure (Figure 7.2) – pioneered in du Pont and General Motors in which day-to-day responsibilities were devolved to profit-accountable divisions. This permitted the separation of divisional operating responsibilities from the headquarters' decisions about overall strategic direction. While Chandler saw the M-form's strength as lying in its capacity to ease management overload,

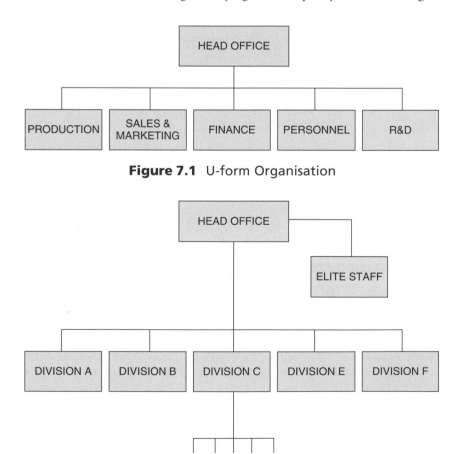

Figure 7.1 U-form Organisation

Figure 7.2 M-form Organisation

Williamson developed a detailed rationale for the superiority of its informational, incentive and transactional properties.

Williamson saw internal transfers of resources, including labour and especially financial capital, as being a means of circumventing some of the difficulties and associated costs of using external markets. Thus he described how the M-form operated as an internal capital market in which profits were remitted from the divisions to the centre and then re-invested as divisions competed for projects. Unlike the external market whose sanctions for poor performance are fairly blunt, the internal process holds managers to continuous account for the progress of their projects with a whole range of punishments and rewards, from dismissal to main board promotion as appropriate. Moreover, he argued that internal scrutiny would be more effective than external appraisal since more information could be released than it would be prudent to divulge to outsiders.

Williamson then developed Coase's argument for the existence of firms into an argument for their expansion. He suggested that vertical integration – that is the expansion of the firm into the ownership and control of successive stages in its production and distribution process – was a means of economising on the transaction costs of using intermediate market transfers. Taking the well-known example of an integrated iron and steel plant, where hot metal passes through a series of adjacent processes, Williamson rejected the traditional thermal economy explanation for integrated ownership. He argued that thermal economy merely required the stages to be physically conjoined; it did not require common ownership. If it is feasible to write and enforce contracts between successive stages, at acceptably low costs, a market solution is appropriate. If the owners of these stages behave uncooperatively towards one another, however, raising costs at the expense of their collective well-being, the market solution becomes unattractive relative to the option of vertical integration. Thus, where Coase had used transaction costs to account for the existence of firms, Williamson posed external and internal transfers, *markets* and *hierarchies* in his terminology, as alternative modes of organisation. The choice between these two being determined by their respective transaction or organisation costs.

In a separate but parallel development, Buckley and Casson (1976), researching the rise of the multinational enterprise, also looked to the costs of using markets to explain internal growth. They suggested that firms successful in their country of origin generally developed assets (technological, human, organisational or other) that could be exploited in new markets. Sometimes these assets were fully protected by intellectual property rights (e.g. patents, trademarks or copyrights) but many assets were imperfectly protected (e.g. general product designs), or so intangible as to defeat market solutions such as licensing. Here they suggested that international expansion by the firm itself was frequently the only viable route for growth. That is, the MNE was seen as a way of internalising the process of exploiting the assets the firm had developed.

After Williamson, TCE developed rapidly. It will be recalled that he had identified small numbers bargaining, uncertainty and asymmetric information as conditions likely to generate high transaction costs. It is here that opportunistic attempts to grab a larger share of the value from exchange are likely to lead to costly haggling, disputes and disruption of trading. Klein et al. (1978) then demonstrated that the problem of small numbers bargaining was typically a derivative condition resulting from asset specificity. Consider an asset which is dedicated to a highly specific use: say a proposed desert pipeline linking an oilfield to a refinery. Almost certainly this will be the cheapest mode of transporting crude oil and hence, once constructed, represents a cost–saving measure and a source of value. The value of such a pipeline in oil transport, however, is overwhelmingly greater than in its next best use (whatever this might be: a child's linear playground?). This difference is called the asset's quasi-rent. It may be thought of as a reward for specificity. Its existence, however, also means that the pipeline's owner faces a considerable range of transport charges across which the oil transport remains the best use for the pipeline. Any pipeline user knows this with the result that they have a strong incentive to bargain for an increased share of the value created. The user possesses the real threat of hold-up; that is any interruption of use leaves the owner with no obvious alternative use and source of revenue.

The obvious solution to the hold-up problem, and its associated transaction costs, is vertical integration. If successive stages are brought under common ownership the incentive to haggle over quasi-rents disappears. Thus an integrated oil company owning oilfield, pipeline and refinery would remedy the problem.

It became apparent that the frequency with which transactions were repeated influenced costs. Many regularly repeated purchases were observed to involve the same buyer and seller who often developed a relationship based on trust. These long-term associations, which might or might not rest on formal written contracts according to local custom and practice, clearly represented an alternative to either one-off market deals or vertical integration. It was clear, however, that the impact of frequency on the mode of organisation is not straightforward and it depends on what other conditions apply. Williamson (1979) developed a transaction governance typology, see Figure 7.3, distinguishing unified governance (i.e. vertical integration) from bilateral governance (i.e. two-way bargaining) and trilateral governance where third part assistance was required.

It was also clear that transactions differ in the residual uncertainty attaching to them. For example, compare the contracting out of an R&D project, where the existence of a feasible solution is not known with certainty, with a car assembler contracting out the supply of tyres. In the former case the problem is to devise a contract that motivates the research laboratory to solve the issue while encouraging it to keep down costs. Payment according to costs incurred risks the kind of cost overruns that are such a frequent feature of defence projects. Conversely, payment on delivery puts all the risk on the contractor who might only take it on in exchange for a very high price.

The TCE, like any evolutionary theory, runs the risk of tautological reasoning. If it is assumed that competition for resources eliminates the inefficient operators then, other things being equal, the survivors must be efficient. This leads to the danger that observed characteristics of survivors are assumed to be desirable and necessary attributes. Since all other things are very rarely equal, this logic can lead to false confidence in TCE and, if acted upon by market participants, to strategic mistakes. Even if all the surviving firms in an industry displayed similar organisational forms, this alone is neither proof of its optimality nor any indication of what disadvantage, if any, would fall to those adopting a different form. It is possible, for example, that the survivors are merely equally inefficient, having copied one another's strategies.

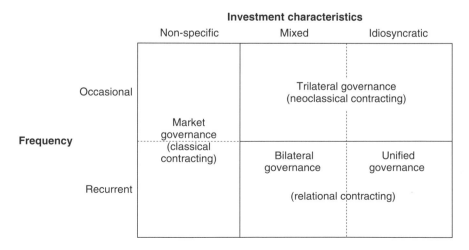

Figure 7.3 Williamson's Model

What was needed to raise TCE above this circularity were empirical tests of its validity across different industries. The problem, however, is that with few exceptions such as in the case of financial markets, transaction costs are rarely directly observed. Moreover, it is likely that managers will have different subjective cost estimates of many of the activities involved in setting up trades, including search, negotiating, monitoring, and so on, while other costly contractual features will be incurred as a safeguard against some non-observed contingency. The result is that tests of TCE have usually taken an indirect form. Researchers try to identify features that are likely to produce high or low transaction costs in the context of make versus buy decisions. This leads to a prediction of where each mode of supply will be preferred. The researcher then collects data on make or buy outcomes in that industry and tests their hypotheses against these data. This involves investigating a relationship of the general type as follows:

$$\text{Organisational form} = f(X, \Upsilon)$$

where Organisational form is a variable that could, say, take a value of 1 where make is observed and 0 for buy outcomes. X is a set of variables associated with cost-influencing attributes, including asset specificity; and Υ is a set of control variables that might impact on the transaction choice but which are not themselves believed to affect transaction costs. The researcher then looks to see if there is a significant relationship between the organisational form outcome and the X variables.

Tests across a series of industries broadly supported the hypothesised role for the assumed cost determinants on the make–buy choice. Monteverde and Teece (1982), for example, found that US carmakers typically contracted out the production of components requiring non-specific assets and manufactured in-house those requiring specific assets. Similarly, Masten (1984) used industry experts to assess asset specificity and component complexity across a set of aircraft parts and then found these features significant determinants of the make option. In an interesting variant Joskow (1987) compared the coal mine–power plant relationship on the east and west coasts of the United States. The eastern mines are smaller, produce homogeneous coal and have access to alternative transport systems, reflecting the area's older history. In the west the typical mine is larger, produces a chemically distinctive coal and usually has access to road transport only. The result is that power plant owners in the east can buy coal from multiple sources and hence use spot markets without difficulty. In the West the generator's choice is much more restricted, raising the possibility of hold-up. As a result, long-term supply contracts dominate.

There have been quite a large number of tests of TCE along the above lines, almost all broadly supportive. However, it is important to remember two limitations. First, these are strictly indirect tests, in that they merely explore a relationship between contractual outcomes and the assumed determinants of transaction costs and not the costs themselves. Second, contractual choices in conformity with the assumption are treated as optimal; although there has been no attempt to quantify the performance outcome of departing from that outcome. Some empirical work (see Shelanski and Klein, 1995) has attempted to address this second objection by using a more sophisticated design that first predicts optimal form choice and then explores the impact of departures from this, on observed firm performance. Early indications from these are generally supportive.[1]

Linking transaction cost economics to strategic management

It should be clear from the foregoing that the TCE perspective is very much concerned with those issues that the strategist confronts when considering the appropriate boundaries of his/her firm. This is most obviously so for the vertical boundary questions, where the make versus buy issue is paramount. Moreover, choices are rarely that simple and a range of buy and make arrangements are frequently available with separate transactional issues attaching to each choice. Thus long-term contracting is distinctively different to spot market sourcing, while full vertical integration might be compared to joint venturing. Horizontal boundary decisions too involve transaction costs. For example, consider a firm that has accumulated valuable but underutilised assets and cannot expand its core activity because of market limitations. Such a firm faces a choice between diversification into a new activity, hopefully thereby enjoying economies of scope as it uses its spare capacities, or selling the services of such assets to other firms.

If the choice between alternatives were as clear-cut as textbook examples in TCE often presents it, there would be a role for strategists but it would be strictly limited. Thus, if conditions such as asset specificity, complexity and uncertainty are objectively measurable and have impact on, say, the make–buy choice in a predictable way, the manager's role becomes a straightforward optimisation decision. Moreover, since there would be a clear right and wrong solution, those mistakenly adopting the latter would soon realise their error and conform. Thus a decision over organisational form would be unlikely to deliver any sustainable competitive advantage.

In fact, real-world decisions are much more difficult than their textbook equivalents as transaction cost outcomes are rarely known with certainty and have to be projected on the basis of the same imperfect information set that gives rise to these costs in the first place.

First, technological and organisational innovations impact directly upon transaction costs across and within organisations. For example, in retailing the checkout scanner/computerised stock monitoring innovations permit a degree of centralised control that would have been unattainable 15 years ago. This has facilitated the development of very large chains such as Wal-mart and Tesco.

Second, it is clear that the costs of using alternative modes of organisation vary across countries and cultures. For example, the choice between international expansion via the establishment of a wholly owned local subsidiary or via an equity joint venture with a local partner is likely to be strongly influenced by the cultural and informational problems of trading in the country concerned. Thus US multinationals setting up in the United Kingdom usually choose between establishing a UK subsidiary from scratch and taking over an existing firm as a vehicle for their operations. The same firms expanding into China might opt for the joint venture route.

Third, the costs of using different modes of organisation also vary across firms, even firms within the same country. Since factors such as trust and reputation can lower transaction costs, firms can develop successful sourcing and/or distribution arrangements that lower their costs relative to rivals. The UK high-street retailer Marks and Spencer built its national position on a close working relationship with a large network of independent producers manufacturing to its specifications with the output sold under its St Michael brand. Ikea, the Swedish household goods manufacturer, built its global empire on designing stylish yet economical products, whose manufacture was then outsourced to producers in the global region of sale (Haskel and Wolf, 2001).

Where a firm is able to develop an organisational advantage, whether favouring market arrangements or internal production, this is likely to be much harder for rivals to replicate; not least because the development of attributes such as trust and reputation, which arise through successful trading, are difficult to acquire since their absence itself retards the growth of such trading. This somewhat reinforces the tendency of firms to develop along separate path-dependent trajectories. When fundamentals do change, requiring a major reorganisation of activities, managers may show a greater or lesser ability to instigate the move to a new trajectory.

Since firms can develop their own expertise at making some set of organisational arrangements work for them, it follows that we frequently observe coexisting solutions to the make–buy decision. Thus in contrast to the starker predictions of TCE, where competitive pressure was expected to produce a dominant organisational form determined by the underlying transactional properties such as asset specificity, alternative arrangements may be used by rivals without either suffering obvious disadvantage. Thus Ford and General Motors jointly dominated the US car industry for much of the twentieth century. However, while the former traditionally followed Henry Ford's preference for full vertical integration, from raw material to vehicle delivery, the latter adopted a much more extensive system of subcontractors.

Case study revisited

From the perspective of TCE the outsourcing decision hinges on the viability of the supply contract with Bogson. The specification of quality and product delivery standards is likely to be difficult, which in turn makes it hard to use sanctions short of non-renewal of the contract. The premature termination of the contract would leave the company without its own product and able, at best, to sell such beers as could be bought at short notice. A limited duration contract may be necessary at the start of the deal with Bogson, but its renewal will pose difficulties if the suppliers seek a major price increase. Before signing the initial agreement, Ramsbottom will need to determine what alternative suppliers are likely to be available at the renewal stage. If the alternatives are very restricted, the company's bargaining power will be weak. If there were to be no viable alternatives at all and the company were to be effectively locked into a deal with Bogson, it would need to be sure that the latter are not merely using a low-ball pricing strategy to bring Ramsbottom in, such that the deal exaggerates the future cost savings from outsourcing.

There are two sides to the outsourcing transaction and Ramsbottom should consider the incentives affecting the other party. How vulnerable will Bogson be to the non-renewal of the contract? If Bogson need to invest in assets (delivery vehicles, distribution facilities, etc.) to fulfil the terms of the deal how specific to the transaction are these? If they are specific in the sense that their disposal or redeployment would hit the company's earnings then there is a quasi-rent that Bogson will be anxious to preserve. If both sides stand to lose from a failure in the contract each has an incentive to make it work, that is they have mutual hostages. It may be that the current level of underutilisation of capacity at Bogson is sufficient to create such an incentive, although this might signal unsatisfactory features to that firm's current operations.

If the proposed deal really works and lowers costs by eliminating redundant capacity and freeing up resources, as the proponents suggest, does it go far enough? If two breweries can be replaced by one, and two distribution systems replaced by one, could not two pub management companies be replaced by one?

Summary

The TCE offers a perspective to analyse organisational arrangements within and between businesses. It is not comparable to those constructs in strategic management which offer a simple checklist of points for decision-making (e.g. SWOT analysis) or even a carefully structured tool for environmental analysis (e.g. Porter's Five Forces framework). In this regard, it is much closer to the resource-based view with which it shares some antecedents, especially in the work of Teece, in providing a more general framework for firm-level analysis. It does possess one advantage over the resource-based view, however, in that much more effort has gone into testing the predictions of TCE.

The weight of evidence in support of TCE, whilst not overwhelming, does point to broad principles which surviving firms tend to follow when structuring their activities. It shows that certain characteristics (e.g. asset specificity, complexity, informational asymmetry) which appear to be associated with high costs in transaction do seem to discourage market solutions to organisational issues and encourage internalisation. However, the extensive quantitative and case-study work which has accompanied the testing of TCE has drawn attention to the diversity of real-world solutions. This work also suggests that transactions costs are not simply exogenously determined by fundamental conditions of technology and information distribution, but are subject to changes directly and indirectly instituted by managers.

In the first place the technology of transacting itself changes over time. Thus new ways of searching out trading partners, formalising deals, monitoring, delivering, and so on all impact on the costs of doing business and so on the optimal way of organising activities. Some of these developments – for example the contraction of search costs generated by the Internet – may be exogenous to individual managers, but the latter still differ with regard to the speed and extent to which they adapt. Other changes may involve idiosyncratic innovations – perhaps very low tech ones – introduced by managers themselves.

Finally, as TCE research has shown that the 'one size fits all' approach is rarely the full answer to organisational design, it has drawn attention to the importance of the firm's individual experience in shaping its opportunity set. As in the resource-based view of the firm, it is recognised here that qualities such as reputation, trust, capability in operating particular systems, and so on develop out of each firm's particular experience. These qualities both distinguish the firm from its rivals and impact directly on its ability to make alternative arrangements work.

In short, an important aspect of the strategist's job concerns shaping the appropriate boundaries of the firm. TCE offers an efficient contracting perspective to this task. It will rarely provide all the answers; however, like any good theory, it may prompt the strategist to ask the right questions.

Note

1. These tests are more problematic than the single equation version reported above in that the researcher needs to identify variables determining some key contractual choice that do not themselves affect performance.

References

Buckley, P. and M. Casson, *The Future of the Multinational Enterprise* (London: Homes and Meier, 1976).

Chandler, A. D., *Strategy and Structure: Chapters in the History of the Industrial Enterprise* (Cambridge: MIT Press, 1962).

Haskel, J. and H. Wolf, 'The Law of One Price: A Case Study', *Scandinavian Journal of Economics*, 103 (2001) 545–558.

Joskow, P., 'Contract Duration and Relationship Specific Investments: Evidence from Coal Markets', *American Economic Review* 77 (1987) 168–185.

Klein, B., A. Alchian and R. Crawford, 'Vertical Integration, Appropriable Rents and the Competitive Contracting Process', *Journal of Law and Economics*, 21, 2 (1978) 297–326.

Masten, S., 'The Organization of Production: Evidence from the Aerospace Industry', *Journal of Law and Economics*, 27 (1984) 403–417.

Monteverde, K. and D. Teece, 'Supplier Switching Costs and Vertical Integration in the US Automobile Industry', *Bell Journal of Economics and Management*, 13 (1982) 206–213.

Shelanski, H. and P. Klein, 'Empirical Research in Transaction Cost Economics: A Review and Assessment', *Journal of Law, Economics and Organization*, 11 (1995) 335–361.

Williamson, O. E., *Markets and Hierarchies: Analysis and Antitrust Implications* (New York: The Free Press, 1975).

Williamson, O. E., 'Transaction Cost Economics: The Governance of Contractual Relations', *Journal of Law and Economics* 22 (1979) 233–261.

CHAPTER 8

Agency Theory Perspective

Duncan Angwin

Basic principles

Agency theory has a wide application across academic disciplines. As Eisenhardt (1989) notes, it has been used by scholars in accounting (e.g. Demski and Feltham, 1978), economics (e.g. Spence and Zeckhauser, 1971), finance (Fama, 1980), marketing (e.g. Basu et al., 1985), political science (e.g. Mitnick, 1986), organisational behaviour (e.g. Eisenhardt, 1985, 1988; Kosnik, 1987) and sociology (e.g. Eccles, 1985; White, 1985). For some it offers a foundation for a powerful theory of organisations (Jensen, 1983) and provides significant insights into strategy.

Agency theory focuses on relationships between parties where one delegates some decision-making authority to the other. In these situations, one party (the 'principal') delegates responsibility to another party (the 'agent') to take decisions on their behalf. In the modern corporation, for instance, the 'principal' would be a shareholder, whilst the 'agent' would be the manager. The principal would delegate some decision-making authority to the agent who, in turn, would be responsible for maximising the principal's investment in exchange for an incentive, such as a fee.

Other agency relationships exist between employers and employees, between professionals such as lawyers and doctors and their clients and between public servants and citizens. In a business setting the nature of the delegation is often a formal contract, but in other circumstances delegation does not need to be explicit.

Agency relationships are designed to increase value to the parties involved. However, there are costs involved including engaging in the relationship, monitoring its progress and enforcing it. These costs are influenced by the different attitudes of principals and agents to risk and their different access to information ('information asymmetries'). The agent, for instance, has private information to which the principal does not have access and cannot observe accurately. This can allow the agent to increase their bargaining power in the relationship.

Where the desires of the principal and the agent conflict and the agents are not provided with proper incentives or are constrained in some manner, perhaps through the terms of contract, agents may act more in their own interests than those of the principal. This is known as an 'agency problem'. In the relationship between shareholders and management the agency problem is often portrayed as shareholder principals having goals of value maximisation whilst management agents' goals are those of self-aggrandisement; the consumption of value to build their own empires.

The ways in which agency problems may be resolved are through the 'market for corporate control'. This external mechanism, the takeover process, acts as a discipline on target firm management, allowing control to be transferred from inefficient to efficient management and encouraging convergence of their interests with their shareholders. Hostile takeover bids in particular are claimed to identify governance structures that have failed to protect shareholder interests. In essence, competing groups of managers are fighting for the right to manage the target firm's scarce and valuable resources. These bids are unwelcome and resisted strongly by target management who are very likely to lose their jobs as a consequence.

So far agency has been discussed in what we may describe as classical terms, 'how capital markets can affect the firm'. However, agency relationships can be seen to operate hierarchically through the levels of a firm and laterally with other firms and partners. For instance, within the multi-business firm, particularly conglomerates, head offices can exert discipline over subsidiary managers by threatening to dismiss them and/or selling off their business. This can be viewed as the firm internalising the market's disciplining role, with the head office acting as principal and business unit managers acting as agents who may be fired if performance is perceived to be inadequate.

The firm itself may act as principal in agency relationships along the value chain, amongst competitors and across industries. For instance, a firm may delegate some decision-making authority to a key supplier or customer. In the formation of a joint venture company with a competitor, the firm as co-owner will be a principal to the manager – agent of the jointly owned firm. Across industries, the firm may be embedded in a network where it has principal–agent relationship(s) with other firms.

Classically, the agency relationship is also generally discussed in dyadic form, either as a contractual or as a political relationship between two interests. However, in some business situations this is an overly simplistic view. For instance, in the syndication of venture capital to entrepreneurs, the venture capitalists themselves can occupy the position of principal to the entrepreneurial agent, principal to other venture capitalists who may syndicate loans to entrepreneurs, as well as agent to institutional investors and other venture capitalists. Such triadic arrangements are more frequent than is commonly supposed.

We began by saying that agency theory may offer powerful insights into strategy and other areas of organisation. However, it is not without its limits. Critics of agency theory, as embedded in an economic perspective, argue that its core assumption of maximising value with human nature as singularly self-interested is only a partial view of the world. It ignores a great deal of the complexity of organisations and is dehumanising and potentially dangerous (Perrow, 1986).

By way of example case study 8.1 describes a hostile bid for the large British cement company, Blue Circle PLC. From the outset an agency problem is raised. The case reveals a number of key issues on which agency theory is based, as it tracks the evolution of the bid and also exposes some of its limitations.

CASE STUDY 8.1

On 31 January 2000 an all-cash hostile bid was launched by the French cement giant Lafarge for Blue Circle PLC, an FTSE 100 company and the sixth largest cement producer in the world. The bid valued Blue Circle at £3.4bn and would make Lafarge the largest cement company in the world (Table 8.1).

Table 8.1 Cement kiln capacity (million tonnes) by largest companies and by region

	Western Europe	Eastern Europe	Africa	Asia	Oceania	North America	C & S America	Total
Holderbank	16.4	6.6	5.7	17.4	1.2	15.3	21.3	83.9
Lafarge	24.7	12.0	12.0	6.0		13.2	8.2	76.1
Cemex	10.4		4.0	10.2		1.1	41.1	66.8
Italcementi	30.2	2.6	3.6	3.9		5.4	0.7	46.3
Heidelberger	33.8	12.5	1.2	3.0		10.5		61.0
Blue Circle	16.7		4.1	12.3		6.7	0.9	40.6
CRH	5.8							5.8
RMC	8.9	6.5			3.1	1.0		19.5
Dyckerhoff	10.7	2.6				4.7		18.1
Cimpor	7.1		2.4				2.8	12.3

Source: European Cement Review, January 2000, HSBC

In 1999 Blue Circle, capitalised at EUR 4.7bn, was parent to an international group of companies involved in cement, aggregates and readymix concrete. Cement was the core business and contributed to the majority of group sales and operating profit. During the 1980s and early 1990s Blue Circle expanded into unrelated business areas. It then struggled to manage these acquisitions which it subsequently sold off in the following decade, incurring substantial losses. Blue Circle then stopped acquiring, reduced its debt levels to zero and slowly raised its dividend levels, although not up to the average for the sector. From 1997 to 1999, Blue Circle doubled its cement capacity with acquisitions in Asia and Greece and disposed of its heating and bathrooms divisions. This later expansion in cement came after its main competitors had been acquiring internationally for some time. In 1999 Blue Circle's financial health was strong with lower levels of gearing than that of its competitors. Its share price had declined consistently throughout the 1990s relative to the FTSE index and the sector.

Haythornthwaite: Blue Circle's new CEO

Haythornthwaite, CEO of Blue Circle at the time of the hostile takeover, joined Blue Circle in October 1997 and had initial responsibility for Heavy Building Materials in Asia where he was the architect of Blue Circle's strategy for investing and acquiring in Malaysia. He became Chief Manager designate in December 1998 and finally CEO in July 1999 on a salary of £390,000.[1]

Just a few months after his appointment, Haythornthwaite had to release a profits warning which severely undermined his credibility. Six weeks later the first rumours of Blue Circle as a potential bid target occurred. Lafarge, the second largest cement producer in the world, was reported to have engaged an investment bank to prepare a bid. Collomb, the Chairman and Chief Manager of Lafarge, telephoned Haythornthwaite during January 2000 to discuss a possible takeover at £4.30 per share – an offer dismissed by Haythornthwaite.

The hostile bid

On 1 February 2000 Lafarge announced a pre-conditional offer for Blue Circle of 420P per share. The offer represented a premium of only 1.4 per cent over Blue Circle's closing middle market price of 414P on 31 January. Analysts agreed that there was a good strategic fit, but felt the price needed to be closer to 500P for success.

Lafarge attacked Blue Circle for mistakes made in the past, including the diversification strategy of the 1980s and early 1990s. By diversifying Blue Circle had fallen behind its international competitors and it was now heavily dependent on 'too few countries'. Lafarge asserted that 'this "over-dependence" on a small number of operating territories means that Blue Circle's profitability is inherently volatile'.

Defence plan

The first critical issue was what value to put on Blue Circle? Analysts' valuations were around 500P. Lazards, Blue Circle's financial advisers, presented their valuation to the board in January 2000, based on the 2000–2002 business plan and profit forecasts. However, Blue Circle tended to achieve actual results lower than the plan forecast, and so Lazards were instructed to reduce the profit forecasts and recalculate the value. On this basis, their discounted cash flow analysis valued the business at a conservative 486P. This supported management claims that the Lafarge bid undervalued the group.

Blue Circle's response

Blue Circle's first formal response to Lafarge's offer document was to assert that the offer undervalued the company and to claim that the bid was a 'quest for our Asian assets which justifies our investment strategy'.

The final dividend for the year was raised to be in line with the industry. Assets were re-valued and a profit forecast issued for the Asian businesses to convince shareholders that those investments would pay off in the short term.

On 6 April, Blue Circle announced its operational improvements programme (OIP). The document announced details of the projected benefits arising from such cost savings and included forecasts of £116m of benefits per annum to be achieved by 2002.

The final salvo in Blue Circle's defence was an announcement on 11 April that it would return £800 million to shareholders. This return of capital was in effect a downpayment to shareholders demonstrating the confidence of management in delivering the promises they had made. Blue Circle's gearing increased significantly (17.2 per cent [1999] to 107.7 per cent [2000]), and free cash flow available for future projects was reduced dramatically.

At the same time Haythornthwaite reviewed a number of other options. 'Many were dismissed because they did not give cash to shareholders, and because of the reluctance of other parties to get involved.' The pressure from shareholders for cash was palpable. 'The only consideration of shareholders was cash. They were not interested in any wider responsibilities to the company and there was a total lack of engagement' (Executive Committee Member).

Options considered but rejected were a management buyout, a large acquisition, a white squire defence (where another firm would invest in new Blue Circle equity) and a white knight (where a friendly company would take them over). For various reasons no other companies wished to be involved in this way.

On 19 April, day 46 of the bid, Lafarge launched a dawn raid and picked up 19.9 per cent of Blue Circle directly and a further 9.6 per cent through its bankers. Lafarge then increased its offer to £4.50 per share and was confident of victory.

During the last 10 days of the offer period Haythornthwaite and his Finance Director held a number of meetings with institutional investors to persuade them to back management and reject the bid. As day 60 approached, the lobbying of shareholders paid off when Schroeder's Bank publicly backed the incumbent management and other shareholders followed. On 3 May the bid lapsed as Lafarge's acceptances and holdings totalled 44.5 per cent of Blue Circle shares. This was the first all-cash bid for an FTSE 100 company to fail in 15 years.

Haythornthwaite was widely fêted by commentators for his successful defence of Blue Circle. 'The smile on Rick Haythornthwaite's face says it all. . . . His success in beating off a cash bid in a market where cash was clearly king has propelled a little known executive into prominence. With the target having seemed doomed at the outset, the escape was seen to be a considerable personal victory for Rick Haythornthwaite' (*Financial Times*, 6 May 2000).

Blue Circle was left with a major competitor effectively owning 32.2 per cent of the firm. To remain independent a major acquisition was needed but potential partners were disinterested with such a large minority shareholder. The group also had to deliver on defence promises which analysts suspected might have been too ambitious. Haythornthwaite also realised that forecast operating profits were significantly below analysts' estimates and earnings quality appeared to be deteriorating.

Haythornthwaite presented three strategy options to the board, dealing with Blue Circle's relative short-term strength but medium-term weakness: (1) achievement of an early deal with Lafarge; (2) an acquisition to move out of Lafarge's reach; (3) a merger with another party. Considerable time and resources had been devoted to evaluating acquisitions of or mergers with various parties but the board decided that negotiations should begin with Lafarge. Lafarge offered 470P with no dividend but Haythornthwaite needed to present the deal as being worth over 500P per share in order to recommend it to shareholders. The advisers to both sides worked in the period up to and over Christmas, finally agreeing to a deal at 495P per share plus a final dividend. A board meeting on 7 January 2001, a Sunday, recommended the offer to shareholders.

The vast majority of Blue Circle's shareholders were institutions and readily agreed to the bid which was regarded by analysts as being '*a sensibly priced deal*'. However, many individual shareholders, who were mainly ex-employees with an emotional attachment, voted against the takeover, as they saw Blue Circle as a 'British Institution'. Nevertheless, the deal was completed and Lafarge's shares responded favourably. As for Haythornthwaite, he left Blue Circle on 11 July 2001, and on 24 July 2001 it was announced he would become CEO of Invensys PLC.

Overview of agency theory

Origins of agency theory

Given a choice between two alternatives, man as a rational actor will choose the option that increases his or her individual benefit. This assumption about man as a rational actor, who seeks to maximise his or her individual benefit (Jensen and Meckling, 1976), can be traced back through 200 years of economic research. It is a key assumption in agency theory which arose to address the problems of risk sharing and conflict that can occur between cooperating parties with different goals. In particular, agency theory aimed to explain and warn of the potential conflicts that occurred with the separation of ownership and control of business during the rise of the modern public corporation.

Rational owners of businesses would prefer to manage their own companies and reap the maximum benefit for themselves. However, as companies grew beyond the means of a single owner, unable to meet the increasing economic obligations of the firm, ownership became dispersed amongst thousands of unorganised stockholders who were removed from day-to-day management of the firm. The control of the firm shifted from entrepreneurs to professional managers. These are the changes which created the modern public corporation which is based on the efficient separation of ownership and managerial control. However, it was this separation of control and ownership, widely dispersed, which Berle and Means (1932), some 70 years ago, warned us 'released management from the overriding requirement that it serve the stockholder'.

The separation of ownership and control of wealth creates an agency relationship where one or more persons (the principal(s)) engage another person (the agent) to perform some service on their behalf. An agency relationship is therefore said to exist when one party delegates decision-making responsibility to a second party for compensation. This relationship is the focus of agency theory and is described using the metaphor of a contract.

The fundamental feature of the contract between principal and agent is the delegation of some decision-making authority to the agent (Jensen and Meckling, 1976). The agent is morally responsible to maximise shareholder utility. They accept the responsibility of managing a principal's investment because they perceive the opportunity to maximise their benefit in comparison with other opportunities. Where the interests of the principal and the agent converge, there is no problem as both enjoy increases in their individual benefits. Figure 8.1 shows a classical principal–agent chain between owners and managers in the firm.

Agency problem

There are several aspects to the agency problem: (1) the interests of the principals and agents diverge or conflict, which occurs when agents have the opportunity to rationally maximise their own benefits at the expense of principals; (2) it is difficult or expensive for principals to know in advance which agents will self-aggrandise or to verify what agents are actually doing. The problem here is how to check that the agents are acting in an appropriate manner; (3) the principal and the agent may have different attitudes to risk sharing, leading to preferences for different actions.

The objective of agency theory then is to reduce agency costs incurred by principals by keeping the agent's self-serving behaviour in check. As the unit of analysis in agency theory

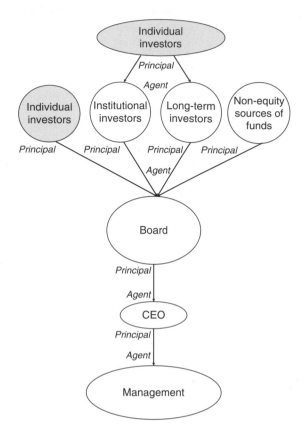

Figure 8.1 Principal–agent chain (Angwin, 2006)

Table 8.2 Agency theory overview

Key idea	Principal–agent relationship should reflect efficient organisation of information and risk-bearing costs
Unit of analysis	Contract between principal and agent
Human assumptions	Self-interest, bounded rationality, risk aversion
Organisational assumptions	Partial goal conflict among participants Efficiency as the effectiveness criterion Informational asymmetry between principal and agent
Information assumption	Information as a purchasable commodity
Contracting problems	Agency (moral hazard and adverse selection) Risk sharing
Problem domain	Relationships in which the principal and agent have partly differing goals and risk preferences (e.g. compensation, regulation, leadership, impression management, whistle-blowing, vertical integration, transfer pricing)

Source: Eisenhardt (1989)

is the contract, which governs the relationship between the principal and the agent, the focus is on determining its most efficient for given assumptions, outlined earlier, that people are self-interested, boundedly rational and risk adverse. There will also be assumptions made about the nature of organisation, information, contracting problems and the problem domain. These are summarised in Table 8.2.

Evidence of the agency problem

Conflicts between principal and agent in a firm can affect the investment, operating or financial policies of the firm. Agency problems can be of the following types: First, effort, where there is less incentive for managers to exert full effort in increasing shareholder value as their ownership of the firm falls (Jensen and Meckling, 1976).[2] This shirking, of not putting in agreed-upon effort, is also known as a problem of *moral hazard*.

Second, time horizon, where managers prefer investment or operating strategies that have lower costs and produce results more quickly than potentially more profitable long-term projects that have higher initial costs, as they are limited in their future employment whereas firm value is determined by a potentially infinite series of future cash flows.

Third, risk, where managers are generally dependent on the firm for which they work for a large part of their wealth and stand to lose much if their firm becomes financially distressed but benefit relatively little if the firm is successful. As a result they tend to prefer less risk than shareholders, who through portfolios eliminate firm-specific risk, and tend to view diversification as reducing their exposure to industry- or market-specific risk, even though diversification is associated with a decrease in firm value (Amihud and Lev, 1981). These different risk profiles are illustrated in Figure 8.2.

The shareholders' curve in Figure 8.2 shows the owners seeking a level of diversification that reduces the risk of the firm's total failure while simultaneously increasing the company's value through

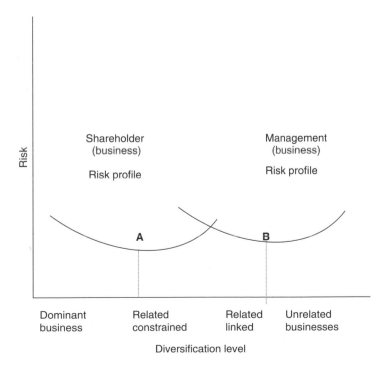

Figure 8.2 Diversification level. Adapted from Hitt et al. (2005)

the development of economies of scale and scope. The optimal position for shareholders is point A, between dominant and related constrained business.[3] Management will prefer a greater degree of diversification as shown by point B in Figure 8.2, to maximise firm size and their compensation and reduce their employment risk. They are unlikely to diversify to the point that their employment risk is increased and reduces their subsequent employment opportunities. Managers may also prefer lower levels of debt and lower dividend payouts than shareholders as less debt lowers the risk of financial distress and lower dividends result in greater cash reserves available for investment.

Fourth, asset use, where they can be expropriated by managers. Some consumption is likely to be beneficial to the firm as it may assist in attracting and retaining good managers, but excessive consumption can destroy shareholder value. Recent cases include former Tyco CEO, Kozlowski, accused of fraud by the Securities and Exchange Commission for failing to disclose multi-million dollar low-interest loans (US SEC, 2002), and even Jack Welch, one of the most fêted of US CEOs, who has been accused of excessive expenses, with a Manhattan apartment, limousine services, security guards, corporate jet and best seats at sporting and artistic events to name but a few (Rayner, 2002).

Managers may have incentives to increase the size of the firm beyond the optimal level, thereby increasing their compensation and prestige. The potential for over-investment by managers is particularly serious when managers have access to free cash flow, that is cash flow in excess of that needed to fund all available projects of the firm with positive net present values (Jensen, 1986). This excess cash should be paid out to investors, but is likely to be reinvested at rates well below the corporate cost of capital, particularly in diversifying acquisitions, which present the greatest opportunity for bidding managers to express non-value-maximising preferences (Shleifer and Vishny, 1988).[4]

The pursuit of managerial self-interest with cunning or guile may be termed managerial opportunism (Hoskisson et al., 2002). It is both an attitude and a set of behaviours. It is difficult for a principal to know beforehand whether an agent will act opportunistically and the prior reputation of top managers is an imperfect predictor. Indeed, there may be an *Adverse Selection* problem as agents may misrepresent their ability where principals are unable to completely verify these skills or abilities at the time of hire. Principals therefore establish governance and control mechanisms to prevent opportunistic behaviour from their agents, but the potential for conflict remains.

Mechanisms for controlling agency costs

Agency costs are the sum of incentive costs, monitoring costs, enforcement costs and individual financial losses incurred by the principals in using governance mechanisms. These mechanisms cannot ensure total compliance by the agent and are likely to increase if a firm is diversified as it is more difficult to monitor what is going on in the firm. The mechanisms which may control agency costs are both internal and external to the firm.

Internal to the firm, financial incentive schemes can bring agent–principal alignment, such as increasing manager share ownership (cf. Denis et al., 1997), and through compensation arrangements based on accounts, markets,[5] and contingencies (such as long-term incentive plans, 'LTIPs' (Shleifer and Vishny, 1997)). If managers receive compensation subject to the successful completion of shareholder objectives, such as long-term rewards tied to firm performance or an earn-out for instance, they will be motivated to behave in a manner consistent with stockholder interests. Such schemes are particularly desirable when the manager has a significant informational advantage and monitoring is impossible. However, these mechanisms can be counterproductive (Byrd et al., 1998; Tosi and Gomez-Mejia, 1994) as in earn-outs for instance, a manager could distort short-run performance in order to obtain personal rewards, but harm the medium-term future of the business in the process.

Other internal mechanisms include improving internal controls (Jensen and Meckling, 1976) and monitoring, through (1) the performance and pay review process (Fama, 1980) and (2) corporate governance (The Cadbury Report, 1992). Boards of directors keep potentially self-serving managers in check by communicating shareholder's objectives and interests to managers and performing audits and performance evaluations.

Agency theorists do not specify total control of the agent as this would mean the agent would have no discretion and the firm would be owner-managed. The crux of agency theory is that the principals delegate authority to agents to act on their behalf (Davis et al., 1997). Thus agency theorists specify an intermediate condition of control which is first delegation and then controls to minimise the potential abuse of the delegation (Jensen and Meckling, 1976). This has led to considerable debate over whether an outcome-oriented contract, based on stock options, commissions, transfer of property rights and so on, is more efficient than a behaviour-oriented contract focusing upon hierarchical governance, salaries and so on.

There are also external mechanisms for controlling agency costs. These include: (1) the managerial labour market as a process of ex post settling up (Fama, 1980); (2) the existence of large minority shareholders and activist investors as they have the incentive to collect information and monitor management and (3) externally the hostile takeover (Walsh and Seward, 1990).

A hostile takeover is an unwelcome bid, which target firm management resists strongly. Hostile takeovers occur to correct certain classes of managerial failure, which are otherwise difficult to rectify. Whilst ex post absolute failure, such as incompetence or dishonesty, can be dealt with through management contracts, ex post failure through inferior relative performance or changing market conditions and ex ante failure through differences in expectations, for example, concerning investment or managerial capabilities, require new management (Franks and Mayer, 1990). This external mechanism for the replacement of underperforming management has become known as the market for corporate control.

Linking agency theory to strategic management

Agency theory addresses vertical links of ownership and control at multiple levels across the borders of firms and within the firm's boundaries. Classically, strategists have focused upon the narrow hierarchical relationship between investors (principals) and top-level executives (agents) on the basis that this relationship is related directly to firm strategy and outcome. However, more recent research has focused upon the implications of a more extended set of agency relationships, both vertically and horizontally. The extent and relevance of agency theory is discussed in the following sections: 'Corporate governance', 'Corporate strategy', 'Competitive strategy', 'Internal control'.

Corporate governance

The central concern of corporate governance is the relationship among stakeholders that is used to determine and control the strategic direction and performance of the firm. Four main mechanisms exist which influence the extent to which an agency relationship may be controlled and monitored. These are (1) the monitoring capacity of investors; (2) the influence of the board of directors; (3) setting executive compensation; (4) the market for corporate control.

The monitoring capacity of investors

The power of the owners in the agency relationship with management is a function of the concentration of ownership.[6] Where there is diffuse ownership of shares, it is difficult for the owners to coordinate their actions, and monitoring of management decisions is weak. However, there has been a continuous growth in the size of institutional shareholders who are able to exert greater influence over management on account of their size. They also have an incentive to monitor management closely and are becoming much more active in their efforts to influence the firm's choice of strategies and overall strategic decisions. Initially these institutional investors and shareholder activists concentrated on the performance and accountability of CEOs and have been instrumental in bringing about their removal (see Angwin, 2006, for discussion and examples). Now they have widened their scope to include the boards of firms. To date research suggests that the effects of stakeholder activism on firm performance are unclear, but there are effects on important strategic decisions such as diversification and innovation (Hitt et al., 1997).

The influence of the Board of Directors

From an agency perspective, the board of directors is a monitoring and controlling device of the shareholders. Shareholders elect members to the board to oversee managers and ensure the firm operates in ways which will maximise shareholder wealth. The primary responsibility of the board is to act in the principals' best interests by formally monitoring and controlling the firm's top managers, exerting leverage over any self-interested tendencies of the agents. Boards have the power to direct the affairs of the organisation, punish and reward managers and protect shareholder rights and interests. An appropriately structured, vigilant and powerful board should protect the owners from managerial opportunism.

Recent corporate scandals have raised questions over the effectiveness of some agency relationships. Criticism has been levelled at some boards as being a managerial tool, uncritical of top manager actions and all too ready to approve managerial self-serving interests. This has focused attention on the composition of boards, with critics believing that boards with a preponderance of Insider executives are more likely to be guilty of ineffective control and monitoring of top managers. The agency relationship may be improved by using more independent Outsider executives in boards to enable more effective monitoring and, potentially, to enable higher quality strategic decisions (Kassinis and Vafeas, 2002). However, whilst Outsiders may be more objective than Insiders, they are less likely to have the level of information available to Insiders, which reduces their awareness of strategic intentions, motivations and anticipated outcomes.

Attention has also focused on the power of the CEO, where high levels of power concentrated in this individual can significantly reduce the effectiveness of outside board members. For this reason the Cadbury report mentioned earlier advocated that the roles of chairman and CEO should not be held by one individual.

Setting executive compensation

Top management strategic decisions may be influenced by executive compensation, which, from an agency point of view, are a set of techniques designed to align managerial interests with those of owners. Compensation can take several forms such as salary, bonuses, stock options and other incentive plans and can range from short- to long-term rewards. Short-term incentives, such as annual bonuses, may cause top managers to manage their firms to achieve short-run improvements in profitability. However, this may also mean that top managers pursue short-term objectives at the expense of long-term interests. Indeed, research by Hoskisson et al. (1993) tends to support this interpretation by showing that bonuses based on annual performance are negatively related to investments in R&D. For this reason it is generally believed that longer-term incentives are more effective in aligning managerial interests with those of shareholders as managers are less likely to under-invest in the short term. These help avoid potential agency problems and, as a consequence, are now a critical part of compensation packages. Some of the consequences of longer-term incentives are that managers are more exposed to uncontrollable risks such as market fluctuation and their wealth more inflexibly tied to the firm. This reduces the value of such long-term incentives to managers and explains the huge rise in compensations to CEOs of this nature. Research shows, however, that despite the huge compensation packages of stocks and options, CEOs are more rewarded for the size of their firm than for firm performance (Tosi et al., 2000), and with increasing ownership of shares, are more difficult to remove. This underlines the difficulty of using compensation as an effective agency mechanism.

Compensation packages are imperfect in their ability to monitor and control the strategies of managers. They focus on financial performance as a measurable outcome, as strategic decision-making itself is complex and non-routine and impossible to supervise directly. Performance outcomes are also the result of an extended period of decision-making and so it is difficult to assess current strategic decisions.

The market for corporate control

Where a firm is underperforming there may be an agency problem. Top management may be guilty of shirking, consuming perquisites, diversification and excessive growth. With a failure in the firm's internal controls, the external governance mechanism of the market for corporate control may become active. Other firms and investors may seek to buy ownership positions in underperforming firms in order to correct the managerial failure of the incumbents. Hostile bids are motivated by the belief that value can be created by restructuring the target, changing its financial policies and reversing earlier diversification strategies (Bhide, 1989). This threat, of hostile a takeover, may in itself be sufficient to act as a discipline on underperforming firms, encouraging convergence of interests between management and shareholders. Examples in the United Kingdom include Lord Hanson's bid for ICI PLC in 1993, which was defeated by political intervention and yet resulted in the subsequent demerger into ICI and Zeneca. Other examples include Hoylake's failed hostile bid in 1989 for BAT Industries PLC which was based on the logic of 'unbundling': that BAT was worth more broken up than kept together. BAT subsequently divested a large number of businesses.

The formulation and execution of the strategy of the underperforming firm is generally held to be the responsibility of top management. As a consequence, where hostile takeovers are successful, top management are frequently removed, with studies estimating rates of 73 per cent (Jenkinson and Mayer, 1994)[7] and 88 per cent (Franks and Mayer, 1990). The market for corporate control can therefore be perceived as rival teams of managers competing for the opportunity to manage unique sets of assets efficiently for their owners.

The market for corporate control has been responsible for significant changes in many firms' strategies. The fear of a bid has been an effective constraint on top manager growth aspirations, and hostile bids have resulted in major changes in firm configurations. The high premium associated with most successful hostile takeovers also results in very significant post-deal restructuring; major drives for rapid cost reduction and divestment are necessary to recover the premium paid.

A hostile takeover then is likely to be the market for corporate control exercising its power to remove underperforming management and replace them with management who will seek to remove excess costs associated with the earlier management, probably through divestments and restructuring.

Corporate strategy

Top managers expect their corporate-level strategy to help their firm gain/maintain a competitive advantage and earn above-average returns for their shareholders and themselves. The businesses in their portfolio should be worth more through their management than if they stood on their own. The central concerns for corporate strategy are: (1) which businesses should their firm be in (and should be exiting) and (2) how to manage the business portfolio which may be in very different industries, products and geographic areas. This raises questions about the extent to which a firm should diversify and here the benefits to managers and owners can vary and can potentially lead to an agency problem.

Diversification generally leads to an increase in the overall size of the firm, which is positively associated with size of executive compensation. This is clearly in the interests of top managers, not only in terms of financial reward but also in terms of status and reputation. The increased complexity of the business may also be a rationale for greater pay. Diversification also serves to reduce risk to managers of loss of employment, earnings and risk, as the firm is less exposed to downturns in a particular industry, product or geography.

The attractions of diversification to managers is such that they may use free cash flow to invest in this way, when shareholders would prefer these funds to be distributed as a special dividend (see Figure 8.1). For shareholders, diversification is easier and less costly than it is for their managers as they can purchase shares in other companies through the financial markets with low transaction costs. For managers to diversify, organic development is slow, expensive and risky, and acquisitions have a much higher transaction cost than do share dealings. Over-diversification by managers then may be perceived, through agency theory, as self-serving and opportunistic action and evidence of a potential agency problem.

Competitive strategy

Firms may improve their competitive position through the use of mergers and acquisitions (M&As) and strategic alliances. Agency theory can give insights into the rationales for entering into these types of deal as well as the way in which the subsequent organisation can work.

M&As are a form of strategic renewal and the quickest and surest way to grow the firm. However, top manager compensation is linked more closely with firm size than with firm performance and indeed there is evidence to show that the incomes of managers rise even with substantial subsequent declines in performance of acquiring companies (Firth, 1991; Fowler and Schmidt, 1989). M&A may therefore 'be undertaken by managers even if they do not promise profit and shareholder wealth increases' (Mueller, 1995, p. 15). The traditional agency issue then is whether the acquiring manager is acting in the shareholders' best interests in entering into an M&A deal and negotiating the level of premium necessary to win. For some, excessive premiums paid are taken to be evidence of an agency problem (Sirower, 1997). The conventional explanation for this overpayment is the concept of hubris, that is the top manager is suffering from overweening pride and self-confidence (Roll, 1986).

Strategic alliances raise interesting agency issues as there may be multiple partners, pooling of ownership assets and a degree of joint management between two or more firms. These may be termed 'multiple agencies' as each principal has different rationales for entering the alliance and each is sufficiently important to require its interests to be respected. Because the owner-partners usually contribute complementary resources, they also in effect become agents for each other in ensuring the viability of the alliance. The managers of the alliance are agents of the principal, but the agency role is complicated by the presence of multiple owners with different expectations. The agency relationship is further complicated if alliance managers are drawn from different principals and if they come from different cultures and traditions. The problem for principals in these multiple agencies is the loss of control arising through managerial role conflict and the likelihood of role ambiguity (Child, 2005). The effect upon strategic outcomes is a risk of opportunism and a breakdown in collaboration, which may help to explain the high rates of failure recorded for strategic alliances.

Recently there has been a trend for large integrated firms to decompose into networked value chains. The result has been a similar disruption in the agency chain. The power of the firm to control behaviour in a network can be severely circumscribed and it also raises the question of who takes responsibility for the behaviour of firms in the network. Dell computers for instance uses the assets of its network partners to produce under its corporate brand name, but is not accountable in law for the conduct of its network producers towards their shareholders (Child, 2005). However, there are examples of MNCs, such as Nike, Marks and Spencers, permitting subcontractors in developing countries to apply practices different to their own and where financial markets and consumer groups deemed them to be principals and the subcontractors their agents. Bad practice in these agents' operations led to both principals sustaining significant damage to their reputations and share prices.

Internal control

Agency relationships are not just limited to the interaction between owners of capital and top managers. The agency relationship extends in a hierarchy down through the firm, so that corporate managers are in a principal–agent relationship with their workforce. Conventional views of agency assume that corporate managers can control the behaviour of their agents within the firm and that strategic control is sufficient to avoid misinformation and will ensure operational effectiveness. Strategic control, or focus on the means and methods on which the firm depends, is seen as underwriting operational control, which is determining and monitoring how the workforce behaves and performs in production or service provision. Generally, a strong hierarchy with clearly defined reporting relationships is the traditional way in which top managers achieve operational control. However, the assumption that the agency relationship is unproblematic is dangerous.

Corporate dysfunction is endemic as subordinates strive for autonomy and control is lost. Agency theory helps to show that subordinates will act in ways to improve their benefits, by reinterpreting orders flowing downwards and presenting information flowing upwards in a positive light. This potential agency problem can be termed a 'double agency problem' and it is present in all forms of organisation that are of a scale to create personal and often physical distance between top managers and agents. The implications for strategy may be perceived in the way firms struggled to manage the complexities of their vast organisations after the wave of diversifying acquisitions which took place during the 1970s–1980s.

In new organisational forms where hierarchy is de-emphasised and greater flexibility achieved through the decentralisation of initiatives, managers have only limited awareness of the transformation processes involved in the organisation. The effect of having initiatives widely dispersed is a dilution of the agency relationship to a scattering of semi-autonomous agents. The consequence can be that the board is helpless in having much impact on the activities of the company even though they may still have considerable influence on the CEO. Indeed, this situation has been used as an explanation for the disastrous series of events at Enron – many of its new businesses had moved beyond top manager control and were the result of entrepreneurial initiatives of middle managers.

Case study revisited

Agency theory provides a rich insight into the Blue Circle case. We shall examine several aspects in turn: (1) the reasons behind the bid; (2) Blue Circle's top management actions in defending the firm; (3) Haythornthwaite as a potential agency problem.

The reasons behind the bid

The launching of a hostile bid by Lafarge for Blue Circle immediately alerts us to a competing managerial group potentially identifying an agency problem, where target incumbent management have not acted in their principal's best interests. Apart from the fact that the bid is hostile rather than friendly, what is the evidence to support the interpretation of an agency problem?

Blue Circle had clearly made many unrelated acquisitions in the past through an active diversification programme. These are generally perceived to be more in the interests of incumbent management than in the interests of their shareholders. The subsequent disposal of these acquisitions realised substantial losses and is further evidence of value-destroying behaviour by incumbent management. Blue Circle's policy in the 1990s was of not acquiring at all and just accumulating cash in order to reduce gearing and not returning much to shareholders by way of dividend. During the 1990s, Blue Circle's competitors were expanding into newly deregulated countries, but Blue Circle was inactive. Their share price fell relative to the FT All share index up until 1999 when they began to make related acquisitions in Asia. Blue Circle's consistent share price underperformance and profits warning may be construed as evidence of a significant period of failure by Blue Circle's management team and an agency problem.

Blue Circle's top management actions in defending the firm

The valuations prepared by a company's financial adviser are normally the most reliable indicator of how much a business is worth as an independent group. If there was an agency problem, we might expect Haythornthwaite to inflate the value of Blue Circle to prevent a takeover.[8] Evidence that he was not upwardly influencing the valuation is seen in the instruction to financial advisers, Lazards, to reduce their profit forecasts. This resulted in a more conservative valuation for Blue Circle and is not the behaviour characteristic of a CEO holding out at all costs.

Many other defences are available to target top management, which have the effect of repelling potential acquirers. However, in extremis, some defences may also damage the target firm and its shareholders – a case of being 'defended to death'. For example, raising dividends to very high levels may discourage an acquirer but will also saddle the target firm with an enormous drain on its financial resources for the future. Prominent amongst extreme defences are shark repellents, designed to make the target so unpleasant that it wards off predators, and poison pills, intended to damage the company in the event of the takeover succeeding. These could include loan covenants, onerous commercial agreements, 'golden parachutes' (where unacceptably high compensation is payable to incumbent directors if control changes hands). All of these defences are of questionable nature as their main objective seems to be the protection of incumbent management whatever the level of the bid. If the bid succeeds in spite of these defences, shareholders of the target and the predator suffer alike. These would be actions of an incumbent top management where there is an agency problem.

Blue Circle's defences included profit reporting, increasing dividend, revaluation of assets, profits forecasting and return of capital. Blue Circle's shareholders might have been damaged if the dividend increase had been excessive, but it was only brought back into line with the sector (see Angwin et al., 2006, for an analysis). They considered other defences such as an MBO, acquisitions, white squire and white knight. They also carried out a vigorous public relations campaign through defence documents and lobbying and considered all legal opportunities.

All of these defences are textbook actions and did not prejudice Blue Circle shareholders in the process. Indeed, some of their actions greatly reduced potential agency costs. For instance, the return of capital greatly increased gearing (from 17.2 to 107.7 per cent) and consequently reduced the potential for misuse of free cash flow.

None of the defences identified earlier as damaging to shareholders, such as poison pills and shark repellents, were adopted by Blue Circle. Indeed, the sale of the heating and bathrooms businesses just prior to the bid might be seen as removing a 'poison pill'.

The absence of takeover defences such as golden parachutes and the restraint in using financial deterrents so that shareholders and the business would not be damaged suggest that the top management were not acting as dysfunctional agents.

Haythornthwaite as a potential agency problem

Considerable empirical evidence shows that CEOs of target companies in hostile takeovers are very likely to lose office and not find a position on the board of the acquirer (Franks and Mayer, 1990; Jenkinson and Mayer, 1994). They are also likely to benefit less, in terms of personal wealth, from a hostile bid than an uncontested offer.[9] Managers with smaller personal wealth changes tend to oppose offers, while those with larger personal gains do not (Walkling and Long, 1984).

Loss of office and lower wealth gain are both reasons for incumbent management to resist a hostile takeover. In addition, there may be resistance as a negotiating tool to solicit additional bids (Lefanowicz and Robinson, 2000) and to drive up prices (Angwin, 2000). A top manager may also be influenced by his age, as a young manager may have less difficulty in finding a new position (Buchholtz and Ribbens, 1994) and older ones have fewer options (Angwin, 1996). These will all be considerations for incumbent management acting more through self-interest.

As the vast majority of Blue Circle's shareholders were institutions, Hawthornthwaite's job was to please 'the City'. In resisting the original hostile bid as too low in value for his shareholders, there was an alignment of agent–principal motives. Post bid, Haythornthwaite's ability to obtain a higher price than from the original bid, and one at the higher end of independent valuations, also pleased shareholders. These actions are consistent with Haythornthwaite being a good agent. However, he must have known that in the subsequent sale he would lose his job, and one where the appointments committee had already greatly increased his base salary and doubled his share options to tie him to the business. This does not fit with a core assumption of agency theory, of self-interested maximisation. It was clear that Blue Circle was paralysed by having the hostile bidder holding so many shares. The sale resolved this position for the good of the business, but at the expense of Blue Circle's top managers. Such self-sacrifice is evidence that a strict agency perspective on the case may be too limiting in its interpretation of human motivation.

Limitations of agency theory

The case study has shown that agency theory gives insight into the relationship between target firm top management, its shareholders and the market for corporate control. For a more extensive treatment which also shows principal/agency issues with suppliers, customers, employees and regulators, see Angwin et al. (2004). However, the case also exposes limitations.

Many economists and sociologists have questioned the monolithic microeconomic behavioural assumptions of short-term advantage and self-interest maximisation. Indeed, attempting to defend these assumptions for descriptive or predictive use has been described by Sen (1991, p. 16) as 'leading a cavalry charge on a lame donkey'.

The limitation of the agency theory of agents as self-interested maximisers is only a partial description of human motivation and does not entirely explain the complexity of human behaviour (Doucouliagos, 1994). People act irrationally as noted amusingly by Etzioni (1988, p. ix): 'People brush their teeth but do not fasten their seat belts' and can be more concerned with the group than with themselves. They can also be motivated by outcomes other than purely personal benefit. In response to the need to consider a more complex conception of man, researchers are experimenting with relaxing core assumptions such as man being entirely a self-interested maximiser.

Stewardship theory considers managers where pro-organisational, collectivistic behaviours have greater value than individualistic self-serving ones (Davis et al., 1997).Where a manager is given the choice between self-serving behaviour and pro-organisational behaviour, a steward's behaviour will not depart from the interests of their organisation. They believe a steward who successfully improves the performance of the organisation generally satisfies most groups (Davis et al., 1997). Stewards therefore believe their interests are aligned with that of the corporation and its owners. Their interests and utility motivations are directed to organisational rather than personal objectives.

The implications for the CEO as steward are structures that facilitate and empower rather than those that monitor and control. Under these arrangements, CEOs as stewards are best facilitated when the corporate governance structures give them high authority and direction, such as when the CEO chairs the board of directors – a situation which would be different under agency theory where these roles should be separate. The reason why there is not always a stewardship relationship is due to the risks principals are willing to take. Where owners are risk averse, they are likely to perceive managers as self-serving and will therefore prefer agency governance prescriptions.

The differences between agency and stewardship theory are helpful for crystallising when agency relationships may be more appropriate. Stewardship assumes that individuals are motivated by intrinsic factors such as opportunities for growth, achievement, affiliation and self-actualisation, factors that correspond to the higher order needs of Maslow's hierarchy. Agency theory assumes that agents are motivated by extrinsic factors such as remuneration and perquisites. Stewards tend to identify with their organisations more than do agents, working towards the organisation's goals and using their initiative to promote the success of the organisation and its principals. Agents are more likely to blame external factors for any organisational problems, avoiding taking responsibility and making decisions that may rectify the problems. There is also a difference in the use of power, with agents relying on institutional power derived from their position in the organisation and stewards relying on personal power derived from interpersonal relationships.

Situational factors that distinguish the two theories include management philosophy and culture. Control-oriented environments respond to increases in risk by implementing more controls and are more likely to produce agency environments. Involvement-oriented environments respond to risk by increased training and empowerment and are more likely to produce stewardship environments. Individualistic cultures emphasise personal goals over group goals whereas collectivist cultures subordinate personal goals to the goals of the collective.

Fundamentally, agency and stewardship theory offer different and opposing perspectives about manager/owner relationships. The implications of these different perspectives are evident in the case study and also highlight a processual dynamic of how shifting interests over time allow for today's agent becoming tomorrow's 'steward' (Albanese et al., 1997). A more detailed review of the tensions between these two theories is contained in Angwin et al. (2004).

The lack of a process dimension to agency theory means that it does not look at the history of engagement. Each exchange is viewed as a new event, un-encumbered by feelings of gratitude, indifference, disloyalty or revenge. Any notion of intended reciprocity for past benefits or damage is excluded. Indeed, moral hazards, or the lack of enthusiastic adherence to contractual agreements, are deemed to be a problem only for the agent, not for the principal, so acts by the principal which might induce negative feelings in the agent are ignored (Hosmer, 1994). Recognising that there may be multiple engagements over time, and that over this period benefits/harms may accrue to the agent, makes explicit the effect on the agent's sense of current benefit and anticipated benefit. This recognition may be a useful addition for assessing on-going levels of trust, commitment and effort from the agent (Hosmer, 1994). In terms of the case study, it is interesting to wonder how prior confrontation between Haythornthwaite and Collomb shaped the subsequent discussion about sale.

Finally, agency theory is rooted in a Western economic conception of man which may not be sustainable in other cultures and national business systems. This should make us wary of assessing international business and cross-border agreements using this approach uncritically. However, this limitation also presents researchers with significant opportunities for elaborating and refining agency theory for different contexts and across different borders.

Summary

Agency theory provides a useful insight into the problems of cooperative effort. It has very wide applications in strategy: (1) vertically across the boundaries of the firm, between owners and managers and a whole host of intermediate positions; (2) between firms along supply chains; (3) between firms in the creation of strategic alliances and other inter-organisational forms; (4) in a wide variety of contexts. These settings also show how the conceptualisation of the principal/agent relationship needs to evolve from a simple dyad into more complex forms to reflect more intricate forms of organising. The advantages of agency theory are that it is testable and has empirical support. However, in its classic form, it presents a partial view of the world that, whilst valid, does ignore a lot of complexity in organisations and managers. Researchers are developing theories to overcome some of these limitations, such as stewardship theory, which relaxes assumptions about self-interestedness. Others are drawing upon complementary perspectives, such as institutional theory and equity theory, in order to gain a greater appreciation of complexity in agency situations.

Notes

1. The discount of 20 per cent to the median level reflected his lack of experience in such a role.
2. The possibility of jeopardising future job, salary or promotion opportunities places an upper limit on the level of effort problem.
3. The optimum position will depend upon firm-specific factors, the nature and competitiveness of the industry and top management experience.
4. The willingness of managers to pay for benefits to themselves that are of no value to shareholders explains why acquisitions often result in negative returns for acquiring firms (Shleifer and Vishny, 1988).
5. There is a positive relationship between firm performance and manager compensation (Lambert et al., 1993).
6. Primarily this has been focused upon equity ownership, but where businesses are in trouble, ownership of debt can assume primacy.
7. These figures may understate actual level of replacement in hostile bids as their interpretation of hostile could include initial posturing/bargaining behaviour by the target.
8. There are some checks and balances against this in law. The financial advisers have to produce an opinion that the valuation they produce is a fair view. For this opinion they are accountable and this responsibility is not taken lightly. However, financial advisers are dependent on information supplied to them by the client and they do have a vested interest in a successful defence.
9. Wealth change for directors in uncontested bids was an average of 8.6 years annual salary, whereas that for directors in contested bids was only 2.3 times annual salary (Walkling and Long, 1984).

References

Albanese, R., M. T. Dacin and I. C. Harris, 'Agents as Stewards', *The Academy of Management Review*, 22, 3 (1997) 609–611.

Amihud, Y. and B. Lev, 'Risk Reduction as a Managerial Motive for Conglomerate Mergers', *Bell Journal of Economics*, 12 (1981) 605–616.

Angwin, D. N., 'After the fall', *Management Today*, April (1996) 56–58.

Angwin, D. N., *Implementing Successful Post-acquisition Management* (New York: Financial Times/Prentice Hall, 2000).

Angwin, D. N., 'Movers and Shakers', in D. N. Angwin, S. Cummings and C. Smith, *The Strategy Pathfinder* (Oxford: Blackwell, 2006), Chapter 2.

Angwin, D. N., P. Stern and S. Bradley, 'Agent or Steward: The Target CEO in a Hostile Takeover: Can a Condemned Agent be Redeemed?', *Long Range Planning*, 37 (2004) 239–257.

Angwin, D. N., P. Stern and S. Bradley, 'Strategic Practice During a Hostile Takeover Process: The Bid for Blue Circle PLC', *Journal of Strategic Management Education*, 3 (2006).

Basu, A. K., R. Lal, V. Srinivasan and R Staelin, 'Salesforce Compensation Plans: An Agency Theoretic Perspective', *Marketing Science*, 4 (1985) 267–291.

Berle, A. and G. Means, *The Modern Corporation and Private Property* (New York: Macmillan, 1932).

Bhide, A., 'The Causes and Consequences of Hostile Takeovers', *Journal of Applied Corporate Finance*, 2 (1989) 36–59.

Buchholtz, A. K. and B. A. Ribbens, 'Role of Chief Manager Officers in Takeover Resistance: Effects of CEO Incentives and Individual Characteristics', *Academy of Management Journal*, 37, 3 (1994) 554–579.

Byrd, J., R. Parrino and G. Pritsch, 'Stockholder–Manager Conflicts and Firm Value', *Financial Analysts Journal*, 54 (1998) 14–30.

Cadbury, 'The Committee on the Financial Aspects of Corporate Governance', *The Financial Aspects of Corporate Governance* (The Cadbury Report, 1992).

Child, J., *Organization. Contemporary Principles and Practice* (Oxford: Blackwell Publishing, 2005).

Davis, J. H., F. D. Schoorman and L. Donaldson, 'Towards a Stewardship Theory of Management', *The Academy of Management Review*, 22 (1997) 20–47.

Demski, J. and G. Feltham, 'Economic Incentives in Budgetary Control Systems', *Accounting Review*, 53 (1978) 336–359.

Denis, D., D. Denis and A. Sarin, 'Agency Problems, Equity Ownership and Corporate Diversification', *Journal of Finance*, 52 (1997) 135–160.

Doucouliagos, C., 'A Note on the Volution of Homo Economicus', *Journal of Economics Issues*, 3 (1994) 877–883.

Eccles, R., *The Transfer Pricing Problem* (Mass: Lexington Books, 1985).

Eisenhardt, K., 'Organizational and Economic Approaches', *Management Science*, 31 (1985) 134–149.

Eisenhardt, K., 'Agency and Institutional Theory Explanations: The Case of the Retail Sales Compensation', *Academy of Management Journal*, 31 (1988) 488–511.

Eisenhardt, K., 'Agency Theory: An Assessment and Review', *Academy of Management Review*, 14 (1989) 57–74.

Etzioni, A., *The Moral Dimension: Toward a New Economics* (New York: Free Press, 1988).

Fama, E., 'Agency Problems and the Theory of the Firm', *Journal of Political Economy*, 88 (1980) 288–307.

Firth, M., 'Corporate Takeovers, Stockholder Rewards and Executive Rewards', *Managerial Decision Economics*, 12 (1991) 421–428.

Fowler, K. L. and D. R. Schmidt, 'Determinants of Tender Offer Post Acquisition Financial Performance', *Strategic Management Journal*, 10 (1989) 339–350.

Franks, J. and C. Mayer, 'Takeovers: Capital Markets and Corporate Control: A Study of France, Germany and The UK', *Economic Policy: A European Forum*, 10 (1990) 189–231.

Hitt, M. A., R. E. Hoskisson and H. Kim, 'International Diversification: Efects on Innovation and Firm Performance in Product-Diversified Firms', *Acadmey of Management Journal*, 40 (1997) 767–798.

Hitt, M. A., R. D. Ireland and R. E. Hoskisson, 'Strategic Management: Competitiveness and Globalization', Thompson Southwestern, 2005.

Hoskisson, R. E., M. A. Hitt and C. W. L. Hill, 'Managerial Incentives and Investment in R&D in Large Multiproduct Firms', *Organization Science*, 4 (1993) 325–341.

Hoskisson, R. E., M. A. Hitt, R. A. Johnson and W. Grossman, 'Conflicting Voices: The Effects of Ownership Heterogeneity and Internal Governance on Corporate Strategy', *Academy of Management Journal*, 45 (2002) 697–716.

Hosmer, L. T., 'Strategic Planning as if Ethics Mattered', *Strategic Management Journal*, 15, Special Issue (1994) 17–34.

Jenkinson, T. and C. Mayer, *Hostile Takeovers, Defence, Attack and Corporate Governance* (London: McGraw-Hill, 1994).

Jensen, M., 'Organization Theory and Methodology', *Accounting Review*, 56 (1983) 319–338.

Jensen, M., 'Agency Costs of Free Cash Flow, Corporate Finance and Takeovers', *American Economic Review*, 76 (1986) 323–329.

Jensen, M. and W. Meckling, 'Theory of the Firm: Managerial Behaviour, Agency Costs, and Ownership Structure', *Journal of Financial Economics*, 3 (1976) 305–360.

Kassinis, G. and N. Vafeas, 'Corporate Boards and Outside Stakeholders as Determinants of Environmental Litigation', *Strategic Management Journal*, 23 (2002) 399–415.

Kosnik, R., 'Greenmail: A Study in Board Performance in Corporate Governance', *Administrative Science Quarterly*, 32 (1987) 163–185.

Lambert, R., D. Larcker and K. Wigelt, 'The Structure of Organizational Incentives', *Administrative Science Quarterly*, 38 (1993) 438–461.

Lefanowicz, C. E. and J. R. Robinson, 'Multiple Bids, Management Opposition and the Market for Corporate Control', *The Financial Review*, 35 (2000) 109–122.

Mitnick, B., *The Theory of Agency and Organizational Analysis*, Unpublished working paper (University of Pittsburg, 1986).

Mueller, D., 'Mergers: Theory and Evidence', in G. Mussatti (ed.), *Mergers, Markets and Public Policy* (Dordrecht: Kluwer, 1995).

Perrow, C., *Complex Organizations* (New York: Random House, 1986).

Rayner, A., 'Divorce Reveals Secrets of E&Y', *The Times*, 16 October 2002.

Roll, R., 'The Hubris Hypothesis of Corporate Takeovers', *Journal of Business*, 59 (1986) 197–216.

Sen, A., *On Ethics and Economics* (Oxford: Basil Blackwell, 1991).

Shleifer, A. and R. Vishny, 'Value Maximisation and the Acquisition Process', *Journal of Economic Perspectives*, 2 (1988) 7–20.

Shleifer, A. and R. Vishny, 'A Survey of Corporate Governance', *The Journal of Finance*, LII, 2 (1997) 737–783.

Sirower, M. L., *The Synergy Trap. How Companies Lose the Acquisition Game* (New York: Free Press, 1997).

Spence, M. and R. Zeckhauser, 'Insurance, Information and Individual Action', *American Economic Review*, 61 (1971) 380–387.

Tosi, Jr, H. L. and L. R. Gomez-Mejia, 'CEO Compensation Monitoring and Firm Performance', *Academy of Management Journal*, 37 (1994) 1002–1016.

Tosi, Jr, H. L., S. Werner, J. Katz and L. R. Gomez-Mejia, 'How Much Does Performance Matter? A Meta-analysis of CEO Pay Studies', *Journal of Management*, 26 (2000) 301–339.

US Securities and Exchange Commission, 'SEC Sues Former Tyco CEO Kozlowski', http://www.sec.gov/news/press/2002-135.htm (16 October 2002).

Walkling, R. A. and M. S. Long, 'Agency Theory, Managerial Welfare, and Takeover Bid Resistance', *Rand Journal of Economics*, 15 (1984) 54–68.

Walsh, J. and J. Seward, 'On the Efficiency of Internal and External Corporate Control Mechanisms', *Academy of Management Review*, 15 (1990) 421–458.

White, H., 'Agency as Control', in J. Pratt and R. Zeckhauser (eds) *Principals and Agents: The Structure of Business* (Boston: Harvard Business School Press, 1985).

CHAPTER 9

The Resource-based View of the Firm

Véronique Ambrosini

Basic principles

The resource-based view of the firm examines the link between the internal characteristics of a firm and firm performance (Barney, 1991). Broadly speaking, this means that the resource-based view is concerned with the relationships between a firm's resources and competitive advantage. It suggests that an organisation can be regarded as a bundle of resources and that resources that are simultaneously *valuable, rare, imperfectly imitable* and *imperfectly substitutable* (Barney, 1991) are a firm's main source of sustainable competitive advantage.

The following are the underlying assumptions on which the resource-based view of the firm is based:

- Resources are heterogeneous across organisations. This means that firms differ with respect to their resources and there is asymmetry in firms' resource endowment.
- This heterogeneity can remain over time, which means that resource transferability is limited. The resource-based view of the firm assumes that resources are not perfectly mobile across firms.

Before we embark on a more detailed elaboration of the approach, the following excerpts provide a practical context within which we can explore this perspective.

CASE STUDY 9.1

THE COMPANY

Delta is part of a Plc. It is a leading supplier of IT software to the finance sector. It was founded in 1986 and is based in London. Delta contributes approximately 33 per cent of the Group's turnover and it employs around 150 staff members. Delta focuses on supplying a unique accounting and settlement system ('The Software') to the wealth management and investment broking community. Its clients include a number of the largest retail stockbrokers and leading client investment managers as well as some small Internet brokers.

The Software is functionally rich and offers a highly automated 'straight-through' processing solution. Built on a modern, client/server architecture, The Software is flexible and scaleable. Internet and WAP enabled, the system allows authorised retail clients to directly enter deals and make enquiries on their accounts.

What underpins Delta's competitive success?

An analysis of Delta revealed a range of factors which contribute to its performance. In summary:

- To operate, Delta relies heavily on IT systems. These systems have not been developed by Delta; most of them were bought. This was easy to do as there is a range of systems available off the shelves, such as back-up systems.

- Delta cares about its offices. These are important in terms of their sizes and their locations. Many of Delta's traditional customers, i.e. the retail stockbrokers, are in the City of London and being located in London was practical for both Delta and its customers.

- One of Delta's major clients is BUS. BUS is a high-profile company, which is the largest provider of online share dealing services in the United Kingdom, and is a subsidiary of the leading 'execution only' stockbroker in the United States. This is a well-known factor, and many of Delta's current clients have used BUS as a referent because of its high profile.

- Sixty per cent of Delta's revenues are generated from providing services (i.e. software development, training, support) to current clients. There are two main sources of revenues. Some revenues come from servicing The Software recently bought by new clients who are just starting to implement the system and from clients who have had to make mandatory legal changes. This suggests that revenues are generated from not getting the product right in the first place.

- When clinching deals with traditional customers (i.e. not Internet based) it is worth noting that The Software, as such, is not central to the discussion. Interviews with Delta's managers revealed that 'the functionality of the software was not considered by X when making their decision to use it'; 'The CEO's decision was based on his feeling that the director knew what she was doing'; 'The CEO never looked at the software'; 'The IT team was available for advice but was not part of the decision making process'. One of these managers also mentioned that in many cases, 'We had personal relationships with people at the top of the organisation' and 'Whenever a problem appeared we compromised'. The managers also mentioned that for such organisations senior staff members were always involved to discuss the clients' business models and hence the selling process was more about discussing business development issues rather than making a 'hard' sell and dedicating all the time to the quality and specifications of The Software.

- Delta has a range of Internet-based customers who are impressed by the suitability of this software for Internet trading (despite the fact that many of Delta's managers wonder about the appropriateness of The Software to Internet brokers). Apart from this it seems that the other reasons Delta is successful in this market is because Delta is part of a Plc and is perceived to really understand their business and the brokerage marketplace.

Issues

This report of some of the factors that underpin Delta's success raises issues about how a firm gets business, keeps business and how it could loose business to rival firms. The resource-based theory of the firm provides a rich perspective for exploring these fundamental business issues. At the end of the chapter we shall return to this case, but as you grapple with the material in the chapter, try to have these three questions at the back of your mind:

- How could you summarise how Delta achieves superior performance?
- Do you think that Delta's success is sustainable?
- What would be your recommendations to Delta?

Overview of the resource-based view of the firm

The origin of the perspective

Before embarking on the study of the resource-based view of the firm it may be worth recalling that strategic management is concerned with how some organisations outperform others, that is how sustained advantage, expressed in the form of above-average levels of profits, or 'super-normal' profits is achieved.

Up to the early 1980s, strategic management was very much dominated by neo-classical economics and notably the structure–conduct–performance paradigm of Industrial Organisation Economics (IO) (Caves, 1980; Caves and Porter, 1977; Porter, 1980). Briefly (see Chapter 5), IO's main thesis is that competitive advantage derives from privileged market positions. It argues that the prime determinant of an organisation's performance is its external environment, the structure of the industry it belongs to. In other words, according to the IO perspective, the source of organisational profits is market positions, positions protected by barriers to entry into the market.

The resource-based theory of the firm takes a different approach. As mentioned in the introduction, it claims that an organisation can be regarded as a bundle of resources (Amit and Shoemaker, 1993; Rumelt, 1984) and it is some of these resources that enable a firm to obtain sustainable competitive advantage. In other words, the resource-based view rests on the assumptions that competitive advantage does not derive from market and industry structures but rather it derives from a firm's internal resources. This means that the resource-based view locates the source of superior profitability inside the firm. Super-profits are called 'rents', and they accrue to the specific assets and resources controlled by the firm.

The resource-based view of the firm is based on Selznick's (1957) seminal work on 'distinctive competences' and on Penrose's (1959) argument that a firm is a collection of resources and that a firm's performance depends on its ability to use them. The resource-based view as such started with Wernerfelt's 1984 article and was developed by Barney (1986) and Dierickx and Cool (1989). However, this perspective really took off in the 1990s and can be argued to be the dominant strategic management perspective if one considers the strategy programmes of conferences such as the Academy of Management meeting or the Strategic Management Society conference. There is a large quantity of academic research published. Some notable early conceptual contributions include Barney (1991), Conner (1991), Mahoney and Pandian (1992) and Peteraf (1993). It is worth commenting that the proportion of conceptual work versus empirical work is disproportionate. The resource-based view arguments are conceptually well developed, but there is a lack of empirical evidence supporting the theory and notably there is a lack of qualitative studies. Many of the empirical studies published consist of quantitative studies with large sample sizes that are subject to statistical analysis (Shimizu and Armstrong, 2004). Examples of empirical studies include Collis (1991), Henderson and Cockburn (1994), Maijoor and van Witteloostuijn (1996), McGaughey and Liesch (2002) and Miller and Shamsie (1996).

The resource-based view perspective is very much consistent with the strategic management tradition as in essence it focuses on the Strengths and Weaknesses elements of the widely used SWOT analysis. This suggests that it would be misleading to argue that the resource-based view is in opposition to IO. These approaches actually describe different aspects of the same world and hence it may be more appropriate to consider the perspectives as complementing each other.

Elaboration of the key principles of the resource-based view of the firm

Barney's (1991) work on the principles of the resource-based view is key to the perspective. His main contribution was to characterise what allows a resource to be a source of competitive advantage and in doing so to highlight the importance of intangible, hard-to-define elements that can be found in organisations. We have structured what follows on Barney's work, while complementing it where necessary.

What is a resource?

There is little controversy about what it is, as actually, it can be anything. For instance it has been defined as 'anything which could be thought of as a strength or weakness of a given firm' (Wernerfelt, 1984, p. 172), or as 'those (tangible and intangible) assets which are tied semi-permanently to the firm' (Wernerfelt, 1984, p. 172). Resources can be categorised as physical resources (e.g. machinery, buildings), as human resources (e.g. knowledge, experience, workers' insights), as organisational resources (e.g. organisational culture, organisational structure, informal processes) and as financial resources (e.g. debt, equity) (Barney, 1991).

It is worth noting that there are numerous terms used to describe resources. They are sometimes called capabilities, strategic assets, organisational competence, competencies or core competence (if the resource is a source of sustainable competitive advantage). Sometimes a distinction is made between resources and capabilities. 'Resource' is understood as resource possession and 'capability' as resource utilisation (Brumagin, 1994). When such a distinction is made resources are usually seen as consisting of inputs into the production process and capabilities the processes by which the resources are utilised. Very often though, the general meaning of 'resources' is used, that is the term encompasses both resources and capabilities.

Another distinction that is frequently made is that between tangible and intangible resources. Tangible resources are physical resources and include, for instance, equipment and finance, whereas intangible resources include resources such as brand, reputation, knowledge and organisational culture. As we shall see in what follows, intangible resources are the resources that are most argued to be a source of competitive advantage because they are usually the most difficult resources to imitate.

Characteristics of a resource

The resource-based view does not propose that any resource can be a source of competitive advantage. It must possess a number of characteristics, and these characteristics must be held simultaneously:

■ Resources must be valuable. A resource is said to be valuable if 'it exploits opportunities and/or neutralises threats in a firm's environment' (Barney, 1991, p. 105) or expressed differently if it 'enable[s] a firm to conceive of or implement strategies that improve its efficiency and effectiveness' (1991, p. 106).

■ Resources must be *rare*, that is they must not be possessed by a large number of firms. A resource that is possessed by a large number of firms cannot be a source of sustainable competitive advantage. Resources that are valuable but not scarce can only be sources of competitive parity (Barney, 1995). Some resources may be essential but they are only prerequisites; they are order-qualifying, not order-winning criteria. This does not imply that these resources do not matter. They do matter as they are needed to be a player in the industry, they are needed for a firm to be able to compete, to survive.

■ Resources must be *imperfectly imitable*, that is others firms cannot copy and then obtain the resources. An organisation's resource cannot be a 'differential ability' (Conner, 1994) if its competitors can copy it, if they were to do so the organisation's advantage would be nullified.

■ There cannot be any strategically *equivalent substitutes* for them. If a resource can be easily substituted by another resource that delivers the same effect then it cannot remain a source of competitive advantage.

A resource that is simultaneously valuable, rare, imperfectly imitable, non-substitutable is called in short a VRIN resource. In a later work, Barney (2002) proposed an alternative to the VRIN framework: the VIRO or VRIO framework. The V relates as before to the question of value, and the R to the question of rarity. The I relates to the question of imitability (and substitutability as in effect a resource that can be substituted for is in essence the same as a resource that can be imitated). The O is about organisation. It is about whether a firm has other policies and procedures supporting the exploitation of VRIN resources (Barney and Hesterly, 2006). In other words, a VRIN resource can be a source of sustainable competitive advantage but to fully be able to exploit the VRIN resource a firm must be organised to do so. In particular, a firm may have complementary assets, that is assets that in combination with the VRIN resources allow the firm to fully exploit the VRIN resources and generate all its potential sources of sustainable competitive advantage. This means that the value of a VRIN resource is often contingent upon the presence of other resources.

Knowing which characteristics are necessary for a resource to be a source of sustainable competitive advantage is only part of starting to understand resources. We need to appreciate what makes a resource rare and hinders its imitation.

Resources can be difficult to imitate for various reasons and the main one is that organisations have 'isolating mechanisms' (Rumelt, 1984). These mechanisms protect the organisation's resources from imitation and preserve the stream of profits accruing to them. Causal ambiguity is one of these mechanisms that have been argued to be an explanation for firm differences (Lippman and Rumelt, 1982). It relates to the uncertainty that 'stems from a basic ambiguity concerning the nature of the causal connections between actions and results, the factors responsible for performance differentials will resist precise identification' (Lippman and Rumelt, 1982, p. 418).

Causal ambiguity limits imitation and mobility because competitors do not know what are the causes of a rival firm's effectiveness; therefore they do not know what they should be imitating (Rumelt, 1987). Moreover, it often occurs that a firm does not itself know better than its competitors the reasons for its competitive advantage, and therefore this advantage is likely to be sustained because imitation cannot take place. Barney (1991) implies that causal ambiguity can only be a real source of competitive advantage if firms themselves ignore the link between their resources and their advantage, the reason being that if an organisation can understand this link then others can also do so. Other firms can just go through the process of purchasing the resources they need and reproduce the same effects, and thus they will be able to have the same advantage as the other organisation. As a result, the first organisation would have lost its competitive advantage through imitation of its resources. Thus, it appears that competitive advantage can really only be sustained if firms ignore its origin, because then, replication is almost impossible. Lippman and Rumelt (1982) acknowledge that immobility can frequently be explained by uniqueness but they affirm that uncertainty and uniqueness are independent, because 'in the absence of uncertainty, the creation of a unique resource could be repeated and its uniqueness destroyed' (1982, p. 420). They state that factors are immobile not because they are unique but because they cannot be replicated because of their causal ambiguity.

Causal ambiguity is certainly of the main reasons for a resource's imperfect imitability but it is not the only one. We could also cite:

- *Time compression diseconomies* (Dierickx and Cool, 1989). Some resources are imperfectly imitable because they are history-dependent. Elements such as routines, organisational culture, past investments and so on impact heavily on the development of resources. This is at the root of the suggestion that inimitability can stem from the difficulty of discovering and repeating the development processes that are responsible for a resource's existence.

- *Asset mass efficiencies and interconnectedness of asset stocks* (Dierickx and Cool, 1989). Resources can remain immobile and cannot be replicated or transferred because first the initial level of an asset influences the pace of further accumulation, and second the accumulation in an existing asset does not depend just on the level of that asset but also on the levels of others. Interconnectedness of asset stocks refers to the situation where a 'lack of complementary assets can often impede a firm from accumulating an asset which it needs to serve its market successfully' (Verdin and Williamson, 1994, p. 87). For these reasons, replicating a resource can be extremely difficult.

All this means that history matters and that VRIN resources may be path dependent. As organisations develop, they acquire resources, develop traditions, ways of doing things, and hence become unique. Their resources can be extremely difficult to imitate because they exist due to the firm's unique history, the unique paths the firm has travelled (founder, employees, critical events, etc.). They have the resources only because of the type of situations they faced. One cannot reproduce the resource accumulation overnight and it may even be impossible to reproduce it at all because circumstances can never be the same again.

- *Specificity.* Some resources 'are specialised to a particular usage or firm' (Castanias and Helfat, 1991, p. 162), and because of that cannot be fully copied. This can be easily understood with Nonaka's (1991) explanation that 'what makes sense in one context can change or even lose its meaning when communicated to people in a different context' (1991, p. 103). This means that some resources could perhaps be transferred from one organisation to another; however, their efficiency or effectiveness would not be as high as it was before, because the context as a whole would be different.
- *Codifiability.* If resources are tangible, or if their structure is defined by a set of identifiable rules (Kogut and Zander, 1992), that is if they can be articulated (Winter, 1987), then resources are likely to be easily imitated and consequently they cannot be a source of competitive advantage.

The fact that resources that are difficult to codify are potential sources of sustainable competitive advantage has led strategy researchers to argue for the central role that tacit knowledge occupies in the development of sustainable competitive advantage. They propose that because of the ability of competitors to quickly acquire resources, 'sustainability of competitive advantage (. . .) requires resources which are idiosyncratic (. . .) and not so easily transferable or replicable. The criteria point to knowledge (tacit knowledge in particular) as the most strategically important resource of the firm' (Grant, 1993, p. 2). Tacit knowledge is best understood with the assertion that 'we can know more than we can tell' (Polanyi, 1966, p. 4). The main characteristics of tacit knowledge that explain why it is so difficult to codify are that tacit knowledge is difficult to express, it is deeply ingrained in people and organisations. It is practical knowledge and is about how to do things in specific contexts.

Linking the resource-based view to strategic management

The resource-based view addresses many aspects of strategic management. Specifically, it informs competitive and corporate strategy. Finally, the perspective also informs strategic change when its logic is applied to changing environment. This development of the resource-based view is called the dynamic capability view of the firm.

Competitive strategy

The resource-based view of the firm is almost entirely focused on how firms can achieve competitive advantage with their resources. The main implications in terms of competitive strategy are that, in order to compete, firms need to manage their resources. This requires three kinds of effort: they must protect current resources, they must continually improve their resources and they must build new resources, because firms cannot solely rely on their current resources. This is because resources may become irrelevant, that is they cease to be 'valuable'. Changes in the environment may render resources obsolete.

A firm must be able to identify its resources, in particular it must try to identify those resources and capabilities 'which are durable, difficult to identify and understand, imperfectly transferable, nor easily replicated, and in which the firm possesses clear ownership and control' (Grant, 1991, p. 129), that is it must identify its VRIN resources.

Once it has done so, a firm can start envisaging strategies. From the resource-based standpoint, strategic choice is limited by what the firms' resources are. If firms adopt strategies that are not based on its VRIN then they have to expect to only be able to realise short-term returns at best. If it is not based on VRIN resources the advantage is going to be short term (and not sustainable) because it is likely to be quickly competed. This is summarised in Table 9.1.

This raises the issue of what 'sustainable' advantage means. Barney (1991) argues that a firm has a competitive advantage when it is implementing a value-creating strategy not simultaneously being implemented by current or potential competitors. A firm has a sustained competitive advantage (SCA) when it is implementing a value-creating strategy not simultaneously being implemented by current or potential competitors and when these other firms are unable to duplicate the benefits of this strategy. This means that sustained advantage is not linked to the time period during which the advantage is achieved. These definitions imply that the resource-based view recognises that competitive advantage may sometimes not derive from rare, non-imitable and non-immobile resources but that sustained advantage does derive from these resource qualities.

The most favourable route for long-term advantage is for firms to envisage strategies that build on their resources. Resources are not product specific and therefore organisations could attempt to leverage their resources: i.e. can the resources be used in different markets? However, strategies also need to address new resources: do we need new resources to exploit our current market? Are there any new market opportunities and do we need new resources to exploit them?

Competitive strategy is conceptually easy to grasp insofar as it is not very original (it incorporates mainstream strategies ideas) and it is fully consistent with the core principles of the resource-based view of the firm: organisations should build on what they are good at and they should establish

Table 9.1 Competitive advantage and the VRIN criteria. Adapted from Hitt et al. (2005)

Valuable	Rare	Imperfectly imitable	Non-substitutable	Outcome
No	No	No	No	▪ Low return ▪ No advantage
Yes	No	No	No/yes	▪ Competitive parity ▪ Average return
Yes	Yes	No	No/yes	▪ Temporary advantage ▪ Superior return
Yes	Yes	Yes	Yes	▪ Sustainable competitive advantage ▪ Superior return

where the gaps in resources lie and try to fill them. There are not, as we shall see later, many tools from the resource-based perspective to help develop competitive strategies. However, it might be worth mentioning Porter's (1996) approach. He asserts that organisations can examine what they are currently doing and identify what makes them unique by answering questions such as the following:

- Which of our product or service varieties are the most distinctive?
- Which of our product or service varieties are the most profitable?
- Which of our customers are the most satisfied?
- Which customers, channels or purchase occasions are the most profitable?
- Which of the activities in our value chain are the most different and effective? (Porter, 1996, p. 76).

When dealing with competitive strategy it is also worth turning our attention to Hamel and Prahalad's (1990, 1994) publications who popularised the RBV principles with their work on competences.

Competences

The resource-based view is a competence-based perspective. It encourages managers to 'look inside for competitive advantage'. It directs attention to critical sources of advantage, which had hitherto been avoided, misunderstood or unrecognised by some other strategic management perspectives. By focusing attention on resources that are rare, imperfectly imitable and imperfectly mobile, the resource-based view recognises that since tangible resources are easily traded (equipment, software, etc. can be bought 'off the shelves'), competitive advantage is likely to derive from intangible/idiosyncratic resources. What is most likely to create a difference between firms is how resources are utilised and not only if the resources are possessed. One consequence of this recognition that intangible resources are the most likely sources of competitive advantage is the acknowledgement that people matter. However, this does not signify that physical resources are irrelevant to organisational success. They are important but they are not likely to be a source of sustained advantage.

Up to now, we have mainly considered the academic development of the resource-based view of the firm. In what follows we set out how these arguments have been translated for practitioners. As we have pointed out earlier Hamel and Prahalad (1990, 1994) made the resource-based arguments widely known to the business community. Instead of employing the expression intangible resources that are a source of sustainable competitive advantage, they talk about core competences. They define a core competence as a bundle of skills and technologies rather than a single discrete skill or technology. It represents the sum of learning across individual skill sets and individual organisational units and is unlikely to reside in its entirety in a single individual or small team. Hamel and Prahalad emphasise that (and this is similar to the resource-based view of the firm criteria) for a competence to be core it must meet three tests:

1. *Customer value.* A core competence must make disproportionate contribution to customer-perceived value. That does not imply that the core competence will be visible to, or understood by, the customer. There is an exception to the 'customer value' rule. Any bundle of skills that yields a significant cost advantage in the delivery of a particular customer benefit may also be termed a core competence.

2. *Competitor differentiation.* To qualify as a core competence a capability must also be competitively unique. This does not mean that to qualify as a core competence a competence must be uniquely held by a single firm, but it does mean that any capability that is ubiquitous across an industry

should not be defined as core. It makes little sense to define a competence as core if it is omnipresent or easily imitated by competitors. Benchmarking an organisation's competences against those of competitors helps guard against a natural tendency to overstate the uniqueness of one's own capabilities.

3. *Extendibility*. In defining core competence managers must abstract the core competence away from the particular product configuration in which the core competence is currently embedded and imagine how the core competence might be applied in new product arenas. A core competence is truly core when it forms the basis for entry into new product markets.

In their work Hamel and Prahalad (1994) make clear what a core competence is not. In doing so they emphasise the difference between tangible and intangible resources. They highlight that core competences are not an asset in the accounting sense; they do not appear on balance sheets. Factories, distribution channels, brands or patents are not core competences, but an aptitude to manage them may be one. Thus, if we were to discriminate between resource and capability, as explained previously, it would be appropriate to use the term capability rather than resource when referring to core competences. Finally, we can also add that Hamel and Prahalad (1994) argue that all core competences are sources of competitive advantage but not all competitive advantages are core competences. For instance, an advantage based on a physical asset or on luck does not derive from a core competence.

Culture

As explained so far the perspective focuses on what is happening inside the firm and notably examines the impact of resources on performance. We have already mentioned that tacit knowledge was often seen to be a VRIN resource, it is also the case of corporate culture and hence it is important within the context of competitive strategy to consider the role of culture.

As suggested, intangible resources are more likely to be sources of sustained advantage than tangible assets. When we discussed the reasons for rarity, imperfect immobility and imperfect imitability we explained that path dependency and social complexity were sources of inimitability and we gave organisational culture as an example of a socially complex phenomenon. Barney defines culture as 'a complex set of values, beliefs, assumptions and symbols that define the way in which a firm conducts its business' (Barney, 1986, p. 657). He argues that culture can be valuable because it can enable things that can positively impact on a firm's performance to happen in the organisation. Culture can encourage innovation, customer focus, flexibility and so on, which help a firm's efficiency.

He also explains that cultures are unique to organisations because they develop in organisations through time. Organisational culture is embedded in a firm's history and heritage. It reflects the unique circumstances of the organisations' birth and growth, the experiences of its employee's and so on. This mix is idiosyncratic to each organisation. Two organisations never follow identical patterns of development. Barney (1986) also argues that culture is very difficult to imitate. It is difficult to imitate because it is socially complex, path dependent and because it is difficult for outsiders to observe and difficult to describe, even for insiders. Culture is often 'taken for granted' and organisational members themselves usually have great difficulties in expressing what their culture is about. This difficulty in articulating and codifying organisational culture means that it is difficult to copy. If people in the organisation cannot 'tell' what their culture is, it is unlikely that competitors can do so and begin imitating the culture. Barney adds that 'because of the subtle multidimensional character of socially complex organisational resources [such as culture], they are not likely to have close strategic substitutes' (Barney, 1992, p. 48).

Corporate strategy

The resource-based view of the firm can have some important implications for corporate strategies, notably in terms of diversification. Proponents of the resource-based view argue that diversifications are most likely to be successful if based on the firms' specific resources. In other words, diversification is recommended to exploit resources that can have uses in markets that are not currently exploited by the firm. This means that the resource-based view supports related diversification, it argues that 'the rationale for multibusiness organisations ultimately lies in sharing strategic capabilities among businesses' (Robins and Wiersema, 1995). It posits that related diversification can increase firm value by sharing specific assets such as production capacity and know-how and that because unrelated diversification is not based on shared resources it will not yield cost or differentiation advantage (Wiersema and Liebeskind, 1995). It could be noted that this argument is not only a theoretical argument. There is empirical evidence that shows that there is a correlation between relatedness within the portfolio of businesses and corporate performance: the economic performance of unrelated diversified organisations is lower than the performance of related portfolio businesses (Robins and Wiersema, 1995; Rumelt, 1974). This position is very much in the tradition of strategic management. Diversification is seen as being a way of matching a firm's resources with market opportunities. The crux of the resource-based view prescriptions is that firms should adopt strategies that their resources can support (Peteraf, 1993).

More precisely, Collis (1996) argues that corporate strategy should be about relatedness. What he calls the three elements of corporate strategy, resources, portfolio of businesses and organisation structure and processes and systems, must be aligned. Resource relatedness is the match between the organisations' resources and what is needed to generate competitive advantage. Business relatedness is about the extent to which the 'activities of the businesses are mutually reinforcing and exploit economies of scope' (Collis, 1996, p. 134) and each of the businesses contribute to the development of the corporation's resources. Finally, organisational relatedness is about how the organisation structure, processes and systems of the corporation are 'used to control and coordinate the corporation fit with the resources it is leveraging across markets' (1996, p. 127) and how relevant the 'dominant logic' (ways of thinking, experience, etc.) of the managers in the corporation is to the business. In short, Collis argues that

> 'when businesses fit the alignment of the elements of corporate strategy, they are related and deserve to be in the corporate portfolio, regardless of how disparate they appear in product market terms. When businesses do not fit this alignment, they do not belong inside the corporation, regardless of how similar the products may be'. (1996, p. 139)

He concludes that 'the best corporate strategies are indeed related – just not related in the traditional way of thinking' (1996, p. 139).

This issue of relatedness implies that outsourcing is a corporate decision that is accepted within the resource-based view of the firm framework. Corporations should not try to do what they cannot do well enough to achieve competitive advantage. Outsourcing activities that are not core to the business are thus a corollary of the focus on valuable resources.

One of the main obstacles that corporations might face when searching for novel ways of using their resources is the problem of the specificity of their resources. As we have seen earlier, specificity is a great isolating mechanism: it hinders resource transferability. However, there is a flip side: corporations may not be able to transfer their own resources. What works in a specific part of the corporation may not work as well (or not at all) in other parts, or what works in one environment may not work in another. Resource idiosyncrasy can have important ramifications for corporations: if what causes success is based on specific, idiosyncratic resources, this suggests that one cannot copy 'recipes' of strategy from one business unit to another or even from one part of a business unit to another. Generic strategies just become the equivalent of tangible resources that are available to any organisations and therefore may not be sources of advantage. Organisations have to be ready to tailor their strategies to each specific situation they are facing.

Change

Before examining the dynamic capability perspective, that is the resource-based view strand that specifically addresses changing environment, it is worth commenting that if intangible resources are a source of competitive advantage it is of prime importance for organisations to know about them: thanks to them, organisations may be able to deploy resources in an effective and efficient manner. Yet, because intangible resources generate casual ambiguity, managers may not know exactly how competitive advantage is generated in their organisation. Causal ambiguity is an important issue for any organisation and it can be seen both as a positive and as a negative phenomenon. If the management does not know where success comes from, they cannot explain to anybody else why the organisation is successful and hence this source of advantage is unlikely to be imitated. However, because of this lack of awareness, managers may also destroy sources of advantage, for instance, when embarking on an organisational change programme. If managers are not aware of what generates success, they may inadvertently change something that is critical, for example, through delayering or business process re-engineering.

Dynamic capabilities

The dynamic capability approach focuses attention on the firm's ability to renew its resources in line with changes in its environment. The turbulent and changing nature of the environment suggests that resources cannot remain static. They must be continually evolving and developing. Therefore, firms must continue to invest in and upgrade their resources to create new strategic growth alternatives. Dynamic capabilities refer to a firm's ability to alter its resources by creating, integrating, recombining and releasing resources (Eisenhardt and Martin, 2000; Teece et al., 1997). In other words, dynamic capabilities are directed at the creation of future valuable resources (Bowman and Ambrosini, 2003). Dynamic capabilities may help firms avoid developing core rigidities (Leonard Barton, 1992), which inhibit development, generate inertia and stifle innovation. Core rigidities are the flip side of VRIN resources, they are resources that used to be VRIN but that have become obsolete and inhibit the development of the firm.

The dynamic capability perspective has lent value to the resource-based view arguments as they transform what is essentially a static view into one that can encompass competitive advantage in a dynamic context (Barney, 2001a,b). It helps to understand how firms evolve over time.

Dynamic capabilities are argued to comprise four main processes: reconfiguration, leveraging, learning and integration (Teece et al., 1997). Reconfiguration refers to the transformation and recombination of assets and resources, for example, the consolidation of central support functions that often occurs as a result of an acquisition. Leveraging might involve replicating a process or system that is operating in one area of an organisation in another, or by extending a resource by deploying it into a new domain, for instance, by applying an existing brand to a new set of products. As a dynamic capability, learning allows tasks to be performed more effectively and efficiently as an outcome of experimentation, failure and success. Finally, integration relates to the ability of the firm to integrate its assets and resources, resulting in a new resource base.

Case study revisited

In light of what precedes, what issues can be raised from the case and how can the three questions be addressed? The resource-based view of the firm perspective encourages us to look at what is happening inside Delta and how that affects its performance.

How could you summarise how Delta's achieve superior performance?

The case may not report all of Delta's sources of performance as many could be causally ambiguous or tacit. That said, the case highlights the following sources:

While being important, the tangible assets of IT systems are not a differential source of performance. They are valuable but are not rare and as they can be bought they are easily imitated. This means that they are most probably a source of competitive parity. The same can probably be said about the locations. With Internet brokers it is unlikely that Delta's physical locations matters most and it is worth questioning whether it matters much for the other customers either.

Reading the case explicitly and interpreting some of the quotes one can suggest that there are three main sources of advantage.

- 'Providing reassurance to customers' can be seen to be key to clinching deals. The text suggests that one of the success-generating causes is that Delta is trustworthy, stable. This is shown when it is said that it matters to clients that Delta belongs to a Plc. This means that it has to declare its accounts and hence its results can be scrutinised; to many belonging to a public company means stability, and hence that Delta can be trusted to be there for the foreseeable future. Two other points can help provide reassurance: because Delta has essentially only one product, it is not going to abandon it or neglect it and having BUS as a customer also matters in this respect. Being able to demonstrate that such a respected company uses The Software also helps reassure the customer: it shows that BUS trusts Delta.

  The question is whether this is a VRIN resource. It is difficult to evaluate without knowing the industry and Delta's competitors but it seems to be valuable; it is probably rare in this sector otherwise it would not be a seemingly important selection criterion. As far as inimitability is concerned one could surmise that it is imitable in the long term as other suppliers could decide to become public or be taken over by a Plc. For the substitutability criterion one could think that having a proven track of success and advertising this success through trusted channels and developing a solid relationship within the brokering community may achieve a similar result and help other firms 'provide reassurance'.

- Another set of success factors seems to be about 'having a business approach rather than an IT approach'. This may, however, be context specific. From the text it appears to be valuable in servicing 'traditional' businesses rather than Internet operation companies. This is linked to the fact that negotiating at the top level seems critical for traditional organisations. In this case, it seems that the product plays a secondary role to senior-level relationships with the clients.

  Is it a VRIN resource? The text shows that the V criterion is matched. The other criteria are difficult to judge as they are very intangible. We can here rejoin the discussion we had earlier on culture and hence one can propose that it is difficult to imitate.

- Finally another cause of success that can be implied from drawing parallels between the two type of clients is Delta's ability to 'adapt the sales pitch to the customer'. Traditional organisations seem to need a business approach, whereas Internet brokers seem to need a technical approach. Considering that both types are Delta's clients we can assume that they both received what they wanted. This success routine is about the ability to identify the right emphasis, that is, either on The Software or on business issues, and being able to deliver it. It would also suggest that the ability to 'sense', which is the right approach early on in the engagement, is critical to progressing the relationships.

Is this VRIN? It is unlikely to be rare as other companies will have the same types of customer base. Moreover as long as Delta's managers and employees are aware that it is a source of success it is likely to be imitable as should they leave Delta they might be able to replicate their ways of doing things.

Do you think that Delta's success is sustainable?

Delta is partly relying on personal relationships with clients to gain business, but unless they keep developing those relationships and have new staff able to do the same things when the current senior staff leaves they may lose this source of advantage. It is also important to question whether everybody at Delta knows about the role of 'providing reassurance to customers' and 'having a business approach rather than an IT approach'. If senior managers are not aware of these sources of advantage they may inadvertently take actions that destroy them, for example, by a strong focus on cost efficiency and imposing a single codified sales procedure, or by re-organising into different, 'more logical' groupings. One also needs to note that if Delta did succeed in understanding and specifying their sources of advantage, by making the 'adapting the pitch' routines explicit so that they can be inculcated into new staff they run a higher risk that other organisations might be more able to copy them. Another point worth noting is how much does the sales staff know about these success factors? Does the sales team know about the importance of adapting the pitch to the customers? Does it fully exploit the fact that BUS is often used as a referent?

When answering the first question one may have wondered why 'providing services' was not mentioned as a source of success. It is clearly a source of revenue and hence it should have been mentioned indeed. However, by playing devil's advocate one can wonder whether it is really about success, considering that Delta makes money by 'fixing' The Software they installed in the first place. They make money by fixing a faulty product. How sustainable is this? If a new team of designers come in and improve The Software this source of revenue may well disappear. We could indeed imagine the situation of a newcomer, a new product manager wanting to improve the product so that it never fails. Such an improvement, as rational as it may seem ('we want to sell a good product'), may jeopardise Delta's main source of income.

What would be your recommendations to Delta?

The first one is that it would be useful for Delta to ensure that they identify what their current sources of advantage are. This is essential but it is a challenge. It is essential because if managers make mistakes in their evaluation they may develop strategies on an unsound basis. Delta's managers need to explore the *how*, the detail of how things are done in the organisation, the 'nitty-gritty' of their operations (Ambrosini, 2003; Ambrosini and Bowman, 2005). This would be the first step towards first protecting what is critical to the business and also for assessing what could be leveraged, or exploited further. It could also highlight what is missing in the business and what they need to change if they want to keep generating superior performance.

Finally, it is interesting to remark that the case report did not reveal any special routines embedded in The Software, or the use of The Software by Delta. For instance, nothing about innovation or research or team skills was mentioned. In order to develop The Software and make it a market leader, they must have existed in the past. However, considering that The Software is a unique product and has been sold to a limited market, it seems that these skills have not been recognised and exploited. It might also be worth asking whether they might even have been lost. If we follow the resource-based view of the firm argument, a product is most unlikely to be a source of *sustainable* competitive advantage. It could be argued that there were some critical routines when the product was developed and created. This is possibly why, for the time being, the product is still so key to Delta, it still has little competition and customers, once they possess The Software, are somewhat locked in. These routines are reflected in the complexity of The Software's architecture that prevents customers from fully understanding what they have, and it makes it difficult for competitors to reverse-engineer the product and imitate it.

Routines that are sources of sustainable competitive advantage are history-dependent. They are based, among others, on Delta's people and past investments. Discovering and repeating the development processes that were responsible for The Software would be impossible for competitors. However, if there is no further development, competitors are going to be able, in time, to catch up and unlock the 'secrets' of The Software. Delta's top management team may need to recognise The Software may not be a market leader forever. They need to preserve it while realising that its future life may be limited.

Finally, to come back to the 'revenues from services' issues. As explained earlier, this may not be sustainable and hence Delta needs to consider how to envisage the future without this source of revenues. What would be the consequences? How can it be replaced?

Summary

Before summarising, it is worth mentioning some of the limitations of the resource-based view (for a full exposé see Priem and Butler, 2001). The two key criticisms are that it currently suffers from a high level of abstraction and that it is tautological. The former relates essentially to the fact that there are little tools and prescriptions that could help managers identify their VRIN resources and manage them meaningfully. For instance, one does not know much about how to deal with causal ambiguity or how to create dynamic capabilities. The latter refers to the fact that as it stands it is explained that a valuable and rare resource is a source of sustainable competitive advantage but yet sustainable competitive advantage is defined in terms of value and rarity, hence the tautology.

So to summarise, proponents of the resource-based view locate the source of superior performance inside the firm and argue that resources that are simultaneously *valuable, rare, imperfectly imitable* and *imperfectly substitutable* are a firm's main source of sustainable competitive advantage. On a practical basis when examining a firm using a resource-based view lens it is worth asking the following questions: What are the firm's sources of competitive advantage? How unique are they? How sustainable are they? Are they difficult to imitate? How do you renew them?

References

Ambrosini, V., *Tacit and Ambiguous Resources as Sources of Competitive Advantage* (Hemel Hempstead: Palgrave, 2003).

Ambrosini, V. and C. Bowman, 'Reducing Causal Ambiguity to Facilitate Strategic Learning', *Management Learning*, 36, 4 (2005) 517–536.

Amit, R. and P. J. H. Shoemaker, 'Strategic Assets and Organizational Rents', *Strategic Management Journal*, 14 (1993) 33–46.

Barney, J. B., 'Organizational Culture: Can it be a Source of Sustained Competitive Advantage?', *Academy of Management Review*, 11, 3 (1986) 656–665.

Barney, J. B., 'Firm Resources and Sustained Competitive Advantage', *Journal of Management*, 17, 1 (1991) 99–120.

Barney, J. B., 'Integrating Organizational Behavior and Strategy Formulation Research: A Resource-Based Analysis', in P. Shrivastava, A. Huff and J. Dutton (eds) *Advances in Strategic Management*, 8 (Greenwich: Jai Press, 1992) pp. 39–61.

Barney, J. B., 'Looking Inside for Competitive Advantage', *Academy of Management Executive*, 9, 4 (1995) 49–61.

Barney, J. B., 'Is the Resource-Based "View" a Useful Perspective for Strategic Management Research? Yes', *Academy of Management Review*, 26, 1 (2001a) 41–56.

Barney, J. B., 'Resource-Based Theories of Competitive Advantage: A Ten Year Retrospective on the Resource-Based View', *Journal of Management*, 27 (2001b) 643–650.

Barney, J., *Gaining and Sustaining Competitive Advantage*, 2nd edn (Englewood Cliffs, MD: Prentice Hall, 2002).

Barney, J. and W. S. Hesterly, *Strategic Management and Competitive Advantage Concepts* (New Jersey: Pearson, 2006).

Bowman, C. and V. Ambrosini, 'How the Resource-Based and the Dynamic Capability Views of the Firm Inform Competitive and Corporate Level Strategy', *British Journal of Management*, 14 (2003) 289–303.

Brumagin, A. L., 'A Hierarchy of Corporate Resources', in P. Shrivastava, A. Huff and J. Dutton (eds) *Advances in Strategic Management, 10A* (Greenwich: Jai Press, 1994) pp. 81–112.

Castanias, R. P. and C. E. Helfat, 'Managerial Resources and Rents', *Journal of Management*, 17, 1 (1991) 155–171.

Caves, R. E., 'Industrial Organisation, Corporate Strategy and Structure', *Journal of Economic Literature*, 18 (1980) 64–92.

Caves, R. E. and M. Porter, 'From Entry Barriers to Mobility Barriers: Conjectural Decisions and Contrived Deterrence to New Competition', *Quarterly Journal of Economics*, 91 (1977) 241–262.

Collis, D., 'A Resource-Based Analysis of Global Competition: The Case of the Bearings Industry', *Strategic Management Journal*, 12 (1991) 49–68.

Collis, D., 'Related Corporate Portfolio', in M. Goold and K. Sommers Luchs (eds) *Managing the Multibusiness Company: Strategic Issues for Diversified Groups* (London: Routledge, 1996) pp. 122–142.

Conner, K. R., 'A Historical Comparison of Resources-Based Theory and Five Schools of Thought Within Industrial Organisation Economics: Do We Have a New Theory of the Firm?', *Journal of Management*, 17, 1 (1991) 121–154.

Conner, K. R., 'The Resource-Based Challenge to the Industry-Structure Perspective', Best Paper Proceedings (Dallas: Annual Meeting of the Academy of Management, 1994).

Dierickx, I. and K. Cool, 'Asset Stock Accumulation and Sustainability of Competitive Advantage', *Management Science*, 35, 12 (1989) 1504–1511.

Eisenhardt, K. and J. Martin, 'Dynamic Capabilities: What Are They?', *Strategic Management Journal*, 21 (2000) 1105–1121.

Grant, R. M., 'The Resource-Based Theory of Competitive Advantage: Implications for Strategy Formulation', *California Management Review*, 33, 3 (1991) 114–135.

Grant, R. M., *Organisational Capabilities Within a Knowledge-Based View of the Firm*, paper presented at the Annual Meeting of the Academy of Management, Atlanta, Georgia (1993).

Hamel, G. and C. K. Prahalad, 'The Core Competence of the Corporation', *Harvard Business Review*, 68, 3 (1990) 79–91.

Hamel, G. and C. K. Prahalad, *Competing for the Future* (Boston, MA: Harvard Business School Press, 1994).

Henderson, R. and I. Cockburn, 'Measuring Competence? Exploring Firm Effects in Pharmaceutical Research', *Strategic Management Journal*, 15 (1994) 63–84.

Hitt, M. A., R. D. Ireland and R. E. Hoskisson, 'Strategic Management: Competitiveness and Globalization', Thompson Southwestern, 2005.

Kogut, B. and U. Zander, 'Knowledge of the Firm, Combinative Capabilities, and the Replication of Technology', *Organisation Science*, 3 (1992) 383–396.

Leonard Barton, D., 'Core Capabilities and Core Rigidities: A Paradox in Managing New Product Development', *Strategic Management Journal*, 13 (1992) 111–126.

Lippman, S. A. and R. P. Rumelt, 'Uncertain Imitability: An Analysis of Interfirm Differences in Efficiency Under Competition', *The Bell Journal of Economics*, 13, 2 (1982) 418–438.

Mahoney, J. T. and J. R. Pandian, 'The Resource-Based View Within the Conversation of Strategic Management', *Strategic Management Journal*, 13 (1992) 363–380.

Maijoor, S. and A. van Witteloostuijn, 'An Empirical Test of the Resource-Based Theory: Strategic Regulation in the Dutch Audit Industry', *Strategic Management Journal* (1996) 549–569.

McGaughey, S. L. and P. W. Liesch, 'The Global Sports-Media Nexus: Reflections on the "Super League Saga" in Australia', *Journal of Management Studies*, 39, 3 (2002) 383–416.

Miller, D. and J. Shamsie, 'The Resource-Based View of the Firm in Two Environments: The Hollywood Film Studios from 1936 to 1965', *Academy of Management Journal*, 39, 3 (1996) 519–543.

Nonaka, I., 'The Knowledge-Creating Company', *Harvard Business Review*, 69, 6 (1991) 96–104.

Penrose, E. T., *The Theory of Growth of the Firm* (New York: Wiley, 1959).

Peteraf, M. A., 'The Cornerstone of Competitive Advantage: A Resource-Based View', *Strategic Management Journal*, 14 (1993) 179–191.

Polanyi, M., *The Tacit Dimension* (New York: Doubleday and Co., 1966).

Porter, M. E., *Competitive Strategy: Techniques for Analysing Industries and Competitors* (New York: Free Press, 1980).

Porter, M. E., 'What Is Strategy?', *Harvard Business Review*, November–December (1996) 61–78.

Priem, R. L. and J. E. Butler, 'Is the Resource-Based View a Useful Perspective for Strategic Management Research?', *Academy of Management Review*, 26 (2001) 22–40.

Robins, J. and M. F. Wiersema, 'A Resource-Based Approach to the Multibusiness Firm: Empirical Analysis of Portfolio Interrelationships and Corporate Financial Performance', *Strategic Management Journal*, 16 (1995) 277–299.

Rumelt, R., *Strategy, Structure and Economic Performance* (Cambridge, Mass: Harvard University Press, 1974).

Rumelt, R., 'Toward a Strategic Theory of the Firm', in R. Lamb (ed.) *Competitive Strategic Management* (Englewood Cliffs, MD: Prentice Hall, 1984) pp. 556–570.

Rumelt, R., 'Theory, Strategy and Entrepreneurship', in D. J. Teece (ed.) *The Competitive Challenge* (Cambridge, MA: Ballinger Publishing Company, 1987) pp. 137–158.

Selznick, P., *Leadership in Administration: A Sociological Interpretation* (New York: Harper and Row, 1957).

Shimizu, K. and C. Armstrong, 'A Review of Empirical Research on the Resource-Based View of the Firm', *Academy of Management Conference*, New Orleans (2004).

Teece, D., G. Pisano and A. Shuen, 'Dynamic Capabilities and Strategic Management', *Strategic Management Journal*, 18 (1997) 509–533.

Verdin, P. J. and P. J. Williamson, 'Core Competences, Competitive Advantage and Market Analysis: Forging the Links', in G. Hamel and A. Heene (eds) *Competence-Based Competition* (Chichester: Wiley, 1994) pp. 77–110.

Wernerfelt, B., 'A Resource-Based View of the Firm', *Strategic Management Journal*, 5 (1984) 171–180.

Wiersema, M. F. and J. P. Liebeskind, 'The Effects of Leveraged Buyout on Corporate Growth and Diversification in Large Firms', *Strategic Management Journal*, 16 (1995) 447–460.

Winter, S. G., 'Knowledge and Competence as Strategic Assets', in D. J. Teece (ed.) *The Competitive Challenge* (Cambridge, MA: Ballinger Publishing Company, 1987) pp. 159–184.

Part III
Behaviouralist Perspectives

CHAPTER 10

The Cognitive Perspective

Gerard P. Hodgkinson

Basic principles

Drawing on concepts, theories and methods from cognitive science (broadly conceived, so as to incorporate cognitive psychology, cognitive anthropology and social cognition), over the past two to three decades a growing number of strategic management researchers and organisation theorists have contributed to the development of an exciting new field of inquiry: managerial and organisational cognition (MOC). As we shall see, this rapidly evolving body of work has created a perspective on strategic management that focuses on the subjectivity and limitations of human information processing. The insights gained from this perspective have led scholars to raise a number of fundamental questions that challenge the very foundations of the strategy field.

The basic principles of the cognitive perspective on strategic management can be summarised as follows:

■ Individuals are limited in their ability to process the rich variety of stimuli contained in the external world. (In Simon's (1947) terms they are constrained by 'bounded rationality'.)

■ Consequently, they employ a variety of strategies in order to reduce the burden of information processing that would otherwise ensue.

■ This culminates in the development of a simplified representation of reality that is encoded within the mind of the individual.

■ Once formulated, these 'mental representations' act as filters through which incoming information is subsequently processed, which in turn may lead to biased and inappropriate decisions, but under certain circumstances may also form the basis of creative ideas and new insights.

Overview of the cognitive perspective

The foundations of the cognitive perspective were laid with the development of cognitive psychology as a major sub-field of study within psychology. Cognitive psychology evolved in part as reaction against behaviourism, the approach advocated by Skinner and his followers (e.g. Mowrer, 1947; Skinner, 1938). Behaviourists believe that since all human behaviour is essentially generated in response to stimuli, it should be possible to develop satisfactory accounts of behaviour in stimulus–response (S → R) terms, without recourse to concepts relating to 'under-the-skin phenomena', such as 'perception', 'attention' and 'memory'. In order to render psychology a truly scientific endeavour, behaviourists argued that such concepts should be eschewed in favour of much simpler concepts, ones that could be readily subjected to direct observation and measurement.

In practice, S → R theories are unable to account for all but the most simple of behaviours, and for this reason behaviourism was subsequently displaced by cognitive psychology, although by no means entirely. Within the field of marketing, for example, there are still researchers who argue that behaviouristic theories of learning can better account for consumer purchasing behaviour than can cognitive theories (e.g. Foxall, 1997).

Human information processing

Rejecting the central theoretical tenets of behaviourism, cognitive psychologists (and cognitive scientists in general) focus on the analysis of the various intervening mental processes that mediate responses to the environment. In order to aid understanding of the complex mental processes performed by the brain in response to environmental stimuli, researchers have found it useful to conceptualise these as a sequence of activities involving a variety of functions, including sensory and perceptual processes, memory (both working memory and long-term memory) and decision-making, culminating in the execution of skilled responses (see, e.g. Broadbent, 1958; Welford, 1976; Wickens, 1984). Although highly simplified, this general approach makes it possible to model the essential processes associated with virtually any task involving human cognition.

This approach suggests that the way in which individuals act is driven ultimately by the way in which they interpret their worlds (perception), this in turn being shaped in part by their past experiences and learning. Often, in an effort to reduce the amount of cognitive activity required, past experience, stored in long-term memory, is influential in determining an individual's responses to current situations or stimuli; actions that worked in the past are routinely applied to the present, so as to free up mental capacity. Cognitive psychologists employ the term 'top-down processing' to denote this type of processing activity.

A second type of processing activity, known as 'bottom-up processing', occurs when incoming environmental stimuli influence actors' cognitions and actions directly, without reference to past memories. In practice, at any given point in time, information processing may be affected by what an individual brings to the task at hand (e.g. prior expectations, influenced by previous experience and contexts) and/or key features of the stimuli present in the current task environment. Clearly, the balance between bottom-up (stimulus-driven) and top-down (conceptually driven) information processing strategies is likely to vary across tasks and situations; in the contexts in which senior managers operate, however, it is the latter that is likely to predominate – see Walsh (1995) for detailed explanations as to why this is the case.

Mental representations: Schemata, cognitive maps and mental models

Precisely how knowledge is represented in the mind and what types of computations can be carried out on these representations in order to bring about such activities as remembering, perceiving, reasoning, problem solving and decision-making are the fundamental questions to which basic and applied research within the field of cognitive science is ultimately addressed (see e.g. Anderson, 1990; Johnson-Laird, 1993). Not surprisingly, therefore, much of the scholarly activity of MOC researchers has been devoted to operationalising the notion of mental representations in such a way as to shed light on issues of primary concern to strategy scholars and organisation theorists more generally.

It is useful at this point to introduce three further preliminary concepts: the related notions of 'schemata' (Bartlett, 1932), 'cognitive maps' (Tolman, 1932) and 'mental models' (Johnson-Laird, 1983). Schemata may be broadly defined as follows:

> Schemata contain collections of knowledge derived from past experience which serve the function of directing perceptual exploration towards relevant environmental stimuli. Such exploration often leads the perceiver to sample some of the available stimulus information. If the information obtained from the environment fails to match information in the relevant schema, then the information in the schema is modified appropriately.
>
> (Eysenck and Keane, 1995, p. 81)

The notion of 'cognitive maps', which originated from work on the ways in which animals and humans navigate the physical world, is similarly intended to capture the idea that knowledge is internally represented in a form which both simplifies reality and provides a basis for subsequent action. Likewise, Johnson-Laird's (1983) theory of mental models, and the pioneering work of Craik on which it is based (e.g. Craik, 1943), asserts:

> The psychological core of understanding . . . consists in your having a 'working model' of the phenomenon in your mind. If you understand inflation, a mathematical proof, the way a computer works, DNA or divorce, then you have a mental representation that serves as a model of an entity in much the same way as, say, a clock functions as a model of the earth's rotation . . . Many of the models in people's minds are little more than high-grade simulations, but they are none the less useful provided that the picture is accurate.
>
> (Johnson-Laird, 1983, pp. 2–4)

MOC scholars have tended to use these notions interchangeably, to convey the general idea that actors develop internal representations of their worlds which in turn are linked to organisational action (e.g. Huff, 1990; Reger and Palmer, 1996; Walsh, 1995). Arguably, these notions are sufficiently similar in meaning to justify this general usage and for present purposes it is convenient to follow this trend. In the remainder of this chapter, therefore, the terms 'schemata', 'cognitive maps' and 'mental models' are employed synonymously, to capture the overarching idea that individuals internalise their knowledge and understanding of organisational life in the form of a simplified representation of reality. In so doing, however, we must also be mindful of the fact that scholars pursuing a variety of research problems in cognitive psychology, albeit centred on the general notion of mental representations, originally developed these terms for differing purposes.

CASE STUDY 10.1

The conversation, below, comprises an extract from a discussion with the owner-manager of a small jeweller's shop in the United Kingdom. The purpose of this discussion is to explore the owner-manager's views as to how he sees his business growing. The content of the discussion provides us with some useful material for gaining insights into the owner-manager's mental model of the business and its longer-term strategy. By using a variety of 'cognitive mapping techniques' – such as those described later in this chapter (see 'Tools and techniques') and reviewed in greater detail in Huff (1990), Fiol and Huff (1992) and Hodgkinson and Sparrow (2002) – we can gain a clearer idea not only of the way in which the owner-manager defines his business and the bases on which he sees it competing with rival firms, but also the way in which he plans to develop the strategy of his business over the longer term.

The conversation

'Fortunately in the UK it's just about possible to be independent; jewellery is the most independent of any retail operation in the high street. This is because people are often buying gifts, so they often want something that is unique, and they're prepared to pay a bit more for that. We decided that there would be no point in trying to sell, as Ratner does, a pair of earrings for ninety pence. Our products aren't particularly price sensitive, because there isn't the direct competition. That's not to say that you don't have to be competitive because, as with any high street shop as we've got, you have to carry a range of goods which are the bread and butter of the market and if we put a chain in the window that's twenty pounds more than a chap down the road, the customers will go down the road.

We get most of our enjoyment out of the special pieces and the commissioned pieces, because that's where we get the real positive feedback from customers and pick up most of our profit. Obviously we do a lot of handmade wedding rings which are very important; it's nice to know when you look in the paper that half the people who got married have your wedding rings on. They know they're unique because we make them specially for them, and that's good advertising for us because if they're happy they'll go and tell four or five people; if they're not happy, they'll tell nine or ten; so it's an important part of our advertising, it's an internal advertisement.'

Issues

The cognitive perspective on strategic management starts from the basic premise that it is the owner-manager's mental representations of his business and its strategy that will drive his actions directed towards the longer-term development of the business. The material presented in 'Case study 10.1' will be revisited later in the chapter, but for the time being, consider the following four interrelated questions when reviewing the substance of the cognitive perspective:

1. What are the key elements (variables and concepts) that inform the owner-manager's view of his business strategy and how are these inter-connected within his reasoning?
2. Which organisations would the owner-manager regard as the major competitors to his business and for what reasons?
3. To what extent are there significant threats and opportunities which may go unnoticed, but which nevertheless may have a major bearing on the longer-term well-being of his organisation?
4. What are the fundamental assumptions underpinning his responses to the above questions and to what extent are these assumptions reasonable?

Key contributors

Although the application of cognitive theory and research to managers and organisations is a relatively recent phenomenon, it can be argued that the need for a cognitive approach to managerial and organisational analysis was implicitly acknowledged in a number of 'classic', earlier works on strategy and organisation theory. Hence, Stubbart (1989) contends that MOC research provides a vital missing link between environmental conditions and strategic action, a link that was implied strongly in the work of early strategy scholars such as Hofer and Schendel (1978) and Andrews (1971), while Weick (1995) notes that Barnard's (1938) seminal text on the functions of the executive introduced the notion that organisations can be viewed as systems of action, consciously co-ordinated by controlled information processing and communication.

At the outset of this chapter I made a brief reference to Simon's (1947) notion of 'bounded rationality'. This concept captures the idea that actors are unable to take decisions in a completely rational manner due to the fact that they are constrained by fundamental information processing limitations. Nevertheless, they strive for rationality within their cognitive limits. Undoubtedly, *Administrative Behavior*, the book in which this notion was introduced, made a seminal contribution that has shaped much of the recent theory and research on MOC. March and Simon's (1958) *Organisations* has also profoundly influenced the development of the MOC field, by drawing attention to the ways in which organisational routines free up attention that can be used to concentrate on non-routine events (see also Cyert and March, 1963). While the origins of the MOC field can be traced back to these earlier works, it is over the past 20 years or so that the analysis of cognition within the field of strategic management, and organisation studies more generally, has come of age.

Drawing on Simon's notion of bounded rationality, Hambrick and Mason (1984) developed a theoretical model of strategic choice, known as 'the upper echelons perspective'. According to Hambrick and Mason, it is the psychological and demographic characteristics of the 'dominant coalition', the group of powerful actors at the very top of the organisation, which ultimately determine its direction and outcomes. Hambrick and Mason posit a three-stage filtration process comprising: (1) a limited field of vision; (2) selective perception; and (3) interpretation, which they argue underpins the tendency for executives to perceive only a limited portion of all potentially relevant information in the internal and external environment, often deriving idiosyncratic interpretations of reality and assigning differential weights to the various potential outcomes.

The first stage of this filtration process, limited field of vision, arises from the fact that decision-makers are exposed to a limited subset of the available stimuli, while the second stage, selective perception, occurs due to the fact that they only actually attend to a portion of the stimulus information within their limited field of vision. The third stage, interpretation, entails the attachment of meaning to stimuli. Starbuck and Milliken (1988) employ the term 'sensemaking' to describe this stage (see also Weick, 1995).

As noted by Finkelstein and Hambrick (1996), much of the empirical work conducted on executive perception has focused on this third stage. As part of a wider programme of research into strategic issue diagnosis, Dutton and Jackson (Dutton and Jackson, 1987; Jackson and Dutton, 1988), for example, have analysed the processes by which managers categorise particular strategic issues as opportunities or threats (see also Dutton et al., 1989). This work has shown that managers are more sensitive to the issues they believe to be threatening than those perceived as opportunities. As another example of the work on sensemaking processes in organisations, Lant and her colleagues (1992) have studied the way in which managers explain poor performance records. This work has demonstrated that within turbulent environments, organisational actors are more likely to attribute past poor performance records to external factors, whereas in stable environments no such tendency is observed. On the basis of these findings, Lant and her colleagues concluded that such biased sensemaking leads ultimately to poor adaptation, not least because managers fail to learn from their experience, that is attributional biases prevent managers from learning about the impact of their behaviour on organisational outcomes.

Weick (1969, 1979) has provided another seminal contribution to this body of work, through his notions of 'enactment' and 'the enacted environment'. Many of the sequential information processing models advanced by cognitive psychologists imply that the environment is an objective entity, and that the reason subjective differences in perception occur is because the objective environment can only be partially comprehended due to limited processing capacity (i.e. 'bounded rationality'). Weick's work challenges this limited view of the environment (which he terms 'the perceived environment'), arguing that theories which stress the notion that reality is selectively perceived over-emphasise the object → subject relationship, at the expense of the idea that often the subject exerts considerable influence on the object:

> ... managers construct, rearrange, single out, and demolish many 'objective' features of their surroundings. When people act they un-randomise variables, insert vestiges of orderliness, and literally create their own constraints ...

> there is a reciprocal influence between subjects and objects, not a one-sided influence such as implied by the idea that a stimulus triggers a response. This reciprocal influence is captured in the organising model by the two-way influence between enactment and ecological change.
>
> (Weick, 1979, pp. 164–166)

By drawing attention to the fact that the environmental constraints and opportunities faced by organisations are actively constructed by the actions of particular individuals and groups, the notions of 'enactment' and 'the enacted environment' have laid an important conceptual foundation for better understanding the processes of sensemaking in organisations (Weick, 1995).

Having outlined the historical background to the development of the cognitive perspective on strategic management, and briefly introduced some of its key principles, concepts and frameworks, it is timely to consider the ways in which this approach is beginning to shed light on specific issues and problems within the wider strategy field.

Linking managerial and organisational cognition to strategic management

In many ways, the analysis of cognitive processes in strategic management is still in its infancy. Nevertheless, the rate and pace of its development over the past 15–20 years precludes a detailed treatment of the many and varied topics within the strategy field that are now being addressed from an MOC perspective. Here, it is only possible to provide a selective overview of several of the more prominent issues, theoretical concepts and empirical findings in strategic management that are currently capturing the attention of MOC researchers, in order to highlight some of the potential insights to be gained from the adoption of cognitive approaches more generally.

Heuristics and biases in strategic decision-making

The recent upsurge of interest in MOC has arisen from a fundamental conviction shared by a growing number of strategic management researchers and organisation theorists that, hitherto, too much emphasis has been placed on the largely unquestioned (although for notable exceptions see Chaffee, 1985; Johnson, 1987; Mintzberg, 1994; Mintzberg et al., 1998) assumption that managers control and define a strategy process that is an inherently rational phenomenon, that is managers will make the best possible decisions, on the basis of all available information, informed by dispassionate, objective analysis. Cognitively oriented theory and research in strategic management has directly challenged this fundamental assumption of rationality, on which many of the dominant theoretical perspectives within the strategy field – such as the design school (e.g. Christensen et al., 1982), the planning school (e.g. Ackoff, 1983; Ansoff, 1965; Steiner, 1969) and the positioning school (e.g. Porter, 1980, 1985) – are, to varying extents, implicitly or explicitly based. Backed by an impressive body of theory and research evidence from the cognitive psychology and behavioural decision-making literatures (e.g. Fischhoff, 1975; Fischhoff et al., 1977; Kahneman et al., 1982; Tversky and Kahneman, 1974), a number of cognitively oriented strategic management researchers (e.g. Das and Teng, 1999; Hodgkinson et al., 1999; Lant et al., 1992; Maule and Hodgkinson, 2002; Schwenk, 1995) have highlighted several key deficiencies in the way in which individuals process strategic information (and information in general) that render such a viewpoint untenable. These researchers have argued that strategic decision-makers employ various heuristics, or 'rules-of-thumb', which enable them to cope with a complex and uncertain business world by making a series of simplifying assumptions that reduce the burden of information processing that would otherwise ensue. While heuristics render the world manageable (by reducing the information processing requirements of the decision-maker), unfortunately, there are several deleterious consequences that may follow from the adoption of these procedures. A number of laboratory experiments have demonstrated that actors' cognitions and judgements may become biased as a result of adopting these heuristics, which in turn may lead to sub-optimal decision choices. Table 10.1 presents a selective summary of the some of the commonly identified heuristics and biases which Schwenk (1988) has argued are of key significance in the context of strategic decision-making.

Table 10.1 An evaluation of selected heuristics and biases in terms of their effects on strategic decision-making

Heuristic/bias	Effects
1. Availability	Judgements of the probability of easily recalled events are distorted
2. Selective perception	Expectations may bias observations of variables relevant to strategy
3. Illusory correlation	Encourages the belief that unrelated variables are correlated
4. Conservatism	Failure to sufficiently revise forecasts based on new information
5. Law of *small* numbers	Overestimation of the degree to which small samples are representative of populations
6. Regression bias	Failure to allow for regression to the mean
7. Wishful thinking	Probability of desired outcomes judged to be inappropriately high
8. Illusion of control	Overestimation of personal control over outcomes
9. Logical reconstruction	'Logical' reconstruction of events which cannot be accurately recalled
10. Hindsight bias	Overestimation of predictability of past events

Source: Adapted from C. R. Schwenk, 'The Cognitive Perspective on Strategic Decision Making', *Journal of Management Studies*, 25 (1988) 44. © Blackwell Publishers. Reproduced with kind permission of the publisher.

The work highlighted above (reviewed more extensively in Das and Teng, 1999; Hodgkinson, 2001; and Maule and Hodgkinson, 2002) suggests that many of the phenomena initially identified by behavioural decision researchers are highly applicable in the context of strategic decision-making. Recently, however, Gigerenzer and his colleagues (e.g. Gigerenzer et al., 1999) have questioned the extent to which mainstream behavioural decision research such as this is *ecologically valid*. They have argued that many of the experimental studies demonstrating the irrationality of human judgement are based on tasks involving probabilistic reasoning and other forms of abstract judgement that are far removed from the real-world environments to which humankind has readily adapted over many years. Based on a fundamentally different conception of bounded rationality, known as *ecological rationality* (Gigerenzer and Todd, 1999, p. 5), which emphasises the adaptive capacities of heuristic processing, they have identified a whole new class of heuristics that makes minimal computational demands on the decision-maker: *fast and frugal* heuristics. These heuristics do not involve probabilities and utilities and are deployed in situations that require individuals to draw inferences with limited time and knowledge. Breiman et al. (1993) have dramatically illustrated the potential power of fast and frugal heuristic processing to enhance decision-making in the field of medicine. This work has reduced the amount of information that needs to be processed to reach a sound clinical judgement in respect of potential heart attack cases from 19 separate cues to a simple three-stage decision tree, involving basic dichotomous (yes/no) questions in respect of: (1) minimum systolic blood pressure over the initial 24-hour period (>91?); (2) the age of the patient (>62.5?) and (3) whether or not sinus tachycardia is present. In the event that the patient's blood pressure is found to fall below 91, he/she is immediately classified as a high-risk case; otherwise, the clinician needs to move on to the second question. Should the answer to this second question prove negative, at that point, the patient is classified as a low-risk case; otherwise, an answer to the third question is required, the presence of sinus tachycardia being indicative of high risk.

The work of Gigerenzer and his colleagues is beginning to reshape the way in which behavioural decision researchers view bounded rationality, re-emphasising the 'up-side' of limited information search and informing the design of artificial systems to aid decision-making. It is still early days in the development of this new body of work; nevertheless, potentially, there is much to be gained by seeking to identify instances of such fast and frugal heuristics in the context of real-life organisational decision-making, with a view to enhancing the strategic choice process.

Understanding the external context: The role of cognition in environmental analysis

The notion that businesses should analyse their external environments if they are to compete effectively is a fundamental and familiar prescription in many of the standard texts on strategic management and marketing strategy (e.g. Abell, 1980; Grant, 1998; Hitt et al., 1996; Johnson et al., 2005; Oster, 1990; Piercy, 1992; Porter, 1980, 1985). The various frameworks and techniques that have been put forward to assist with this endeavour are predicated on the implicit assumption that business environments are objective entities waiting to be discovered through formal analysis. However, the notions of selective perception and the enacted environment challenge this basic premise. Perhaps this is best illustrated with reference to the enduring SWOT framework (Andrews, 1971), which recent survey evidence suggests is one of the most popular analytical tools employed in strategy workshops or 'away days' (Hodgkinson et al., 2005, 2006).

As we saw earlier, the way in which managers classify strategic issues into 'threats' and 'opportunities' entails a considerable degree of interpretation; this is essentially a sensemaking process in which meaning is actively assigned to ambiguous and uncertain stimuli, rather than an 'objective' analysis based on the 'facts' of the situation (Dutton and Jackson, 1987; Dutton et al., 1989; Jackson and Dutton, 1988). If we are to take the notions of selective perception, enactment and sensemaking seriously, the fundamental question that needs to be addressed when considering the results of any form of environmental analysis is: 'from whose perspective has the analysis been undertaken?' Different findings are likely to emerge depending on where particular actors are located within the wider social arena. Thus, for example, it is highly likely that a SWOT analysis undertaken by a CEO would yield rather different findings from a similar analysis undertaken by a maintenance engineer within the same firm (cf. Dearborn and Simon, 1958).

The role of cognition in shaping the external context: Mental models in the social construction of competitive industry structures

Much of the conventional literature on business competition has been dominated by attempts to refine techniques for the analysis of competitive structures in industries and markets, based on the notion of strategic groups (for a review see McGee and Thomas, 1986). The commonly accepted definition of the strategic groups concept is that provided by Porter:

> A strategic group is the group of firms in an industry following the same or a similar strategy along the strategic dimensions. An industry could have only one strategic group if all the firms followed essentially the same strategy. At the other extreme, each firm could be a different strategic group. Usually, however, there are a small number of strategic groups which capture the essential strategic differences among firms in the industry.
>
> (Porter, 1980, p. 129)

In recent years, there has been a growing recognition that this predominantly economic approach is limited fundamentally in terms of its ability to explain how or why competitive structures in industries and markets come to develop and on what basis particular strategies are chosen (e.g. Barney and Hoskisson, 1990; Pettigrew and Whipp, 1991). In response to these criticisms a growing number of theorists have developed 'social constructionist' accounts of the formation of strategic groups centring on the notion of 'competitive enactment' (for recent reviews see Hodgkinson, 2005; Hodgkinson and Sparrow, 2002). Drawing on the work of Berger and Luckmann (1967) and Weick (1979),

Porac and colleagues (e.g. Porac and Thomas, 1990; Porac et al., 1989) have argued that over time, within a given industry, individuals' beliefs about the identity of competitors, suppliers and customers become highly unified through mutual enactment processes, in which subjective interpretations of externally situated information are objectified via behaviour. In keeping with the notion of enactment in general, competitive enactment captures the continual objective → subjective → objective cycle underpinning the development of competitive structures. Viewed from this perspective, 'industries', and 'strategic groups' are socio-cognitive constructions, created through a shared interpretation of reality among business rivals, which come to define the boundaries of the competitive arena and on what bases the battles for competitive success are to be fought.

Porac et al. (1989) have demonstrated empirically the basic features of competitive enactment in a study of the Scottish knitwear industry (see also Porac et al., 1995). In this study the senior executives from a number of firms were interviewed in order to ascertain the structure and contents of their mental models of the competitive arena. While the combined efforts of Scottish knitwear producers account for a mere 3 per cent of the total amount of knitted outer-wear manufactured on a worldwide basis, when asked to define their competitors the research participants in this study tended to focus exclusively on other Scottish firms. Despite the fact that producers from Italy, the Far East, the United States and other parts of the United Kingdom far outstrip the Scots in total output, firms from these other geographical areas were not typically regarded as serious competitors.

Porac and his colleagues reasoned that the Scottish firms have came to regard one another as major competitors due to the existence of a strongly held collective mental model which has directed the managers' attention inward, towards firms highly similar to their own, that is other Scottish knitwear producers of high-quality, expensive cashmere sweaters in classic designs. In the words of Huff (1982) and Spender (1989), an 'industry recipe' developed, informing rivals on what bases they were to compete with one another. This group-level mental model had come to define the boundaries of the competitive arena and led individual firms to consider a relatively narrow range of strategic options and competitors. Only firms within the immediate locality of Scotland that produce a similar range of goods to one another and use similar technological processes of production and common channels of distribution were regarded as serious competitors. Porac and his colleagues employed the term 'cognitive oligopoly' to describe this state of affairs. The fact that the participants in this study only considered a subset of all competitors potentially available to pose a serious threat to their businesses is entirely in keeping with the notions of 'bounded rationality', 'limited field of vision' and 'selective perception' introduced earlier in this chapter and is borne out by a number of other studies that have investigated managers' mental models of competitive industry structures (e.g. Clark and Montgomery, 1999; de Chernatony et al., 1993; Gripsrud and Gronhaug, 1985; Johnson et al., 1998).

In the previous section on the role of cognition in 'understanding the external context' a theoretical argument was briefly outlined that implies that rather different findings are likely to emerge from an analysis of the competitive environment depending on where particular actors are located within the wider social arena. Following this line of reasoning, the seemingly high levels of cognitive convergence observed by Porac and his colleagues in the Scottish knitwear study, which concentrated on the views of a sole informant from each organisation that took part in the investigation (typically the CEO), might not have been so apparent if the range of participants had been expanded to include multiple representatives from each participating firm, drawn from a variety of functional backgrounds. For example, a group of senior managers located within the headquarters of a given firm might well have held different views to, say, a group of managers located in the sales field. In keeping with this logic, in recent years a growing number of studies adopting such multi-informant, multi-organisation research designs have found striking differences in cognitive maps of competitor definition within and between organisations in a given sector (e.g. Daniels et al., 1994; Hodgkinson and Johnson, 1994; Johnson et al., 1998). This has led some researchers (most notably Daniels et al., 1994) to challenge the cognitive foundations of strategic groups theory, as advanced by Porac and his colleagues. However, there are several methodological weaknesses associated with these studies that render premature such an interpretation at this stage (for details see Hodgkinson, 1997a, 2002, 2005). Moreover, as noted by Porac and Rosa (1996), the notion that competitive fields are socially constructed entities need not necessarily imply that actors' mental representations of competition should be identical in all respects. Indeed, more recent work (e.g. Daniels et al., 2002; Hodgkinson, 2005; Porac et al., 2002) has been more nuanced in its underlying theoretical foundations, based on a recognition that the extent to which and in what ways actors develop common conceptions of business rivalry is a function of a variety of influences, some internal and others external to the organisation.

The role of mental models in organisational decline: Cognitive inertia in strategic analysis and change

Business history is littered with organisations that have become extinct because they were unable to adapt successfully to major environmental shifts. Population ecology theorists such as Hannan and Freeman (1977, 1988) contend that inertial forces often prevent organisations from achieving such adaptation. In recent years a number of MOC researchers have argued that one possible source of such inflexibility is the 'cognitive inertia' often found among key individuals and groups in situations where there is clearly an urgent requirement for actors to radically alter their thinking and behaviour.

Earlier we drew attention to the fact that in an effort to reduce the amount of cognitive activity required, experience, captured in long-term memory, can be influential in determining an individual's responses to current situations or stimuli. Actions which worked in the past are routinely applied to the present, so as to free up mental capacity. While such top-down processing is ordinarily functional, an associated danger is that actors may become overly dependent on their extant mental models of their situations, to the extent that they fail to notice the requirement for change until the key environmental stimuli signalling this requirement have become so widespread, or significant in other ways, that their organisation's capacity for successful adaptation has been seriously undermined (see, e.g. Baden-Fuller and Stopford, 1992; Morecroft, 1994; Senge, 1990). A growing number of empirical studies lend support to this notion (e.g. Barr and Huff, 1997; Hodgkinson, 1997b, 2005; Reger and Palmer, 1996).

An investigation into the impact of environmental change on organisational performance by Barr et al. (1992) illustrates the importance of this stream of research. This study suggests that it is not the degree of attention to environmental changes per se that delineates the extent to which a firm is able to harness its adaptive capabilities and thereby survive the rigours of a turbulent environment. Drawing on documentary sources of evidence, these researchers examined the views of top managers of two US railroad companies (the C and NW and the Rock Island), both facing deregulation over an extended time period. This study revealed that the executives of both companies recognised the threats deregulation posed to their businesses (as evidenced by changes in their mental models), but only one of the organisations concerned was able to understand how to re-align its business strategy in order to respond effectively to these environmental changes. Not surprisingly, it was this organisation which ultimately survived over the longer term. Barr and her colleagues contend that although the mental models of the executives of both companies changed over time, ultimately only the C and NW, the organisation which survived over the longer term, exhibited a true learning process, in marked contrast to the Rock Island, the company which failed to survive. While the former remains viable to this day, the latter sought bankruptcy protection in the mid-1970s and was wound up accordingly.

Cognitive mapping for the analysis of organisational competences (resources/capabilities/skills/knowledge)

Eden and Ackermann (1998, 2000) use a cognitive mapping approach to help managers elicit the distinctive competences of organisations. Their work has focused on enhancing strategic thinking through the use of cognitive mapping techniques:

Our experience suggests that a necessary part of the journey of strategy making is for any management team in any type of organisation to jointly reflect upon the organisation's competencies which are distinctive. However, the crucial activity is to go on and discover the *patterns* of distinctive competencies so that *core* competencies can be identified.

(Eden and Ackermann, 1998, p. 102)

Bowman and Ambrosini (2002) employ cognitive mapping techniques to explore organisational-level tacit knowledge. Core competencies are context dependent and therefore need to be understood within a specific organisational situation. One of the advantages of using cognitive mapping techniques as a basis for exploring the nature of core competencies is that they 'impose structure on vague situations' (Weick and Bougon, 1986, p. 107). Another important dimension of the cognitive perspective and the mapping tools it has encouraged (see 'Tools and techniques') is that it has permitted the explicit linking of higher-level competencies to organisational action. In turn, this has allowed managers to bring greater clarity to bear on the way in which they identify and influence the critical competencies of the organisation.

Tools and techniques

How then can we facilitate individual and collective 'learning' so as to minimise the potentially catastrophic impact of cognitive bias and inertia? Ultimately what is required is the development of intervention techniques that will enable individuals and groups to explore the largely taken-for-granted assumptions that drive their day-to-day behaviour, in order that they are able to change and re-frame their mental representations in such a way that they not only register the nature and significance of new events or situations, but also are able to ensure that the strategic capabilities of the organisation are realigned accordingly. Here, the various mapping techniques that have been employed in order to shed light on the nature and significance of cognition in the strategy process may have an invaluable role to play. The application of these procedures as a practical means for facilitating strategic conversations may enable those charged with the responsibility for strategy-making and implementation to overcome their potential blind spots and ensure that they question the appropriateness of their organisation's modus operandi on a continuous basis.

In recent years a large number of cognitive mapping techniques and related procedures have been developed and used in an effort to further the theory and practice of strategic management. A detailed review of the available alternatives is beyond the scope of this chapter. Here, I can only provide a brief illustration of three of the more popular techniques available for use as research tools and bases of intervention, namely, causal mapping, repertory grids and scenarios. Comprehensive overviews of these and the many additional techniques currently available for mapping strategic thought are provided by Eden and Spender (1998), Fiol and Huff (1992), Hodgkinson and Sparrow (2002), Huff (1990), Huff and Jenkins (2002) and Walsh (1995).

Causal mapping techniques

Ranked among the most popular of cognitive mapping procedures, causal mapping techniques are designed to capture actors' causal belief systems. In their most basic form, cause maps are depicted graphically, using the medium of the influence diagram (Diffenbach, 1982), the pathways interconnecting the concepts contained in the diagram denoting patterns of causality within the reasoning of the participant(s) concerned. Causal mapping procedures have been employed fruitfully not only in order to investigate individual thinking (Cosette and Audet, 1992) but also in an effort to represent the collective logics of organisations and wider communities as a whole (Roberts, 1976).

Figure 10.1 shows an example of a cause map, taken from the Barr et al. (1992) study of US railroad companies outlined above. In this diagram, variables which are thought to be causally related

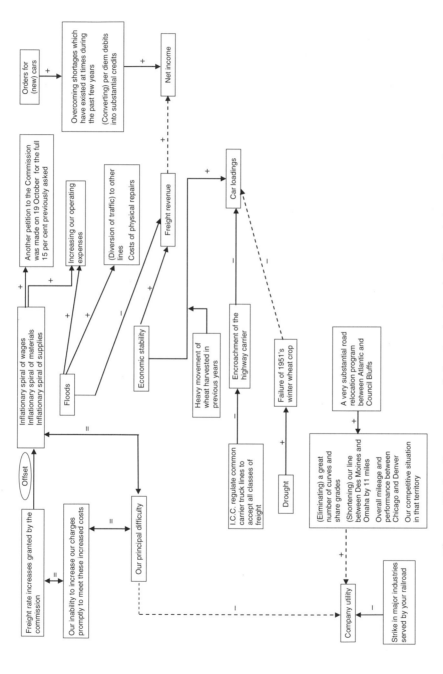

Figure 10.1 Cause map of the Rock Island Railroad Company in 1951

Source: Barr et al. (1992)

to one another directly and indirectly are connected by means of a series of lines which emanate from the independent variables and terminate on the dependent variables, the arrowheads depicting the directions of causality. Perceived positive causal relationships, in which increases in one variable are thought to cause an increase in one or more other variables, are depicted by means of plus signs which accompany the arrow-headed pathways linking the variables in question. Conversely, perceived negative causal relationships, in which increases in one variable are thought to cause decreases in one or more other variables, are depicted by means of arrow-headed pathways accompanied by minus signs.

Causal maps can be far more complex than that illustrated in Figure 10.1. Increasingly sophisticated variants of causal mapping procedures are available in which a range of different types of relationship between variables are evaluated, that is in addition to basic positive and negative causality. While relatively simple cause maps can be represented in diagrammatic form, as the number of variables and relationships contained within a map increases this greatly complicates our ability to capture adequately the information contained within a map. Fortunately, however, such maps are amenable to a variety of quantitative analyses, based on the mathematics of graph theory, and increasingly researchers are developing software which can be readily implemented in order to facilitate such analyses (e.g. Clarkson and Hodgkinson, 2005; Eden et al., 1992; Laukkenan, 1994; Markoczy and Goldberg, 1995). For further illustrations and a discussion of some of the methodological issues associated with the wider application of causal mapping techniques see Jenkins and Johnson (1997a,b), Jenkins (1998), Hodgkinson et al. (2004) and Hodgkinson and Clarkson (2005).

Increasingly, causal mapping procedures are being used as a basis for intervening in the strategy process. For example, as noted earlier, Eden and his colleagues have used this form of mapping as a basis for identifying organisational competencies (Eden and Ackermann, 1998, 2000) and Bowman and Ambrosini (2002) have used this approach as a basis for revealing tacit knowledge within organisations. Despite the growing popularity of these techniques in these and other practitioner contexts, there is virtually no evidence (other than basic anecdotal evidence) demonstrating that such applications actually improve the quality of strategic decision-making (for a notable exception in this regard see Hodgkinson et al., 1999; Hodgkinson and Maule, 2002).

Repertory grid techniques

Another set of techniques that has proven highly popular in the analysis of strategic thought is known as 'repertory grid'. These techniques originated in the field of clinical psychology, based on the notions of *personal construct theory* (Kelly, 1955). This theory asserts that individuals navigate their intra- and inter-personal worlds using a series of bipolar dimensions (termed 'personal constructs') which they employ in order to make sense of the stimuli (known as 'elements') which they variously encounter. According to this theory, individuals, by and large, construe their worlds differently from one another, hence the term 'personal construct theory'. Personal construct theory is based on the fundamental premise that individuals behave in a manner akin to natural scientists as they go about their everyday business, formulating hypotheses about their worlds, which they then seek to verify through observation. To the extent that their hypotheses are confirmed, individuals' personal construct systems are said to be validated. In the event that their hypotheses are falsified, however, ordinarily individuals will set about the task of revising their construct systems.

The primary strength of the repertory grid technique lies in its inherent flexibility, from the point of view of both data collection and analysis (see, e.g. Dunn and Ginsberg, 1986; Fransella and Bannister, 1977; Fransella et al., 2004; Ginsberg, 1989; Reger, 1990a,b; Slater, 1976, 1977; Smith and Stewart, 1977) and in recent years this approach has come to enjoy considerable success in applied studies of social cognition, in a wide variety of domains well beyond its clinical roots and ideographic origins (e.g. Forgas, 1976, 1978; Forgas et al., 1980; Smith and Gibson, 1988; Stewart et al., 1981).

In its original form, each participant is required to draw up a list of elements (e.g. alternative strategies for growing a business), which are used to elicit the constructs (e.g. the attributes differentiating the various growth strategies). The elements are randomised by the researcher and presented to the participant in triads. The participant is required to explain the ways in which any two of the three elements so presented are similar to one another but different from the third. This exercise is continued until it becomes evident that all possible constructs have been elicited. The constructs elicited in this way are used as a basis for forming a series of bipolar rating scales which the participant is required to use in order to evaluate each of the various elements in turn. The end result is an $n \times m$ matrix (or 'grid') for each participant that contains their complete set of evaluative judgements. These matrices form the basis for conducting subsequent statistical analyses (usually involving the application of one or more multivariate techniques) in order to represent the participants' cognitive maps of the phenomenon under investigation. Repertory grid techniques in a variety of forms have been employed successfully in a number of the studies of mental models of competitive industry structures and cognitive inertia reviewed earlier in this chapter (e.g. Daniels et al., 1994, 1995, 2002; Hodgkinson, 1997b, 2005; Reger and Palmer, 1996; see also Reger, 1990a; Reger and Huff, 1993).

Scenarios

One technique in particular that has been popularised in the practitioner-oriented literature as a means for overcoming the potentially deleterious consequences of cognitive bias and cognitive inertia is the method of scenario planning (e.g. Mobasheri et al., 1989; Shoemaker, 1995; Wack, 1985a,b). In contrast to traditional strategic planning techniques, which seek to forecast the future in probabilistic terms in an attempt to plan for a predetermined future, scenario planning techniques seek to develop a series of stylised portraits of the future, which capture what may or may not happen, thereby providing a basis for developing a strategy for dealing with the various contingencies so identified, thus directly incorporating uncertainty in the analysis (van der Heijden, 1994). According to van der Heijden (1996, p. 41) the benefits stemming from the application of a scenario planning approach are twofold:

- In the longer term development of a more robust organisational system, better able to withstand the unexpected shocks that will come its way.
- In the shorter term increased adaptability by more skilful observation of the business environment.

Eden and colleagues (e.g. Eden and Ackermann, 1998; Eden and Radford, 1990; van der Heijden, 1996) have developed a variety of cognitive mapping approaches that can be readily incorporated within the scenario planning process. Building on the technique of causal mapping, outlined above, Eden and his colleagues have devised a range of procedures for eliciting in systematic and structured ways managers' views of the future which can be developed into graphical representations using specialist support software. The object of such an exercise is to help individuals and teams to share and reconcile multiple ideas about the future environment. Whilst scenario planning appears to have high face validity as a means for overcoming cognitive bias and cognitive inertia, as with the related causal mapping procedures which are increasingly being used as a key element within the scenario process, thus far very little supporting evidence has accumulated, other than basic anecdotal evidence, for its efficacy (though for a notable exception in this respect see Shoemaker, 1993.)

One of the main drawbacks of cognitive mapping and scenario planning procedures in general is that they rely on what individuals or groups are prepared to say. The assumption that these tools and techniques adequately capture, let alone enrich, the strategic thoughts of individuals or groups (cf. van der Heijden et al., 2002) is highly questionable. As recently documented by Hodgkinson and Wright (2002) for a variety of reasons participants may be unwilling, or unable, to confront the future in the manner that scenario techniques require (Hodgkinson and Wright, 2006). Moreover, it is not always possible to identify viable alternatives to the extant strategy, even in situations where strategic change is clearly warranted. At the time of writing this chapter, work is ongoing to identify potential processes and mechanisms that might stimulate appropriate changes in participants' mental models of the strategic situations confronting their organisations (Chattopadhyay et al., 2006) and the organisational contexts which are more or less conducive for the successful application of scenario-based techniques (Healey and Hodgkinson, 2005). In the meantime would-be users of these tools and techniques for intervention purposes should proceed with due caution.

Case study revisited

Before concluding this chapter, it is instructive to return briefly to the series of questions posed earlier in connection with the case conversation with the owner-manager of the small jewellery business. One way of approaching the issues raised by these questions is to analyse the text of the conversation (previously reported in 'Case study 10.1'), using one or more cognitive mapping procedures. Figure 10.2 presents a representation of this conversation, based on the technique of causal mapping.

■ What are the key elements (variables and concepts) that inform the owner-manager's view of his business strategy and how are these inter-connected within his reasoning?

It can be seen from Figure 10.2 that the owner-manager's view of his business strategy is centred on the manufacture of bespoke jewellery. As such, this business is vertically integrated and the fact that all the pieces they make are both designed and manufactured by them creates a niche strategy which focuses on offering differentiated products for significant occasions such as weddings:

It's really on the special pieces and the commissioned pieces that we can actually get most of our enjoyment, because that's where you get the real positive feedback from customers and that's where we pick up most of our profit.

From a cognitive point of view this statement makes a set of causal connections which seem to summarise the basis of the business. The concept 'commissioned jewellery' is central to the strategic

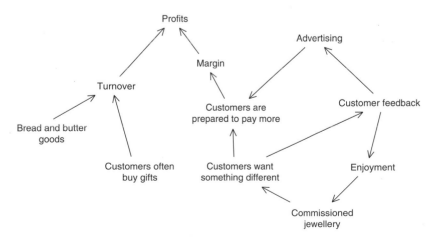

Figure 10.2 Cause map representing the strategic conversation with the owner-manager of a jeweller's shop

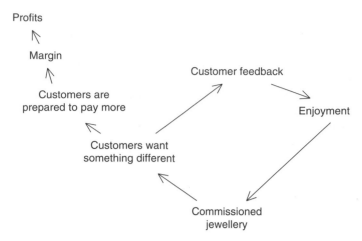

Figure 10.3 Section of causal map revealing the fundamental basis of the owner-manager's business strategy

vision of the owner-manager because it is central to the identity of his business (as a niche player) and ultimately creates the marginal revenue from which the company derives its profits. This becomes clearer when we edit the cause map in order to remove the less central elements (Figure 10.3).

■ Which organisations would the owner-manager regard as the major competitors to his business and for what reasons?

While at one level the owner-manager is acknowledging competition in terms of the jewellers 'down the road', the implication seems to be that because they make their own jewellery they have no direct competition for this part of the business. Although no competitors are actually named as such, it is evident that other niche players specialising in the design and manufacture of commissioned jewellery constitute the greatest competitive threat. This can be inferred from the fact that the concept 'commissioned jewellery' is the key source of revenue and central to the market identity of the organisation, as viewed from the perspective of the owner-manager.

■ To what extent are there significant threats and opportunities which may go unnoticed but which nevertheless may have a major bearing on the longer-term well-being of his organisation?

The most likely threats to this company's strategy would come in the form of competition or substitution. For example, the jeweller does not seem to consider the fact that other jewellers may offer this service as a possibility. Presumably, he employs skilled staff who could either move to other jewellers or set up on their own. Another possibility is that the jewellery craftsman may offer a similar service to a range of retail outlets, both large and small. The threat of substitution will vary according to the buying situation; for weddings this is probably low, but for gifts, new technologies and social trends may move the emphasis away from the value of jewellery.

■ What are the fundamental assumptions underpinning his responses to the above questions and to what extent are these assumptions reasonable?

An examination of the conversation reveals that a number of assumptions are inherent within this strategy, ones that may or may not be explicitly recognised by the owner-manager. One of the strengths of the cognitive perspective on strategic management is that it helps reveal such assumptions and addresses the implications they raised for strategy-development. Some of the main assumptions underpinning the owner-manager's strategy relate to the nature and characteristics of buyers:

> This is because people are often buying gifts, so they often want something that is unique, and they're prepared to pay a bit more for that . . . . Our products aren't particularly price sensitive, because there isn't the direct competition.

These statements reveal several highly questionable assumptions concerning: (1) the regular availability of demand; (2) the desirability of being 'different'; (3) the price insensitivity of buyers and (4) a lack of competition.

It is clear from this brief illustration that the cognitive perspective in general, and the technique of causal mapping in particular, provides a potentially effective method for identifying the core assumptions of the owner-manager that underpin his strategy for the business. The above analysis has revealed a number of limitations in his thinking, which, left unchecked, must surely threaten the longer-term viability of this venture.

Summary

The cognitive perspective on strategic management highlights a number of potential weaknesses in the way in which individuals and groups handle information, weaknesses that can and frequently do undermine the strategy process. In drawing attention to these potential dangers, I do not wish to imply that selective attention and limited information search are invariably dysfunctional. In the absence of such filtering strategies, decision-makers would be greatly overwhelmed by the sheer complexity of the world. Indeed, there is evidence to suggest that strategies which are simple, coherent and easily understood may lead to better performance than those which are sophisticated and highly complex (Pettigrew and Whipp, 1991). A simplified view of the world can help unite organisation members, undoubtedly a key factor in successful strategy implementation. This discussion highlights a fundamental tension within the strategy process: increasingly, actors must not only be open enough to consider new and innovative ideas and approaches, but also be single-minded enough to provide the commitment and focus needed to implement such ideas.

The adoption of a cognitive perspective on strategic management shifts the focus of analysis away from the objective characteristics of firms, industries and markets to consider the subjective and inter-subjective worlds of individuals and groups. In so doing, the cognitive perspective challenges two of the core assumptions of neo-classical economics, namely, that all firms have equal access to information about the marketplace and that they will invariably respond to such information in similar ways. It is clear that the core assumption that business environments are objective entities waiting to be discovered through the application of analytical procedures and techniques, implicit within much of the mainstream literature on competitive strategy and strategic planning, does not stand up to theoretical and empirical scrutiny.

Further reading

Like many of the perspectives underpinning the field of strategic management, there are a number of distinctive interpretations of the MOC field. Unfortunately, there are relatively few overviews of the field as a whole. A notable exception, however, is the *Organization Science* article by Walsh (1995): 'Managerial and Organizational Cognition: Notes from a Trip Down Memory Lane'.

Possibly one of the most comprehensive surveys of the MOC field as it relates specifically to strategic management, encompassing the very latest theory, methods and research findings connected to the themes introduced in the present chapter, is to be found in Hodgkinson and Sparrow's (2002) book: *The Competent Organization: A Psychological Analysis of the Strategic Management Process*. The core thesis advanced in this book is that the many changes currently confronting organisations are placing unprecedented informational burdens upon those responsible for strategy formulation and implementation and that cognitive competence is thus becoming increasingly central to the adaptive capabilities of the organisation. Strategic competence, as viewed from this perspective, implies that organisations need to be able to acquire, store, recall, interpret and act upon information with sufficient alacrity to be able to adjust to rapidly shifting environmental contingencies. A welter of theory and evidence from a wide range of scholarly sources is surveyed, both in order to advance the basic thesis and in order to identify a number of promising future research directions. The strengths and limitations of a number of cognitive mapping techniques are also explored in considerable depth.

Although now more than 15 years old, Huff's (1990) volume, *Mapping Strategic Thought*, an edited collection of specially commissioned chapters with accompanying commentaries, provides another useful basis for considering some of the empirical research which has been undertaken within the strategy field from a cognitive perspective. It also continues to be an invaluable guide to management researchers as the second part of the book provides useful step-by-step introductions to a wide variety of alternative cognitive mapping procedures. The themes in this book have been taken up and combined with a more specific focus on mapping approaches and their use in strategy in the book *Mapping Strategic Knowledge* by Huff and Jenkins (2002). The book edited by Eden and Spender (1998), *Managerial and Organizational Cognition: Theory, Methods and Research*, in many ways serves as another useful update to the earlier Huff (1990) volume.

References

Abell, D. F., *Defining the Business: The Starting Point of Strategic Planning* (Englewood Cliffs, NJ: Prentice Hall, 1980).

Ackoff, R. L., 'Beyond Prediction and Preparation', *Journal of Management Studies*, 20 (1983) 59–69.

Anderson, J. R., *Cognitive Psychology and its Implications*, 3rd edn (New York: Freeman, 1990).

Andrews, K. R., *The Concept of Corporate Strategy* (Homewood, IL: Irwin, 1971).

Ansoff, H. I., *Corporate Strategy* (New York: McGraw-Hill, 1965).

Baden-Fuller, C. and J. M. Stopford, *Rejuvenating the Mature Business* (London: Routledge, 1992).

Barnard, C. I., *The Functions of the Executive* (Cambridge, MA: Harvard University Press, 1938).

Barney, J. B. and R. E. Hoskisson, 'Strategic Groups: Untested Assertions and Research Proposals', *Managerial and Decision Economics*, 11 (1990) 187–198.

Barr, P. R. and A. S. Huff, 'Seeing Isn't Believing: Understanding Diversity in the Timing of Strategic Response', *Journal of Management Studies*, 34 (1997) 337–370.

Barr, P. S., J. L. Stimpert and A. S. Huff, 'Cognitive Change, Strategic Action, and Organizational Renewal', *Strategic Management Journal*, 13, Summer Special Issue (1992) 15–36.

Bartlett, F. C., *Remembering: A Study in Experimental and Social Psychology* (London: Cambridge University Press, 1932).

Berger, P. L. and T. Luckmann, *The Social Construction of Reality* (Harmondsworth: Penguin, 1967).

Bowman, C. and V. Ambrosini, 'Mapping Successful Organizational Routines', in A. S. Huff and M. Jenkins (eds) *Mapping Strategic Knowledge* (London: Sage, 2002), pp. 19–45.

Breiman, L., J. H. Friedman, R. A. Oshen and C. J. Stone, *Classification and Regression Trees* (New York: Chapman and Hall, 1993).

Broadbent, D. E., *Perception and Communication* (London: Pergamon Press, 1958).

Chaffee, E. E., 'Three Models of Strategy', *Academy of Management Review*, 10 (1985) 89–98.

Chattopadhyay, P., G. P. Hodgkinson and M. Healey, 'Of Maps and Managers: Toward a Cognitive Theory of Strategic Intervention', in K. M. Weaver (ed.) *Academy of Management Best Paper Proceedings* (2006).

Christensen, C. R., K. R. Andrews, J. L. Bower, G. Hamermesh and M. E. Porter, *Business Policy: Text and Cases*, 5th edn (Homewood, IL: Irwin, 1982).

Clark, B. H. and D. B. Montgomery, 'Managerial Identification of Competitors', *Journal of Marketing*, 63 (1999) 67–83.

Clarkson, G. P. and G. P. Hodgkinson, 'Introducing CognizerTM: A Comprehensive Computer Package for the Elicitation and Analysis of Cause Maps', *Organizational Research Methods*, 8 (2005) 317–341.

Cosette, P. and M. Audet, 'Mapping of an Idiosyncratic Schema', *Journal of Management Studies*, 29 (1992) 309–348.

Craik, K., *The Nature of Explanation* (Cambridge: Cambridge University Press, 1943).

Cyert, R. M. and J. G. March, *A Behavioral Theory of the Firm* (Englewood Cliffs, NJ: Prentice Hall, 1963).

Daniels, K., G. Johnson and L. de Chernatony, 'Differences in Managerial Cognitions of Competition', *British Journal of Management*, 5, Special Issue (1994) S21–S29.

Daniels, K., L. de Chernatony and G. Johnson, 'Validating a Method for Mapping Managers' Mental Models of Competitive Industry Structures', *Human Relations*, 48 (1995) 975–991.

Daniels, K., G. Johnson and L. de Chernatony, 'Task and Institutional Influences on Managers' Mental Models of Competition', *Organization Studies*, 23 (2002) 31–62.

Das, T. K. and B.-S. Teng, 'Cognitive Biases and Strategic Decision Processes', *Journal of Management Studies*, 36 (1999) 757–778.

Dearborn, D. C. and H. A. Simon, 'Selective Perception: A Note on the Departmental Identification of Executives', *Sociometry*, 21 (1958) 140–144.

de Chernatony, L., K. Daniels and G. Johnson, 'A Cognitive Perspective on Managers' Perceptions of Competitors', *Journal of Marketing Management*, 9 (1993) 373–381.

Diffenbach, J., 'Influence Diagrams for Complex Strategic Issues', *Strategic Management Journal*, 3 (1982) 133–146.

Dunn, W. N. and A. Ginsberg, 'A Sociocognitive Network Approach to Organizational Analysis', *Human Relations*, 40 (1986) 955–976.

Dutton, J. and S. Jackson, 'Categorizing Strategic Issues: Links to Organizational Action', *Academy of Management Review*, 12 (1987) 76–90.

Dutton, J., E. J. Walton and E. Abrahamson, 'Important Dimensions of Strategic Issues: Separating the Wheat from the Chaff', *Journal of Management Studies*, 26 (1989) 379–396.

Eden, C. and F. Ackermann, *Making Strategy: The Journey of Strategic Management* (London: Sage, 1998).

Eden, C. and F. Ackermann, 'Mapping Distinctive Competencies: A Systematic Approach', *Journal of the Operational Research Society*, 51 (2000) 12–20.

Eden, C. and J. Radford, *Tackling Strategic Problems: The Role of Group Decision Support* (London: Sage, 1990).

Eden, C. and J.-C. Spender (eds) *Managerial and Organizational Cognition: Theory, Methods and Research* (London: Sage, 1998).

Eden, C., F. Ackermann and S. Cropper, 'The Analysis of Cause Maps', *Journal of Management Studies*, 29 (1992) 309–324.

Eysenck, M. W. and M. T. Keane, *Cognitive Psychology: A Student's Handbook*, 3rd edn (Hove: Psychology Press, 1995).

Finkelstein, S. and D. C. Hambrick, *Strategic Leadership: Top Executives and Their Effects on Organizations* (St Paul, MN: West, 1996).

Fiol, C. M. and A. S. Huff, 'Maps for Managers. Where Are We? Where Do We Go From Here?', *Journal of Management Studies*, 29 (1992) 267–285.

Fischhoff, B., 'Hindsight and Foresight: The Effect of Outcome Knowledge on Judgment under Uncertainty', *Journal of Experimental Psychology: Human Perception and Performance*, 1 (1975) 288–299.

Fischhoff, B., P. Slovic and S. Lichtenstein, 'Knowing with Certainty: The Appropriateness of Extreme Confidence', *Journal of Experimental Psychology: Human Perception and Performance*, 3 (1977) 552–564.

Forgas, J. P., 'The Perception of Social Episodes: Categorical and Dimensional Representation in Two Subcultural Millieus', *Journal of Personality and Social Psychology*, 34 (1976) 199–209.

Forgas, J. P., 'Social Episodes and Social Structure in an Academic Setting: The Social Environment of an Intact Group', *Journal of Experimental Social Psychology*, 14 (1978) 434–448.

Forgas, J. P., L. B. Brown and J. Menyhart, 'Dimensions of Aggression: The Perception of Aggressive Episodes', *British Journal of Social and Clinical Psychology*, 19 (1980) 215–227.

Foxall, G., 'The Explanation of Consumer Behaviour: From Social Cognition to Environmental Control', in C. L. Cooper and I. T. Robertson (eds) *International Review of Industrial and Organizational Psychology*, 12 (1997), pp. 229–287.

Fransella, F. and D. Bannister, *A Manual for Repertory Grid Technique* (New York: Academic Press, 1977).

Fransella, F., R. Bell and D. Bannister, *A Manual for Repertory Grid Technique*, 2nd edn (Chichester: Wiley, 2004).

Gigerenzer, G. and P. M. Todd, 'Fast and Frugal Heuristics: The Adaptive Toolbox', in G. Gigerenzer, P. M. Todd and the ABC Research Group (eds) *Simple Heuristics that Make Us Smart* (New York: Oxford University Press, 1999).

Gigerenzer, G., P. N. Todd and the ABC Research Group (eds) *Simple Heuristics that Make Us Smart* (New York: Oxford University Press, 1999).

Ginsberg, A., 'Construing the Business Portfolio: A Cognitive Model of Diversification', *Journal of Management Studies*, 26 (1989) 417–438.

Grant, R. M., *Contemporary Strategy Analysis*, 3rd edn (Oxford: Blackwell, 1998).

Gripsrud, G. and K. Gronhaug, 'Structure and Strategy in Grocery Retailing: A Sociometric Approach', *Journal of Industrial Economics*, XXXIII (1985) 339–347.

Hambrick, D. C. and P. A. Mason, 'Upper Echelons: The Organization as a Reflection of Its Top Managers', *Academy of Management Review*, 9 (1984) 193–206.

Hannan, M. and J. Freeman, 'The Population Ecology of Organizations', *American Journal of Sociology*, 82 (1977) 929–964.

Hannan, M. and J. Freeman, *Organizational Ecology* (Cambridge, MA: Harvard University Press, 1988).

Healey, M. and G. P. Hodgkinson, 'Exploring the Dynamics and Effectiveness of Scenario Planning Workshops: Evidence from a Critical Incident Study', Paper presented in a Strategy as Practice Symposium entitled: 'Research On Strategy Workshops (Strategy Away-Days)', at the *Annual Conference of the British Academy of Management* (University of Oxford, Said Business School, September 2005).

Hitt, M. A., R. D. Ireland and R. E. Hoskisson, *Strategic Management: Competitiveness and Globalization*, 2nd edn (St Paul, MN: West, 1996).

Hodgkinson, G. P., 'The Cognitive Analysis of Competitive Structures: A Review and Critique', *Human Relations*, 50 (1997a) 625–654.

Hodgkinson, G. P., 'Cognitive Inertia in a Turbulent Market: The Case of UK Residential Estate Agents', *Journal of Management Studies*, 34 (1997b) 921–945.

Hodgkinson, G. P., 'Cognitive Processes in Strategic Management: Some Emerging Trends and Future Directions', in N. Anderson, D. S. Ones, H. K. Sinangil and C. Viswesvaran (eds) *Handbook of Industrial, Work and Organizational Psychology: Volume 2 – Organizational Psychology* (London: Sage, 2001), pp. 416–440.

Hodgkinson, G. P., 'Comparing Managers' Mental Models of Competition: Why Self-Report Measures of Belief Similarity Won't Do', *Organization Studies*, 23 (2002) 63–72.

Hodgkinson, G. P., *Images of Competitive Space: A Study of Managerial and Organizational Strategic Cognition* (Basingstoke, UK: Palgrave Macmillan, 2005).

Hodgkinson, G. P. and G. P. Clarkson, 'What Have We Learned from Almost Thirty Years of Research on Causal Mapping? Methodological Lessons and Choices for the Information Systems and Information Technology Communities', in V. K. Narayanan and D. J. Armstrong (eds) *Causal Mapping for Research in Information Technology* (Hershey, PA: Idea Group, 2005), pp. 46–79.

Hodgkinson, G. P. and G. Johnson, 'Exploring the Mental Models of Competitive Strategists: The Case for a Processual Approach', *Journal of Management Studies*, 31 (1994) 525–551.

Hodgkinson, G. P. and A. J. Maule, 'The Individual in the Strategy Process: Insights from Behavioural Decision Research and Cognitive Mapping', in A. S. Huff and M. Jenkins (eds) *Mapping Strategic Knowledge* (London: Sage, 2002), pp. 196–219.

Hodgkinson, G. P. and P. R. Sparrow, *The Competent Organization: A Psychological Analysis of the Strategic Management Process* (Buckingham: Open University Press, 2002).

Hodgkinson, G. P. and G. Wright, 'Confronting Strategic Inertia in a Top Management Team: Learning from Failure', *Organization Studies*, 23 (2002) 949–977.

Hodgkinson, G. P., N. J. Bown, A. J. Maule, K. W. Glaister and A. D. Pearman, 'Breaking the Frame: An Analysis of Strategic Cognition and Decision Making under Uncertainty', *Strategic Management Journal*, 20 (1999) 977–985.

Hodgkinson, G. P., A. J. Maule and N. J. Bown, 'Causal Cognitive Mapping in the Organizational Strategy Field: A Comparison of Alternative Elicitation Procedures', *Organizational Research Methods*, 7 (2004) 3–26.

Hodgkinson, G. P., G. Johnson, R. Whittington and M. Schwarz, *The Role and Importance of Strategy Workshops: Findings of a UK Survey* (London: ESRC/EPSRC (UK) Advanced Institute of Management Research (AIM) and the Chartered Management Institute (CMI), 2005).

Hodgkinson, G. P., R. Whittington, G. Johnson and M. Schwarz, 'The Role of Strategy Workshops in Strategy Development Processes: Formality, Communication, Coordination and Inclusion', *Long Range Planning*, 39 (2006) 479–496.

Hodgkinson, G. P., and G. Wright, 'Neither completing the Practice Turn, Nor Enriching the Process Tradition: Secondary Misinterpretations of a Case Analysis Reconsidered', *Organization Studies*, 27 (2006) 1895–1901.

Hofer, C. W. and D. Schendel, *Strategy Formulation: Analytical Concepts* (St Paul, MN: West, 1978).

Huff, A. S., 'Industry Influences on Strategy Formation', *Strategic Management Journal*, 3 (1982) 119–131.

Huff, A. S. (ed.), *Mapping Strategic Thought* (Chichester: John Wiley, 1990).

Huff, A. S. and M. Jenkins (eds), *Mapping Strategic Knowledge* (London: Sage, 2002).

Jackson, S. E. and J. E. Dutton, 'Discerning Threats and Opportunities', *Administrative Science Quarterly*, 33 (1988) 370–387.

Jenkins, M., 'The Theory and Practice of Comparing Causal Maps', in C. Eden and J. C. Spender (eds) *Managerial and Organizational Cognition* (London: Sage, 1998), pp. 231–249.

Jenkins, M. and G. Johnson, 'Linking Managerial Cognition and Organizational Performance: A Preliminary Investigation Using Causal Maps', *British Journal of Management*, 8, Special Issue (1997a) S77–S90.

Jenkins, M. and G. Johnson, 'Entrepreneurial Intentions and Outcomes: A Comparative Causal Mapping Study', *Journal of Management Studies*, 34 (1997b) 895–920.

Johnson, G., *Strategic Change and the Management Process* (Oxford: Basil Blackwell, 1987).

Johnson, P., K. Daniels and R. Asch, 'Mental Models of Competition', in C. Eden and J. C. Spender (eds) *Managerial and Organizational Cognition* (London: Sage, 1998), pp. 130–146.

Johnson, G., K. Scholes and R. Whittington, *Exploring Corporate Strategy: Text and Cases*, 7th edn (London: FT Prentice Hall, 2005).

Johnson-Laird, P. N., *Mental Models* (Cambridge: Cambridge University Press, 1983).

Johnson-Laird, P. N., *The Computer and the Mind*, 2nd edn (London: Fontana, 1993).

Kahneman, D., P. Slovic and A. Tversky (eds) *Judgment under Uncertainty: Heuristics and Biases* (Cambridge: Cambridge University Press, 1982).

Kelly, G. A., *The Psychology of Personal Constructs* (in 2 volumes) (New York: Norton, 1955).

Lant, T. K., F. J. Milliken and B. Batra, 'The Role of Managerial Learning and Interpretation in Strategic Persistence and Reorientation: An Empirical Exploration', *Strategic Management Journal*, 13 (1992) 585–608.

Laukkenan, M., 'Comparative Cause Mapping of Organizational Cognitions', *Organization Science*, 5 (1994) 322–343.

March, J. G. and H. A. Simon, *Organizations* (New York: John Wiley, 1958).

Markoczy, L. and J. Goldberg, 'A Method for Eliciting and Comparing Causal Maps', *Journal of Management*, 21 (1995) 305–333.

Maule, A. J. and G. P. Hodgkinson, 'Heuristics, Biases and Strategic Decision Making', *The Psychologist*, 15 (2002) 68–71.

McGee, J. and H. Thomas, 'Strategic Groups: Theory, Research and Taxonomy', *Strategic Management Journal*, 7 (1986) 141–160.

Mintzberg, H., *The Rise and Fall of Strategic Planning* (London: Prentice Hall, 1994).

Mintzberg, H., B. Ahlstrand and J. Lampel, *Strategy Safari: A Guided Tour Through the Wilds of Strategic Management* (London: Prentice Hall Europe, 1998).

Mobasheri, F., L. H. Orren and F. P. Sioshansi, 'Scenario Planning at Southern California Edison', *Interfaces*, 19, 5 (1989) 31–44.

Morecroft, J. D. W. 'Executive Knowledge, Models and Learning', in J. D. W. Morecroft and John D. Sterman (eds) *Modelling for Learning Organizations* (Portland, OR: Productivity Press, 1994).

Mowrer, O. H., 'On the Dual Nature of Learning: A Reinterpretation of "Conditioning" and "Problem Solving" ', *Harvard Educational Review*, 17 (1947) 102–148.

Oster, S., *Modern Competitive Analysis* (Oxford: Oxford University Press, 1990).

Pettigrew, A. M. and R. Whipp, *Managing Change for Competitive Success* (Oxford: Blackwell, 1991).

Piercy, N., *Market-Led Strategic Change* (Oxford: Butterworth-Heinemann, 1992).

Porac, J. F. and A. Rosa, 'Rivalry, Industry Models, and the Cognitive Embeddedness of the Comparable Firm', *Advances in Strategic Management*, 13 (1996) 363–388.

Porac, J. F. and H. Thomas, 'Taxonomic Mental Models in Competitor Definition', *Academy of Management Review*, 15 (1990) 224–240.

Porac, J. F., H. Thomas and C. Baden-Fuller, 'Competitive Groups as Cognitive Communities: The Case of Scottish Knitwear Manufacturers', *Journal of Management Studies*, 26 (1989) 397–416.

Porac, J. F., H. Thomas, F. Wilson, D. Paton and A. Kanfer, 'Rivalry and the Industry Model of Scottish Knitwear Producers', *Administrative Science Quarterly*, 40 (1995) 203–227.

Porac, J. F., M. J. Ventresca and Y. Mishina, 'Interorganizational Cognition and Interpretation', in J. A. C. Baum (ed.) *The Blackwell Companion to Organizations* (Oxford: Blackwell, 2002), pp. 579–598.

Porter, M. E., *Competitive Strategy: Techniques for Analyzing Industries and Competitors* (New York: Free Press, 1980).

Porter, M. R., *Competitive Advantage: Creating and Sustaining Superior Performance* (New York: Free Press, 1985).

Reger, R. K., 'Managerial Thought Structures and Competitive Positioning', in Huff, A. S. (ed.) *Mapping Strategic Thought* (Chichester: John Wiley and Sons, 1990a), pp. 71–88.

Reger, R. K., 'The Repertory Grid for Eliciting the Content and Structure of Cognitive Constructive Systems', in Huff, A. S. (ed.) *Mapping Strategic Thought* (Chichester: John Wiley and Sons, 1990b), pp. 301–309.

Reger, R. K. and A. S. Huff, 'Strategic Groups: A Cognitive Perspective', *Strategic Management Journal*, 14 (1993) 103–124.

Reger, R. K. and T. B. Palmer, 'Managerial Categorization of Competitors: Using Old Maps to Navigate New Environments', *Organization Science*, 7 (1996) 22–39.

Roberts, F. S., 'Strategy for the Energy Crisis: The Case of Commuter Transport Policy', in R. Axelrod (ed.) *The Structure of Decision: Cognitive Maps of Political Elites* (Princeton NJ: University Press, 1976), pp. 142–179.

Schwenk, C. R., 'The Cognitive Perspective on Strategic Decision Making', *Journal of Management Studies*, 25 (1988) 41–55.

Schwenk, C. R., 'Strategic Decision Making', *Journal of Management*, 21 (1995) 471–493.

Senge, P., *The Fifth Discipline: The Art and Practice of the Learning Organization* (London: Century Business, 1990).

Shoemaker, P. J. H., 'Multiple Scenario Development: Its Conceptual and Behavioral Foundation', *Strategic Management Journal*, 14 (1993) 193–213.

Shoemaker, P. J. H., 'Scenario Planning: A Tool for Strategic Thinking', *Sloan Management Review*, 36, 2 (1995) 25–40.

Simon, H. A., *Administrative Behavior* (New York: Macmillan, 1947).

Skinner, B. F., *The Behavior of Organisms* (New York: Appleton-Century-Crofts, 1938).

Slater, P. (ed.), *The Measurement of Intrapersonal Space by Grid Technique: Vol. I – Explorations of Intrapersonal Space* (Chichester: John Wiley and Sons, 1976).

Slater, P. (ed.), *The Measurement of Intrapersonal Space by Grid Technique: Vol. II – Dimensions of Intrapersonal Space* (Chichester: John Wiley and Sons, 1977).

Smith, M. and J. Gibson, 'Using Repertory Grids to Investigate Racial Prejudice', *Applied Psychology: An International Review*, 37 (1988) 311–326.

Smith, M. and B. J. M. Stewart, 'Repertory Grids: A Flexible Tool for Establishing the Contents and Structure of a Manager's Thoughts', in D. Ashton (ed.) *Management Bibliographies and Reviews*, 3 (1977), pp. 209–229.

Spender, J.-C., *Industry Recipes: The Nature and Sources of Management Judgement* (Oxford: Basil Blackwell, 1989).

Starbuck, W. H. and F. J. Milliken, 'Executives' Perceptual Filters: What They Notice and How They Make Sense', in D. C. Hambrick (ed.) *The Executive Effect: Concepts and Methods for Studying Top Managers* (Greenwich, CT: JAI, 1988), pp. 35–65.

Steiner, G. A., *Top Management Planning* (New York: Macmillan, 1969).

Stewart, V., A. Stewart and N. Fonda, *The Business Application of Repertory Grids* (London: McGraw-Hill, 1981).

Stubbart, C. I., 'Managerial Cognition: A Missing Link in Strategic Management Research', *Journal of Management Studies*, 26 (1989) 325–347.

Tolman, E. C., *Purposive Behaviour in Animals and Men* (New York: Century, 1932).

Tversky, A. and D. Kahneman, 'Judgment under Uncertainty: Heuristics and Biases', *Science*, 198 (1974) 1124–1131.

van der Heijden, K., 'Probabilistic Planning and Scenario Planning', in G. Wright and P. Ayton (eds) *Subjective Probability* (Chichester: Wiley, 1994).

van der Heijden, K., *Scenarios: The Art of Strategic Conversation* (Chichester: Wiley, 1996).

van der Hiejden, K., R. Bradfield, G. Burt, G. Cairns and G. Wright, *The Sixth Sense: Accelerating Organizational Learning with Scenarios* (Chichester: Wiley, 2002).

Wack, P., 'Scenarios: Uncharted Waters Ahead', *Harvard Business Review*, 63, 5 (1985a) 73–90.

Wack, P., 'Scenarios: Shooting the Rapids', *Harvard Business Review*, 63, 6 (1985b) 131–142.

Walsh, J. P., 'Managerial and Organizational Cognition: Notes from a Trip Down Memory Lane', *Organization Science*, 6 (1995) 280–321.

Weick, K. E., *The Social Psychology of Organizing* (Reading, MA: Addison-Wesley, 1969).

Weick, K. E. *The Social Psychology of Organizing*, 2nd edn (Reading, MA: Addison-Wesley, 1979).

Weick, K. E., *Sensemaking in Organizations* (Thousand Oaks, CA: Sage, 1995).

Weick, K. E. and M. G. Bougon, 'Organizations as Cognitive Maps: Charting Ways to Success and Failure', in Sims, H. P. and Gioia, D. A. (eds) *The Thinking Organization* (San Francisco: Jossey-Bass, 1986), pp. 102–135.

Welford, A. T., *Skilled Performance* (Glenview, IL: Scott Foresman, 1976).

Wickens, C. D., *Engineering Psychology and Human Performance* (Columbus, OH: Merrill, 1984).

CHAPTER 11

Knowledge Perspective

J. C. Spender

Basic principles

Not all strategy theorists see knowledge as a useful concept; indeed, it is not at all obvious what people even mean by the term. It seems simple enough, but on close examination of the everyday notion of having something in one's head that corresponds to some objective fact about the world beyond, one cannot resist asking the question 'how do you know what you think you know is true?' The boostering knowledge-based literature skips over these quicksands and shouts that the Internet changes everything, that knowledge has become the economic and political feature of our age and that computerising information will change the human condition. Alas, we are ever the same muddlers, as susceptible to rumour, error and mendacity when surfing the web or Enron's accounts as when cruising the halls of Westminster or the Stock Exchange floor.

Recognising problems with what managers know and how they think lets us cut strategy several ways, and inasmuch as this leads to new insights we can propose a knowledge view of strategy. Eventually, this might evolve into a knowledge-based theory of strategy; indeed, some argue we already have a knowledge-based view of the firm (Grant, 2003), but it is not clear we are there yet. The main weakness resides in our not really knowing what knowledge is or how it relates to our practices. So our theory of strategy might begin by suggesting that one gather such knowledge of the world as one can, what we might call 'business intelligence'. Clearly, intelligence can be faulty, rendering the resulting strategies inappropriate. But with good information about the world and our firm in hand we can define strategy as about deciding rationally and rigorously how best to respond to what we see of the world's opportunities and threats. Chandler's (1966) notion of 'strategic fit', how we should match our strengths and weaknesses to the world, is a variation on this theme. Alternatively, we can focus on 'sense-making', on knowing, for example, what a competitor's new product might 'really mean for us', will it diminish our market share or expand our market (Weick, 2001)? The assumption here is that the competitor's view of the world probably differs from ours and, as a result, our action choices may turn more to our interpretation of their actions rather than to their own interpretation, or to anyone else's. Or, we might focus on communications within the firm, recognising that knowledge is often 'sticky', leading the firm to 're-invent the wheel' when the people in Department X do not know what those in Department Y already know (Szulanski, 2003). We see that communications breakdowns and disagreements about knowing and the meaning of what is known arise at every level, between individuals, departments, firms, cultures and nations.

Rather than solving these problems we might notice that these different ways of firm's strategy bring up different assumptions about the world. In the first exam knowable in an objective sense that makes our knowledge of it independent of us. but the facts and, barring errors, one firm's view of the market should be much marketing consultant's work applies to either. In the second example, knowledge i perhaps a characteristic of the firm as a system of knowing and practice. GM's vie different to Toyota's, else their strategies would be more similar. Now the mar

to fashion his or her advice to the firm's perceptions. In the third example, the firm's knowledge is even more problematic, leading us to question whether a firm can ever have a single coherent view or strategy. Then the emphasis might be more dynamic, on the processes by which those participating in the strategic process resolve their differences and eventually dispose of the firm's resources which belong to the firm rather than these individuals (Cyert et al., 1958; Johnson et al., 2003; March and Simon, 1958). Our strategic consultant would then spend more time focused internally, facilitating the discussion process, than externally, directing it with research findings. The resulting theory would pay attention to the firm's administrative structures, cognitive invariants like corporate culture or industry recipe and the organisational routines that shape the firm's strategising (Nelson and Winter, 1982). These framings differ, and lacking any overarching meta-model we are obliged to begin theorising about strategy by choosing from among them, or perhaps some others, in ways that cannot be justified objectively as the 'best'. Should we couch our analysis within the first, or within one of the others? Of course, this is itself a strategic choice (Child, 1972) and is our rhetorical trick to surface a special meaning of the term strategy – as managerial choice under conditions that cannot be analysed rigorously. Not all theorists take this view of strategy, of course, but our point here is that ahead of the very idea of strategy comes a strategic choice of the problem that strategy is supposed to address, and not all strategy theorists are open or honest about how they deal with this.

A little history

In the field's early days many defined strategy as the grand decisions that had lasting impact on the firm, such as HP's decision to merge with Compaq, while lesser decisions, like HP's notebook implementation of IEEE 802.11 WiFi technology, were tactical (Gilmore, 1970; Learned et al., 1965; Taylor and Macmillan, 1973). This metaphor was drawn from the military, where generals make big decisions and commanders in the field work the tactics with the non-commissioned ranks (see Chapter 3). While the same vertical division of labour sometimes applies in business, the metaphor does not show us the essence of strategising because, clearly, not everything senior executives do is strategic. At the same time, we have problems with the implied Benthamite calculus; we seldom know for sure the eventual consequences of our actions and much of what we think of initially as tactical turns out in retrospect to be strategic, in the sense of having a long-term impact – and *vice versa*. As the field matured into Chandler's research programme (Channon, 1973), strategy came to mean the firm's choice of engagements with its markets, and the distinction between what is or is not strategic lay in the decision's content (Spender, 2001). If the decision relates to the firm's competitive or market position it is strategic, if it relates to corporate structuring or to changes in its production function it is not. Such Chandlerian notions, perhaps modified in the light of Porter's (1980) work, still dominate the literature, especially for practicing managers. The theorising has moved ahead, as the various chapters in this book attest. Among practitioners we see increased use of the term 'business model'. This broadens the notion of the firm's strategy to embrace a complex of choices about market positioning, resource allocation, organisational structuring and administration that has been operationalised as the Balanced Scorecard (Kaplan and Norton, 1996). Two specific theories, transactions cost economics (TCE) and the resource-based view (RBV), are also currently popular among strategy academics (see Chapters 7 and 9). But note that these theories still focus on strategy's content, in the first by comparing the costs of conducting a transaction within the firm or across the market, and in the second by identifying and managing the firm's rent-earning resources and resource-generation capabilities. Some contrasting views can be found in the Chapter 13 (Balogun, Jarzabkowski and Seidl).

A rather different alternative to the strategy-as-content position has co-existed uneasily in our field ˜˜many decades. Curiously, it is most evident when we teach strategy for we reassure our students ˜˜e is no one 'correct answer' to the cases. We see strategising is somehow more open than ˜lysis. For instance, we would not normally talk about a strategy when searching for the cheapest flight between New York and London – it is a matter of price alone and a simple decision. But when we bring in some other objective functions, such as the airline's on-time record or the quality of the food, things get messier. We might then define a 'personal strategy' in terms of our preferred pay-offs between these attributes, especially complex if these values cannot be calculated by, say, equating 10 per cent of the fare to a 50 per cent improvement in the food quality. Facts and values differ (Simon, 1997) and if decisions are about facts what should we call choosing values as we set up the rationality of our decision?

Strategy is one term and sense-making is another and the difference is not just a matter of one type of content rather than another. It points to the very different process of setting up the framework within which we make decisions. We see 'making a decision' is dangerously ambiguous; it can be a one-step affair, doing the calculation, or it can involve two steps: first creating the calculation's framework and then doing the calculation. The content approach to strategy takes the framework for granted, grounded perhaps in the financial or market share pay-off. But is this appropriate? How can anyone know the future and its surprises, or even the present and its unknowns, so well that we can calculate the financial consequences of, say, investing in a new technology? Is strategy more like sense-making, requiring managers to construct a framework for their decisions because it is not already available, lying open and obvious for all to see? Is strategy-making noticeably different from rational decision-making? Few researchers have followed senior managers closely, but those that have do not give us a clear picture of what managers really do (Mintzberg, 1973).

Strategy-making

Strategy seems an interesting topic largely because business people know the decisions with which they guide their firm have many different facets and there is no obviously right way to bring them all together into a rigorous quantitative model. That quantitative models dominate our academic literature can be read in two ways: either as evidence of what we believe strategists should better spend their time doing or as evidence of some deeper weakness in our strategic theorising. Surely the underlying questions are always about the nature and extent of the strategists' knowledge? If they have perfect knowledge of the firm's situation and possibilities then strategy can only be distinguished from management generally on the basis of its content; it becomes a subset of management's activity and management theory. But if strategy-making managers do not have perfect knowledge, but still wish to make thoughtful or 'mindful' decisions, a preparatory step is needed to bridge the gap between their imperfect knowledge and the fully specified state necessary for rigorous decision-making. For many of us this bridge is the intellectual locus of strategy.

Simon's (1982, 1997) concept of 'bounded rationality' helped give the bridging process a name but he is less than clear about the reasons why it is necessary. On the one hand, we cannot gather information about everything that could conceivably matter to the firm. Surprises, such as those that precipitated Toyota's production crisis when their brake P-valve sub-contractor's factory burnt out (Watts, 2003: 254), are by definition things not known ahead of the time they demand management decision. At the same time, we often lack the capacity to process the information we already have available, now famously named 'connecting the dots' (Baron, 2006). Simon's approach, supported by Child's (1972) article on 'strategic choice', and Weick's (1979) work on sense-making helped move the field on from Chandler's views, convincing many that strategy is more about concept formation than about rigorous decision-making, this author included. Computers, we said, can clean up the tactical stuff once the heavy-lifting conceptual strategic work has been completed; only people can do that (Dreyfus, 1979).

With this more open framing we see two questions which, if answered, would bear on a theory of strategy: (1) can we describe what or who determines the sense-making's outcome and (2) what is the theoretical status of the process's outcome? Again, Simon's work is helpful, introducing the notion of 'satisficing' (March and Simon, 1958: 140). In a rigorous framework, the conclusion seems to be in the data and business schools give their students the tools to extract it. The result is optimal and appears as a fact, independent of the decision-makers. The numbers, we say, do not lie. They drive the decision. Satisficing engages the decision-makers in a different way, for the search for answers terminates when an acceptable solution emerges. It seems more subjective, given that the choice criterion is chosen by the decision-maker. But there is less here than one might think, for satisficing merely reminds us that rigorous decision-making also requires us to put decision criteria into the analysis, they do not get there by themselves and so long as they are not the output of another decision; this is no more than another way of describing sense-making. The criteria of even the most rigorous of models must be chosen with a strategic choice.

Once alerted to this need for sense-making, whether by our bounded rationality or by our partial perceptual 'lenses', we cannot readily wish it away. From a managerial point of view rather than from a philosophical point of view, it may make no great difference what we regard as the source of the problem that such sense-making solves. For instance, if, as many realists do, we suppose the world to be coherent and knowable, sense-making is necessary because of our inability to know this knowable world in its entirety. Aside from our natural modesty, the notion that Man cannot have complete knowledge of the world is not new with Simon; it has been a fundamental religious and philosophical tenet for centuries. We might take a different view, postmodernist perhaps, and say that there is no reason to suppose right thinking is necessarily coherent, and that the coherence of rigorous modelling is something we impose on the fragments of knowledge that we have (Hatch, 1997; Rose, 1991). Whatever the cause or causes of our knowledge problems – and these may be forever unknown – we need to theorise how to address them rather than ignore them.

Human agency

Our first objective is to show that strategy theory comes in these two very different flavours. One is a subset of managerial decision-making, distinguished by its special content rather than by any variation from the perfect rationality approach that dominates our theorising. The second flavour is more puzzling. It stands apart from and logically prior to any rational decision-making, apparently more to do with the construction of the rationality within which strategic decisions are made, and this knowledge view will occupy the rest of the chapter. The two flavours might seem mutually exclusive, but only for those whose philosophical and methodological assumptions lead them to ignore human agency. This is the main point of this chapter so we shall make it several times and in several ways. Human agency is the notion that we can make a difference in the world, that everything that happens is not already determined or written, that we have choices and, of course, with these choices come responsibilities to others who might be affected by them. We might see human agency as the middle ground between free will and determinism. Once we admit agency we can no longer plead objectivity, saying that the numbers determine our decisions, for we must admit the decisions are ours, part of who we are.

As agents we stand between causes and their effects, having an impact that cannot be explained in terms of purely external or objective causes. Our initial sections are no more than a set-up for this discussion about the nature of managerial knowledge, but even more about the relationship between that knowledge and the manager, the person with the knowledge. In the first flavour of strategy theory there is no relationship, it is denied. Adopting a realist stance presumes some variant of what philosophers call 'correspondence theory': that knowledge is an objectively testable or falsifiable representation of something out there in reality. The knowledge is grounded in reality and remains independent of us or our knowing, so we are constrained to gathering information about what we presume exists, and to processing it 'objectively' to reveal the best options reality allows. This flavour of theory is not about the person or group doing the processing or about them as actors in the world. The conclusions are objective in that they are independent of them, and the only knowledge defects considered arise from inadequate research or incorrect processing of the information gleaned.

The second flavour of strategy starts by presuming we cannot ever know the essence or truth of reality, and the theorists telling us to pursue Truth actually divert us from the real agenda, which is about acting effectively in the world as we find it. Broadly speaking, we act within the world of our imaginings, implying a close relationship between who we are and the strategies we adopt; indeed, there may be no real difference. The firm's strategy may be no more than its identity and the analysis is never independent of the knower. This point seems complicated in ways many find difficult, especially when we have been trained into 'rigour' and 'objectivity'. The first position is associated with positivism. The application of positivist methods in the social sciences has been much criticised and we shall not engage this matter directly. Rather, we suggest that while positivist methods dominate our research and journals, and have been clearly successful for the natural sciences, they may not serve the field of strategy well, especially if human agency is the central axiom of the theory.

Sense-making is 'agency-lite', for it is clearly about us making the sense. We move away from naive correspondence into something more complicated as our perceptual apparatus and perceptions mediate what our senses tell us. So what we perceive may be contingent on the reality we are trying to understand, and lots of perceptual psychology and philosophising hinges on the 'may'. From our managerial point of view we need only admit our hand in creating our perceptions, for in its essence this is the hand of the strategist. One theory of leadership is of the person who comes up with the perceptual framework that communicated to those around them becomes the firm's sense of itself. We might as easily call this outcome the firm's strategic knowledge, the touchstone against which every managerial decision can be tested – what should we do with this complaining customer or with that under-performing plant?

Much has been written along these lines, and a fair amount of it within the strategic genre. But the relationship between the individuals and groups doing the sense-making and what they produce is far from clear. There is a long tradition of searching for leadership traits (Hunt, 1999) and we might think of categorising strategists as, for instance, 'risk takers', or 'cautious'. The implication is a psychologically grounded theory of strategy along these lines. We build an overall model with independent variable measures of reality like 'market turbulence' or 'sector profitability' and introduce mediation by the strategist's psychological variables. The question here is about how to describe the human agent making the difference, and the temptation is to come up with an alternative set of independent variables and in this way slide away from thinking directly about agency. Strategy theorists have other avoidance mechanisms in their tool-kit and lately institutional theory has overtaken cultural theory as a system of independent variables determining managerial choices (Powell and DiMaggio, 1991).

Some of those interested in considering agency directly frame it in three ways: personal, proxy and collective (Bandura, 2000). Each suggests some ways of framing the mediation above: the first being an individual acting in their own interest, as an entrepreneur might; the second being an individual acting in the interest of another, as in principal–agency theory (Pratt and Zeckhauser, 1991); the third being the agency generated at the collective level. The last is both the basis of new institutional theory and the core of North's (1990, 1991) theory of social institutions as emergent responses to the society's experienced and perceived uncertainties. We can build non-positivist sense-making theories of strategy incorporating all of these kinds of mediation. But it is difficult to know what to make of them if we have no independent explanations of why the agent's mediation is this way rather than that, and this, of course, is to misunderstand entirely what is meant by agency. It cannot be understood within the objective deterministic framework so familiar in our field's research.

Man as entrepreneur

The literature of human agency goes back millennia, but today's interpretation is largely the result of the Enlightenment philosophers such as Locke and Hume. The point here is to realise that agency is not so much an identified thing or even attribute with an identifiable cause, but rather an epistemological device to point beyond the realm of reason and causal explanation. Locke writes:

'the faculty which God has given Man to supply the want of clear and certain knowledge in cases where it cannot be had, is judgement ... The Mind sometimes exercises this judgement out of necessity, where demonstrative proofs and certain knowledge are not to be had, and sometimes out of laziness, unskillfulness or haste, even when demonstrative proofs are to be had'. (1928: 298)

Here we have what we now call 'heuristics' (Kuehn and Hamburger, 1970). Recall also that Hume argues causality itself cannot be discovered in the world, it is what we impress upon it to make sense of being able to predict our experiences (Dow, 2001). Adam Smith presents the same thought in a rather different way when he argues that Man is endowed with at least three distinct faculties: reason, reflection and imagination (Skinner, 2001).

As Simon (1957) reminds us, it is to do with the 'model of man' that we choose, strategically, to underpin our theorising. If we ignore values and focus only on reasoning and our senses we align ourselves with positivism. In contrast, the Enlightenment model of agency is that which goes beyond the senses and reason to embrace the imagination. This is not to be explained, it is to be assumed, just as we assume and do not explain our power to reason. Positivism minimises and may even eliminates the role of the imagination, prioritising our reasoning demanding a universal logic. In Popper's falsificationism the hypotheses tested are generated randomly, they are not logically related steps towards anything in the way 'problemistic search' suggests (Daft and Weick, 1984). The Enlightenment philosophers assume all of us have imaginations, without which we could not make our way through the world, for it enables us to deal with the shortcomings of our knowledge about the world. Strategy is evidence of our imagination, not our reason, and to chase our tails endlessly looking for a positivist theory of strategy is to busy ourselves so much that we miss its essence. The knowledge view is useful because it helps us see that strategising is about the creation of knowledge, the process of dealing with knowledge absences rather than with knowledge assets (Spender, 2005a,b). Many other theorists struggle to bring imagination to the centre of the analysis and not all are successful. The creativity research within psychology seems to have fallen victim to the positivist methodological hegemony and so into the chasm of its own paradoxes as it attempts an uncreative explanation of creativity (Sawyer et al., 2003). More useful for us is the work on 'personal construct theory' (Kelly, 1955) and Kelly describes each of us as an exploratory scientist bringing our limited faculties to bear on an unknowable world. But we cannot make much sense of this without first considering where we go if we reach beyond the realm of reason (Crowther-Heyck, 2005; Simon, 1983).

Tacit knowledge

We might argue the knowledge view's most characteristic axiom is the distinction between the explicit knowledge presumed and required by reason and the tacit knowledge evident in our practice. There is a huge literature seeking clarification of this term, and we might summarise it by suggesting four shades of meaning. The most widely accepted is that explicit knowledge is fully codified while tacit knowledge is under-codified. Both imply knowledge of the same basic type that can be melded and transformed into each other (Boisot, 1998). The next most familiar is that tacit refers to human or organisational skills that cannot be verbalised and made explicit, most famously riding a bicycle, but also implied in organisational routines. This is the thrust of the 'we know more than we can say' maxim. A third variant requires us to think of the relationship between bounded rationality and attention, and understand that the way we select what to pay attention to, selected from everything that we might pay attention to, establishes the boundary of our bounded rationality, and is what is tacit about our knowledge (Gourlay, 2004). As such our tacit knowledge is mediating our explicit knowledge and is orthogonal to it; the explicit and the tacit cannot be converted into each other. Our selections are also evidence of a heuristic since there is no rational explanation or logical justification for our choice. Note that selection is the obverse face of the trade-offs we mentioned earlier in this chapter.

The final variant is related to the third, but hinges more obviously on the role of practice. First, heuristics evolve from practice. While this is learning by doing, what is learned is not held by the reason, explicitly, which is what this term generally means. On the contrary, it is held elsewhere; precisely where, of course, remains a puzzle, with some speaking of our second 'gut' memory. But note that we imply a wedge between practice as (1) purposive, always explainable and rational in terms of the ends towards which it is directed, but which must be known ahead of action, and (2) that taken to be a defining or axiomatic characteristic of our natures, as in *homo ludens*, in the sense of orthogonal to and supplementing reason and imagination (Huizinga, 1955). Being an outcome of practice, tacit knowledge is situated, embedded in specific contexts, while explicit knowledge is always an abstraction from the situated presentness of practice (Tsoukas and Mylonopoulos, 2004). So as we reach beyond our reason we find only practice, just as Wittgenstein tells us we must turn to practice to grasp meaning. There is more to be said along these lines, of course. But leaving the philosophising to one side we can see that this notion of strategy is intimately tied into practice and as such goes far beyond the kind of mental model framed within the sense-making tradition (Spender, 1998). In this sense strategy is not a product of pure reason that can be captured in a causal theory, it is a heuristic derived from practice-situated imagination and reflection.

The constraints to the imagination

The challenge is to theorise practice so that we might theorise the kinds of strategy that it gives rise to. Again, like creativity, there is much literature here and we can tentatively align ourselves with Bourdieu (1998) and the actor network theory (Law and Hassard, 1999). Perhaps the most useful way to think about practice, from the point of view of strategy theory, is as the experience of bringing imagination into the situation that then leads towards situated knowledge (Chaiklin and Lave, 1993; Rogoff and Lave, 1984; Schatzki et al., 2001). We can distinguish creativity, making a difference in the world, from imagination, which, like reason, is an aspect of our thinking, an abstraction, and not the world. From a philosophical point of view we are here edging towards 'radical constructivism' (Pickering, 1995; von Glasersfeld, 2002) as opposed to 'social constructionism' (Gergen, 1995). Under the press of our imagination we experience boundaries and barriers in the contexts in which we seek to act with reason. These may be psychological and collective, as suggested previously, but they might be physical such as gravity and the Second Law of Thermodynamics, or religious or legal.

We might propose a knowledge view of strategy as a system of selections and trade-offs but if we do this we can never get behind it enough to explain the acts of imagination that generate it. Learning by doing (Cohen and Sproull, 1996) tends to prioritise the domain of reason, presuming we learn explicitly from experience in ways that are accepted uncritically or can subsequently be explained. But if we prioritise practice there is either nothing to be said, beyond assuming that practice is one of our natural defining characteristics, learned by observation perhaps, or speak to the limits of practice and so associate them with the limits to rationality. In this sense a theory of strategy emerges as an inventory of the limits to the organisation's imagination and creative practice. It is encouraging to realise this theory converges with Barnard's (1968) definition of the executive's function. One angle on this, not well explored in Barnard's book, is the degree to which corporate law, by acting as a constraint over corporate action rather than corporate sense-making, becomes an important dimension of any real strategy. An examination of the history of corporate and employment law provides insights into the limits to strategic practice inside the firm and in its markets, which are all too often ignored in our literature (Barley and Kunda, 2006; Fligstein, 2001; Horwitz, 1992). Likewise, many non-formal codes of social practice are strategically relevant limits (Jacobs, 1992, 2006). At this point we want to show that a knowledge view of strategy, far from being bounded by mental mapping and sense-making, actually provides the necessary leverage to reach beyond reason and into practice. In the concluding section we show this is not news to economists though it might be news to our organisation and strategy theorist colleagues.

Ah, the economics of it all

Strategy theorising has recently been much influenced by 'organisational economics' (Barney, 1997; Barney and Hesterly, 1999; Barney and Ouchi, 1986). While economics appears to many to be the defining rigorous methodology it is not that simple and, like strategy theorists, economists are sharply divided on whether to recognise or ignore uncertainty and bounded rationality, the issues germane to the second flavour of strategy. A common assumption in economics is that the manager's knowledge is adequate to his or her rational decision-making. The resulting positivist research questions and methodologies dominate our business schools and journals. The minority of economists who presume that the manager's knowledge is problematic normally hang their hats on the work of Frank H. Knight. His PhD thesis, first published in 1921 as *Risk, Uncertainty and Profit* (Knight, 1921), eventually won him the 1957 Walker Medal – the prize awarded by the American Economic Association before the Nobel (or rather the Bank of Sweden Prize in Economic Sciences) was established. His argument turns on the distinction between risk as 'randomness with knowable probabilities' and uncertainty as 'randomness with unknowable probabilities'. Likewise, we might say uncertainty is whatever arrests the rational decision-making process, preventing its coming to a rigorously demonstrable conclusion.

Having introduced uncertainty, Knight explains profit as the entrepreneur's return to dealing with it, thus disagreeing with the economic theorists who see risk-return issues as explaining profit. To emphasise this, economists now refer to 'Knightian uncertainty' to distance themselves from the conventional sense of uncertainty as dealing with probabilistic data (Camerer and Weber, 1992; Dempster, 1999; Nash, 2003). As a result three knowledge conditions come into view: when managers have (1) certain knowledge of cause and effect, (2) knowledge encapsulated in population statistics and (3) no knowledge of the relations between cause and effect. In practical terms we can imagine the first condition as, for instance, having enough knowledge of the market size and product attributes to be more or less certain that the new Jeep Grand Cherokee will take 9 per cent of the mid-size SUV US market in the next 12 months. The second condition might be believing that, adequately promoted, a new margarine typically takes 7 per cent of the UK retail market within 3 months of its introduction. The third condition might describe one's wondering about the consequences of introducing the iPod. In terms of the previous sections the positivistic flavour of strategy refers to the first two situations, while the more open, practice-oriented flavour inclines to the last. The weakness of the Knightian literature is that while it admits the imagination and so provides the basis for Schumpeter's (1961) work on entrepreneurship and much 'radical subjectivist' literature (Shackle, 1972), it does not reach forward to psychological, institutional or practice-based theories of creativity. Consequently, it tends to fizzle out on combination of unexplained creativity and uncritically comprehended experience. Kirzner (1997), as a leading exponent of this school, flirts with a psychological theory, arguing that entrepreneurs have a special 'alertness' to profit opportunities, but behind this lies something profound about how we might frame the imagination and thus develop an inclusive non-positivistic theory of strategy.

Evolutionary methods

There is increasing interest in evolutionary approaches to both organisational and economic theory. But there is also widespread recognition that evolutionary theory does not fit into the familiar causal framework. We agree something will evolve and move into niches vacated, and we understand that surviving species get selected after evolving capabilities that, retrospectively, seem to fit them for their context. But there is little predictive power to it. In the theory's Darwinian version the variations that lead to this change arise randomly, as opposed to the Lamarckian perspective in which they are determined and problemistic. From an epistemological point of view Darwin's randomness is specifically designed to cut his theory off from any identifiable cause or agency, for it would bespeak a goal and be teleological: species evolve towards their ultimate perfection, for instance.

The whole point of randomness is to bring the model in from the transcendental to the presupposed realism of science, hence the widespread social reaction to Darwin's work. The reality of the natural world is presumed and, at the same time, its changes are placed beyond the theorising. Evolutionary theory provides the mechanism through which unexplained changes in the environment work their way through as enactments on the species populations within them. Since we do not, maybe cannot, predict these changes we cannot predict the species' future condition. As an aside, we see similar questions about the sources of value and change in the resource-based view (Priem, 2001). This shifts the agency behind the change from us, acting on the world, to some unspecified entity behind the environment. In Kirzner's theory of strategy the creativity is shifted from the entrepreneur's imagination, working against unexplained and undiscovered constraints in the world, and into the natural world itself. The special alertness at the centre of his model is not the agentic imagination but mere sensing by the passive observer watching a horn of plenty with Nature herself the imaginative agent. So the resulting theory of strategy is just another sense-making one, competitive advantage going to the firm that moves first to take up a newly emerging need, such as delivering music in a new way made possible by a technology that did not previously exist (Baron, 2006). This view completely neglects other situated sources of uncertainty that manifest themselves as constraints over the firm's imagination, especially those arising from equally imaginative others (Spender, 1989).

To conclude we can provide some sense of how this knowledge-based theory of strategy works at the managerial level. Whatever their deficiencies, the positivist theories so eagerly promoted in our journals are wonderfully clear on this. Our discipline's intent is to generate tools or procedures to help managers gather information about their world in the expectation of turning up under-exploited rent opportunities. Depending on the school we belong to we focus on transactions costs, rent-earning resources, dynamic capabilities to generate rents, quasi-monopolistic markets, emerging technology or otherwise driven opportunities, changes in consumer tastes, the legal interstices between different nations' trade law and so forth. While some alertness is necessary, none of these call for entrepreneurial creativity, the acts of imagination within a situation's constraints. As soon as we shift into a more open framework, either to balance exploitation with some exploration (March, 1991) or because we begin to think about exploring the world peripheral and that strategy may be more about getting our innovative internal vision out into the world, the game changes. There is a subtle version of this in the micro-economic literature which takes off from a critique of the conventional view that competing firms are invariably at the efficient frontier of their production function. As we have seen above, the implication is they are able to balance the different costs and benefits perfectly, thus manifesting a particular variant of perfect knowledge. There is only one solution and strategic choice is not necessary. In practice, of course, the different inter-objective pay-offs are difficult to understand in themselves, and the idea that the entire set comprising the business model will be optimal is totally unrealistic (Klein, 2001). Strategising here calls for a special kind of internal imagination able to press forward towards the efficient frontier.

The core to our model of strategy is about recognising knowledge absences that provide managers the opportunities to apply their agentic imagination. But the firm is a community of agents and to engage employees in this endeavour requires managerial encouragement and some care to avoid disincentives and dysfunctionality (Amabile, 1998). But that is not managing people's creativity. But it can be managed indirectly by manipulation of the constraints and attention as imagination is brought into the world as creativity. Many constraints are beyond immediate management control, such as the applicable corporate law, cultural and religious attitudes, the presence of necessary infrastructure, the physical and chemical constraints and so forth. But many are subject to management's control, such as employee attitudes, care for the business model and its proximity to its efficient frontier.

Most important, of course, is management's ability to change the attitudes and expectations of those comprising the firm's environment and with whom the firm interacts.

There is nothing surprising here; it is pretty old hat and any manager worth their salt can tell us all about it. But that is not really what we are trying to do here. Rather, we are trying to save strategy theory from its own handiwork. Under the press of our discipline's methodological choices, what we might call our strategy for progress, we have developed a set of professional practices that are increasingly remote from those of our real constituency, practicing managers. If we are really trying to address these managers, our principal tasks are both to legitimate modes of non-positivistic thinking among them and to speak to our discipline's evident problems (Spender, 2005c). We seem to have two strategies available. One, obvious in this book, is to engage managerial practice directly, as the strategy as practice movement suggests. The other, which this chapter proposes, is to pay attention to the deeper assumptions on which our theorising is based and, having some axiomatic issues surface, to construct a more appropriate type of theory. Both, of course, imply the bankruptcy of the rational cognitive theorising so popular in the strategy literature.

References

Amabile, T. M., 'How to Kill Creativity', *Harvard Business Review*, 76, 5 (1998) 76–88.

Bandura, A., 'Exercise of Human Agency Through Collective Efficacy', *Current Directions in Psychological Science*, 9, 3 (2000) 75–78.

Barley, S. R. and G. Kunda, 'Contracting: A New Form of Professional Practice', *Academy of Management Perspectives*, 20, 1 (2006) 45–66.

Barnard, C. I., *The Functions of the Executive*, 30th Anniversary edn (Cambridge, MA: Harvard University Press, 1968).

Barney, J. B., *Gaining and Sustaining Competitive Advantage* (Reading, MA: Addison-Wesley, 1997).

Barney, J. B. and W. S. Hesterly, 'Organizational Economics: Understanding the Relationship between Organizations and Economic Analysis'. In S. Clegg and C. Hardy (eds), *Studying Organization: Theory and Method* (London: Sage, 1999), pp. 109–141.

Barney, J. B. and W. G. Ouchi, *Organizational Economics: Toward a New Paradigm for Understanding and Studying Organizations* (San Francisco, CA: Jossey-Bass, 1986).

Baron, R. A., 'Opportunity Recognition as Pattern Recognition: How Entrepreneurs "Connect the Dots" to Identify New Business Opportunities', *Academy of Management Perspectives*, 20, 1 (2006) 104–119.

Boisot, M., *Knowledge Assets: Securing Competitive Advantage in the Information Economy* (Oxford: Oxford University Press, 1998).

Bourdieu, P., *Practical Reason: On the Theory of Action* (Stanford, CA: Stanford University Press, 1998).

Camerer, C. and M. Weber, 'Recent Developments in Modeling Preferences: Uncertainty and Ambiguity', *Journal of Risk and Uncertainty*, 5, 4 (1992) 325–370.

Chaiklin, S. and J. Lave (eds), *Understanding Practice: Perspectives on Activity and Context* (Cambridge: Cambridge University Press, 1993).

Chandler, A. D., *Strategy and Structure: Chapters in the History of the American Industrial Enterprise* (Garden City, NY: Doubleday and Company Inc., 1966).

Channon, D. F., *The Strategy and Structure of British Enterprise* (London: Macmillan, 1973).

Child, J., 'Organisation Structure, Environment and Performance', *Sociology*, 6 (1972) 1–21.

Cohen, M. D. and L. S. Sproull (eds), *Organizational Learning* (Thousand Oaks, CA: Sage Publications, 1996).

Crowther-Heyck, H., *Herbert A. Simon – The Bounds of Reason in America* (Baltimore, PA: Johns Hopkins University Press, 2005).

Cyert, R. M., W. R. Dill and J. G. March, 'The Role of Expectations in Business Decision Making', *Administrative Science Quarterly*, 3, 3 (1958) 307–340.

Daft, R. L. and K. E. Weick, 'Toward a Model of Organizations as Interpretation Systems', *Academy of Management Review*, 9 (1984) 284–295.

Dempster, G. M., 'Austrians and Post-Keynsians: The Questions of Ignorance and Uncertainty', *Quarterly Journal of Austrian Economics*, 2, 4 (1999) 73–81.

Dow, S. C., 'Hume: A Reassessment'. In P. L. Porta, R. Scazzieri and A. Skinner (eds), *Knowledge, Social Institutions and the Division of Labour* (Cheltenham, Glos: Edward Elgar, 2001), pp. 75–92.

Dreyfus, H. L., *What Computers Can't Do: The Limits of Artificial Intelligence*, Revised edn (New York: Harper and Row, 1979).

Fligstein, N., *The Architecture of Markets: An Economic Sociology of Twenty-First-Century Capitalist Societies* (Princeton, NJ: Princeton University Press, 2001).

Gergen, K. J., 'Social Construction and the Educational Process'. In L. P. Steffe and J. Gale (eds), *Constructivism in Education* (Hillsdale, NJ: Lawrence Erlbaum and Associates, 1995), pp. 17–39.

Gilmore, F. F., *Formulation and Advocacy of Business Policy*, Revised edn (Ithaca NY: Cornell University, 1970).

Gourlay, S., 'Knowing as Semiosis: Steps Towards a Reconceptualization of Tacit Knowledge'. In H. Tsoukas and N. Mylonopoulos (eds), *Organizations as Knowledge Systems* (Basingstoke, Hants: Palgrave Macmillan, 2004), pp. 86–105.

Grant, R. M., 'The Knowledge-Based View of the Firm'. In D. O. Faulkner and A. Campbell (eds), *The Oxford Handbook of Strategy* (Oxford: Oxford University Press, 2003), Vol. 1, pp. 197–221.

Hatch, M. J., *Organization Theory: Modern, Symbolic, and Postmodern Perspectives* (Oxford: Oxford University Press, 1997).

Horwitz, M. J., *The Transformation of American Law, 1780–1860* (New York: Oxford University Press, 1992).

Huizinga, J., *Homo Ludens: A Study of the Play-Element in Culture* (Trans. R. F. C. Hull) (Boston, MA: Beacon Press, 1955).

Hunt, J. G., 'Transformational/Charismatic Leadership's Transformation of the Field: An Historical Essay', *Leadership Quarterly*, 10, 2 (1999) 129.

Jacobs, J., *Systems of Survival: A Dialogue on the Moral Foundations of Commerce and Politics* (New York: Random House, 1992).

Jacobs, J. B., *Mobsters, Unions, and Feds: The Mafia and the American Labor Movement* (New York: New York University Press, 2006).

Johnson, G., L. Melin and R. Whittington, 'Guest Editors' Introduction: Micro Strategy and Strategizing: Towards an Activity-based View', *Journal of Management Studies*, 40 (2003) 3–22.

Kaplan, R. S. and D. P. Norton, 'Using the Balanced Scorecard as a Strategic Management System', *Harvard Business Review*, 74, 1 (1996) 75.

Kelly, G. A., *The Psychology of Personal Constructs* (New York: W. W. Norton, 1955).

Kirzner, I. M., 'Entrepreneurial Discovery and the Competitive Market Process: An Austrian Approach', *Journal of Economic Literature*, 35 (1997) 60.

Klein, D. B., *A Plea to Economists Who Favor Liberty: Assist the Everyman* (London: Institute of Economic Affairs, 2001).

Knight, F. H., *Risk, Uncertainty and Profit* (Boston, MA: Houghton Mifflin Company, 1921).

Kuehn, A. A. and M. J. Hamburger, 'A Heuristic Program for Locating Warehouses'. In L. A. Welsch and R. M. Cyert (eds), *Management Decision Making* (Harmondsworth, Middx: Penguin Books, 1970), pp. 228–258.

Law, J. and J. Hassard (eds), *Actor Network Theory and After* (Oxford: Blackwell, 1999).

Learned, E. R. Christensen, K. Andrews and W. Guth, *Business Policy: Text and Cases* (Homewood, IL: Richard D. Irwin, 1965).

Locke, J., *Selections* (New York: Scribner's, 1928).

March, J. G., 'Exploration and Exploitation in Organizational Learning', *Organization Science*, 2 (1991) 71–87.

March, J. G. and H. A. Simon, *Organizations* (New York: John Wiley, 1958).

Mintzberg, H., *The Nature of Managerial Work* (New York: Harper and Row, 1973).

Nash, S. J., 'On Pragmatic Philosophy and Knightian Uncertainty', *Review of Social Economy*, 61, 2 (2003) 251–272.

Nelson, R. R. and S. G. Winter, *An Evolutionary Theory of Economic Change* (Cambridge, MA: Belknap Press, 1982).

North, D. C., *Institutions, Institutional Change, and Economic Performance* (Cambridge: Cambridge University Press, 1990).

North, D. C., 'Institutions', *Journal of Economic Perspectives*, 5, 1 (1991) 97–112.

Pickering, A., *The Mangle of Practice: Time, Agency, and Science* (Chicago IL: University of Chicago Press, 1995).

Porter, M. E., *Competitive Strategy: Techniques for Analyzing Industries and Competitors* (New York: Free Press, 1980).

Powell, W. W. and P. J. DiMaggio, *The New Institutionalism in Organizational Analysis* (Chicago, IL: University of Chicago Press, 1991).

Pratt, J. W. and R. J. Zeckhauser, 'Principals and Agents: An Overview'. In J. W. Pratt and R. J. Zeckhauser (eds), *Principals and Agents: The Structure of Business* (Boston, MA: Harvard Business School, 1991), pp. 1–35.

Priem, R. L., 'Tautology in the Resource-Based View and the Implications of Externally Determined Resource Value: Further Comments', *Academy of Management Review*, 26, 1 (2001) 57.

Rogoff, B. and J. Lave (eds), *Everyday Cognition: Its Development in Social Context* (Cambridge, MA: Harvard University Press, 1984).

Rose, M. A., *The Post-Modern and the Post-Industrial: A Critical Analysis* (Cambridge: Cambridge University Press, 1991).

Sawyer, R. K., V. John-Steiner and S. Moran, *Creativity and Development* (Oxford: Oxford University Press, 2003).

Schatzki, T. R., K. Knorr Cetina and E. von Savigny (eds), *The Practice Turn in Contemporary Theory* (London: Routledge, 2001).

Schumpeter, J. A., *The Theory of Economic Development: An Enquiry into Profits, Capital, Credit, Interest, and the Business Cycle* (New York: Oxford University Press, 1961).

Shackle, G. L. S., *Epistemics and Economics: A Critique of Economic Doctrines* (New Brunswick, NJ: Transaction Publishers, 1972).

Simon, H. A., *Models of Man: Social and Rational* (New York: John Wiley and Sons, 1957).

Simon, H. A., *Models of Bounded Rationality* (Vols 1 and 2) (Cambridge, MA: MIT Press, 1982).

Simon, H. A., *Reason in Human Affairs* (Stanford, CA: Stanford University Press, 1983).

Simon, H. A., *Administrative Behavior: A Study of Decision-Making Processes in Administrative Organization*, 4th edn (New York: Free Press, 1997).

Skinner, A., 'Adam Smith, the Philosopher and the Porter'. In P. L. Porta, R. Scazzieri and A. Skinner (eds), *Knowledge, Social Institutions and the Division of Labor* (Cheltenham: Edward Elgar, 2001), pp. 35–51.

Spender, J.-C., *Industry Recipes: The Nature and Sources of Managerial Judgement* (Oxford: Blackwell, 1989).

Spender, J.-C., 'Workplace Cognition: The Individual and Collective Dimensions'. In C. Eden and J.-C. Spender (eds), *Managerial and Organizational Cognition: Theory, Methods and Research* (London: Sage, 1998), pp. 13–39.

Spender, J.-C., 'Business Policy and Strategy as a Professional Field'. In H. Volerba and T. Elfring (eds), *Rethinking Strategy: Beyond Fragmentation* (London: Sage, 2001), pp. 26–40.

Spender, J.-C., 'An Overview: What's New and Important about Knowledge Management? Building New Bridges between Managers and Academics'. In S. Little and T. Ray (eds), *Managing Knowledge: An Essential Reader* (London: Sage, 2005a), pp. 127–154.

Spender, J.-C., 'Review of Amin, Ash, and Cohendet, Patrick "Architectures of Knowledge: Firms, Capabilities, and Communities" OUP 2004; Patriotta, Gerardo "Organizational Knowledge in the Making" OUP 2004, and Tsoukas, Hari and Mylonopoulos, Nikolaos "Organizations as Knowledge Systems: Knowledge, Learning, and Dynamic Capabilities" Macmillan Palgrave 2004', *Prometheus*, 23, 1 (2005b) 101–116.

Spender, J.-C., 'Speaking about Management Education: Some History of the Search for Legitimacy and the Ownership and Control of Management Knowledge', *Management Decision Incorporating the Journal of Management History*, 43, 10 (2005c) 1282–1292.

Szulanski, G., *Sticky Knowledge: Barriers to Knowing in the Firm* (London: Sage Publications, 2003).

Taylor, B. and K. Macmillan, *Business Policy: Teaching and Research* (Bradford: Bradford University Press, 1973).

Tsoukas, H. and N. Mylonopoulos, 'Introduction: What Does it Mean to View Organizations as Knowledge Systems'. In H. Tsoukas and N. Mylonopoulos (eds), *Organizations as Knowledge Systems* (Basingstoke: Palgrave Macmillan, 2004), pp. 1–26.

von Glasersfeld, E., *Radical Constructivism* (London: Routledge/Falmer, 2002).

Watts, D. J., *Six Degrees: The Science of a Connected Age* (New York: W. W. Norton and Co., 2003).

Weick, K. E., *Social Psychology of Organizing*, 2nd edn (Reading, MA: Addison-Wesley, 1979).

Weick, K. E., *Making Sense of the Organization* (Malden, MA: Blackwell, 2001).

CHAPTER 12

Network Perspective

Silviya Svejenova and José Luis Álvarez

Basic principles

In explaining why some firms are more competitive than others, strategic management perspectives have often emphasized either external aspects of the firm, such as the structure of its industry, or its internal characteristics, for example, its strategic resources and capabilities. The former view is known as an industry structure view and positions the analysis of the source of competitive advantage at industry level. The latter view is the resource-based view (RBV) of the firm, for which the relevant unit of analysis is the firm. In this chapter we outline the main tenets of a relational or network perspective to strategy, which argues that another useful way to understand the differences in firms' profitability and conduct is by examining the network of relationships in which firms are embedded. A network perspective combines a focus on external aspects of the firm, such as its partners and their resources, with attention to its internal characteristics, such as the firm's ability to identify, engage in collaboration with, learn from and create value through, its partnerships.

A network view on strategy conceives of the firm as an interdependent, rather than an autonomous, entity. It argues that a firm's economic activities are both enabled and constrained by its relationships. From such a viewpoint the boundaries between the 'inside' and the 'outside' of the company become less relevant, both analytically and practically. What matters most is the role a firm's relationships play in achieving and sustaining its competitive advantage. The value that a firm can generate through its partnerships depends on a number of factors, among which is its position in the inter-firm network, the partners' resources and reputation, as well as the firm's experience in partnering and its ability to integrate and exploit the resources of its partners. Thus unlike RBV, which focuses on the strategic resources and capabilities of the firm that can confer a competitive advantage, a network perspective on strategy zeroes in on who the firm's partners are and what they are good at. More importantly this perspective focuses on how a firm can bring together the partners' inputs and its own resources in a value-creating way. Further this collaboration results in relational rents, that is profits generated jointly by the partners and which cannot be generated by either partner individually (Dyer and Singh, 1998). From a network perspective, what is hard, costly and timely to imitate and therefore constitutes potential source of sustainable competitive advantage is a firm's network of relationships and the mechanisms for integration of the firm's unique resources and capabilities with those of its partners.

There are at least three main areas of attention from a network perspective: first, the influence of a firm's cooperative relationships on its competitive advantage and performance (Jarillo, 1988); second, the form of organization these inter-firm relationships take (Nohria and Eccles, 1992); and third, the 'company behind the chart' (Krackhardt and Hanson, 1993), which denotes the firm's informal channels and lateral connections for getting things done. In this chapter we focus mostly on the strategic networks' impact on a firm's competitiveness and profitability and, to a lesser extent, on the organizational form these partnerships take. The third aspect, the informal connections, deserves a chapter on its own, and the interested reader could further explore some pertinent issues in Cross and Parker's (2004) book *The Hidden Power of Social Networks: Understanding How Work Really Gets Done in Organizations.*

A network perspective of competitive advantage poses that the social structure in which a firm is embedded is its source of social capital, which in turn creates inter-firm performance differences. There are two essential mechanisms that lead to some firms outperforming others: brokerage and closure (Burt, 2005). Brokerage is manifested in situations in which a firm creates value by connecting groups and/or organizations that will otherwise remain disconnected. The broker company identifies new opportunities in the network structure's empty space. Closure is revealed when a firm acts in a network, in which partners are tightly connected to one another and, as a result, information sharing within the network is enhanced and inter-firm cooperation takes place in concert. In a closed, cohesive network the risk of behaviors that can de-stabilize the partnership is lower, as there are usually collective sanctions for defection. While brokerage is about value creation by bridging disconnected parts of the social structure, closure is about the realization of value through repeated and stable exchanges in a network of trust-based relationships. The former mechanism is associated with the work of Burt and what he calls 'structural holes' (Burt, 1992), kinds of empty spaces in a social structure that when 'bridged' by a 'broker' have a value-creating potential. The latter mechanism is related to the contribution of Coleman (1988) that networks, in which all members are connected, are the sources of social capital and relational stability, as they sanction undesirable behavior. In the brokerage mechanism, value resides in the increased variation (the non-redundant contacts that a broker firm connects). In the closure mechanism, value appears in the decreased variation through norms shared in the closed and densely connected network. Thus closure within a group and brokerage beyond it could together, in integration, define social capital (Burt, 2005). Burt's 2005 book *Brokerage and Closure: An Introduction to Social Capital* provides an insightful account of the possible integration of the two network mechanisms, brokerage and closure.

Another key question from a network perspective is how a firm's portfolio of partnerships can be optimized in the quest for competitive advantage. For this it is important not only to understand a firm's position in a network of relationships, but also to examine the nature of its partnerships. For example these relationships can be horizontal, when the firm cooperates with competitors, and vertical, when it partners up with companies that specialize in activities at different stages of the industry's value chain. Horizontal networks involve access to complementary technology and innovative capabilities. Vertical networks create opportunities for backward integration providing a firm with access to R&D and design engineering or for forward integration that allows it to reach out to new markets. Further horizontal and vertical alliances can be symmetrical when firms of similar size partner together or asymmetric when formed, for example, between a big, established incumbent and a small, entrepreneurial firm. For example the keiretsu, a traditional form of collaboration among Japanese firms that involves both ownership and network relationships, can be either vertical or horizontal. Horizontal keiretsu networks are diversified, 'intermarket' forms, while vertical keiretsu consist of a large parent firm and its dependent affiliates, which are situated upstream and downstream in the industry value chain.

Thus a network perspective requires managers to adopt a dynamic stance on the firm's partnerships, understanding and managing a firm's portfolio of relationships. It demands that executives constantly review whether their alliances fit the firm's strategic intent and direction, as well as which partnerships are worth maintaining and strengthening and which need to be weakened or exited. It calls for decision-making on what the core of the firm is, which value-adding activities should be kept in-house, and what activities could be performed by or together with partners from the network. It also puts a significant emphasis on the importance of a firm's absorptive capacity in learning from its partners and its collaborative capability in order to better manage its partnerships.

The following case study of InnoCentive LLC, an independent online venture established in 2001 by Eli Lilly and Company, illustrates some of the key issues under consideration when adopting a network perspective. First we provide an overview of the pharmaceutical industry and of Eli Lilly's situation at the time of InnoCentive's founding. Next we highlight the essential elements of Inno-Centive's business model. Finally we conclude the case with some challenges the company is facing, 5 years after the commencement of its activities.

CASE STUDY 12.1

By harnessing the Web, InnoCentive has built a virtual community of scientists that puts the organization 'within one or two degrees of separation from every single organic chemist in the world'.

(Darren J. Carroll, Chairman of InnoCentive)

InnoCentive's efforts to foster collaboration and to become a bridge between major R&D companies and the leaders in the worldwide scientific research community.

(Ali Hussein, InnoCentive's Chief Marketing Officer and Vice-President of Global Markets)

The pharmaceutical industry of the twenty-first century and the birth of InnoCentive

In the late 1990s the pharmaceutical industry was riding the consolidation rollercoaster, with merger waves bringing together one-time rivals such as Glaxo Wellcome and SmithKline Beecham, Pfizer and Warner-Lambert and a number of other major players. In 2001 amidst the high consolidation activity, pharmaceutical giant Eli Lilly had to face a patent protection loss for its star drug – the antidepressant Prozac – which had come to rival the popularity of painkiller aspirin and had generated hefty profits for the company over the years. (According to Maiello, 2004, profits were peaking at $3 billion in 2000.) Estimates suggested that as it was launched on the Belgium market in 1986, Prozac had been taken by at least 38 million people. Despite the battle Lilly fought to get its patent extended until 2003, in 2001 the competition authorities at the Federal Drug Administration gave Barr Pharmaceuticals permission to sell fluoxetine, the generic name for Prozac, which pushed Lilly's star drug off the shelf. At its peak Prozac had accounted for 34 per cent of Lilly's annual sales (Breen, 2002). As a result of the patent expiration, Lilly lost 90 per cent of its Prozac prescriptions over a year and $35 billion of its market value in a single day (Maiello, 2004). While profit erosion from the patent protection loss is almost immediate, the quest for a new blockbuster drug takes much longer (according to industry statistics, about 12–15 years on average) and demands a huge R&D budget and an army of scientists.

Amidst the loss of Prozac's major revenue stream, Eli Lilly and Company not only urged its ranks of scientists to work harder on the next new thing. It also launched an experiment which sought to create incentives for innovation by forming a wholly owned subsidiary called *InnoCentive LLC* and incubating it through its e.Lilly division. As explained on the division's website (http://e.lilly.com), e.Lilly relied on 'the Internet technology and new business models to radically speed up and improve the implementation of the company's strategy in the new economy'. At the heart of e.Lilly were notions such as 'connections' and 'connectivity' – with researchers, clinicians, healthcare providers, payers and patients, regulators, suppliers and employees.

InnoCentive was expected to speed up and lower the cost of the R&D process by connecting *Seekers of Solutions* (companies in science-driven industries) with *Solvers of Challenges* (scientists from around the world). Scientists who unraveled a problem receive an award, and companies that post a challenge get the intellectual property rights to the solution for the award they pay. Thus Lilly was doing something unusual for the industry: 'We're punching a hole in the side of the laboratory and exposing mission-critical problems to the outside world. This isn't sock puppets or Super Bowl advertising. It's using the Net to communicate, collaborate, and innovate', explained Darren J. Carroll, President and CEO of InnoCentive at the time and its current chairman (Breen, 2002).

The InnoCentive model

InnoCentive operates the largest network of scientists in the world. As explained on the company's website, it is 'the first online forum that allows world-class scientists and scientific companies to collaborate in a global community to achieve innovative solutions to complex challenges'.

InnoCentive connects the Seekers (companies, such as Lilly, DuPont, Novartis, Henkel, P&G, Syngenta, Nestlé Purina, Dow, Boeing, Ciba, Rhodia) and the Solvers (independent scientists as well as university and scientific partners from around the world) via a web-enabled platform, creating a distributed R&D organization that any member company can use. *Quovix LLC*, a 10-person outfit and a virtual workforce of 455 free-agent programmers, designed the software that enables InnoCentive to set up web-based workspaces (Breen, 2002). Here is how such a system works.

The member companies, called Seekers, post challenges describing problems that need to be resolved. The scientists, labeled Solvers, sign a confidentiality agreement that allows them to access the data and product specification related to a problem in what is known as a secure project room. They work on a challenge at their own risk and, only if they resolve it, receive awards ranging from $10,000 to $100,000 depending on the difficulty of the problem. Hence it is by spreading the risk to outside scientists that InnoCentive cuts the cost of drug discovery: 'So now it's up to solvers to decide whether the risk is worth the reward', InnoCentive's CEO explains. 'But ideally, they already know the answers. They've just been waiting for us to come along and ask the right questions.'

Intellectual property is an essential factor in InnoCentive's model and therefore zealously protected throughout the entire process. From the outset anonymity and confidentiality is guaranteed to Seekers when working closely with InnoCentive's Scientific Operations Group on the development of the challenge description and the check of its compliance with legal, scientific and commercial requirements. Confidentiality agreements are also signed with Solvers and they work on the challenges in private online project rooms. When solutions are received, they are validated by InnoCentive's Scientific Operations Group and also by the Seeker organization, which lead to the selection of the winning solution and the reward for the Solver.

InnoCentive generates revenues from the Seekers. They pay an *annual access fee* for the right to use InnoCentive's network; *a posting fee* for the problems they post; and *a commission fee* when they choose a solution. Lilly was the first Seeker company at InnoCentive to provide challenges and awards. InnoCentive is incorporated as an independent company and at present partners up with Seeker companies in a number of science-driven industries.

There is no fee for scientists' registration and they can participate freely, without any obligation, in the solution of challenges they find attractive. According to Darren Carroll, Solvers 'can continue to work for large, R&D-based organizations, or they can become free agents and work for themselves. Under certain circumstances, they might even do both. Free agency has never been an option in the hard sciences – until now' (Breen, 2002). Werner Mueller is one of those independent chemists, formerly head of technology for the specialty chemicals group of pharmaceuticals giant Hoechst/Celanese before it became part of Clariant (Breen, 2002). Mueller devised a two-step synthesis for the compound 4-(4-hydroxy-phenyl) butanoic acid, an intermediate for a drug that Lilly is developing. For this he earned a $25,000 reward. In his view, under the InnoCentive model, the Solver assumes too much risk: 'You have to be willing to work for 3 months and possibly come up with nothing', he says and suggests that 'The Seeker should do more to share the risk. Right now, there's high risk for the Solver and zero risk for the seeker.'

Despite the risk transfer to Solvers, however, the number of scientists continues growing. InnoCentive allows Seekers to tap into its unique virtual R&D network of over 110,000 scientists and scientific organisations spanning more than 60 disciplines and 175 countries. Through this so-called 'democratization' of science,

InnoCentive has been able to achieve a success rate of problem solution far higher than its Seekers' in-house R&D performance and at about one-sixth of their cost (*Business Week*, 2005). As explained by Dr Dan Kittle, Vice-President of R&D for The Dow Chemical Company: 'Our relationship with InnoCentive gives us access to an unparalleled global community of scientists. We renewed our contract with InnoCentive because it has accelerated the pace of our R&D innovation by fostering scientific collaboration that crosses traditional boundaries.'

InnoCentive seeks to improve its model continuously. In the years that followed its beginnings, with Eli Lilly as the only Seeker company, it has substantially increased the number of problem-posting member firms. As revealed by the company's chairman, Mr Carroll, expanding the model to Seekers from a number of industries is facilitated by major trends in the environment, which InnoCentive's business model allows them to address:[1]:

First, there are significant pressures on the R&D budgets of nearly every one of the R&D leaders that we speak to around the world, no matter what the industry and no matter what the company, and we know that R&D leaders are being asked to do more and more with less.

Second, we know that there are some key demographic variables that companies are going to have to contend with. There are fewer and fewer people going into science education in the United States and Western Europe, while at the same time, there is a tremendous bubble of talent that's about to retire at the PhD and Masters level in all of these companies. The InnoCentive model provides R&D leaders with the ability to manage all of these very fundamental shifts that they are going to be dealing with over the next five, 10, or 20 years. We provide them with dramatically expanded access to talent that includes all the retirees who are going to be leaving the regular work force.

InnoCentive has also expanded the ranks of its Solvers. From 7000 scientists registered with InnoCentive during the first year of its operation, in 2006 their numbers reached 110,000 and continue growing. Scientists from around the world have the option to register individually or through their research centers. The effort to tap talent on a global scale is seen in the fact that the company website is available in a number of languages, among which are English, Chinese, Spanish, Russian, German, Japanese and Korean. As explained by Mr Carroll, Chairman of InnoCentive:[2]

we've been able to establish partnerships with research institutes and research based universities throughout the world. We've done it with the Chinese Academy of Sciences, with the National Natural Science Foundation in China, as well as with leading universities like Beijing University and Fudan University. Likewise, we've done it now with about 25 universities throughout Russia, including such stellar institutions as Moscow State University and St. Petersburg University. And then finally, we have significant relationships in India with the Council of Scientific and Industrial Research, which is India's collection of national laboratories, as well as with the Indian Institute of Chemical Technology and various Indian Institutes of Technology around the nation.

In a press release on 1 February 2006, the company reported that it had secured $9 million USD in venture capital funding to support its platform development and further commercial expansion. 'This investment is an endorsement of the strength of our global scientific network and each and every researcher who contributes to its success', affirmed Dr Alpheus Bingham, the company's President and Chief Executive Officer. Darren Carroll, Senior Managing Director of Lilly Ventures and Chairman of the InnoCentive Board of Directors added, 'As a founding executive of InnoCentive, I have seen the network significantly reduce financial risk for innovation-driven companies and deliver cutting-edge solutions since its inception in 2001.' According to Doug Solomon, Vice-President for Investments at Omidyar Network, 'InnoCentive is removing the barriers of distance, specialization and organization from the sciences, facilitating global collaboration that is driving scientific discovery'.

While in 2001 InnoCentive was definitely a unique (and uniquely positioned) venture, by 2006 a number of other related or completely unrelated companies have appeared that offer similar services in democratizing science. For example *YourEncore* Inc., which counts Lilly and P&G among its founding fathers, provides its member companies with the services of retired scientists, engineers and product developers. Yet 2.com is an IP (intellectual property) broker which, rather than connecting Seekers with challenges and Solvers with solutions or member companies' complex and urgent projects with a network of retired scientists, engineers and product developers, helps companies to identify and capture the full value of their intellectual property assets. Whether InnoCentive will continue growing its network, while preserving its unique position of broker within it, remains to be seen.

Overview of the network perspective

A network perspective zeroes in on the relational aspects of economic activities. Well before a network perspective was acknowledged insightful for strategic management (Jarillo, 1988), interest in and research on relationships and networks were thriving among psychologists, anthropologists, sociologists and mathematicians. Thus unlike the industry structure perspective on strategy, which is based on insights from Industrial Organization, the network perspective on strategy acts from a social sciences background.

The social scientists who have developed critical insights that have advanced the network perspective are numerous. Here we briefly review a selected number of contributors. In 1922 Bronislaw Malinowski, the British anthropologist of Polish origin, published his work on the complex system of visits and gift exchanges that enhanced social solidarity among the Trobriand Islanders. In the 1930s Jacob Moreno, an Austrian-born psychotherapist who had moved to the USA, developed *sociometry* (the science and art of measuring relationships) and the *sociogram* as a method for graphical representation of individuals as points and their relationships as lines, which allowed advances to be made in the systematic explorations of social structures. In 1929 Hungarian writer Frigyes Karinthy in a short story called 'Chains' planted the seeds of what would later come to be known as the small-world phenomenon and the six degrees of separation. The terms themselves were coined and inspired in 1967 by the behavioral psychologist Stanley Milgram, who conducted an experiment in which he found that only six steps were needed to deliver letters from random people in the American Midwest to a stranger located in Massachusetts. Six degrees of separation is the theory that anyone on earth can be connected to any other person on the planet through a chain of acquaintances that has no more than five intermediaries.

Efforts to further disentangle the effect of relationships on behavior led to the introduction of a number of important distinctions and concepts. In a 1974 book, *Getting a Job*, Mark Granovetter revealed rather counter-intuitive findings that people got the jobs they hold through their acquaintances rather than through their friends, a phenomenon he denoted as the strength of weak ties. In 1985, he came up with the notion that the economic activities of firms are embedded in a network of relations and, in order to be understood, attention should be paid to firms' relationships. In a 1988 paper on human and social capital, James Coleman put forward the concept of network closure, which is the degree to which everyone knows everyone else in a network. In his 1992 book, Structural Holes, Burt described the theory of structural holes, the gaps between two groups in a social network, arguing that competition is a matter of relations, not attributes. He affirmed that the structural hole argument is a theory about competition for the benefits that relationships can provide. Network closure brings reputation effects, while structural holes are sources of entrepreneurial opportunities for those that connect the gaps in the network structures.

In the 1990s a growing number of scholars were adopting the network perspective, examining informal social networks that knitted together companies' hierarchies through horizontal and lateral connections (Krackhardt and Hanson, 1993) or influenced processes of change. Network structure needed to be not only understood, but also measured. Comprehensive packages for the analysis of social network data, such as UCINET (http://www.analytictech.com/ucinet.htm) by Borgatti et al. (1999), appeared and spread rapidly among the ranks of academics.

Linking the network perspective to strategic management

Why and how did these predominantly sociological contributions to the development of a network perspective trespass on the terrain of strategic management, traditionally occupied by the economists? In 1988, José Carlos Jarillo proposed the concept of strategic network as a tool for understanding the firm's cooperative relationships and the latter's role in the competitive strength of the firm. He argued that firms are entities operating not in isolation but in a context of social and business relationships that influence the development of deliverable strategies. Twelve years later, Gulati et al. (2000, p. 19) acknowledged that 'the time was ripe to seriously address the question of how strategic networks influence the relative profitability of firms', and that there are important insights that result from adopting a network perspective on strategy.

A network perspective provides new insights into competition, competitive advantage and performance differences. It suggests that a firm's relationships and location in a network are its unique and most difficult to imitate strategic assets. The firms that occupy the most central positions in their respective networks are able to achieve superior returns because of their access to opportunities that may not be available to peripheral firms. So the rents that accrue to firms depend not only on how attractive their industries are or what unique resource endowments they have. They also depend on the resources and capabilities of the firm's partners and the way in which these are integrated with the focal firm's strategic assets in the joint value creation. Thus there are many ways in which a firm's network can be a valuable and hard to imitate strategic resource that yields a differential return. One reason for the unique character of a firm's network is that a firm usually creates its relationships in an idiosyncratic and path-dependent way, which is difficult to replicate by its competitors, at least in the short to medium run. It is not only the network creation that is hard to imitate. So are the capabilities and experience a firm develops in building the network and managing and creating value through it. An essential reason for this difficulty is the development of a trust-based relationship between the parties in the network (especially with the so-called closure mechanism, discussed earlier), which usually takes a long time and repeated satisfactory exchanges and so is both difficult and timely for competitors to replicate. Below we explore the sources of relational advantage as well as the network's benefits and drawbacks.

Sources of relational advantage

There are a number of essential factors and characteristics to which a network perspective is attentive and which can lead to relational advantage and rents: the network structure, the tie modality and the network's membership (Gulati et al., 2000).

The *network structure* is characterized by the overall size of a firm's network (the number of firms and other organizations in its relational portfolio); the number of relationships that exists among its partners (the higher the number of these relationships, the higher the network's density, which as discussed earlier leads to higher level of closure (Coleman, 1988) as a source of social capital for the firm); the gaps or lacks of connections that exist between parts of the networks (the structural holes [Burt, 1992], which are a source of brokerage advantage for the firm that brings the disconnected parts of the network together), as well as the distinction between core and peripheral firms in the network (a core firm could be one that integrates the contributions of other network partners and serves as a hub of network activities).

Tie modality refers to the strength of the connections (e.g. weak or strong ties – see our earlier discussion), their stability (e.g. stable or dynamic networks), their intent (e.g. exploration or exploitation) and their nature (e.g. cooperative and/or competitive). A firm can take part in stable or dynamic networks (Snow et al., 1992). Stable networks arise from embedding the firm in repeated inter-organizational exchanges, such as those in the high-tech networks in Silicon Valley (Saxenian, 1990). Dynamic networks can thrive on the interface between the hierarchy and the market, as in the case of investment banking, where client-focused teams of professionals with heterogeneous inputs are activated out of the internal structure of the bank (Eccles and Crane, 1988). Where network relationships are more fluid and dynamic, the role of a network integrator can be likened to that of a broker, who temporarily (usually for the duration of a particular project or product) connects the assets owned by other independent companies. The network is disbanded with the project's completion. A new network is formed (possibly) with different members and different relationships in response to the needs of the new project.

Depending on its strategic intent, a firm can shape exploration and exploitation partnerships (Koza and Lewin, 1998). As Koza and Lewin explained, exploitation partnerships pool together complementary resources for purposes that the partners are not interested in or capable of developing on their own. In turn exploration partnerships are a means for probing or co-developing new markets, products or technological opportunities and have rather open-ended performance goals. The two partners may have symmetrical strategic intents (e.g. both share exploitation or an exploration strategic intent) or, alternatively, have asymmetrical intents, where one partner considers the collaboration as an exploitation opportunity while the other aims at exploration. Koza and Lewin (2000) provide a refinement of the alliance typology along the distinction of high–low exploration and exploitation intent. Using a co-evolutionary perspective, they discuss three different types of alliances: a learning alliance, in which both companies share a strong exploration intent; a business alliance that links companies with strong exploitation intents and limited need for exploration; and a hybrid alliance formed by companies with simultaneous exploration and exploitation objectives (Koza and Lewin, 2000). A firm's absorptive capacity is essential for recognizing the value of, assimilating and making use of new, external information (Cohen and Levinthal, 1990). From a relational perspective, what matters most is the firm's partner-specific absorptive capacity, which denotes a firm's ability to recognize and assimilate valuable knowledge from its network partners (Dyer and Singh, 1998).

The *network's membership* refers to the firm's partners in the network and the status and other resources they possess. Thus young biotech firms were found to receive higher market valuation by analysts (Powell, in Dyer and Singh, 1998) or to show higher innovative performance in terms of patenting and R&D spending growth (Baum et al., 2000), if they had formed beneficial partnerships with rivals and/or established firms.

Benefits and drawbacks

Networks have to be understood in terms of both the benefits they bring and the constraints they may impose on a firm's activities. Among the main benefits from operating in a network are the access to partners' value-adding or value-creating resources; a better awareness of what partners are like through repeated inter-firm exchanges; the speeding up and enhancing innovation outcomes; the possibility of achieving economies of scale and scope by tapping into the partners' locations and capacities; shared uncertainty. Further network structures allow to achieve high levels of flexibility, decentralized planning and control (Baker, 1994). Constraints could be the preclusion of cooperation with other firms because of current partners, as well as learning races that could lead to the loss of know-how.

A firm's rent generation capacity can increase if it is able to optimize and manage its network. As suggested by Gulati et al. (2000), this could involve the choice of appropriate governance mechanisms for the firm's partnerships; the development of specific knowledge-sharing routines that allow the firm to learn from its partners; the making of relationship-specific investments that can enforce the inter-firm relationship; managing the partners' expectations, as well as initiating the necessary changes to the partnership when needed.

As already discussed a network perspective on strategy emphasizes the co-creation of sustainable competitive advantage by integrating the strategic resources and capabilities of the firm with those of its partners. Inter-firm partnerships evolve (or co-evolve) with firms' strategies, competitive conditions, technological advances and the overall environment, as well as changes in the top management team committed to the joint undertaking (Koza and Lewin, 2000). Hence one of the natural connections of the network perspective is not only with the RBV (see Chapter 9) but also with the co-evolutionary perspective, which calls attention to the interaction of a firm with its environment in the shaping of its strategy. In general terms a network perspective on strategy focuses on the notion of social capital, which emphasizes the resources and capabilities available to a firm from its network of relationships.

Overall the network perspective can be applied to different levels of strategic analysis, both external and internal to the firm: the overall industry structure, the strategic groups within an industry, inter-firm relationships, intra-firm structure and informal intra-organizational social systems. These levels provide a useful taxonomy for distinguishing between the phenomena associated with the concept 'network' and for appreciating their dynamics.

Case study revisited

The case of InnoCentive illustrates the usefulness of a network perspective to strategy. First, the company's source of advantage cannot be understood by simply applying an RBV of the firm or thinking about the attractiveness of the pharmaceutical industry through an Industrial Organization framework. What makes InnoCentive's value proposition unique for both Seekers and Solvers is its position in a network structure of contacts, which would otherwise have remained disconnected. Thus the first insight that a network perspective provides to the case is that InnoCentive is able to create value through its brokerage role, in which it connects individuals and organisations that lack direct contact and can benefit from it.

Yet the issue is not only the firm's unique brokerage role and position, but also how InnoCentive has established this position and what it does to sustain it. To start attracting Seekers and Solvers and building the bridge between them, initially the company relied on the reputation of its corporate parent, Eli Lilly and Company, and the financial support it provided to its new e-venture. Having Lilly as a parent allowed InnoCentive to convince a number of prestigious companies to post their challenges on the company website, as well as leading scientific minds and research institutions to register as Solvers. Reputable Seekers such as P&G and Dow Chemicals became further endorsers of the business, commenting on their satisfaction with the improved innovation and renewing their subscriptions to InnoCentive's service.

So in the first place, InnoCentive's competitive advantage resides in the creation and management of the network and the construction of a seamless and secure (for intellectual property) bridge between Solvers and Seekers that would have otherwise remained disconnected. Second, it is also due to the size of this network and the features of those companies and scientists that it connects, their reputation and visibility in the industry's network, their talent and thus their ability to endorse the quality of service provided. Furthermore in playing this brokerage role InnoCentive has been willing and able to learn, constantly seeking to formalize and improve the processes through which Solvers and Seekers work together, facilitating the challenge and the solution definition, guaranteeing confidentiality and anonymity when required. In that learning process the company has clearly demonstrated a high absorptive capacity that comes from having the people and processes in place to learn from its partnership relationships.

Last but not least, the value created for the Seekers by providing them with access to potential Solvers has decreased the cost, increased the number of solutions and speeded up the R&D process, in comparison with the results of their in-house R&D operations. Examined from the perspective of the Seeker companies such as P&G or Dow Chemicals, InnoCentive is a partner that allows them to seamlessly outsource certain problems. Yet in order to continue benefiting from this cheaper and faster process, these companies need to redefine the role of their well-integrated and resourced R&D units, to allow them to capture the opportunities provided by the solutions they receive through distributed innovation. Hence from a network perspective, partnering with InnoCentive gives them access to a key resource in the industry – the global, seamless and timeless access to talent. From the perspective of the Solvers, InnoCentive provides an opportunity to participate in the global pharmaceutical industry from their home or research institutions.

Summary

A network perspective on strategy provides a relational view of competitive advantage. While a network perspective itself is able to provide additional insight and understanding on performance differences, we suggest that it be employed in combination with RBV. The combination of the two perspectives allows us to identify what Zaheer and Bell (2005) call 'network-enabled capabilities', capabilities that allow the firm to gain superior rents when it possesses both a superior set of internal resources and a beneficial network structure (one that gives the firm access to structural holes). In using this perspective to understand a firm's potential to outperform competition, the following questions are worth further exploration:

1. How big is our company network? What companies form part of it?
2. What is our position in the network? Is our firm a core, central player? Do we integrate the inputs of others? Or is it a rather peripheral actor?
3. What firms are our strategic partners? What are their strategic resources and capabilities? How do they fit with those of our firm? What is the nature of our relationships with them? How are we going to jointly create value?
4. If we are about to enter a new alliance, would it add value to our relational portfolio? Or would it rather lock us into a relationship that will not allow us to partner with other important industry players?
5. Given the changes in our strategic direction, which partnerships do we need to strengthen? What are those to which we can pay less attention or even exit?
6. Do we have the right capabilities, processes and structures in place in order to learn from our partner in and about the process of collaboration?

Experienced managers realize the importance of the network realities of their organizations. In addition they also have the ability to create, manage, renew and add value through partnerships. As Krackhardt and Hanson (1993, p. 111) point out: 'Understanding relationships will be the key to managerial success.' For that purpose, a network perspective to strategy is a useful tool.

Notes

1. Excerpts from The Wall Street Transcript: Company Interview – InnoCentive, Inc., 29 March 2005.
2. Ibid.

References

Baker, W., *Networking Smart: How to Build Relationships for Personal and Organizational Success* (New York: McGraw-Hill, 1994).

Baum, J. A. C., T. Calabrese and B. Silverman, 'Don't Go it Alone: Alliance Network Composition and Startups' Performance in Canadian Biotechnology', *Strategic Management Journal*, 21 (2000) 267–294.

Borgatti, S. P., M. G. Everett and L. C. Freeman, 'Ucinet UCINET 5 for Windows: Software for Social Network Analysis', Analytic Technologies, Inc. (1999) (Last revised: 5 March 2006).

Burt, R., *Structural Holes: The Social Structure of Competition* (Cambridge, MA: Harvard University Press, 1992).

Burt, R., *Brokerage and Closure: An Introduction to Social Capital* (Oxford, UK: Oxford University Press, 2005).

Cohen, W. and D. Levinthal, 'Absorptive Capacity: A New Perspective on Learning and Innovation', *Administrative Science Quarterly*, 35 (1990) 128–152.

Coleman, J. S., 'Social Capital in the Creation of Human Capital', *American Journal of Sociology*, 94 (Supplement) (1988) 95–120.

Cross, R. and A. Parker, *The Hidden Power of Social Networks: Understanding How Work Really Gets Done in Organizations* (Boston, MA: Harvard Business School Press, 2004).

Dyer, J. and H. Singh, 'The Relational View: Cooperative Strategy and Sources of Interorganizational Competitive Advantage', *Academy of Management Review*, 23, 4 (1998) 660–679.

Eccles, R. W. and D. B. Crane, *Doing Deals* (Boston, MA: Harvard Business School Press, 1988).

Gulati, R., N. Nohria and A. Zaheer, 'Strategic Networks', *Strategic Management Journal*, 21 (2000) 203–215.

Jarillo, J. C., 'On Strategic Networks', *Strategic Management Journal*, 9 (1988) 31–41.

Koza, M. P. and A. Y. Lewin, 'The Co-Evolution of Strategic Alliances', *Organization Science*, 9, 3 (1998) 255–264.

Koza, M. P. and A. Y. Lewin, 'Managing Partnerships and Strategic Alliances: Raising the Odds of Success', *European Management Journal*, 18, 2 (2000) 146–151.

Krackhardt, D. and J. R. Hanson, 'Informal Networks: The Company Behind the Chart', *Harvard Business Review*, 71 (1993) 104–111.

Nohria, N. and R. G. Eccles (eds), *Networks and Organizations: Structure, Form, and Action* (Boston, MA: Harvard Business School Press, 1992).

Saxenian, A. L., 'Regional Networks and the Resurgence of Silicon Valley', *California Management Review*, Fall (1990) 89–112.

Snow, C., R. Miles and H. Coleman, 'Managing 21st Century Network Organizations', *Organizational Dynamics*, 20 (1992) 5–20.

Zaheer, A. and G. G. Bell, 'Benefiting from Network Position: Firm Capabilities, Structural Holes, and Performance', *Strategic Management Journal*, 26, 9 (2005) 809–825.

Sources used in the case study

Breen, B., Lilly's R&D Prescription, *Fast Company*, 57 (April 2002) 44.

Business Week, 'The Power of Us', 20 June 2005.

Howell, D., 'Online Forum Helps Firms Find Answers', *Investor's Business Daily*, 13 November 2002.

Kaihla, P., 'Building a Better R&D Mousetrap', *Business 2.0*, September 2003.

Maiello, M., 'Prozac Hangover', *Forbes.com*, 5 October 2004.

Raynor, M. E. and J. A. Panetta, 'A Better Way to R&D?' *Strategy & Innovation*, March–April (2005) 3–5.

www.innocentive.com

CHAPTER 13

Strategy as Practice Perspective

Julia Balogun, Paula Jarzabkowski and David Seidl

Basic principles

Strategy-as-practice (SAP) is a developing field on strategising in organisations. Broadly speaking, it focuses on the work of the strategist with the aim of understanding the everyday processes, practices and activities involved in the making and doing of strategy and strategic change in organisations. As we shall discuss in more detail later in the chapter, this field brings together a range of scholars working from different theoretical backgrounds, but with a shared interest in 're-humanising' strategy in response to the dominance of micro-economics-based research in strategic management. Whilst those working within the SAP perspective acknowledge the major contribution of individuals such as Michael Porter, they also recognise that strategy research has been increasingly criticised on the basis that it is not relevant to practice, and argue that strategy-research contributions are paradigmatically constrained by the positivistic assumptions and research traditions of micro-economics, which avoid the messy realities of *doing* strategy. Human action disappears as strategy is reduced to a series of causally related variables. Strategy-as-practice seeks to redress the balance. It is concerned with the detailed and intricate aspects of the doing of strategy, or 'strategising', such as how strategists think, talk, act, interact and emote, with a concern also for the tools, technologies and events used by strategists, be it 5-force analyses, post-it notes and specialised planning and analysis software, or workshops and away days (see Balogun et al., 2003; Jarzabkowski, 2004, 2005; Johnson et al., 2003; Whittington, 2003, 2006).

The SAP website (www.strategy-as-practice.org) points out that despite their diverse backgrounds, individuals working within this field agree that to move the strategic management field forward, we need to focus more on the processes and practices constituting the everyday activities of organisational life and that relate to strategic outcomes at the level of the firm and the wider environment. The linkage through to strategic outcomes is an important component as ultimately we need to be able to link the outcomes of (multiple) strategising activities, events and behaviours within the firm to more macro-organisational, institutional and, possibly, even broader social contexts and outcomes. As such, this perspective shares with traditional strategy research a concern for firm performance, but also emphasises the significance of potentially intermediate outcomes. In addition, this perspective argues that strategy research is rife with false dichotomies, such as a separation of the content of ___egy from the process of doing strategy, and the separation of the formulation of strategy from ___tegy, and the separation of the planned and intentional design of strategy ___ements of strategy. Rather we need to acknowledge the interlinked nature ___ Therefore, this perspective typically leads to in-depth qualitative research ___ examine the inside of strategising processes, and recognises the interlinked ___d process, and intentional and emergent activities and outcomes. ___ studies to illustrate the range of studies that are incorporated within the ___ctive. The first is a more traditional study of strategists and their strategising, ___ses on the detailed dialogue that occurs as part of strategising activity, and ___ the presentation of the strategy under discussion.

CASE STUDY 13.1

STRATEGISING AT ÖSTGÖTA ENSKILDA BANK

Östgöta Enskilda Bank (OEB) was a medium-sized Swedish bank operating mainly in one region in Sweden. During the 1990s the bank developed a strategy of geographical expansion within Sweden. The vision was for OEB to become a provincial bank with the establishment of a number of (independent) local banks providing customised services through greenfield investment. The aim was to grow into a national bank, yet make customers feel that they were dealing with a bank that offered rapid decision-making and personal service. Top management's challenge was to focus the local banks on the corporate strategy at the same time as enabling them to develop a local identity and approach: 'We want the customer to feel that all the decision power is in the local bank, even if the decision process on larger credits is standardised and centralised' (Local bank manager).

Top management put in place a centralised framework of standardised controls for issues such as risk-taking and credit decisions. Whilst these provided guidelines, the local banks were free to take individualised strategic actions in other areas. Importance was attached to the recruitment of a well-established, proficient local bank manager from a competitor, who was then tasked with the creation of his own bank, including the recruitment of his staff. During the first year of a new bank's operation, headquarters also provided a pilot computer system to ensure the new, local bank provided the standard information required by the head office on its activities. However, the key to the success of shaping local strategising lay in top manager's use of active engagement with those delivering the strategy on the ground. Once recruited, the new bank manager was engaged in dialogue with the top management team, leading to the evolution of shared meanings. In addition, the top managers continued to exert influence on local interpretations of their vision through ongoing formal and informal dialogues with local bank managers, including regular face-to-face meetings. Yet significant local discretion was allowed in order to tailor services to local customer needs, since each local bank could, for example, choose their own name, the location and design of premises, what staff to recruit and the range of products to offer.

The process of developing common goals between the head office and the local banks comprised a two-way process. Top managers had a vision of the goals but needed to allow local bank managers to adapt these into local activities through which the goals could be realised. Strategic goals and appropriate local activity were progressively interpreted and reinterpreted through the dialogues with local bank managers: 'No manager from the centre came down to tell us how to do it. . . . They were very supportive and interested, but they let us do things based on our own thinking' (Local bank manager). Through the ongoing formal and informal dialogue, the top management team and local bank managers gradually developed a set of shared meanings about OEB as a network of largely independent local banks with common views on personalised customer service, profitability, risk-taking and credit decisions.

Adapted from 'Leadership: the role of interactive strategising' by L. Achentenhagen et al. (2003: 49–71), and Jarzabkowski (2005).

Questions: Strategising at Östgöta Enskilda Bank

1. Who do you consider to be the strategist(s) here?

2. What strategic activities are these different strategists engaged in?

3. How do the different strategic activities affect strategic outcomes a) at the local level and b) at the organisational level?

4. To really understand what is happening here, what else do you need to know about the strategists, their actions and activities, and the resources they are drawing on?

CASE STUDY 13.2

WRITING STRATEGY: SHAPING THE STORY

This vignette takes a look at the detailed work of strategists. Precise details about the company from which it is taken are not revealed to preserve anonymity and confidentiality. The vignette is based on a regular strategy meeting. It focuses on the work of a Director of Strategy (DS) and a Strategic Planner (SSP) engaged in writing the annual strategic plan. They had already spent a lot of time on the development of the plan in the previous few months (through formal meetings, corridor and phone conversations and so on, often observed by the researcher) and were now carefully refining it further for the next PLC board meeting. As SSP noted, they were 'shap[ing] the story'. The strategists were engaged in a 'line-by-line' scrutiny of the document, altering it in minute detail in order to influence its reception by the board. The extract provides a glimpse of this interpersonal process.

DS: So we really need to make this (*pause*) something *like that one* it needs to be about the economic downturn and impact on market structure

SSP: um

(*pause and silence as both read*)

DS: What did you say on that (*pause*) when you say [name of division] do you mean [Group name]?

SSP: Er yeah [name of company] and the organisation, the external market

DS: I'd think I'd call that recent trends (*quietly speaks as reads*) 'survival' (*reads*) its another bit that goes in there, I think you've got it somewhere else but the um the dirt-cheap asset prices need to go in there

SSP: Yeah I've got that in the main body of the report and the competition but yeah we can put that in there as well

DS: I think its part of the (*pause*) if you made that into market structure . . .

SSP: . . . Yes . . .

DS: What that says is (*pause*) here's a big consolidation piece . . . its (*pause*) consolidation (*as he writes*)

(*and less than a minute later . . .*)

DS: So some of that um (*pause*) er I would call that (*pause*) mobilising our strategy

SSP: um um right . . .

DS: . . . I'd call that (*as he writes he slowly says*) 'mobilising' (*pause*) and I'd make that the last one

SSP: Sure

DS: In the hope that they'd got bored by then and won't read it properly (*pause*) I'd call that mobilising our strategy or a sub-heading . . . 'business transformation' (*writes as reads*)

Adapted from 'Understanding our world as it happens and re-conceptualising strategising as a "kinda" magic', Organisation Studies Summer Conference, Santorini, 2005, and 'Its a "kinda..." *magic* or alternatively, strategising to project the self and organisation into the future', EGOS Conference, Ljubljana, 2004b, both by D. Samra-Fredericks.[1]

Questions: Writing strategy – Shaping the story

1. What is the difference in the focus of this case study in comparison to the case study on OEB?

2. What do you learn about the doing of strategy from this extract? What does it suggest about the role of formal versus informal strategising activity?

3. What are the strategic outcomes that those involved are trying to influence?

Overview of strategy as practice

An initial conference in 2002 followed by a special issue on micro-strategising (Johnson et al., 2003) in the *Journal of Management Studies* took up the challenge of reintroducing the strategist into strategy research by emphasising the importance of studying the myriad of micro-actions through which human actors shape activity in ways that are consequential for organisational strategic outcomes. The editors called for contributions to strategy that would be explicitly based on human activity; for example, research that, like our two mini cases above, focuses upon strategists and how their interactions shape strategy. Strategy, according to this view, is not something that an organisation *has* but something its members *do*: 'strategising' is the 'doing of strategy'. They suggested the label 'Activity-Based View' to express this micro-focus. A further important aspect of the strategy-as-practice approach, however, was not really addressed in the special issue – that is the *contextualisation* of the micro-activities (Whittington, 2006). Micro-phenomena need to be understood in their wider social context: actors in their micro-situations are not acting in isolation but are drawing upon the regular, socially defined modes of acting that arise from the plural social institutions to which they belong. Much of the social infrastructure, such as tools, technologies and discourses, through which micro-actions are constructed has macro- and institutionalised properties that enables its transmission within and between contexts, whilst being adopted and adapted differently within micro-contexts (Wilson and Jarzabkowski, 2004). In this sense the strategy-as-practice approach tries to establish explicit links between micro and macro perspectives. In order to account for this dual focus on micro and macro, the label 'Activity-Based View' was later on replaced by the current label 'Strategy as Practice', where 'practice' refers both to the concrete doings of the individual human beings (micro) and to the different socially defined practices (macro) that the individuals are drawing upon in their concrete doings.

The special issue's call appealed to individuals working from multiple perspectives, including the institutional and RBV perspectives, but in particular the call for a focus on the individual practitioner has had a resonance with those following the wider 'practice' and 'linguistic' turns in management studies. The practice turn broadly refers to research grounded in the practical activity and reason of human actors, with a focus on activity, actors and practices (Whittington, 2006), whereas the linguistic turn focuses on language, with society, organisations, and so on conceived of as 'discursively constructed ensembles of texts' (Alvesson and Karreman, 2000, p. 137). The linguistic turn is particularly apparent in studies of strategic change, where the application of a variety of approaches using terms such as 'dialogue', 'narrative', 'rhetoric', 'conversation' and 'language' has become popular. It is also fair to say that those interested in the field are approaching it from two different entry points – a practical interest in what strategists do versus an interest from a more ontologically motivated practice perspective which draws on the practice turn. As the strategy-as-practice call for a rehumanisation of strategy has had a growing resonance with these different groups of researchers, the field has acquired momentum, with regular workshops, conference tracks, books (Jarzabkowski, 2005; Johnson et al., 2007) and additional special issues (Balogun et al., 2007; Pye and Pettigrew, 2007; Whittington and Cailluet, 2007). However, since strategy as practice is populated by a group of eclectic individuals, the field faces several challenges. Questions that are consistently raised – particularly by newcomers to the field – include the following:

1. What is strategy?
2. Who is a strategist?
3. What do strategists do?
4. What does an analysis of strategists and their work explain?
5. How can existing organisation and social theory inform an analysis of strategy as practice?

To be able to address these questions we need a framework to help us appreciate the different elements of 'strategising' that we are studying. The following conceptual framework (Whittington, 2006) can be used to tease out the difficulties and deepen the research agenda (see Figure 13.1). Whittington (2006) suggests we need to focus on three elements – praxis, practices and practitioners, each of which comprises a different entry point into the study of strategy as practice. *Praxis* is 'an emphatic term to describe the whole of human action' (Reckwitz, 2002, p. 249). More specifically, it comprises the interconnection between the actions of different, dispersed individuals and groups and those socially, politically, and economically embedded institutions within which individuals act (Sztompka, 1991). Put more simply, praxis is about actual activity – what people actually do. Therefore praxis is dynamic. It consists of a flow of activity over time, constructed by the actions of multiple individuals in interaction with each other and with the institutions of their society. This temporal dimension of praxis – the focus on actions, interactions and negotiations through time – contains within it a connection of past, present and future, since the past is drawn on in creating the present (and thus shapes and constrains present action), yet the present also reconstructs and amends the past, creating new future possibilities. The OEB mini case provides a small example of this as it deals with strategy as a practice that is shaped over time by the multiple interactions between individuals at different levels of the firm. Within strategy as practice, *praxis* encompasses all the activities to do with the formulation and implementation of strategy (Whittington, 2006), and includes not just, for example, consulting interventions and workshops, but also more mundane aspects of the strategists' work such as board meetings and team briefings.

Practices are defined as 'routinised types of behaviour which consist of several elements, interconnected to one another: forms of bodily activities, forms of mental activities, "things" and their use, a background knowledge in the form of understanding, know-how, states of emotion and motivational knowledge' (Reckwitz, 2002, p. 249). 'Practices' refers to shared routines of behaviour, traditions, norms, and ways of thinking and acting – the things people draw on when doing praxis. Practices provide the behavioural, cognitive, procedural, discursive and physical resources through which actors construct activity. Put more simply, practices include the tools, technologies and know-how of the

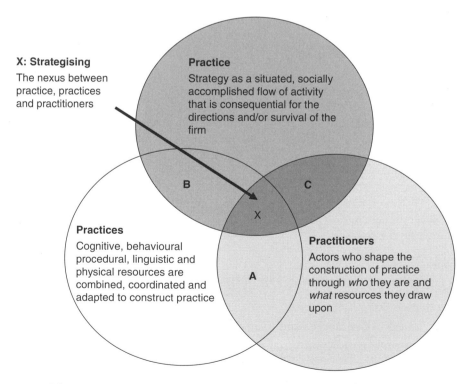

Figure 13.1 Strategy-as-practice: A conceptual framework

practitioner – the things the strategist uses when engaged in strategising. However, the concept of practices also alerts us to the need to examine what types of mental activities, things, know-how and motivations are drawn upon by strategists in constructing strategy and their implications for the practice of strategy. Thus here we might be concerned with the tools of the strategist, like ways of doing environmental scanning, or industry analysis, but we also need to include, for example, the discourses and language that informs how we do strategy, which might be organisation specific, or more general societal-level discourse, and organisational routines of decision-making such as committees. The second vignette on writing strategy provides an example of this since it examines how the strategists are manipulating the words used in the strategy document in order to shape the reactions of the Board.

Practitioners are the actors of strategy; those individuals who draw upon practices and do actions. Practitioners shape such activity through *who* they are, *how* they act and *what* resources they draw upon in that action.

As Figure 13.1 indicates, while these concepts are discrete they are also interconnected, so that it is not possible to study one without also drawing on aspects of the others. Strategising occurs as the union of praxis, practices and practitioners, and any research agenda has to take this into account. Therefore, this framework can be used to help answer the other questions posed above.

What is strategy?

Drawing on the above definition of praxis, we can see that from a strategy-as-practice perspective, strategy is conceptualised *as a situated, socially accomplished activity, while strategising comprises those actions, interactions and negotiations of multiple actors and the situated practices that they draw upon in accomplishing that activity.* As with the more general definition of praxis, a particularly important component of this definition is that it is dynamic, and about a flow of activity over time between multiple individuals, incorporating a temporal dimension in which the past, current and future are connected. Therefore, to study strategy, we need to be concerned with understanding how associated activity is *constructed and shaped*, by both past and present actions, and also how this activity has a future impact upon the directions and survival of the firm. However, this definition is very broad, encompassing *all* organisational activity. So which activity is strategic and which is not? And what do we study? We can answer this question in two different ways. First, we can focus on activities associated with recognised and accepted organisational strategic practice, such as strategic planning and strategy workshops. Since strategy is a particular type of activity (Barry and Elmes, 1997; Hendry, 2000; Knights and Morgan, 1991) connected with particular practice, we can consider strategy to be about the activities involved in a particular practice. So, for example, we can study what strategists do in strategy workshops and their implications for strategy, with a focus on the tools and techniques, the technologies (whiteboards, post-it notes, computer systems) and other activities such as brainstorming, game playing and in general the talk or discourse (Hendry and Seidl, 2003; Hodgkinson et al., 2005). Such research would be focusing on area B of Figure 13.1, since it has little to do with who a strategist is, and more to do with their practices (e.g. what is done, how and why) within the strategic praxis (workshop).

Alternatively, we can consider activity to be strategic if it is consequential for the strategic outcomes, survival and competitive advantage of the firm (Johnson et al., 2003). This is true when the activity is connected with an intended and formally articulated strategy, and when activity is more unintended and emergent. So, for example, we could study the role of a group of strategists in the formulation or implementation of strategy, and how they through their role shape the outcomes achieved (Balogun and Johnson, 2004, 2005). This would be more of a focus on sector C – the intersection between practitioners and praxis. This highlights an important point. Whilst all studies are likely to focus on strategising, within that, there is likely to be a predominant focus on the interconnections marked either A, B or C on Figure 13.1, dependent on what the researcher puts in the foreground, and what the researcher puts in the background.

Who is a strategist?

The question of who may be considered a strategist clearly indicates the practitioner as a unit of analysis from which to study the practice of strategy. However, there are two aspects to this question – first, which types of individuals do we consider to be strategists (i.e. who does strategy work), and second, given that the above framework suggests that practitioners shape praxis through who they are, how they act and what resources they draw upon, what do we study about strategists?

Who do we consider to be strategists?

The literature is still dominated by top-down conceptualisations of strategy, with an emphasis on formulation, and the role of top managers, their demographics and their decision-making processes (e.g. Hambrick and Mason, 1984; Wiersema and Bantel, 1992). First, this focus fails to deal with issues raised by the framework above, such as how the identity of a strategist might affect what they do and how, which connects to the second question, what do we study about strategists? Second, as we argue above, the practice perspective acknowledges linkages between formulation and implementation, content and process, emergent and deliberate, which in turn requires a consideration of a much wider group of actors (Balogun et al., 2003). The intention is not to suggest that it is not useful to study senior managers, as there is still much to be learnt from studying them, and they are often the most significant strategists (e.g. Jarzabkowski, 2003, 2005; Pye, 1995; Samra-Fredericks, 2003, 2004a). However, a growing stream of research dating from the 1970s and 80s indicates that others, such as middle managers, may also be important strategic actors (e.g. Burgelman, 1983, 1996; Floyd and Wooldridge, 1992, 1997; Huy, 2002). Thus some strategy-as-practice scholars have focused on understanding how such actors are able to shape strategy even though they lack a formal strategic role (e.g. Balogun, 2003; Balogun and Johnson, 2004, 2005; Regner, 2003; Rouleau, 2005). Then, of course, there are those actors outside of the firm who also influence strategy and merit attention – consultants, business gurus, non-executive directors and so on.

What do we study about strategists?

As the above framework shows, understanding the strategist requires us to consider the embodied nature of agency, in which *who* a person is, is innately connected to how that person acts and the consequences of that action for the construction of activity (Blackler, 1995). So, for example, how strategy is defined, and therefore what is studied is affected by the identity of individuals. So, for example, in a paper on 'The Mayor, the street-fighter and the insider-out', Beech and Johnson (2005) show how an individual's identity, and the (potentially different) identities imposed on them by others, has an impact on what they do and how. They also show how an individual's identity may shift through time and the impact of this on actions. Similarly, Rouleau (2005) shows how gender impacts on a strategist and what they do. Therefore, one important avenue for analysing strategy as practice involves identifying who is a strategist in terms of what individuals bring to their strategising role. Again – we see the interrelationship between praxis, practices and practitioners. To understand how who a person is affects what they do, requires either a simultaneous focus on the doing (the praxis) or a simultaneous focus on how it affects the practices they are drawing on. Thus by showing how the identity of the strategist affects strategic change, Beech and Johnson (2005) are focusing on sector C. Whereas if they had focused on how the identity of the strategist affected the tools, techniques and know-how drawn on (by, for example, showing that their background as a marketer as opposed to an economist gave them a different repertoire to draw on), this research would have focused on sector A.

What do strategists do?

This question goes beyond simple lists of activities and classificatory schemes. Rather, it focuses upon what the doing of strategy involves and, most importantly, how that doing shapes strategy. The question may appear to be underpinned by the concept of praxis, since we are asking a question about what strategists do. In fact this question is underpinned, theoretically, by the concept of *practices*; that is, it focuses upon those bodily actions, mental activities, talk, 'things' and their use, know-how, emotions and motivations that practitioners engage in when they are doing strategy. In other words, here we are concerned with *how* strategists do what they do. What is the situated knowledge or their person-specific knowledge that they draw on? How do their emotions, intentions and interpretations affect what they do? How do existing organisational discourses shape strategic practice? This suggests that what strategists do is strongly connected to who strategists are and the situation in which they act. In other words, a focus on how strategists do what they do leads to research focus on sector B or A of Figure 13.1. As we argue above, research that explores what strategists do in strategy workshops or meetings and their implications for strategy (e.g. Hendry and Seidl, 2003; Hodgkinson et al., 2005) has less to do with who a strategist is and is more about the practices of doing strategy – a focus on section B of Figure 13.1, the intersection between praxis (e.g. workshops) and practices (e.g. what is done, how and why within the workshop). Whereas research that explores, for example, how an individual's identity influences their strategy work suggests a stronger focus on section A of Figure 13.1, the intersection between practitioners and practices.

The above paragraph may suggest we are going round in circles here – we have already discussed sectors A and B. However, this is also about what is in the foreground as the primary unit of analysis or the starting point, and what is in the background. So, for example, those starting with *praxis* would be interested in strategy workshops as a phenomenon, and then may focus on the practices within those workshops, or the roles of different strategists within the workshops, moving the research towards sector B or C. Whereas those starting with *practices* would be interested in how strategy is done, and would then choose, for example, strategy workshops as a context for the focus on the how, or how who the strategist is affects the how, moving the research towards sector B or A. Whilst this all becomes rather complex, it is all about levels of abstraction. So just as one can study the phenomenon or *praxis* of strategy workshops, one could equally study strategy workshops as *practices* in their own right: we could, for example, examine the role of strategy events in stabilising or destabilising strategic activity (Jarzabkowski and Seidl, 2005) – again sector B, but a different starting point.

What does an analysis of strategists and their work explain?

To be credible within the field of strategic management research, particularly since the field is dominated by an economics-based focus on outcome measures at the firm and industry level such as 'firm performance' (e.g. McGahan and Porter, 1997; Rumelt, 1991), the SAP field must be clear about the 'so what' that comes from research. This problem is partly resolved by our definition of strategy as a situated, socially accomplished flow of activity that has *consequential outcomes for the direction and/or survival of the firm*. The objective of strategising research is, therefore, to explain some aspect of activity which may be considered, plausibly, to be consequential for the firm. While such outcomes can be distinct from firm-level outcomes, since they might explain a strategic decision (Samra-Fredericks,

2003) or the failure to develop a strategic direction (Maitlis and Lawrence, 2003), they are nonetheless outcomes of strategising research that are clearly consequential for the firm. Indeed, Regner's (2003) longitudinal study of inductive strategising behaviour by actors at the periphery of firms serves to explain outcomes as consequential as Ericsson's entry into the mobile telephony market. Thus, the outcomes of strategising studies, rather than focusing upon the firm level, may be explanations of some aspect of organisational activity that is a 'micro mechanism' in transforming the strategy of the firm (Tsoukas and Chia, 2002).

However, as discussed above, the SAP approach also tries to establish explicit links between micro and macro perspectives – and has a concern for whether these micro-level explanations are consequential at more macro levels of the firm and the industry. Thus whilst we don't want to be drawn into a debate as to what constitutes micro and macro, strategising research can provide explanations at many different 'levels', such as the evolution of strategies (Jarzabkowski, 2005; Sminia, 2005) and capabilities (Salvato, 2003), or the implementation of firm-level change (Balogun and Johnson, 2004, 2005; Rouleau, 2005) or firm renewal (Regner, 2003). But the research can also provide even more macro explanations through the examination of practices of institutionalisation and their consequences for firms within an industry, such as alliances within the airline industry (Vaara et al., 2004).

How can existing theory inform an analysis of strategy as practice?

The last challenge regularly revisited by individuals in the strategy–as-practice field, at both conferences and workshops, is the theoretical basis of strategy-as-practice research and how the field can draw on existing organisation and social theory approaches to develop findings of consequences. As we discuss above, the field has naturally populated itself with a diverse range of theoretical perspectives given its appeal to all those taking different approaches to the reintroduction of the strategist to, or humanising, strategy research. Therefore, strategy as practice is characterised less by what theory is adopted and more by the central research focus on explaining who strategists are, what they do and why and how that is influential for the practice of strategy. As such, many problems posed in existing strategy research, and reviewed within this book such as the resource-based view, or managerial and organisational cognition might be illuminated by a practice based approach to their study (Antonacopoulou and Ferdinand, 2004; Hodgkinson and Clarke, 2004; Jarzabkowski, 2005; Johnson et al., 2003).

Table 13.1 summarises some existing empirical work in the strategy-as-practice area. It reveals how organisation theories in areas such as practice, sense-making, cognition, culture, power, narrative and discourse can provide valuable theoretical resources for strategising research drawing, as with much other organisation theory, from the meta-theoretical principles of sociology, social psychology, anthropology and ethnomethodology, among others, to understand the construction of activity within organisations. Table 13.1 also shows that there is a clear tendency towards those organisation theories that adopt a broadly social construction approach to help frame and interpret work. What is noticeable in these studies is a consistent effort to theorise from rich data, drawing upon those sense-making, process, narrative, discourse and social theories that help to frame and explain a particular practice phenomenon. Many studies adopt a focus upon discourse, language and narrative to explain the construction of strategic activity, suggesting that such theories are a particularly fruitful avenue for exploring the construction of strategy as practice. It appears, therefore, that there is room to incorporate a diverse range of organisation theories within a practice research agenda. The common point of such studies is their concern to explain some aspect of the nexus between praxis, practitioners and practices in the construction of strategy as a socially accomplished and consequential activity.

Table 13.1 A summary of how empirical strategising research operationalises key concepts in the SAP agenda[i]

Exemplars	Dominant practitioner focus (Who is a strategist?)	Main practices examined (What do strategists do?)	Level of Practice (What does it explain?)	Dominant analytic focus (Figure 1)[ii]	What theoretical bases are used?
Balogun and Johnson, 2004, 2005	Middle managers in multiple divisions	Sense-making specific to what role (e.g. engineer or services) the strategist occupies Social practices of interaction	Firm-level: implementation of strategic change	C	Sense-making/ schema theory
Balogun and Jarzabkowski, 2005	Top, middle and operational managers	Strategic planning as a practice for constructing and distributing strategy knowledge	Activity level: distributing strategy making within and between levels	B	Perspective-making and perspective-taking; social theory of practice
Hodgkinson et al., 2005	Multiple organisational levels according to workshop participation	Workshops	Activity-level: impact on strategy development	B	Institutionalisation and diffusion of a practice
Jarzabkowski, 2003, 2005	Top managers	Formal administrative practices and face-to-face interaction and their uses in phases of the evolution of activity	Activity-level: evolution of streams of strategic activity over time	B	Social theories of practice Strategy process theory
Jarzabkowski and Seidl, 2005	Top managers	Strategy meetings	Activity-level: role of meetings in stabilising or destabilising strategic activity	B	Social theories of practice
Maitlis and Lawrence, 2003	Top managers, board members, other employees	Use discursive resources specific to the context and political practices according to their power bases	Firm-level: failure in strategy formation	A	Discourse theory Theories of power and politics

Table 13.1 Continued

Exemplars	Dominant practitioner focus (Who is a strategist?)	Main practices examined (What do strategists do?)	Level of Practice (What does it explain?)	Dominant analytic focus (Figure 1)[ii]	What theoretical bases are used?
Mantere, 2005	Top, middle and operational managers	Strategy formation practices; organising practices; and control practices specific to what role the strategist occupies	Individual level: construction of the self as a strategist	A	Structuration theory
Regner, 2003	Top and peripheral (SBU) managers	Sensemaking practices and localised know-how specific to whether the strategist is a peripheral or top manager	Firm-level: strategy creation and renewal over time	B	Strategy process theory
Rouleau, 2005	Middle managers	Engage in sense-making and sense-giving narratives that are specific to who the strategist is Gendered embodiment of agency in interpreting and selling change	Firm-level: implementation of strategic change	C	Sense-making theory Narrative theory

This table is adapted from Jarzabkowski et al., 2007

i These exemplars are neither exhaustive nor exclusive but illustrate how some key studies have addressed the challenges of strategy-as-practice research

ii A, B and C relate to Figure 13.1. A: interconnection practices / practices. B: interconnection practitioners / practice. C: interconnection practitioners / practice

Case Studies Revisited

Strategising at Östgöta Enskilda Bank

Who do you consider to be the strategist(s) here?

This question explores issues related to the practitioner. Obviously the senior managers at ÖEB were strategists, setting a strategic direction for the bank, and a context within which local bank managers had to operate. However, the case also encourages consideration of to what extent the local bank managers were also strategists. By their actions, their local interpretations of the senior managers' strategy for the bank, and their dialogue with the senior managers they created an incremental, bottom-up adaptation of the original senior manager top-down strategy, illustrating clearly how formulation and implementation can be intertwined through time and the connections between the content and process of strategy.

What strategic activities are these different strategists engaged in?

This question focuses more on issues to do with praxis and practices. Overall, we are concerned with the praxis of developing and implementing the strategy: to become a provincial bank through the establishment of a number of (independent) local banks providing customised services. Within this we can see that the different strategists are engaging in a range of different, separate, but also joint, strategic practices. The senior managers are setting the strategising context for local managers through the imposition of centralised systems and controls and through ongoing formal and informal 'conversations' with the local bank managers. The local bank managers are engaged jointly in the conversations, but are also separately engaging in a range of local activities aimed at creating something different or unique, tailored to their customer needs.

We can see how this leads to one set of strategic outcomes locally, and another set organisationally. At the organisational level, there is a strategic vision, set by the senior managers, that endures through time. Locally, the actions of the local bank managers lead to a multiplicity of different customer strategies, and thus there are multiple peripheral strategies, all contributing to the organisational strategic vision. Through this local adaptation, the detail of the overall organisational strategy is also shaped in an emergent, bottom-up fashion by the actions of the local managers and their conversations with the senior managers. Thus the local and organisational outcomes are interlinked.

To really understand what is happening here, what else do you need to know about the strategists, their actions and activities, and the resources they are drawing on?

The case in particular gives us limited information about the strategists, other than to explain that the bank managers recruited are experienced bank managers with good knowledge of local customer needs. So, for example, the whole mechanism here relies on trust, with the senior managers heavily reliant on the skills and know-how of the local managers for the successful delivery of their intended strategy. However, it also gives us limited information of the practices, for example the dialogues engaged in between senior and local managers, how the senior managers arrived at their strategy, and the local practices engaged in to deliver local customised services. Whilst we are left with a good impression of how strategising occurs through two-way dialogue, with the senior managers setting the context and framework for local actions through imposed centralised systems and face-to-face interaction (a focus on sector B of Figure 13.1), to really understand what is going on here, we need to know a lot more about the strategists and their practices, and in particular about the local strategists and their praxis and practices.

Writing strategy: Shaping the story

What is the difference in the focus of this case study in comparison to the case study on ÖEB?

In the second case we are more concerned with exploring the strategist and their resources (practices) – sector A of Figure 13.1 – to understand the practice of strategy presentation. As we argue above, this puts the focus on the tools, technologies and know-how, including the discourses and language, which strategists draw upon to formulate this thing called strategy, and in this particular case a plausible strategy document. As Samra-Fredericks (2004b, 2005) comments, given that the speakers are individuals vested with a formal duty to develop strategy, it is not surprising that they utilise knowledge gained through executive development, for example MBA programmes or executive short courses, in their strategic praxis. Such detailed case studies enable us to appreciate how the language of strategy-making and strategic management is used in practice to realise certain effects during interaction. These two vignettes therefore complement each other, showing how research motivated by both the practice turn and the linguistic turn can inform the SAP agenda. Different theoretical perspectives enable us to learn different things about strategists and what they do.

What do you learn about the doing of strategy from this extract?

Samra-Fredericks (2004b, 2005) argues that by examining such extracts we can see how through working out 'what to put in (*highlight*) or leave out (*hide*)' strategists attempt to seduce their various audiences – strategy emerges through a 'kinda magic'. Yet she also points out that we learn about other aspects of presenting strategy, such as the importance of front-stage and back-stage performances, humour, play and role-modelling. The front- and back-stage activity comes through particularly clearly in the vignette presented here as the strategists are building the document knowing all too well that the document 'will 'stand in' for them in other places where significant (powerful) 'others' will consume them' (Samra-Fredericks, 2005). They need to develop a document that will influence the thinking of others in their absence, and are therefore choosing their words very carefully. To show this, Samra-Fredericks (2004b, 2005) focuses on the use of the strategists' vocabulary and their reliance upon taken-for-granted (local) meanings, highlighting the use of euphemisms such as 'market consolidating', which in this case is being used to disguise yet simultaneously convey the fact of financially weaker companies going 'for a song'. The vignette therefore gives us a direct insight into how strategists 'craft strategy' (Mintzberg, 1987).

The importance of back-stage preparation for front-stage performances, for example considering how to act and talk to influence others, and whom to invite and not invite to meetings, also brings into focus the division between formal, set strategy events, such as workshops, and informal events that occur around the more formal events in preparation. To understand the formal, and typically studied, strategy events, we have to understand the informal events that have occurred in the run-up to these events – be they story-writing meetings, as shown in the case study, or corridor conversations. In other words, in considering the resources strategists draw on, and how they are influenced by their context, we are also considering the politics of strategic decision-making and change. This quote from a different case study (Bate et al., 2000) on change in the National Health Service (UK) illustrates well the need to understand these informal activities as much as the formal:

'It's all about who shouts the loudest, who wields the biggest stick. It's like a playground ... The real power is with the bullies and the empire-builders. And you're asking me about strategy?' (An NHS Manager)

What are the strategic outcomes that those involved are trying to influence?

Clearly the strategists observed by Samra-Fredericks are about trying to influence the acceptance of their strategy by the board. What they put into the document will determine what gets adopted as the organisation's intended strategy. However, as she points out (2005), another aspect of this activity is apprenticeship. DS is clearly the leader talking about what 'I' would or wouldn't do. The language use is subtle, with no explanation of why 'I' would do this or that, but at the same time, DS is passing on to SSP his experience in how to word and present things.

Summary

In this chapter we have tried to show how the strategy-as-practice perspective encourages researchers to dig deeper into the lived world and experiences of strategists in order to 're-humanise' strategy. We are concerned with studying strategy as a *situated social activity, constructed through the actions, interactions and negotiations of multiple actors and the situated practices that they draw upon.* However, we have also emphasised the importance of being able to link the mundane and micro-level aspects of what strategists do to strategic outcomes at the firm level and beyond if the research is to have impact. We must also consider the actual strategic practitioner. Another outcome of the SAP agenda must be to improve the skills and capabilities of those actually doing strategy within organisations. The discussion in this chapter highlights the fact that whilst there are many well-known and almost taken-for-granted techniques and frameworks that we expect strategists to have within their toolkits, our actual knowledge of how strategists deploy their toolkits is limited. The two mini case studies illustrate the potential within SAP research to help practitioners understand better their craft and develop their skills. The field embodies challenges to some of the conventions of the strategy field, in terms of how we think about strategy, who we consider to be strategists and how we think about their work.

The SAP field is still in its infancy. Our consideration above of how we need to further explore praxis, practices and practitioners shows the extent of research that is still needed if we are to advance this field and, for that matter, our knowledge of strategic management. It reveals just how much we don't know about strategists and what they do. Whilst the SAP field has made a considerable impact over the last four years, many challenges remain.

Note

1. We would like to thank Dalvir Samra-Fredericks for allowing us to include this case study material and subsequent analysis.

References

Achentenhagen, L., L. Melin, T. Mullern and T. Ericson, 'Leadership: The role of interactive strategizing', in A. M. Pettigrew, R. Whittington, L. Melin, C. Sanchez-Runde, F. A. J. van den Bosch, W. Ruigrok and T. Numagami (eds) *Innovative Forms of Organizing: Interpersonal Perspectives* (London: Sage, 2003), pp. 49–71.

Alvesson, M. and D. Karreman, 'Taking the Linguistic Turn in Organizational Research: Challenges, Responses, Consequences', *Journal of Applied Behavioral Science*, 36, 2 (2000) 136–158.

Antonacopoulou, E. P. and J. Ferdinand, 'Dynamic Capability Development: The Politics of Strategic Learning Practices', Paper presented at the *24th Annual Conference of the Strategic Management Society* (San Juan, Puerto Rico, USA, 2004).

Balogun, J., 'From Blaming the Middle to Harnessing its Potential: Creating Change Intermediaries', *British Journal of Management*, 14, 1 (2003) 69–84.

Balogun, J. and P. Jarzabkowski, *European Group for Organization Studies Conference* (Berlin, 2005).

Balogun, J. and G. Johnson, 'Organizational Restructuring And Middle Manager Sensemaking', *Academy of Management Journal*, 47, 5 (2004) 523–549.

Balogun, J. and G. Johnson, 'From Intended Strategies to Unintended Outcomes: The Impact of Change Recipient Sensemaking', *Organization Studies*, 26, 11 (2005) 1573–1602.

Balogun, J., A. S. Huff and P. Johnson, 'Three Responses to the Methodological Challenges of Studying Strategizing', *Journal of Management Studies*, 40 (2003) 197–224.

Balogun, J., P. Jarzabkowski and D. Seidl, 'Strategizing: The Challenges of Practice Perspective', *Human Relations*, Special issue, 60, 1 (2007).

Barry, D. and M. Elmes, 'Strategy Retold: Toward a Narrative View of Strategic Discourse', *Academy of Management Review*, 22, 2 (1997) 429–452.

Bate, P., R. Khan and A. Pye, 'Towards a Culturally Sensitive Approach to Organization Structuring: Where Organization Design Meets Organizational Development', *Organization Science*, 11, 2 (2000) 197–211.

Beech, N. and P. Johnson, 'Discourses of Disrupted Identities in the Practice of Strategic Change: The Mayor, the Street-fighter and the Insider-out', *Journal of Organizational Change Management*, 18, 1 (2005) 31–47.

Blackler, F., 'Knowledge, Knowledge Work and Organizations: An Overview and Interpretation', *Organization Studies*, 16 (1995) 1021–1046.

Burgelman, R. A., 'A Process Model of Internal Corporate Venturing in the Diversified Major Firm', *Administrative Science Quarterly*, 28 (1983) 223–244.

Burgelman, R. A., 'A Process Model of Strategic Business Exit: Implications for an Evolutionary Perspective on Strategy', *Strategic Management Journal*, 17 (1996) 193–214.

Floyd, S. W. and B. Wooldridge, 'Middle Management Involvement in Strategy and its Association with Strategic Type: A Research Note', *Strategic Management Journal*, 13 (1992) 153–167.

Floyd, S. W. and B. Wooldridge, 'Middle Management's Strategic Influence and Organizational Performance', *Journal of Management Studies*, 34, 3 (1997) 465–485.

Hambrick, D. C. and P. A. Mason, 'Upper Echelons: The Organization a Reflection of its Top Managers', *Academy of Management Review*, 9, 2 (1984) 193–206.

Hendry, J., 'Strategic Decision Making, Discourse, and Strategy as Social Practice', *Journal of Management Studies*, 37 (2000) 955–977.

Hendry, J. and D. Seidl, 'The Structure and Significance of Strategic Episodes: Social Systems Theory and the Routine Practices of Strategic Change', *Journal of Management Studies*, 40, 1 (2003) 175–196.

Hodgkinson, G. and I. Clarke, 'Toward a Cognitive Research Theory of Organizational Strategizing', *AIM Working Paper Series, WP No. 004* (2004).

Hodgkinson, G., G. Johnson, R. Whittington and M. Schwarz, 'The Role and Importance of Strategy Workshops', *Advanced Institute of Management Research (AIM) and Chartered Management Institute (CMI)* (July 2005).

Huy, Q. N., 'Emotional Balancing of Organizational Continuity and Radical Change: The Contribution of Middle Managers', *Administrative Science Quarterly*, 47 (2002) 31–69.

Jarzabkowski, P., 'Strategic Practices: An Activity Theory Perspective on Continuity and Change', *Journal of Management Studies*, 40, 1 (2003) 23–55.

Jarzabkowski, P., 'Strategy as Practice: Recursiveness, Adaptation and Practices-in-use', *Organization Studies*, 25, 4 (2004) 529–560.

Jarzabkowski, P., *Strategy as Practice: An Activity-based Approach* (London, UK: Sage, 2005).

Jarzabkowski, P. and D. Seidl, 'Meetings as Strategizing Episodes in the Becoming of Organizational Strategy', *European Group for Organization Studies Conference* (Berlin, 2005).

Jarzabkowski, P., J. Balogun and D. Seidl, 'Strategizing: The Challenges of a Practice Perspective', *Human Relations*, 60 (2007).

Johnson, G., L. Melin and R. Whittington, 'Micro Strategy and Strategizing: Towards an Activity-based View?', *Journal of Management Studies*, 40, 1 (2003) 3–22.

Johnson, G., A. Langley, L. Melin and R. Whittington, Strategy as Practice: Research Directions and Resources, Cambridge University Press, 2007.

Knights, D. and G. Morgan, 'Corporate Strategy, Organizations, and Subjectivity: A Critique', *Organization Studies*, 12, 2 (1991) 251–273.

Maitlis, S. and B. Lawrence, 'Orchestral Manoeuvres in the Dark: Understanding Failure in Organizational Strategizing', *Journal of Management Studies*, 40, 1 (2003) 109–140.

Mantere, S., 'Strategic Practices as Enablers and Disablers of Championing Activity', *Strategic Organization*, 3, 2 (2005) 157–284.

McGahan, A. M. and M. E. Porter, 'How Much Does Industry Matter?', *Strategic Management Journal*, 18, Summer Special Issue (1997) 15–30.

Mintzberg, H., 'Crafting Strategy', *Harvard Business Review*, 65, 4 (1987) 66–75.

Pye, A., 'Strategy Through Dialogue and Doing: A Game of "Mornington Crescent"?', *Management Learning*, 26, 4 (1995) 445–462.

Pye, A. and A. Pettigrew, 'Special Issue of Long Range Planning', *Strategizing and Organizing*, 39, 6 (2007).

Reckwitz, A., 'Towards a Theory of Social Practice: A Development in Cultural Theorizing', *European Journal of Social Theory*, 5, 2 (2002) 243–263.

Regner, P., 'Strategy Creation in Practice: Adaptive and Creative Learning Dynamics', *Journal of Management Studies*, 40, 1 (2003) 57–82.

Rouleau, L., 'Micro-practices of Strategic Sensemaking and Sensegiving: How Middle Managers Interpret and Sell Change Every Day', *Journal of Management Studies*, 42, 7 (2005) 1413–1441.

Rumelt, R. P., 'How Much Does Industry Matter?', *Strategic Management Journal*, 12, 3 (1991) 167–185.

Salvato, C., 'The Role of Micro-strategies in the Engineering of Firm Evolution', *Journal of Management Studies*, 40, 1 (2003) 83–108.

Samra-Fredericks, D., 'Strategizing as Lived Experience and Strategists' Everyday Efforts to Shape Strategic Direction', *Journal of Management Studies*, 40 (2003) 141–174.

Samra-Fredericks, D., 'Managerial Elites Making Rhetorical and Linguistic "Moves" for a Moving (Emotional) Display', *Human Relations*, 57, 9 (2004a) 1103–1143.

Samra-Fredericks, D., 'Its a "Kinda..." Magic or Alternatively, Strategizing to Project the Self and Organization into the Future', *EGOS Conference*, Ljubljana (2004b).

Samra-Fredericks, D., 'Understanding Our World as it Happens and Re-conceptualising Strategising as a "Kinda" Magic', *Organization Studies Summer Conference* (Santorini, 2005).

Sminia, H., 'Strategy Formation as Layered Discussion', *Scandinavian Journal of Management*, 21, 3 (2005) 267–291.

Sztompka, P., *Society in Action: The Theory of Social Becoming* (Cambridge, UK: Polity Press, 1991).

Tsoukas, R. and Chia, H. 'On Organizational Becoming: Rethinking Organizational Change', *Organization Science*, 13, 5 (2002) 567–82.

Vaara, E., B. Kleyman and H. Seristo, 'Strategies as Discursive Constructions: The Case of Airline Alliances', *Journal of Management Studies*, 41, 1 (2004) 1–35.

Whittington, R., 'The Work of Strategizing and Organizing: For a Practice Perspective', *Strategic Organization*, 1, 1 (2003) 119–127.

Whittington, R., 'Completing the Practice Turn in Strategy Research', *Organization Studies*, 27, 5 (2006) 613–634.

Whittington, R. and L. Cailluet, 'The Crafts of Strategy: Strategic Planning in Different Contexts', *Long Range Planning*, Special Issue (2007).

Wiersema, M. F. and K. A. Bantel, 'Top Management Team Demography and Corporate Strategic Change', *Academy of Management Journal*, 35, 1 (1992) 91–121.

Wilson, D. C. and P. Jarzabkowski, 'Thinking and Acting Strategically: New Challenges for Interrogating Strategy', *European Management Review*, 1 (2004) 14–20.

Part IV
Emerging and Integrating Perspectives

CHAPTER 14
Complexity Perspective

Jean Boulton and Peter Allen

Basic principles

The notion that the world is complex and uncertain and potentially fast-changing is much more readily acceptable as a statement of the obvious than it might have been 30 years ago when complexity science was born. This emerging worldview sits in contradistinction to the view of the world as predictable, linear, measurable and controllable, indeed *mechanical*; it is the so-called mechanical worldview which underpins many traditional approaches to strategy development and general management theory (see Mintzberg, 2002 for an overview).

The complexity worldview presents a new, integrated picture of the behaviour of organisations, marketplaces, economies and political infrastructures; these are indeed complex systems as we will explain below. Some of these behaviours are recognised in other theories and other empirical work. Complexity theory is unique in deriving these concepts through the lens of a coherent, self-consistent scientific perspective whilst nevertheless applying it to everyday, practical problems.

These key principles can be summarised here:

■ There is more than one possible future
This is a very profound point. We are willing to accept the future may be too complicated to know, but the notion that the way the future may evolve is, generally, *unknowable in principle* fundamentally changes our notion of reality as being something that is unfixed and emergent. The future does not yet exist; it is created and not merely discovered.

■ Tipping
Organisations, economies or other complex systems may *tip* into new forms with radically new characteristics; some of these characteristics may not previously have existed. Such tipping may be triggered by small, seemingly unimportant events or changes and the new state may be different in kind from the old

■ Need for interconnectivity
Complexity theory is systemic in perspective. It asserts that organisations which allow diversity and encourage interconnectivity are more able to respond to changing environments than those which are too controlled and too finely honed around a single purpose. Indeed it demonstrates that change and creativity can *only* occur if there is diversity

■ Variation as a prerequisite for novelty
Change, evolution and innovation result from events that happen *locally* – through non-average interactions and events at particular points in time and space; the nature of these local events are not predictable from the 'average' general situation. Again, the fundamental importance of local variation is a very profound insight. Allowing this so-called micro-diversity is an essential prerequisite for change (even if the change is, ultimately, global) and local variation should not be unintentionally eradicated through too great a focus on standardisation, efficiency and a search for repeatability and control.

■ Unfixed, emergent, self-organising, co-evolving

We are working all the time with the idea of systems that are interacting, nested, evolving, fuzzy and overlapping; nothing, neither boundaries, nor characteristics, nor communities, nor connecting forces, nor constituent elements, are fixed. It is this spatial and temporal complexity that we are at pains to embrace as it contains the potential for change. Indeed the characteristics develop essentially bottom-up, not top-down. Any attempt at global imposition will be treated by the system as merely an intervention, but whether it leads to the intended outcome is another matter; the theme of unintended consequences is central.

■ Both–and

Embracing the message of complexity does not infer chaos and helplessness. The conclusion is *both* to create clear intentions and actions based on the best data available *and* yet recognise that plans may not lead where intended and chance ideas and impulses we unintentionally make on the environment may work beyond our wildest dreams. Strategy development and strategy implementation become much more entwined as we see what works and build on successes. It suggests portfolios are generally preferable to too great a reliance on one theme (see Allen and Boulton, 2005; Boulton and Allen, 2004); we need *both* to exploit cash cows whilst they exist *and* to invest in potential new stars. We need constantly to scan the environment in the broadest sense for potential changes and constantly to interact with the organisation at its deepest levels to see what is really happening, for good or bad.

Before getting immersed in the technical details of complexity theory, we introduce two short case studies. The first, text messaging, is the story of an unintended strategy that was 'pulled' by consumers, grew massively in value over a few short years and radically changed communication processes; not a story easily explained through an analyse–plan–do–review model. The second describes how a small organisation can influence larger structures whilst both keeping to a core mission and yet being opportunistic. Both should be read with complexity theory in mind.

CASE STUDY 14.1[1]

On 3 December 1992, an engineer called Neil Papworth sent the text 'Merry Christmas' to colleagues at Vodafone. Texting had been invented as a way of testing mobile phones remotely. However, after the Christmas message, employees at Vodafone enjoyed sending texts to each other and interest grew. Texting was offered free by many networks, initially, as part of the mobile phone package and for the first 7 years phone owners could only send messages to people on the same network. Then someone found a loophole, which involved sending messages overseas and then back again, and the networks recognised that they would have to collaborate.

In June 1999, just under 600,000 text messages were sent in the UK. By 2004, 26 billion texts were sent in the UK alone. By January 2005, 78 million texts were sent per day. The popularity is put down to its simplicity; they are cheap, do not demand all the ritual attached to a telephone call or all the grandeur of a letter. Text messaging also came of age when it found its natural market, young people. Coupled with the arrival of prepaid phone cards in the late 1990s, texting made the money go further.

The advent of texting has had quite an impact on the communication mechanisms chosen by young people, on the development of language and on the ways parents keep in touch with their children. It is reported in Japan that texting is leading to a new form of neurosis – a fanaticism about being available. A recent (2005) report suggests that texting is replacing direct conversation amongst young people! It also creates the sense that people are always available. It is felt to be immediate, accessible, private and gives unprecedented control. Another survey suggested it has had, in the main, a positive effect on the social interactions and social skills of the young.

Texting is fast becoming a business tool. Within the banking sector the UK bank First Direct says its text message banking has proved 'phenomenally successful'.

The following recent (2005) headlines give a sense of the breadth of the potential for texting:

9 million young people in Nigeria are to be sent texts to raise awareness of HIV/aids

A teenager is treated for text messaging addiction

The Bible has been translated into text messaging speak in Australia

Merseyside police launch a campaign urging the public to text images of vandalism to them

Malaysians vote by text for astronaut candidate

Drivers get roadwork text alerts

Police launch 999 text service for deaf people

Texting is fast taking off in Asia and in the developing world, with forecasts far in excess of those for Europe, although the Swedes send the most texts in the world per person. In the USA, texting is not popular; this is felt to be due to a large degree the fact that in the USA, local calls are free – and Americans, reputably, love to talk! The US record for texting in 1 day is 26.4 million, compared with 133 million in the UK.

It is expected that mobile phones will be used increasingly for a whole range of uses covering voice, data, pictures and video, emails and storage for both business and personal. To what extent will these extended uses take off and how will they affect the popularity of texting?

Questions to consider: Could the exponential growth in texting have been planned for or predicted? Could we have foreseen how it would appeal to the young and how it would have such a wide impact – from mobile phone sales volumes through to changing social norms? How does this story fit with traditional notions of strategic planning and what should you do to 'manage' in these types of markets?

CASE STUDY 14.2[2]

Social Action for Health (SAfH) is a small (£1m turnover) charity based in the East End of London (see www.safh.org.uk). It was established in 1985 and its raison d'etre is to work with marginalised communities to increase people's ability to improve their own health and well-being. In order to achieve this, SAfH in part focuses on the relationship of these communities with the Health Service: Are the services provided appropriate? Are they provided in a way that fits the needs of the communities? Do people in these communities understand what is available and how to access the services? SAfH also teaches self-management, that is, how individuals can take more responsibility for living a healthy lifestyle and, in many cases, cope with chronic diseases such as diabetes and asthma. Part of this work is based on a method developed by Lorig et al. (1996) and has been modified to make it appropriate for Moslem men and women.

SAfH values:

■ We start with the people

■ We encourage self-determination

- We believe poor health is allied to social inequity – poverty, racism, unemployment, powerlessness
- We believe in the right to overall well-being, not just absence of illness

The organisation has 96 staff, 16 of whom are on short-term, project-related contracts, 10 are full-time and 70 are part-time workers, drawn from the local communities; 30 of these are health guides, as they are called, working with their communities to teach people about healthy living, about exercise routines which are culturally acceptable for those from traditional Moslem backgrounds and about how to engage with the Health Service in all its intricacies.

Strategy for such a small organisation has two interrelated strands. The first centres on sustainability. How can the organisation obtain sufficient funds to ensure projects gathering momentum and demonstrating success do not come to a premature end; equally how can the organisation per se ensure its own survival? The Executive Director reports she spends nearly 70 per cent of her time on funding applications, supported by 50 per cent of the time of one of the two other senior managers. Much of the funding at present comes from the public sector, both national and local; the organisation needs to keep abreast of changing agendas, be aware of growing and diminishing pots of money and monitor what topics are 'in fashion' in order to modify approaches and hence gain access to what money is available.

Equally, SAfH clearly has to work out how to fulfil its mission. What *are* the needs of the local communities and what methods are going to work best in order to help these communities?

These two strategic influences can pull against each other. If SAfH becomes too willing to try and track the moving targets of public sector interests and structures, it could end up with no coherent thrust and lose its focus as it manoeuvres and adapts around the hunt for funding. And of course it will become of less interest to funders if it seems too diffuse and overly reactive. Equally, if it becomes too fixed on either what communities or issues are most pressing or on what methods are best to adopt, it could end up with a laudable strategy but no money.

SAfH personnel have very strong beliefs around methodology. They believe very strongly in self-determined, community-led initiatives, training members of those communities to work with existing local structures in their own languages and respecting their own customs. They believe that the start has to be about the communities' issues as seen through their own eyes; only when the relationship has developed and trust has been established can the focus be shifted to introduce new ideas and new ways of working. They experience that it is really important to judge the pace of the enterprise: too fast and trust is not built, too slow and the hopelessness and helplessness experienced by many migrant and marginalised groups is exacerbated. One of their recurrent frustrations is that just when they perceive initiatives are really gathering pace and starting really to make an impact, the focus of funders may change and projects may end too soon, with valued and trained staff having to move on due to lack of funds.

SAfH managers have clear beliefs about change; they see the importance of the interplay between bottom-up and top-down influences. They feel strongly that change is only sustained if it captures the imagination and passion and energy of the people at the grass roots and is *shaped* by them; equally, the ideas for change and the vision of what is possible and how it might fit together requires imagination and strategic vision. This bottom-up to top-down theme (clarified in the 'spiral' model they have developed, see Figure 14.1) is also replicated in the stated intention for SAfH to influence strategic thinking and policy within the NHS. So a recent AGM is designed partly to show the range and effectiveness of current projects, partly not only to enthuse local participants and engender a sense of pride in what they have achieved, but also subtly to influence key Health Service policy-makers and provide another perspective on the art of the possible. Their work has penetrated the most marginal of societies in a way that the NHS itself has struggled to do; for example, 7000 Bengali, Somali and Turkish/Kurdish men and women have participated in Health Guide sessions. Intentions to influence NHS policy seems to be gathering momentum, as symbolised by the fact that the Health Guides project formed the central theme for the editorial of the Chief Executive of the North East London Strategic Health Authority in a recent journal.

Questions to consider: Can such a small organisation indeed influence the NHS? Can it impact on the health and social practices of such dispossessed groups? What is the role of strategy development in such a situation and what else (relationships, power, fashion, changing social norms) might influence success?

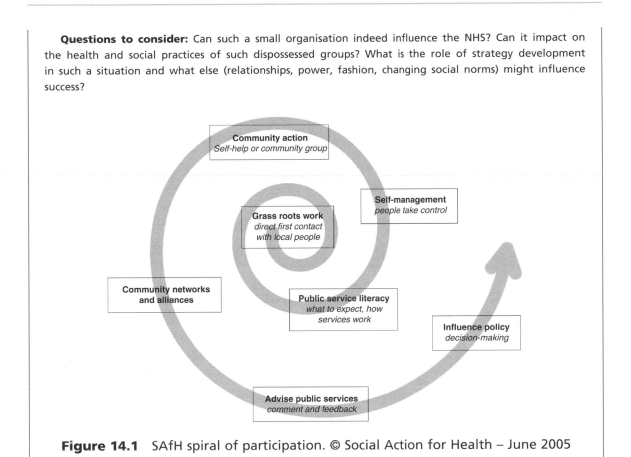

Figure 14.1   SAfH spiral of participation. © Social Action for Health – June 2005

Overview of the complexity perspective

What is complexity science?

It could be argued that many, if not most, of the tenets of complexity science do not seem in themselves to be 'new'. What *is* new, however, is that the science of complexity provides a self-consistent, coherent, scientific perspective which sheds some light on *how* seemingly distinct attributes of structures and systems are related and *why* these attributes occur (see Allen, 1990, 1994, 2001; Allen et al., 1977; Capra, 1996; Futures Special Edition on Complexity and Knowledge, 2005; Garnsey and McGlade, 2006; Goodwin, 1994; Maguire and McKelvey, 1999; Middleton-Kelly, 2003; Richardson, 2005).

This worldview stands in contrast to traditional perspectives which are, consciously or unconsciously, derived from the assumption that the world behaves like a predictable and measurable machine. Complexity theory suggests that to be successful in a fast-changing, complex and uncertain world, we must approach life in a radically different way.

Much has been written about the so-called complexity and chaos over the last 15 years (e.g. Cohen and Stewart, 1994; Gleick, 1987; Lewin, 1995; Pratt et al., 2005; Rihani, 2002); some of this writing takes the original science as 'read' and hence leaves the reader uncertain as to the validity of what is being proposed. In the following sections we seek to elucidate the core theory, returning to the fundamentals of the science. Following this historical and scientific perspective, the core fundamentals of complexity theory are explained and explored.

Where does complexity science come from?

As with many concepts that change our view of what is 'normal', work leading to the realisation that determinism (things being causal, predictable and going to plan) is not the norm came from a number of directions. This started in the late nineteenth century with some American philosophers (Buchler on Peirce, 1955; James, 1995), a mathematician (Poincaré, 1890) and several physicists, through the advent of quantum physics. Cybernetics (Ashby, 1956), General Systems Theory (von Bertalanffy, 1968), Lorenz's (1963) mathematical exploration of weather patterns, Haken's (1977) work on synergetics and Prigogine's non-equilibrium thermodynamics (Nicolis and Prigogine, 1989) built on this theme of uncertainty. They, variously, were able to develop the ideas further through the advantage of increased computer power which allowed the exploration of situations of interest through mathematical modelling.

Prigogine's work, for which he was awarded the Nobel prize in chemistry in 1977, is key (see Prigogine and Stengers, 1984). He was intrigued by the mystery of evolution. How can it be, he asked, that evolution takes species into new and generally more sophisticated forms, when theories of physics seem to indicate something quite to the contrary?

Physics had at the time essentially two ideas on offer. The first built on Isaac Newton's clarification of the laws of motion of mechanical objects. It states that systems are entirely predictable and continue forever without change. The other fundamental physics theory defines 'entropy'. It states that systems will eventually 'run down', lose their diversity and structure and die.

These two theories are clearly in themselves inconsistent in their pure forms; in practice, in real life, things are not so polarised, as Prigogine recognised. The missing ingredient was the realisation that both theories applied to closed systems, that is to systems that do not interact with the wider environment in which they sit. Systems of interest in the real world are in general open, not closed; they exchange information, energy and material with their environment. In these circumstances, he was able to show that such systems do indeed have the propensity to 'self-organise', that is, to develop new structures out of either existing structures or out of so-called random chaos. Non-equilibrium thermodynamics was born and was a key step in the development of complexity theory.

As well as recognising the fundamental importance of being open to the environment, Prigogine emphasised that most natural systems are not linear and mechanical. Complex systems combine 'things' or elements which do not have to be identical; even when of the same type, the connections can be non-linear – and the elements, the forces between them and the nature of any boundaries can change with time.

The important point for those interested in social systems is that, with this most general definition of a complex system, it is impossible *not* to conclude that systems of people are indeed complex systems and can be likened to mechanical systems only in specific, stable circumstances. Therefore it is of interest for us to understand how complex systems in general behave, in order to inform ourselves how best to handle such social systems. Thus a new paradigm has evolved, called variously whole systems thinking, living systems thinking, complexity theory or chaos theory.

How is complexity science developed? Mathematical modelling

Whilst Prigogine's inspiration initially came from chemistry experiments, complexity theory in general derives its substance from studying computer models which seek to describe 'real-life' situations. There are many approaches to such modelling, and debates between practitioners often centre on the validity of various approaches and the degree to which conclusions can be generalised.

The first type of models took an equation which described a system as a whole and explored how the characteristics of the system developed with time. Lorenz's (1963) investigation of weather patterns falls into this category, and out of this the so-called chaos theory was born. Chaos theory is regarded as a subset of complexity theory. Some complexity theorists, including the authors, question the general applicability of some of the concepts deriving from this work; this will be discussed in a later section.

Then there are multi-agent models. They try to model the distinct elements and interactions in detail. A multi-agent model applied to a group of people, for example, would represent each person separately and the interactions that applied to each person would also be represented uniquely. Such multi-agent modelling is associated in particular with the Santa Fe Institute, founded in 1988 by Gell-Mann (1994) and Philip Anderson, and also characterises Allen's early work (1997), in the late 1970s and early 1980s, on cities. Multi-agent models such as these have been used to explore biological systems, ecologies and economies.

A more recent development of multi-agent models allows the agents (i.e. the constituent parts of the system) to learn over time and change their responses in the light of their experiences. This mirrors, of course, in the social realm, the reality that people do learn and change with time and do change the way they interact both with each other and with the environment. Allen (1988), Holland (1992) (through the use of genetic algorithms) and others have developed methods to explore these so-called co-evolutionary processes.

A note of warning

We must remember that systems, models of systems and boundaries are all simplifications; they are in effect figments of our imagination, helpful in that they help us label and think about a situation and dangerous if we give them too much credence. Stacey (2003) and colleagues (Stacey et al., 2002) have been at pains to point out this potential pitfall.

In practice, the notion of system merely represents a collection of 'things' related by some sort of interactions; no restrictions need be made as to the position of the boundaries or the consistency of qualities over space or time. Let us take an organisational example. By talking about a particular organisation, such as a particular bank, we are suggesting that a collection of people and resources exists and is distinct from the general population and distinct from, let us say, another bank. This is obviously helpful. However, in calling attention to the 'system', that is bank A, it is not suggested that the boundaries are fixed and unequivocal (are outsourced cleaners part of the bank or not, is a wholly owned insurance company separate or not?), nor that characteristics are consistent over the whole (to continue the example, is the culture in the Property division the same as in the IT division, in the north as in the south?).

If we go on to consider what happens when we try to model systems, it is true that modelling inevitably simplifies things and no modeller can ever be sure he or she is not ignoring critical aspects of the problem in the attempt to represent 'reality'. However, we must remember that thinking itself is a form of modelling, inevitably limited by language and experience. Modellers merely use modelling as an extension of thinking and use models to try out ideas and experiments, create pictures and allow inadequacies, gaps and errors to be identified. The modeller is, in general, extremely critical of his method and its results and will spend considerable time experimenting with choice of boundaries, time steps and any other simplifications.

What is reassuring for the reader and the user of the results of complex systems modelling, however, is that a number of common principles and characteristics are derived from a whole range of different methods of exploration. Whilst the details may vary, the principles in general do not. Furthermore, these principles, whilst they differ from traditionally held views as to what is scientific and how best to engage with the world, are often comfortably in accord with our personal experiences; in a sense notions derived from complexity theory tend to re-empower our common sense and native wisdom.

Principles of complexity theory

Before embarking on a description of the key principles, it is helpful to introduce the notion of 'state space'. This will allow us to describe certain aspects of complex systems thinking in a consistent fashion.

State space

State space is a well-defined and well-established tool used in mathematics and physics. It is defined as the collection of all possible states in which a system can exist. So if we consider the simplest possible mechanical system, a pendulum, its state is defined by its angular momentum. As its angular momentum does not change with time, the behaviour of a particular pendulum will be a point in state space; this is called a *point attractor*.

More generally, complex systems will need a number of so-called state variables to describe them and the state space will have multiple dimensions. State space can be considered as the terrain available to a system and over which it can roam. It could be applied to represent all the possible strategies an organisation could inhabit, for example, where the state variables in this case would be things such as type of technology, organisation structure, product type, supply chain and so on. What seems to happen in many cases is that the behaviour over time of a complex system settles in one region of state space – that is, a particular type of strategy, at least for a time, becomes stable, successful and self-consistent. This region is called an *attractor basin*. When the system has settled into that region it will tend to remain there; it is said to self-regulate or be homeostatic or in dynamic equilibrium.

In general state space will contain a number of attractor basins; that is more than one combination of characteristics will be stable; in our strategy example, there will be more than one group of available strategic options in the marketplace. There may also be regions of turbulence, where any possible structures do not self-reinforce and patterns of connectivity are constantly shifting and changing. The constant shifts in power and forming and breaking of structures and alliances in unstable political regimes are examples of such turbulent behaviour.

The final, and perhaps the most crucial, point to make about the state space 'landscape' is that it can itself change and evolve – not only through the attractors changing shape and forming new patterns amongst themselves (as the values of existing state variables shift) but more radically through the emergence of new characteristics and dimensions. This latter process *is* evolution. When we look at an evolutionary tree describing the emergence of new species or, in the economic world, we consider new technologies or working methods, we are looking at a picture of an expanding state space, with potential characteristics that did not exist before. So in a pre-amphibian world, the concept of 'legs' did not exist until there were land animals; equally, in a pre-telephone and pre-computer world, the ways of communicating were clearly much more limited than now; state space required many fewer dimensions in the past to describe the options.

So there are in effect two ways that a complex system can change behaviour. The first is that some atypical event (such as the so-called 'noise') can 'tip' the system into a new region. This could be into a turbulent region or into another attractor basin. So, relating this to the field of strategy, changes in the rules applied to chassis design for Formula One racing in 1980 'tipped' the dominant technological characteristic from engine design to aerodynamics and caused Ferrari to lose its leading position for 20 years. Equally, the death of key politicians can in certain circumstances tip regimes into periods of turbulence.

The second way a complex system can change behaviour is when the dimensions, characteristics and attributes of state space themselves change. This could occur through changes in the environment or through learning and evolution of the system per se. In this so-called co-evolutionary phase, what had been a stable attractor basin may either develop new additional characteristics or may disappear altogether. Major so-called disruptive technologies (Christensen, 1997), such as the motor car or the

Internet, which cause a radical shift in social structures and ways of life are examples of triggers which can lead to such co-evolutionary change where the whole landscape of possibilities itself re-forms.

With these concepts defined we can now explore some of the key principles of complexity theory.

Key principles

Path dependency and unpredictability; there is more than one possible future

The trajectory or path of a complex system is irreversible and non-deterministic – that is, it is impossible to retrace one's steps and end up in the same place and it is impossible reliably to predict what will happen in the future. However, that is not to say that the behaviour of a complex system is random. Beguilingly, for much of the time the path of the system will unfold in a relatively causal fashion, with the past forming quite a reliable predictor of the future. The 'problem' occurs at so-called points of tipping or bifurcation; at these points, there is more than one possible path the system could take; which path it will take may be open to guidance or influence but it is not entirely predictable; in other words at that point there is more than one possible future. What is more, it is both hard to predict when these points of bifurcation will be met as well as into which future state the system will tip when it reaches such a point. After such a 'tip' the system may have completely different characteristics than before. The relevant qualities or parameters needed to describe what is happening may also be quite different.

This notion of path dependency is profound. Mechanical science suggests that if we work hard enough we can collect enough data to predict the future reliably, given the right methods and analytical tools. Complexity theory, in contrast, states that the future is created in the future and all we know at a given point in time can *never* be enough to tell us what will unfold. Modelling, scenario planning and foresighting can help us explore possible futures and craft strategies that seem likely to succeed and develop defensive contingency plans – but we can never be absolutely certain what will work and what will not.

Another important nuance is this concept of irreversibility – that there is no going back. It is enticing to feel that if the future is not to our liking we can go back to the methods and structures we had before. But path dependency tells us that even if we attempt to do this, we can never reliably return to a previous state. So, relating this to the organisational world, if we find that an adopted strategy is not giving us what we wanted, we may feel we can merely return to what we were doing previously. But the organisation itself has had a different experience; new lines of reporting and new power structures will have developed; going back will not take the organisation to the same place. In addition, the competition, customers, suppliers and distributors will have changed their expectations, choices and routines and will not seamlessly return to past behaviours.

Furthermore, if the system has tipped into a new, stable attractor basin, it may indeed be very difficult to move on or move back. For example, when one product is chosen in comparison with a competitor (such as petrol cars rather than electric cars or VHS videotape over Betamax) there can be a so-called *lock-in effect* (Arthur, 1983). The interplay of the change with the broader environment (who, to develop our example, have got used to certain technologies and the changes have spawned other related technological advancements) is such that conditions can make it virtually impossible, with time, for what had initially constituted another option to make any headway.

Small things have big effects

Conventional mechanical thinking suggests that future follows rationally from the past and that the future is influenced according to the magnitude of the relevant factors. So, for example, we would expect large firms or dominant political groups to have more impact than individuals or small players. Complexity theory suggests that the cause of change is often quirky, small and local. If a system is near the edge of an attractor basin or if the whole landscape in state space is shifting, it may not take very much to tip the system into a new form, into a new attractor basin. What causes one line of development to succeed rather than another is often dominated by chance events, actions of particular individuals, behaviour of small non-average groups or *unintended consequences* of well-thought-through 'rational' decisions. We can consider the importance of certain key historical figures, such as Hitler or Mandela or the impact of events such as September 11. Equally, if the system is 'locked in' to a stable position, it may resist change no matter what pressure is brought to bear. The impact of the knowledge that smoking causes cancer had remarkably little effect on tobacco sales for many, many years due, in part, to the position of dominance of the tobacco firms and their ability to cast enough doubt on the research findings and perhaps influence governments not to play too strong a part in health education on this point. The collective denial of smokers unwilling to relinquish 'their only pleasure' was also, clearly, part of this 'lock-in'.

Micro-diversity: The importance of 'local'

One of the most exciting and important findings of complex systems modelling is to show how creativity, evolution and change can occur *only* if there is diversity and if elements within the system are strongly inter-related (Allen and McGlade, 1987). In other words, systems or structures where individuals, to look at it from a social systems perspective, are identical and where interactions are controlled by rigid structures can neither adapt to changing circumstances nor develop new characteristics and qualities. In practice the mechanisms for evolution and change come from synergistic interactions of differing qualities that happen at certain locations. For example, if a food source in a lake disappears, it will not do so uniformly; equally the response of a particular species to a given change will not be a uniform one over the lake and over time. Different groups may try out different responses, healthier animals may survive better than weaker individuals, what happens to one species locally will depend on the response of other species and on the density of that species at a particular place. If we only consider average responses to average events or if we seek to minimise variety and control interactions we will destroy the very mechanisms that lead to change (see Kay and Schneider, 1994; Ulanowicz, 1980).

We can make an analogy with hydrodynamics, which describes flow patterns in fluids. The dynamically stable swirling patterns that occur in water going down a plug-hole or in a tornado are the slow patterns that settle down and become stable after the fast dynamics have neutralised themselves. We may never know what the fast dynamics were, and certainly the individual molecules will have no control over these patterns, but they are fundamental to what emerges at a more global level.

Snowden (2002) warns us against what he calls retrospective coherence. When we look back on events we often think we see causal links. What we may not see are the attempts at synergies that failed and the excursions the system made, which left little trace but were nevertheless vital in what transpired. Some work on evolutionary theory (Raup, 1992) similarly emphasises the importance of extinctions in the process of change and shows that evolution happens in bursts not in a gradual fashion. This is punctuated equilibrium (Gould, 1989).

Self-regulation or homeostasis

If a system is in a condition of dynamic stability, it will be robust against relatively small shifts in the environment or small changes from within and will be able to *self-regulate* (Maturana and Varela, 1987). In effect the system is stable, for a time, with respect to its own fluctuations. The conditions for effective self-regulation as for creativity generally, are where the elements of the system are free to shift and change both internally and in relation to each other, where there is diversity and rich interconnectivity. If the system is too rigid, too regimented, too standardised, such adaptability becomes difficult. With respect to state space, we are describing a situation whereby the system adapts to stay within the same attractor basin.

The mechanisms for such self-regulation result from shifting balances between positive feedback loops and negative feedback loops in the interactions between elements within a system. Take, for example, the human body. Most of the time, this is an excellent example of a self-regulating complex system (see Briggs and Peat, 2000). The state parameters, such as temperature or weight, remain steady, despite the person eating or moving from place to place. In that way the negative feedback loops are keeping the body in dynamic equilibrium. However, if the changes are too great, if the person gets a serious disease or is subjected to extreme temperatures, this dynamic equilibrium will break down; certain positive feedback loops will dominate and take the system out of control; in this example, the person may die.

The current debate (2006) on climate change is another example. Mechanical thinking suggests that climate change creeps on gradually and can be slowed down or even reversed if we make gradual incremental improvements. Complexity thinking suggests that there will be a point of no return, a 'last straw', after which the self-regulatory potential of the earth to maintain temperature control in the face of substantial changes will not be enough to resist the tipping into a new era – and that this new era is likely to be irreversible and 'lock in'. This may not be in the best interests of the human animal. Lovelock's recent book (2006) and a recent UK government report (Tirpack, 2006), suggest we may be closer to this point than we would like to think.

The dilemma is that, for stability, we want to restrict positive feedback loops and for creativity, we want to allow and enhance the possibility for synergistic positive loops between qualities within the system and allow them to grow.

Self-organisation

Self-organisation describes the situation where new emergent structures and properties may arise without being imposed from above or from without; as with self-regulation it is a distributed response of a system.

The same mechanisms are at play as with self-regulation, but in this case what may come out of the subtle shifts in the connectivity of qualities and characteristics in the system is that certain combinations of these may find new ways to interact. These new synergistic groupings (formed through positive feedback loops) may create new characteristics which start to assume dominance. Thus the set of system characteristics may *tip* into a new set; this is self-organisation and new properties are said to *emerge*. In terms of state space, we would say that the system has reached a point of bifurcation and tipped into a new attractor basin. In strategy terms we would say that a new type of strategy has been discovered – maybe due to tackling a new marketplace with the same products or changing the distribution process – but that the change has not changed the marketplace or social behaviours out of all recognition, in contrast to a co-evolutionary process, as described below.

Arthur (1999) makes the point, and we would agree, that there is no a priori reason why this new form of the system may be what we wish. The process of tipping does not, as a matter of course, take the system to somewhere that is necessarily 'better' or 'appropriate'. For example, consider the novel *Lord of the Flies* (Golding, 1954). Here is an example of a loosely structured group in a new environment which did find a new form, but at the expense of one of its members. Similarly ecological systems will respond to changes in food supply by changing who eats whom – not necessarily in the best interests of the weak. So in extending these ideas into the organisational world, we must be careful not to conclude that leaderless, loose, diverse structures necessarily lead to something better – it all depends on what we regard as 'better' and from whose perspective. We thus need to encourage diversity and interconnectedness, but still develop shared intents and values; we need to move with the way the system is changing and yet be prepared to intervene when necessary.

Co-evolution

This brings us to the final type of organisation change, where the elements themselves and the interactions between them may both evolve (Allen et al., 1985). This corresponds to the situation where the 'terrain' in state space itself shifts and changes. We are no longer moving within an attractor basin nor shifting between attractor basins; *everything* is shifting. In such processes of radical change, the way the range of possibilities re-forms itself is through an interplay between the environment, the systems within it and the elements within the systems. Co-evolution is said to occur as everything creates change in everything else in an inter-related and recursive fashion. In such circumstances, the future may bear little resemblance to the past. Such radical change is most likely when both system and its environment are least stable and most open to re-forming. Radical new technologies such as the Internet can precipitate such radical change, where the world from both social and economic perspectives can be regarded as substantially different compared with a pre-Internet world, and equally the interplay between the technology and its users has significantly shaped the development of the World Wide Web per se.

Commonly held concepts of more questionable importance, in the view of the authors

Chaos theory

Chaos theory is regarded as a subsection of complexity theory. It was developed from the work of Lorenz (1963). He showed that deterministic (i.e. predictable) but highly irregular flow patterns existed within a particular set of equations used to simulate weather systems. He found that whilst the behaviour with time *looks* random or chaotic, the solutions in fact stay within relatively well-defined regions in state space, called *strange attractors*. The behaviour is called deterministic chaos and should not be confused with the more general and normally accepted use of the word 'chaos' to mean 'random', totally unpredictable behaviour. Confusingly, it is this everyday, latter use of the word that is inferred by Prigogine, in his book *Order out of Chaos* (Prigogine and Stengers, 1984) and by Kaufman (1995) and others in the definition of the 'edge of chaos'. What Lorenz also showed was that the solution was very sensitive to initial conditions; this is often called the *butterfly effect*. Fractal geometry (Mandelbrot, 1977) is another derivation from chaos theory. More recently, questions have been raised as to the general applicability of these ideas deriving from deterministic chaos (see Allen, 1988; Cilliers, 1998; Stacey, 2002).

Edge of chaos

Let us start with Prigogine's phrase, 'order out of chaos'. Prigogine, in considering chemical and biological systems, placed focus on the movement from a state of molecular chaos, where there is no structure, as in a gaseous state, towards the region where spontaneous structure may form – the so-called 'order out of chaos'. The potential for this transition is due to energy being available through connection with the environment; this is referred to as 'pumping' the system. At the point where this energy flow from the outside is sufficient, spontaneous structures may appear; this is the region of self-organisation, already discussed. If the system is pumped to too high a degree, it may enter a region of turbulence. That is where structures may form and break in random fashion but do not settle into stable forms. The region of turbulence is equivalent to the behaviour of choppy water or of turbulent swirls and flows in the body of liquids. To summarise, in the regime where there is intermediate environmental 'pumping' between microscopic chaos and macroscopic chaos (i.e. turbulence), new configurations and structures can spontaneously emerge and evolve.

Let us now compare this perspective with the notion of the 'edge of chaos'. The phrase was coined as a result of work undertaken by Chris Langton using cellular automata, a particular form of multi-agent modelling (Waldrop, 1992). Langton found there was a so-called phase transition, a well-defined shift between order and chaos, in experimenting with such models. Confusingly, order, here, is taken to mean the situation where everything is in equilibrium, which is, in fact, equivalent to what is found where there is random molecular chaos! The extended region where structures can spontaneously emerge and evolve described by Prigogine accords with the notion of the 'edge of chaos' – except that the word 'edge' implies something much sharper, narrower and well defined than may be helpful.

The problem comes when we try and apply this notion to real-life situations. How might we find this region or edge? Is being there necessarily beneficial? This nascent state is felt most likely to lead to new possibilities and hold greatest potential (McMillan, 2004; Rihani, 2002). It is, however, further suggested – in applying these ideas to social systems – that groups with a minimum of structure, focus and leadership, allowing for greatest flexibility and indeed most potential for chaos are most likely to find this state. In other words, chaos is 'sold' as a precursor to change and evolution. It is with this last statement that the authors would disagree. To be somewhat technical, to have the potential for emergence and evolution, we require strong interconnectivity of the non-linear type and self-reinforcing feedback loops; not too tight and not too loose. In addition there must be some degree of 'noise' – that is random inputs, variations or some sort of non-averageness. These variations will in effect test the stability of any emerging structure and, in the event of a revealing instability, drive the system to a new structure or state.

When continuing to apply these ideas to social systems, what seems most beneficial in approaching change is to seek to shift smoothly from one attractor basin to another. The move from apartheid to non-apartheid in South Africa could be regarded as such a shift. The shift did create new structures and characteristics but it was not turbulent but constrained to some degree by the presence of Mandela and others and by the way it was handled. We must also be careful not to conclude, as exemplified by *Lord of the Flies* (Golding, 1954), that providing minimal structure together with maximum flexibility will necessarily be a 'good thing' and result in a positive outcome. Clearly too much structure will constrain the ability of a system to adapt to changing circumstances and find new solutions, but too little structure can be equally dangerous.

Simple rules

Self-organisation can be shown through simulation to be achieved through the use of so-called *simple rules* of interaction. An analogy is made, for example with termite mounds (Bonabeau et al., 1999). Termites follow simple rules of interaction and these rules allow them to modify the shape and structure of the termite mound to suit the local terrain. This is obviously an interesting process and in principle, it implies that if this notion is then transferred to organisational life and organisations are run on 'simple rules', they will be adaptable and re-shape themselves in the light of changing circumstances (see Eisenhardt and Sull, 2001). This is okay as far as it goes. Our first difficulty in putting this into operation is to try and define at what level our suggested 'simple rules' apply. Do they apply to the behaviour of individuals towards each other or to the behaviour of organisations or markets? What happens if rules contradict each other or are ambiguous?

Second, from the point of view of complexity theory, simple rules are emergent, not imposed. They are a consequence of self-organisation, not a prerequisite. We cannot know in advance what types of interactions between elements faded and failed – so choosing simple rules to apply seems problematic, even if better than imposing too great a degree of control.

Finally, we must remember that the rules termites follow still only allow them to make termite mounds! In times of fast-change the simple rules themselves may need to evolve. How do we set up situations whereby we can ensure the rules of engagement continue to evolve? Perhaps the fact that many companies held up as examples of good practice in the work of Peters and Waterman (1982) did not sustain their success.

Linking the complexity perspective to strategic management

What does a complexity theory perspective imply for strategy development?

The notion that the world, generally, is unpredictable and interconnected is hardly a surprise. What perhaps *is* a surprise is the extent to which traditional methods of strategy development are still predicated on the belief that the future is, to a large part, predictable and open to analysis.

So what does a complexity theory perspective imply for strategy development? The first point to make is that the answer to this question is *contingent* on the environment and the nature of the business. For circumstances of relative stability, to assume that yesterday's knowledge of the market, customer requirements and outcomes of previous plans will be good indicators of the future is reasonable and helpful. For example, if we are aiming to develop a strategy for dealing with car insurance claims or with retailing kettles in western Europe, it is reasonable to expect that, provided we ensure there is no relevant new technology on the horizon which could revolutionise the business, or so much adverse consumer opinion that consumers are desperate for something new, we can plan the future in traditional ways.

If, however, we are in situations where the technology or the environment more generally is unstable and fast-changing, then relying on the past to inform the future is more than unhelpful, it can be positively dangerous. Our case study about text messaging is a good example of being in this emergent, co-evolutionary phase of strategy.

In some ways, if it is possible to know which of these two extreme positions characterises a particular environment and a given business situation, then things are relatively straightforward. Either we are in an analyse–plan–do–review situation or we are focused on experimentation, agility, adaptability and co-evolution. Both extremes suggest different types of organisation structure, culture and leadership style; the first is about exploiting economies of scale, being efficient and exerting good controls; the second suggests decentralisation, networks, project teams, empowerment and innovation. Our great difficulty is that we cannot always know for how long our environment will remain stable. Are we near a tipping point? Will a single crisis event or a surge of consumer frustration or a new technology we did not take seriously suddenly tip our industry into a new era? Equally, at the opposite extreme, when will the unstable emergent market we are in settle down into something more knowable and predictable? Has the airlines' response to 9/11 now stabilised or not? Should followers in a market sector wait for the dust to settle and see what happens to the leader who changed the territory and then set up a focused strategy when the new form of the marketplace has taken shape, or should followers help to shape that market and enter the fray as soon as possible? Perhaps the important point to take from this discussion is that, whatever state of play is occurring, we can never reliably know how long it will last.

To recognise that not only do we not know the answers to these questions, but there *are* no firm answers is, in itself, helpful, if frustrating. It suggests that we should regard any strategic thrust as potentially temporary and have some growing strategic shoots in the wings in case things change. It suggests we should spend effort in scanning our environment to at least do the best we can to spot potential changes that may cause tipping. This is extremely difficult to do. Sometimes, situations should, we think, tip and they do not. Consider how long it took between discovering smoking causes cancer, tobacco companies admitting smoking causes cancer and then smoking habits beginning to change. Consider how certain organisations can sometimes be that their technology will take off and it does not. The Betamax–VHS videotape battle is an example of this. Scenario planning is an effective 'scanning' and thinking process, but, again, our difficulty is that it is hard to imagine things that are radically different and have not as yet existed; even with scenario planning we can only think the thinkable, so to speak.

The other side of the coin, of course, is that sometimes strategies take off in ways which we never envisaged or even dreamt could happen. Text messaging was developed to test mobile phones remotely; it was never designed as a strategy. There is a case discussed in Gladwell's book, *The Tipping Point* (2000), about Hush Puppies shoes becoming fashionable again in the 1990s in New York, where they were used on the catwalk. Production shifted from 30,000 pairs per year in 1992 to 400,000 pairs per year in 1996 without the company either intending this as a strategy or promoting these shoes in any way; the strategy came to them.

Summary checklist

The strategy process in the light of complexity theory starts to look something like this:

Take a view as to whether the environment for your products and services seems stable or potentially fast-changing, and take a view as to whether the status quo is likely to change.

Develop your key strategy accordingly (i.e. exploitative/mechanical or adaptive/emergent/agile or poised to respond if things suddenly change).

Have other strategic elements in play and regard these as experiments; some may take off beyond your wildest dreams; some may flop despite evidence to the contrary.

Be agile enough to back strategic threads that are taking off beyond expectations and be prepared to pull the plug on threads that 'should' work, according to the analysis, but don't.

Scan your own organisation for unintended successes, good ideas, hidden resources and be prepared to back winners, even if they were not what you were intending.

Keep scanning the environment and respond and adapt to changing needs, crises that shift the status quo, new competitors, new technology and so on.

Use scenario planning and foresighting to envisage possible futures and, importantly, to identify potential early warning signs of fundamental change – but remember that you may still not think the unthinkable!

Allow some 'slack' and diversity in the organisation and beware of streamlining the organisation to too great a degree around one purpose. This efficiency minimises the ability to respond to changing circumstances or to try out something new. It can result in destroying good intrinsic capabilities which may be just what are needed in a changing and emergent market.

Recognise that sometimes the world changes beyond recognition and what worked in the past will not work in the future; sometimes adapting is the only option and yet proactive innovative strategic thrusts may also win out in changing times.

We would like to raise at this point the concept of the 'dominant firm' (Miller, 1976). This is a very beguiling concept strategically. If we are big enough, we can dominate the marketplace and control what the consumer can have and what other suppliers can give. This strategy can work very well for a time and can indeed strangle innovation and change in the marketplace. However, it seems to be the case that, in the end, the consumers' desires win. Some chink appears, typically through a tiny competitor with a new approach, and consumers vote wholesale with their feet. The ex-dominant dinosaur has little potential to adapt and often struggles to survive. It will be interesting to see (2006) whether Google is able to threaten the giant Microsoft.

How do these ideas relate to other approaches to strategy development?

Complexity theory offers a 'scientific' theoretical lens through which to view many other perspectives, derived more empirically (see Wheatley, 1992). The ideas encompass the notion of learning and adapting, with strategy viewed as an emergent process developed by learning through experience. This so-called learning approach to strategy development encompasses a sense of incremental change, however (see Quinn, 1980, and logical incrementalism). The underlying dynamic from the perspective of complexity theory may be much more sudden and dramatic if the situation in the environment is at a tipping point. So the adaptation implied in such circumstance may be more radical and extreme than the notion of learning may imply. However, the idea that implementation is in part a way of testing strategy and not separate from it, is certainly of importance.

Equally, complex systems thinking is in tune with aspects of a resource-based view (see Chapter 9 for references). Complexity theory emphasises the need for maintaining a diversity of resources and recognising the resources that are hidden or unacknowledged may indeed be the very resources that, in combination with other factors, provide the creative opportunity in a changing environment. As certain synergistic combinations of resources take precedence and others fade, factors that used to be minor and unimportant may take centre stage (see Streatfield, 2001 for an excellent case study of this concept).

In a complex systems perspective there is perhaps more focus on the interplay between organisation and environment than in much of the literature on core competencies (Hamel and Prahalad, 1989), although the notion of dynamic capabilities (Eisenhardt and Martin, 2000; Teece et al., 1997) does indeed recognise that the mechanisms through which firms accumulate and dissipate new skills and capabilities are the source of competitive advantage. Hamel and Prahalad (1989) also emphasise the concept of strategic intent. This need for this proactive assertion on the marketplace is embraced within a complexity perspective.

The idea of strategy and structure are contingent on the nature of the environment is a well-established concept (e.g. Burton and Obel, 1998; Duncan, 1972; Lawrence and Lorsch, 1967; Thompson, 1967). And a recognition of the need to study the co-evolution of firms with their environment dates back to Weber (1978), who argued that the bureaucratic form of organisation arose at a particular time of history in response to the confluence of forces of change that ushered in the industrial age. Lewin et al. (Lewin and Volberda, 1999; Lewin et al., 1999) define co-evolution as the joint outcome of managerial intentionality, environment and institutional effects and state that such studies are still rare.

Conclusion

What, in particular, do the authors feel complexity theory has to offer to the field of strategy development? First of all, it places central importance on adopting an integrative viewpoint and underlines the dangers of single lens perspectives; it is often in the integration of factors both within firms, between firms and with other aspects in the environment, that change, the potential for change, the likely nature of that change, and indeed the possibility for no change are all held. Second, it shows that creativity and adaptation are derived locally and through allowing diversity and interconnectivity to exist; we are warned against overly streamlining and controlling strategies and structures and equally warned against too much looseness and chaos. Third, it emphasises irreversibility and the limits of replicability which brings into question the use of standard solutions and indeed too great a belief in the lessons to be gleaned from case studies.

Perhaps the most important contribution from complexity science centres around the concept of the tipping point. Change can often be fast, radical, triggered by chance or small events and irreversible. After such changes the perspectives of the past no longer hold; it is a new world with new characteristics. The strategist must try and see the signs of instability and impending shifts and tread a fine line between riding the wave and shaping the fall.

Case studies revisited

Text messaging is a prime example of a spectacularly successful innovation that never was a strategy! Text messaging was designed for testing mobile phones remotely; it was not perceived as an important new communication process by either its inventors or its manufacturers. It is an excellent example of consumer pull rather than marketing push. It was non-average consumer 'anoraks' who worked out how to beat the system by sending texts abroad and this forced the hand of the networks who were forced to allow texting between networks. This 'beating the system' – not planned and leading to a strategy adopted reluctantly – was what allowed the texting to take off in leaps and bounds with a 6000-fold increase in traffic in the UK in 6 years. The key market created itself; no one seemingly intended the market focus on young people and the market grew with very little focus or advertising. So we have a clear example of a spectacular growth created because something became accidentally available, something which a new market sector found it really liked and wanted. Manufacturers had to adapt to this growing need rather than go out to create it or even give it shape.

The text messaging story is also an example of co-evolution between the technology and marketplace; both changed in the process. Text messaging has created social changes in communication habits and parenting methods; it has changed the language; it has created a brand new market for mobile phones; it is changing business processes as well as influencing personal communication patterns. Equally, the demand for the technology has produced a response in mobile phone manufacturers in relation to tariff strategies and product design. So the strategy landscape post the advent of texting has a new attractor basin – that of young people, and the landscape as seen from the social perspective has new behaviours; these two changes have co-evolved.

We also have an example here where the world following the introduction of text messaging has new characteristics and behaviours that were not there before and could not easily have been predicted from analysing a pre-texting world. Communications in developing countries, for example, are radically different in kind and in degree from what they were before and communication processes between young people and with their parents have a completely different flow and frequency than in the past. So texting has tipped us into a new era of interaction from which, one might suspect, there is no going back.

The emerging story of *Social Action for Health* (SAfH) is an example of the need, in strategy development, to both adapt and respond to the wider marketplace and yet also to impact their marketplace with a coherent strategic focus; in this case the wider marketplace includes both the Health Service and the local communities. So this is a 'both–and' strategy which must synthesise reactive with proactive elements. The strategy also demonstrates the need to continually refine itself in the light of experience and changing strategic direction in the Health Service in particular. The strategic intent itself embraces a bottom-up approach to working with local communities at the same time as harnessing this experience to influence the Health Service to change methods and priorities. The impact of this small organisation seems out of kilter with its size and provides such a good example of a systemic and empowering way of working that it could perhaps tip the balance of opinion in the health sector and pave the way for new approaches and methodologies.

Summary

The real message of complexity is that of change – not just the superficial growth or decline of different elements in the system, but qualitative structural change involving new entities, new attributes and new possibilities, and therefore creating new threats and new opportunities. The question at its heart is this: how did things become what they are, and more importantly, what might they become in the future? Can we understand what is changing around us and how it might affect us, and can we transform ourselves and our knowledge fast enough to keep up? This co-evolution of the world, of our knowledge and consequently of our aims and goals is the real framework of our existence, and it means that we must live permanently in a real-time, learning process. This means that as fast as change erodes our knowledge, we must be experimenting and exploring and re-constructing our knowledge on a permanent basis – indeed the need to do this is the only thing that will be unchanging!

Notes

1. Information derived from BBC Website.
2. Derived from internal papers and discussions with SAfH personnel.

References

Allen, P. M., 'Dynamic Models of Evolving Systems', *System Dynamics Review*, 4 (1988) 1–2.
Allen, P. M., 'Why the Future Is Not What it Was', *Futures*, 22, 6 (1990) 555–569.
Allen, P. M., 'Coherence, Chaos and Evolution in the Social Context', *Futures*, 26, 6 (1994) 583–597.
Allen, P. M., *Cities and Regions as Self-Organising Systems: Models of Complexity* (Amsterdam: Gordon and Breach, 1997).
Allen, P. M., 'What Is the Science of Complexity?', *Emergence* 3, 1 (2001) 24–42.
Allen, P. M. and J. G. Boulton, 'The Implications of Complexity for Business Process and Strategy', in K. A. Richardson (ed.) *Managing Organizational Complexity* (Greenwich, CT: IAP Publishing, 2005), pp. 397–419.
Allen, P. M. and J. M. McGlade, 'Evolutionary Drive: The Effect of Microscopic Diversity, Error Making and Noise', *Foundation of Physics*, 17, 7 (1987) 723–788.
Allen, P. M., I. Prigogine and R. Herman, 'The Evolution of Complexity and the Laws of Nature', in E. Laszlo and J. Bierman (eds) *Goals for a Global Society* (New York: Pergamon Press, 1977).
Allen, P. M., M. Sanglier, G. Engelen and F. Boon, 'Towards a New Synthesis in the Modelling of Evolving Complex Systems', *Environment and Planning B*, 12 (1985) 65–84.
Arthur, W. B., 'Competing Technologies and Lock-In by Historical Events: The Dynamics of Allocation Under Increasing Returns', *IIASA Paper WP-83-90* (Laxenburg: Austria, 1983).
Arthur, W. B., 'Coming from Your Inner Self', *Interview with W. Brian Arthur, Dialog on Leadership* (Palo Alto, CA, April 16, 1999).
Ashby, W. R., *An Introduction to Cybernetics* (London: Chapman and Hall, 1956).
Bonabeau, E., M. Dorigo and G. Theraulaz, *Swarm Intelligence: From Natural to Artificial Systems* (New York: Oxford University Press, 1999).
Boulton, J. G. and P. M. Allen, 'Strategic Management in a Complex World', *British Academy of Management Conference* (2004).
Briggs, J. and F. Peat, *Seven Life Lessons of Chaos: Spiritual Wisdom from the Science of Change* (New York: Harper Perennial, 2000).
Buchler, J., *Philosophical Writings of Peirce* (New York: Dover Publications Inc., 1955).
Burton, R. and B. Obel, *Strategic Organizational Diagnosis and Design: Developing Theory for Application*, 2nd ed (Boston: Kluwer, 1998).
Capra, F., *The Web of Life* (London: Harper Collins, 1996).
Christensen, C. M., *The Innovator's Dilemma* (Boston, MA: Harvard Business School Press, 1997).
Cilliers, P., *Complexity and Postmodernism: Understanding Complex Systems* (London: Routledge, 1998).
Cohen, J. and I. Stewart, *The Collapse of Chaos* (London: Penguin, 1994).
Duncan, R. B., 'Characteristics of Organizational Environments and Perceived Environmental Uncertainty', *Administrative Science Quarterly*, 17, 3 (1972) 313–327.
Eisenhardt, K. M. and J. A. Martin, 'Dynamic Capabilities: What are They?', *Strategic Management Journal*, 21, 10/11 (2000) 1105–1121.
Eisenhardt, K. M. and D. N. Sull, 'Strategy as Simple Rules', *Harvard Business Review*, January (2001) 107–116.
Futures 37 (7) Special Edition on Complexity and Knowledge (2005).
Garnsey, E. and J. McGlade, *Complexity and Co-evolution, Continuity and Change in Socio-economic Systems* (Cheltenham: Edward Elgar, 2006).
Gell-Mann, M., *The Quark and the Jaguar* (New York: W. H. Freeman, 1994).
Gladwell, M., *The Tipping Point* (London: Little, Brown and Company, 2000).

Gleick, J., *Chaos* (London: Abacus, 1987).

Golding, W., *Lord of the Flies* (London: Faber & Faber, 1954), 1996 reprint.

Goodwin, B., *How the Leopard Changed Its Spots* (London: Weidenfeld and Nicholson, 1994).

Gould, S. J., 'Punctuated Equilibrium in Fact and Theory', *Journal of Social Biological Structure*, 12 (1989) 117–136.

Haken, H., *Synergetics, an Introduction: Non-equilibrium Phase Transitions and Self-Organization in Physics, Chemistry and Biology* (Berlin: Springer-Verlag, 1977).

Hamel, G. and C. K. Prahalad, 'Strategic Intent', *Harvard Business Review*, 67, 3 (1989) 63–76.

Holland, J. H., *Adaptation in Natural and Artificial Systems* (Ann Arbor, MI: University of Michigan Press, 1992).

James, W., *Selected Writings* (London: Everyman, 1995).

Kaufman, S. A., *At Home in the Universe: The Search for the Laws of Self-Organization and Complexity* (New York: Oxford University Press, 1995).

Kay, J. and E. D. Schneider, 'Embracing Complexity, the Challenge of the Ecosystem Approach', *Alternatives* 20, 3 (1994) 32–38.

Lawrence, P. and J. Lorsch, *Organization and Environment* (Boston, MA: Harvard University Press, 1967).

Lewin, R., *Complexity* (London: Phoenix, 1995).

Lewin, A. Y. and H. W. Volberda, 'Prolegomena on Coevolution: A Framework for Research on Strategy and New Organizational Forms', *Organization Science*, 10, 5 (1999) 519–534.

Lewin, A. Y., C. P. Long and T. N. Carroll, 'The Coevolution of New Organizational Forms', *Organization Science*, 10, 5 (1999) 535–550.

Lorenz, E. N., 'Deterministic Nonperiodic Flow', *Journal of the Atmospheric Sciences* 20, 2 (1963) 130–141.

Lorig, K., R. Stewart, P. Ritter, D. Gonzalez, V. Laurent and D. Lynch, *Outcome Measures for Health Education and Other Health Care Interventions* (London: Sage, 1996).

Lovelock, J., *The Revenge of Gaia* (London: Penguin Allen Lane, 2006).

Maguire, S. and B. McKelvey, 'Complexity and Management; Moving from Fad to Firm Foundations', *Emergence: A Journal of Complexity Issues in Organizations and Management*, 1, 2 (1999) 19–61

Mandelbrot, B., *Fractals – Form, Chance And Dimension* (San Francisco, CA: W. H. Freeman, 1977).

Maturana, H. and F. J. Varela, *The Tree of Knowledge* (Boston, MA: Shambhala, 1987).

McMillan, E., *Complexity, Organizations and Change* (London and New York: Routledge, 2004).

Middleton-Kelly, E., 'Ten Principles of Complexity and Enabling Infrastructures', in E. Middleton-Kelly (ed) *Complex Systems and Evolutionary Perspectives on Organisations: The Application of Complexity Theory to Organisations* (London: Elsevier, 2003).

Miller, D., *Strategy Making in Context: Ten Empirical Archetypes* (PhD thesis) (Montreal: Faculty of Management, McGill University, 1976).

Mintzberg, H., *The Strategy Safari* (Harlow: Financial Times/Prentice Hall, 2002).

Nicolis, G. and I. Prigogine, *Exploring Complexity: An Introduction* (New York: Freeman, 1989).

Peters, T. and R. H. Waterman, *In Search of Excellence: Lessons from America's Best-Run Companies* (London: Harper and Row, 1982).

Poincaré, H., 'Sur Le Problème Des Trois Corps Et Les Equations De La Dynamique', *Acta Mathematica*, 13 (1890) 1–270.

Pratt, J., P. Gordon and D. Plamping, *Working Whole Systems; Putting Theory into Practice in Organisations* (Oxford: Radcliffe Publishing Ltd, 2005).

Prigogine, I. and I. Stengers, *Order out of Chaos: Man's New Dialogue with Nature* (New York: Bantam, 1984).

Quinn, J. B., *Strategies for Change: Logical Incrementalism* (Homewood, IL: Richard D. Irwin, 1980).

Raup, D. M., *Extinction: Bad Genes or Bad Luck?* (London: W. W. Norton and Co., 1992).

Richardson, K., 'The Hegemony of the Physical Sciences: An Exploration in Complexity Thinking', *Futures*, 37 (2005) 615–653.

Rihani, S., *Complex Systems Theory and Development Practice* (London: Zed Books, 2002).

Snowden, D., 'Complex Acts of Knowing: Paradox and Descriptive Self-Awareness', *Journal of Knowledge Management*, 6, 2 (2002) 100–111.

Stacey, R. D., *Strategic Management and Organisational Dynamics: The Challenge of Complexity* (Harlow: Financial Times/Prentice Hall, 2003).

Stacey, R. D., D. Griffin and P. Shaw, *Complexity and Management: Fad or Radical Challenge to Systems Thinking?* (London: Routledge, 2002).

Streatfield, P., *The Paradox of Control in Organisations* (London: Routledge, 2001).

Teece, D. J., G. Pisano and A. Shuen, 'Dynamic Capabilities and Strategic Management', *Strategic Management Journal*, 18, 7 (1997) 509–533.

Thompson, J. D., *Organizations in Action* (New York: McGraw-Hill, 1967).

Tirpack, D., 'Avoiding Dangerous Climate Change', *Scientific Symposium on Stabilisation of Greenhouse Gases*, February 1–3 (2006).

Ulanowicz, R. E., 'An Hypothesis on the Development of Natural Communities', *Journal of Theoretical Biology*, 85 (1980) 223–245.

von Bertalanffy, L., *General Systems Theory* (New York: Braziller, 1968).

Waldrop, M. M., *Complexity: The Emerging Science at the Edge of Order and Chaos* (Viking, 1992).

Weber, M., *Economy and Society* (Berkeley, CA: University of California Press, 1978).

Wheatley, M. J., *Leadership and the New Science* (San Francisco, CA: Berrett-Koehler, 1992).

CHAPTER 15

Critical Management Perspective

Mahmoud Ezzamel and Hugh Willmott

'It is important to remember that no one has ever seen a strategy; every strategy is a figment of someone's imagination, whether conceived of as intentions to regulate behaviour before it takes place or inferred as patterns to describe behaviour that has already occurred'.

(Mintzberg, 1995, pp. 18–19)

Basic principles

The 'critical management perspective' has been developed in opposition to mainstream accounts of 'strategic management', many of which are represented in this volume. From a critical perspective, mainstream thinking provides an idealised, de-contextualised, normative and self-aggrandising picture of how organisations are, or should be, managed strategically. Mainstream strategic management literature is criticised for (1) failing to acknowledge the *particular*, normative basis of its truth claims (i.e. its largely unquestioning adoption of a managerialist worldview); and (2) assuming the adequacy of its reliance upon a *particular* ('positivist' or 'neopositivist') model of scientific investigation in which research is understood to examine a pre-given universe of objects that exist independently of their investigation and representation (Knights and Morgan, 1991; Levy et al., 2003). An outcome of these failings is that mainstream perspectives abstract strategic management from the wider relations of inequality and power – of domination, exploitation and subjection – in which knowledge is produced, and where what passes for 'strategic management' in organisations and in academic and consultancy texts is accomplished. By privileging these *particulars* as the sole legitimate path to knowledge of strategic management, mainstream thinking effectively excludes or suppresses the claims of other (e.g. critical) conceptions and associated accounts of the field.

What, then, of a 'critical' perspective on strategic management? Of course, no one has a monopoly over the term 'critical', any more than any executive, fund manager or academic has a monopoly over the meaning of such terms as 'strategy' or 'management'. Take the quotation from Henry Mintzberg that opens this chapter. Mintzberg is critical of those who forget that 'strategy' is, first of all, a *concept*. In this sense, 'strategy' is, as he puts it, a 'figment of the imagination', not something that exists 'out there' in the world. Mintzberg's reflection on the ontological status of strategy resonates with a 'critical management perspective' insofar as it cautions against confusing reified concepts (e.g. 'strategy') with the referents ('the world') that they aspire to know, yet can only know by deploying certain concepts – such as 'strategic' and 'management' – words that have diverse and unstable meanings, depending upon the particular group of practitioners or academics that have made them 'figments' of their 'imagination'. This diversity and associated instability is evident in the varied 'perspectives' on, or constructions of, 'strategic management' that appear in this volume. What 'strategic management is' then depends, first, on the (theorising) of power that (re)presents it in a particular way, as illustrated by the chapters in this text; and, second, upon the power to persuade others, such as the readers of this collection, of its merit which, of course, depends not upon intrinsic merit but, rather, upon its resonance with what they/you conceive to be credible and relevant. The production and reception of knowledge is, from a critical management perspective, understood as an articulation of power, not as a reflection of what it aspires to reflect or capture.

So, do Mintzberg's criticisms of mainstream thinking about strategic management contribute to a 'critical perspective'? Possibly, but arguably only inasmuch that he questions whether strategic management exists 'out there' and thereby jolts us into questioning what we may have taken for granted – that is, the assumption that accounts of, or 'perspectives' on, strategic management more or less adequately capture its 'out-there-ness' – whereas, according to Mintzberg, it is more credibly understood as an 'intention' or an 'inference' that serves either to regulate or to rationalise actions identified as 'strategic management'. Or, to translate this claim into the framing provided by a critical perspective, 'strategic management' is an articulation of power that animates the particular contents of intentions and inferences. What distances Mintzberg's analysis from a critical perspective is the absence of any exploration of the relations of domination, exploitation and subjection that privilege the particular 'intentions' or 'patterns' attributed to 'strategic management' by practitioners and/or academics, let alone the power relations that result in strategy being conceptualised in such terms. Nor, despite a recognition that 'no one has ever seen a strategy', does Mintzberg problematise the assumption that scientific study can *reflect or capture* what strategic management really is. Rather, he champions the idea that 'real-world' strategies are divisible into those that are 'deliberate' (realised as intended) and others that are 'emergent' (realised despite, or in the absence of, intentions), and that studying a larger number of cases (his argument is based upon an intensive study of 11 organisations) would allow the propositions advanced to be tested (Mintzberg and Waters, 1985). By stressing the indivisible connections of knowledge and power, critical analyses point to the theory-dependent nature of empirical findings and would therefore be much more sceptical about truth claims based upon tests of hypotheses.

What counts as a 'critical management perspective', for the purposes of this chapter, is guided by a radical challenge to orthodox conceptions of the relationship between knowledge and power. More specifically, it challenges the assumption that a more inclusive sense of rationality, in the case of 'strategy-as-organisational-conduct', and/or a more exacting method, in the case of 'strategy-as-academic-field',[1] can cleanse knowledge of its dependence upon power – a dependency conventionally identified as 'bias' that is removable by the application of the scientific method. Because the constituent elements of a 'critical perspective' problematise strategic management in diverse ways, what is regarded as a 'central' or a 'basic principle' will differ with the particular approach. It is possible only to convey a flavour of their distinctiveness. Critical approaches:

1. Connect strategic management with wider structures of domination, exploitation and subjection. They challenge the apparent impartiality and objectivity of orthodox accounts of strategic management.

2. Relate strategic management to the reproduction of structures of inequality, including patriarchy, class and post-colonialism. For example, the language of strategic management is seen to be 'macho' or masculinist in its emphasis upon means–end rationality and control.

3. Assess mainstream accounts of strategic management as suppressing or avoiding issues of subordination and conflict in organisations by presenting its content and operation as politically neutral.

4. Diagnose the limitations of mainstream approaches in terms of their reliance upon (1) a positivist conception of scientific investigation in which there is a naturalisation of its objects of enquiry and/or (2) an allegiance with managerial values that limits and compromises the knowledge of strategic management that is generated.

5. Highlight how, as a discourse, the analyses and prescriptions of 'strategic management' are constitutive of the field that they aspire to describe. This discourse provides a seemingly authoritative specification of what are the most pressing or real of strategic problems to which it also

provides its particular, favoured solutions. Most potently, it tells senior managers that they are responsible for 'strategy', and how they should think, and often what they should do, to pass as competent 'strategists'.

It is probably fair to say that with one notable exception (Pettigrew et al., 2002), the existence of contributions to a critical perspective on strategy has gone largely unrecorded even in ostensibly comprehensive reviews of the strategic management literature (e.g. Hoskisson et al., 1999; McKiernan, 1996). Given this neglect, it is important to bear in mind that these contributions have been wide-ranging and include those grounded in critical theory (e.g. Shrivastava, 1986), labour process analysis (e.g. Hyman, 1987), constructionism (e.g. Mir and Watson, 2000), Gramscian analysis (e.g. Levy, 1997) and discourse analysis (e.g. Thomas, 1998). So, the 'critical management perspective' is not so much a perspective as a varied group of commentaries on, and interrogations of, strategic management which, for convenience, have been labelled 'critical'. The variant considered in this chapter is Foucauldian analysis (e.g. Hoskin, 1990; Knights and Morgan, 1991, 1995), a critical perspective on strategic management identified by Whipp (1999, p. 13) as 'one of the most instructive attempts to link the fields of organisation studies and strategy'. It should therefore be borne in mind that Foucauldian discourse analysis is an element within, and is not representative of, a broad range of 'critical management perspectives' on strategic management. As we argue later, sense can be made of discourse only when it is analysed within the context in which it was produced and which such discourse also articulates. For this reason the following section provides a discursive account of the context of our case study company, which we later draw upon in an illustrative example in which we analyse a particular fragment of strategy discourse produced by the CEO of the company.

CASE STUDY 15.1

StitchCo[2] was established in the early 1950s as a 'kitchen table', family business. Its distinctive product range has been characterised as combining classical features with contemporary appeal. By 1985 there were 171 StitchCo stores, a number of production facilities and a turnover of £96 million with after-tax profits of £14 million. Yet, despite the rapid growth and financial strength of the company, it lacked basic financial management at this time, let alone any explicit or 'deliberate' strategy: 'Nobody knew whether we had money in the bank, what was round the corner, nobody had a bloody clue' (Retailing Manager). Nonetheless, StitchCo prospered and became a household name, a success attributed by senior executives to 'having the Midas touch' (Buying Manager).

StitchCo's rapid growth stimulated city interest in the company. In turn, this fostered the formulation of a growth strategy based upon the development of its product range through the acquisition of other brands that would form the basis of five strategic business units (SBUs) (see below), with the expansion being financed by public flotation (oversubscribed 34 times). This strategy was premised upon an expanding retail market; customers who simply could not get enough of StitchCo's distinctive, lifestyle products; and, above all, a belief in StitchCo's successful brand development. Opening more stores, it was anticipated, would produce corresponding increases in revenues, a belief affirmed in 1988 by the rise in turnover to £200 million and an increase in after-tax profit to £23 million, with the number of stores doubling to 360. Within a year there were 439 stores with £250 million turnover, but with a fall in after-tax profit to £20 million. Instead of confirming (the self-deprecating conceit of) the 'Midas touch', the annual accounts cast doubt upon the company's invincibility. Various explanations were offered but the object of blame was deduced from a strategy–structure framework in which (the legacy of) StitchCo's centralised structure was held responsible for a failure to exploit market opportunities.

Strategic business units

The SBU structure had become a fashionable idea during the 1970s and 1980s for stimulating and disciplining business development (Hall, 1978). It was identified as the way of combining 'the micro flexibility of smaller, specialised firms in serving dynamic and fragmented markets with the financial strength and macroflexibility of large diversified groups able to invest in the latest technologies, exploit international market opportunities and transfer resources into or out of specific business sectors' (Kilduff, 2000, p. 8).

Creating five SBUs at StitchCo was intended to give senior managers greater discretion and promote entrepreneurship. It was expected to 'increase the level of financial awareness throughout the business and allow increased control over working capital and investment decisions' (Annual Report, 1989).

The following year, the company posted its first loss before tax of £4 million and current trade creditors rose to over £80 million compared to £8 million in 1989. These unexpectedly poor results again stimulated a re-examination of the company's strategy. A shortage of 'core competencies' was invoked to account for the dissonance between expectation and performance: 'What we tried to do was to manage brands that we didn't know anything about' (Group Treasurer). Any suggestion that StitchCo possessed a 'Midas touch' was discarded, as was the belief that its earlier success as a single brand company could be replicated by other business units. Enacting the SBU formula brought the company to the brink of collapse, resulting in a change of ownership and replacement of its senior managers.

There was then an *inter regnum* as StitchCo awaited the appointment of a new CEO, as 'the focus of the strategy was really one of survival. No more, no less. It was purely aimed at keeping the company afloat' (Group Accountant). Borrowing was reduced substantially, partly through a major closure programme. Many staff were replaced by new managers who were expected to embrace, flesh out and influence the implementation of the new strategy, devised primarily by the incoming CEO, that was distilled in the phrase 'simplify, focus and act' (SFA).

During his lecture tours of the retailing and manufacturing sites to disseminate SFA, the CEO demonstrated his avowed commitment to listen actively to people at all levels: 'the amount of buying (into the new strategy) from people on the shop floor is large because at the end of the day you've listened to them' (Finance Director). The success attributed to the internal marketing of SFA was also explained in terms of the use of broad terms to communicate the new strategy because 'Everyone can buy simplify, focus and act . . . it was essentially vision stuff' (Buying and Manufacturing Director). The SFA strategy was subsequently inscribed in documents, copies of which were circulated throughout StitchCo, and was also translated into performance metrics.

The SFA discourse problematised the previous phase of expansion-through-acquisition as one of complexity[3] and diversification that exceeded the skills of its senior managers to deliver it. By simplifying, costs were to be slashed; by focusing, valuable expertise in the single brand was to be exploited; by acting decisively, an effective response to customer demand was to be promoted rather than endlessly debated. The new strategy emphasised transparency in a vertically integrated business to enable cost reductions through greater simplification of activities. Performance measures were developed that identified and quantified key success factors for every manager, with the claim that they would demonstrate individual contribution to the new strategic vision. The niche customer was courted by using quantified spend targets in an effort to reveal and reward achievement against what the SFA strategy demanded.

Overview of the critical management perspective

'[S]trategy is not simply a technique or body of knowledge . . . [but] a discourse. In other words, the very language, symbols and exchanges around the subject of strategy have important outcomes. Strategy is a *mechanism of power*'.

(Whipp, 1999, p. 13, emphasis added)

Within orthodox approaches, different conceptions of strategy – classified, for example, as 'Classical', 'Evolutionary', 'Processual' and 'Systemic' (Whittington, 1993) – are deemed to provide 'ways of seeing' a distinctive domain of activity: the domain of strategic management. From the standpoint of Foucauldian discourse analysis,[4] in contrast, each perspective is conceived to be 'embedded in social practices that reproduce the "way of seeing" as the "truth" of the discourse' (Knights and Morgan, 1991). Accordingly, 'strategic management' is converted from 'a descriptive label' that is understood to represent a distinctive domain of researchable objects (e.g. 'strategies', 'environments') 'out there' in the world to a discourse that is actively engaged in construing and constituting what strategy analysis commonsensically appears, or aspires, to capture or reflect:

> '[S]trategy as a discourse is intimately involved in constituting the intentions and actions from which it is thought to be derived. Strategy, then, is an integral part, and not independent, of the actions or practices that it is frequently drawn upon to explain or justify'.
>
> (Knights and Morgan, 1991, p. 268)

The key point to be grasped is how, as a discourse, strategy and its enactment as strategic management constitute the social reality that it is understood to describe or justify. In other words, by examining strategic management as a discourse, it becomes possible to appreciate its 'truth effects' in terms of encouraging identification with, and enactment of, the particular 'figment of the imagination' (Mintzberg, 1995, p. 19) that its articulation projects. For Foucault (1979, p. 27), discursive practices articulate social relations in which knowledge and power are inextricably intertwined and *mutually constitutive*: 'there is no power relation without the correlative constitution of a field of knowledge, nor any knowledge that does not presuppose or constitute at the same time power relations'.

Foucauldian discourse analysis rejects a dominant conception of the language–reality relationship in which signs (e.g. the terms 'strategic' and 'management') are understood to capture reality. The departure from a picture theory of language is signalled as Foucault maintains that discourse 'is not a slender surface of contact, or confrontation, between a reality and a language (*langue*)' (1982, p. 48). To treat discourse as a sign that designates things is, he insists, to disregard or neutralise its *constitutive* force. Such neutralisation is a feature of perspectives on strategic management that are inattentive to how they are constitutive of the phenomena that they study.

What is identified as strategic management is conceived as a contested, rather than settled, domain or field whose identity and significance is (precariously) secured through relations of domination, exploitation and subjection. It is not assumed that lay and academic knowledge of strategic management simply confirms and legitimises these relations as it can also act to discredit or subvert them. 'Discourses', Foucault argues, 'are not once and for all subservient to power or raised up against it . . . discourse can be both an instrument and an effect of power, but also a hindrance, a stumbling-block, a point of resistance and a starting point for an opposing strategy' (1990, pp. 101–101). Thus, the quote from Whipp (1999) with which this section begins neatly acknowledges that strategy is a mechanism of power but ignores the equally important point that strategic discourse is also an effect of power. Discourse is not a mere formulation of knowledge; rather, it operates to control and manipulate knowledge by constituting particular fields, such as strategic management, and inviting actions in specific directions. In this way, 'regimes of truth' are established that act to discipline thought and conduct, yet remain vulnerable to alternative thinking and lines of action. For example, a discourse of labour productivity or a discourse of exchange rate movements may be invoked to explain changes in demand for exports and thereby to cast doubt upon putative moves to restore or augment productivity through the restructuring of work and/or the (further) intensification of manufacturing activity. The ascription of truth to such a discourse may then reinforce or dampen enthusiasm for discourses that had previously absorbed the energy and constituted the identity of senior managers. Later we illustrate such dynamics by reference to our study of StitchCo.

Linking the critical management perspective to strategic management

In this section, we compare and contrast rationalist and processualist with discursive perspectives on strategic management as a way of drawing out the distinctiveness of Foucauldian analysis. Comparisons cannot, of course, be undertaken from some neutral, omniscient God-like position, so it is relevant to acknowledge that Foucauldian thinking informs both the depiction and the assessment of each approach.

Rationalist analysis

The field of strategic management has been dominated by rational conceptions of its formulation and implementation, as exemplified in Michael Porter's thinking in which managing strategy is conceived of as an outcome of a rational calculation about competitive advantage in relation to buyers, suppliers, competitors, new entrants and the availability of substitutes. As Porter (1979, p. 137) puts it, 'the corporate strategist's goal is to find a position in the industry where his or her company can best defend itself against these forces or can influence them in its favor'. Minimal attention is paid to the institutional context – such as the distinctive cultural values and organisational politics – within and through which decisions are made and implemented, including the values that bestow legitimacy upon rational models as a key component of top managerial ideology (see Chapter 2). In short, strategy is largely disassociated from the conditions and consequences of its construction and management.

Porter's thinking is illustrative of a dominant, rationalist conception of 'strategy' as 'the pattern or plan that integrates an organization's major goals, policies, and action sequences into a cohesive whole' (Quinn, 1995, p. 5). Note how 'goals, policies and action sequences' are attributed to an organisation and are, in principle, objectively knowable by the architects of strategy. There is either no acknowledgement of possible, and indeed likely, differences of interpretation amongst organisational members occupying different positions and specialisms within corporate hierarchies; or it is assumed that such differences will evaporate with the creation of the strategy. In effect, the term strategy is invoked to *ascribe* and convey coherence and rationality where, arguably, there are more or less manifest relations of compliance, domination, exploitation and subjection, albeit ones that have become so naturalised as to be routinely unrecognisable as such.

Quinn's definition of strategy as '*the pattern or plan . . . into a cohesive whole*' (see above) exemplifies a form of domination: a *particular* view of strategy assumes the authoritative appearance of a *universal* truth. It denies differences of priority (or 'interest') amongst organisation members by suggesting that the architects of strategy alone know what the 'goals, policies and action sequences' are. Quinn's definition also conflates and confuses knowledge that aspired to be descriptive with knowledge that is amenable to prescriptive application. For it implies that the goals, policies and action sequences are inherently mutually consistent and therefore capable of being integrated and that it simply takes the identification of a 'pattern', or the construction of a 'plan', to ensure that this potential is realised. There is a certain grandiosity associated with the term 'strategy'; and it is seductive in its rationalistic, masculinist suggestion that senior managers are in control. In Quinn's words, as competent strategists, senior managers are able to 'marshal and allocate an organisation's resources into a unique and viable posture' (ibid.) – a posture that is developed on the basis of sound information about internal strengths and weaknesses, 'anticipated changes in the environment, and contingent moves by intelligent opponents' (ibid.). Yet, even if this were possible, it might still fail to achieve its own objectives if, as some commentators have argued, planning displaces the vision required to develop anything distinctive (Mintzberg, 1994).

Processualist analysis

Commentators who would probably not welcome an association of their work with a critical perspective have noted how mainstream thinking depends upon static models and methods, naive assumptions, an infatuation with new angles at the expense of substance and an inclination to advocate prescriptions before undertaking in-depth diagnoses (see Daft and Buenger, 1990; Hambrick, 1990). Similar criticisms have been levelled at 'classical' or 'deliberate' conceptions of strategy by more 'processual' or 'emergent' approaches to strategic management (e.g. institutional theory, strategy as practice). They highlight the failure of imposed, formulate-then-implement approaches to get to grips with the messy (processual) complexities of organisations where, for example, unpredictable changes occur and skilful interventions are required to retain the 'core competences' of key staff. They are concerned about showing how strategic decision-making emerges from contextually specific understandings and processes of bargaining – features of organising that are conceived to govern the formulation and acceptability of strategic visions as well as their implementation.

What we are calling 'processualist' analysis of strategic management places greater emphasis upon culture and leadership, for example, in framing and addressing challenges, overcoming resistances and thereby accomplishing strategies, whether deliberate or emergent. When it is not reduced to the examination of mental models and cognitive scripts (e.g. Hodgkinson and Johnson, 1994), processualist analysis aspires to appreciate how managing strategically involves wrestling with a range of ingrained and difficult-to-manage issues – rather coyly characterised as 'political/cultural considerations' (Pettigrew, 1985, p. 46) – that are unacknowledged by rationalistic prescriptions for achieving competitive advantage (e.g. Porter, 1985). In his study of ICI, for example, Pettigrew (1985) makes direct reference to the way dominant groups are protected by the 'existing bias of the structures and cultures of an organization' (ibid., p. 45); he observes how these groups actively mobilise this socioeconomic context to 'legitimize existing definitions of the core strategic concerns, to help justify new priorities, and to delegitimize other novel and threatening definitions of the organization's situation' (ibid., p. 45). However, Pettigrew's account of process is largely abstracted from the historically distinctive, politico-economic organisation – that is, the relations of domination, exploitation and subjection – of processes that shaped the development and direction of strategic management at ICI. In Whittington's (1992, p. 701) words, 'the limits of feasible change within ICI were defined not simply by the personal competencies and organizational advantages of particular managers ... but also by the evolving class structures of contemporary British society'. Yet, Pettigrew's analysis is silent about such considerations (cf. Nichols and Beynon, 1977).

Processualists share with rationalist analyses of strategic management a managerialist concern to generate knowledge that will enhance calculative control over a host of factors that are deemed decisive for managing complexity in order to enhance performance. Processualists continue to take for granted the adequacy of established measures of performance, rather than questioning whether, for example, profitability or growth are, in themselves, necessarily laudable objectives. In this regard, Whittington (1993), for example, subscribes to this normative approach when suggesting that managers can draw from broader, less visible sources of power, such as 'the political resources of the state, the network resources of ethnicity, or, if male, the patriarchal resources of masculinity' (ibid., p. 38). In such thinking, the extra-organisational conditions of strategic management are identified as neglected yet potentially decisive weapons for its effective advance.

Processualists also conceive of strategic management as a set of elements of the world 'out there' to be captured by analysis – for example, as the constituent elements of practitioners' worldviews. Thus, Whittington advocates a 'practice perspective' that is 'concerned with finding out what strategists' and organizers' jobs *really* are' (2003, p. 121, emphasis added). Likewise, Mintzberg and Quinn (1995, p. xi, emphasis added) commend a processual approach which, they claim, provides 'a sophisticated understanding of *exactly what the context is* and how it functions'. From a discursive perspective, there is a basic and insurmountable difficulty with such 'realist' claims that analysts can *know* reality. For the plausibility of such claims is seen to rely upon an inattentiveness *to*, and possibly a denial of, *the interrelationship of the subjects and objects of knowledge*. It is assumed that the world 'out there' is entirely separate from, and uninfluenced by, how this world is understood or theorised by inescapably imperfect and partial perspectives. 'Old' (e.g. rational) and 'new' (e.g. processual and practice) perspectives share the presumption of being able to know what the world is 'really like' in advance, and, independently, of the generation of the knowledge. There is an assumption that the objects of 'observation' – that is, the constituent elements of the social world – are both transparent to, and unchanged by, the theory/methodology that accounts for them, thereby (perversely) disregarding how analytic processes of interpreting, evaluating and appropriating influence the 'realness' of the world that theories purport to describe and explain. The endemic problem with the ambition to achieve 'a *genuine* understanding of how [an] organization *really* works' (Mintzberg et al., 1995, p. xi) is that the reality of the object (e.g. 'organisation' or 'strategy') is necessarily conditioned by the language used to articulate the preoccupations and perspectives of the subject (e.g. researcher): the use of language to describe the world is inescapably divisive, partial and incomplete. Language is not treated as a group of 'signs (signifying elements referring to contents and representations) but as practices that *systematically form the objects of which they speak*' (Foucault, 1990, p. 49, emphasis added). Included in these 'objects' are the social and self-identities of those 'experts' (e.g. academics, consultants, managers) who develop, promote, enact and resist strategy discourse. In short, Foucauldian analysis is more alert to, and reflexive about, the constitutive, 'truth' effects of strategy discourses with respect to, for example, the realities they construct and the actors and actions that they discipline. The differences are summarised in Table 15.1.

The analytical gauntlet thrown down by Foucauldian discourse analysis is to acknowledge and investigate the power/knowledge relations that are productive of *particular* ways of accounting for complex processes. It is not simply that discourse is contextually interpreted. Rather, it is *indexical* in the sense that discourses are rendered meaningful by connecting their claims to the discursively constituted contexts of their articulation. Discourses appeal to a context whose contours they invoke and reproduce. So when, in the following section, we interpret the brief extract taken from some press coverage of StitchCo, we necessarily invoke a context – for example, a broad understanding of what businesses are and what CEOs do as well as our account of the history of the company that preceded the CEO's statement. Yet, in doing so, we stress that it is implausible to assume that 'context' and its interpreters can be objectively mirrored by language. Both context and discourse are understood to be continuously (re)identified through discursive practices. This, to be clear, is not to deny the reality of what is discursively identified as 'history', 'context', 'strategy' or 'management' but, rather, to recognise how it is through discursive practices that we produce (a sense of) reality that is reproduced and transformed through this constitutive process.

Moreover, our analysis appeals to a regime of truth – in the guise of strategy talk – that we aspire to scrutinise. Our interpretations of the extract are constructed from our knowledge of other empirical data, including interviewees' accounts and company documents, that inform *our* 'strategising' about how to deliver our argument to you as a member of an imagined audience. Our identification of

Table 15.1 Rationalist, processualist and discursive accountings of strategic management

	Rationalist	**Processualist**	**Discursive**
Strategic management is	Rational calculation	Cultural negotiation	Complex of power–knowledge relations
Focus of examination	Variables	Meanings	Discursive practices
Objects of examination	Pre-given, external to analysis	Pre-given, external to analysis	Constituted through analysis

relevant data, as well as our own account of its significance, is inflected by a strategy discourse with which 'research subjects' engage in strategising and which enables them to present accounts of their strategising activity.

Case study revisited

Shortly after his appointment, the new CEO of StitchCo released the following statement, which we consider in some detail as an example of discourse analysis:

> 'I have had a unique opportunity to carry the company forward into the Nineties. It is a privilege to participate in this driving, entrepreneurial and creative environment and with so many people that have also been part of its history and development'.

(press coverage)

The CEO's statement, we suggest, is illustrative of the kinds of discursive practices that comprise the micro (re)production of 'strategy'. It is an articulation of the social practice of (managerial) communication through which relations of power – between the CEO and his audience of consumers and investors as well as employees – operate to promote a particular kind of knowledge, and membership, of StitchCo. In this process, distinct subjects, notably, the CEO as occupier of the chief (and 'unique') executive position, as well as objects, such as 'the company', its 'history' and 'environment', are discursively constituted. To the extent that such claims are accepted and normalised, they operate not only to (re)produce discourses of strategy and strategic management but also to forge a regime of truth that disciplines the thought and conduct of those who identify with its call. The statement alludes, we suggest, to the 'strategic management' of StitchCo, both in its reference to moving 'forward' and in associating this movement with a 'driving, entrepreneurial and creative environment'. A discursive practice of strategising operates to position the activity and identity of employees within a process of 'carrying the company forward' into a new era – 'the Nineties' – but in which the CEO ascribed to himself a key, and perhaps sovereign, role. While favourably emphasising StitchCo's history and development, the temporal focus of the CEO's drive 'the Nineties' nonetheless signals some departure from past practices with the intention of developing StitchCo in such a way that it could compete effectively in a changed 'environment'. The use of the term 'environment' is ambiguous: it construes an operating context that is 'driving', presumably in the sense that the market punishes those who fail to respond effectively to its changing demands; it also signals an aspiration and demand that StitchCo employees are themselves driving, entrepreneurial and creative. The strategy favoured by the CEO sought to harness entrepreneurship and creativity in ways that would build upon and extend, rather than replace, a distinctive account of the history and development of the company.

For employees, customers, suppliers and investors alike, however, the press statement is likely to be placed in the context of their interpretation of the context of StitchCo, as reflected in their recent experiences of the company – uncertainties and layoffs, unavailability of stock and unreliable service, erratic demands on suppliers and rapidly deteriorating returns on capital. When placed within this discursive regime of truth, the CEO's statement can also, and perhaps primarily, be heard as an upbeat message of reassurance to StitchCo's stakeholders that a careful and considered diagnosis of previous failures has been achieved, that the basis for quick recovery is firmly established and that a resurgence of creativity, drive and entrepreneurialism will ensure the reversal of the company's recent fortunes.

This is, of course, just *one reading* of the CEO's statement. His words may be interpreted in many other ways. They could, for example, be read as a celebration of the implementation of a *rationalist* strategy intended to foster an 'entrepreneurial and creative' corporate culture capable of exploiting opportunities and parrying risks or as an integral part of a strategy of 'product differentiation' combined with 'focus' (Porter, 1980) that was intended to consolidate or retrieve the unique selling point ascribed to StitchCo's merchandise. Alternatively, the CEO's statement could be interpreted as part of a *process* of negotiation and promotion of a particular vision based upon his 'recipe knowledge' of the industry. In such a reading, the opportunity of press coverage could be interpreted as a way of disseminating a particular vision of strategy in which its dynamic ('carry forward', 'driving') meaning, and means of implementation, is given emphasis.

From a Foucauldian standpoint, however, whatever reading becomes dominant or 'taken for granted' evidences the play of power relations (e.g. by privileging particular discursive practices) rather than approximating what strategy 'is'. Communications do not simply explain or justify the intentions or actions of managers to whom the task of formulating and implementing strategy is assigned. They also exert truth effects insofar as they operate to constitute employee intentions and actions that they are generally assumed to describe. The discourse of this CEO can be read to signal a clear expectation or requirement that employees, himself included, will be assessed within, and will examine their own performance against, a corporate and business 'environment' that is represented as 'driving, entrepreneurial and creative'. Such expectation of employee compliance with the new regime of truth is given greater impetus by appealing to past contributions made by, and the loyalty of, StitchCo's staff, as the CEO claims to be relishing the prospect of working 'with so many people who have been part of its [StitchCo's] history and development'. The implication is that employees who are construed as not demonstrating their commitment to, and delivery of, this discipline will no longer have the 'opportunity' to 'participate', indeed would have no 'right to participate', having been constituted to have acted contrary to the requirements of a new environment and to corporate tradition. The CEO is thus equally tied to, and disciplined (i.e. both constrained and enabled) by, a strategy discourse that he promotes and with which he and his appointees (are) strongly identified by StitchCo's directors, major shareholders and employees. His repeated and amplified articulations of the strategy, distilled in the acronym SFA, operate to fuel the expectations of staff and investors that the CEO would himself exemplify and demonstrate what it means to be 'driving, entrepreneurial and creative'.

It should not be assumed, however, that such discourse is unequivocally coercive or constraining in the expectations it places upon employees; and people may be committed to other discourses (e.g. family, leisure) that render such discourse more or less plausible and appealing. Investment in other discourses and associated identifications (e.g. family or career goals) can result in considerable scepticism and resistance with respect to proposed and enacted strategic change. But ambivalence is perhaps a more common response. Some elements of innovation may be welcomed, when, for example, changes are perceived to be enabling and/or identity-confirming. Elements of the SFA strategy were welcomed by many StitchCo employees who interpreted it as a return to a formula that had succeeded in the past and was now reinvigorated by a personable, charismatic CEO – a role occupied in an earlier era by the highly respected, visionary co-founder of the business. The terrain on which the new strategy discourse at StitchCo was propagated and distributed had previously been 'occupied by a variety of social relations and forms of subjectivity' that relate to the discursively constituted context of StitchCo (Knights and Vurdubakis, 1994) to which the CEO, an outsider, contrived to make selective appeals. The resonance of his vision with the sentiments and aspirations of many employees was registered in their overtly enthusiastic response, though some were privately dubious or even suspicious, and a minority of managers were hostile to the CEO's truth claims with respect to identifying the strategy that would rescue StitchCo from its parlous state. As we have stressed earlier, power works on recalcitrant material.

Reflection

There is a paradox of discursive analysis identified by Knights and Morgan (1991, p. 260) when they note that the 'truth effects' of orthodox thinking about strategy are powerful, making it 'exceedingly difficult for us to disengage ourselves from such a view'. We agree that such disengagement is difficult;

indeed we cannot envisage a worthwhile empirically based analysis of strategy that makes little reference to events (e.g. the appointment of a CEO or a financial crisis) and contexts (e.g. recession).

The issue, then, is less one of how to avoid references to established elements of orthodox thinking, such as events and contexts, but, rather, of how to signal the power/knowledge relations that are productive of *particular* ways of accounting for complex processes. It is not simply that discourse is contextually interpreted. Rather, it is *indexical* in the sense that it is rendered meaningful by connecting its claims to the discursively constituted context of their articulation. The CEO's statement, for example, is placed in the context of what is (discursively) constituted as the history of StitchCo and the position of its CEO. This context is not objective but, rather, is produced through discourse. Discourse analysis exemplifies and stimulates an awareness of how the identification and privileging of particular conditions is itself the product of a contingent, discursively produced way of depicting the emergence of strategising practices.

Summary

Many programmes in business schools are crowned by a 'capstone' course in strategic management, placing it at the very apex of management. Yet, it is only comparatively recently that 'strategic management' has been labelled, studied and privileged as a field of managerial practice and scholarly attention (Bracker, 1980). This observation begs the questions of how managers were able to manage without the benefit of 'strategic management' and, more abrasively, whether 'strategic management' is as much, and perhaps more, about elevating and legitimising the identity and activity of senior managers as 'strategists' than it is about elucidating, let alone guiding, what they do. Strategies may, as Mintzberg (1995, p. 19) claims, be 'figments of the imagination' but they nonetheless have come to exert powerful and privileging truth effects upon practitioners and students of management.

Processualist analysis explores how, for example, the values or interpretative frameworks of key decision makers inform their actions in ways that place in doubt the diagnostic and prescriptive adequacy of impersonal 'rational' calculations about strategy. Institutional analysis, for example, emphasises the importance of what is taken for granted (see Chapter 2) but it sheds little light upon how *particular* forms of taken-for-grantedness become privileged and institutionalised. This is possibly because what is taken for granted is assumed to be legitimate rather than hegemonic. Nor does processualist analysis consider how discourses of strategy, articulated by practitioners and academics, are constitutive of their actions as the discourses render their actions intelligible in a distinctive way. Foucault's thinking invites us to develop an alternative conception of strategic management where the focus is upon 'a group of rules' or a 'grid of intelligibility' that produces the 'truth effect' of *identifying and ordering objects in particular ways*. Instead of understanding the signs that comprise the field of strategic management – such as 'firms' and 'markets' – as conveying (more or less) accurate images of an external social reality, these terms are conceived to constitute the world in inescapably particular, partisan, politically charged ways. Discursive analysis goes to the heart of strategising activity where, for example, certain ideas are conceived to be 'strategic' and various artefacts, such as statements made by CEOs, are discursively imbued with 'strategic' significance.

It is possible, and hopefully likely, that, as a contribution to a critical perspective on strategic management, Foucauldian discourse analysis will prompt some questioning, perhaps leading to a reassessment, of some of the claims that are made in the name of 'strategic management'. It may encourage and enable the development of a more reflective understanding of how the actions of senior managers are represented by orthodox accounts of 'strategic management'. It may foster an increased awareness of how mainstream accounts of 'strategic management' take for granted the historical and political conditions under which managerial priorities are determined and enacted. And it may facilitate consideration of how ideas developed within, or drawn into, the ambit of 'strategic management' are invoked to reform and regulate the ever-widening spheres of activity deemed suitable for its management – from public sector and non-profit management to regional economic development and business school accreditation.

A concern of such discursive analysis is to better appreciate 'how', as forms of power/knowledge, strategy talk and texts are actively involved in the constitution of what, for example, rational and processual models contrive to prescribe or describe. There is, however, no aspiration to offer a substitute or corrective for rationalist or processualist approaches to strategy. An appreciation of this diversity serves as a timely caution against any suggestion that the disciplinary force of any particular strategy discourse is totalising, rather than merely pervasive or hegemonic within specific historical and organisational settings. As we have noted, as discursive formations are founded upon dynamic relations of power, some room for contest and manoeuvre invariably exists within what Foucault (1972, p. 66) terms 'a field of possible options'. Diverse accounts of strategic management have credibility and value within their own (discursive) terms of reference. Their limitations, as constituted from within a discursive approach, stem from a lack of reflexivity (and humility) about claims to rationalise strategy or to accurately reflect its processes, shortcomings that are also evident in a disregard for their truth effects. While an incorporation of greater reflexivity within rationalist and processualist analyses would operate to qualify its objectivism – whether in respect of industry structures or 'managers' meanings – there would remain pragmatic or expedient reasons for retaining forms of knowledge that pay less attention to their discursive production and political effects.

A discursive approach, we acknowledge, is neither self-evidently valuable nor easily undertaken; and this is not least because, in order to discuss any topic (e.g. strategy), it is necessary to treat the topic as if our knowledge of it exists independently of the discursive practices that identify and explore it as a topic. Moreover, the truth effects of established strategic discourse, which find their echo in rational and processual models of strategy, are particularly powerful. Nonetheless, following the lead given by Knights and Morgan (1991, 1995), we believe that by striving to do so offers the possibility of opening up and extending new and challenging ways of understanding strategic management.

Notes

1. This distinction is drawn from Booth (2003). Of course, the two are interrelated, as knowledge of strategy-as-organizational-conduct depends upon some interpretive scheme drawn from 'strategy-as-academic-field'. And 'strategy-as-academic-field' informs the practical theorising that is expressed of strategy-as-organizational-conduct.
2. The authors conducted an intensive case study of StitchCo during a period of 3 years, beginning in 1994. Visits were made to all StitchCo's major administrative and production sites and to a number of retailing outlets. In total, 35 interviews (each lasting between one and one and a half hours) were held with most senior managers in addition to many middle managers, supervisors, team leaders and shop floor workers, with a few 'key informants' interviewed more than once. We also gained access to a number of internal documents that supplemented information drawn from company reports and other publicly available information.
3. Its operational complexity was reflected, we were told, in international sourcing, international distribution, vertical integration, breadth of product range and the company's involvement in manufacturing, retailing, wholesale, licensing and franchising.
4. There are, however, numerous varieties of discourse theory and analysis (for reviews, see Alvesson and Karreman, 2000; Howorth, 2000). In contrast to forms of analysis in which the nature of the objective world determines the character and veracity of discourses, Foucault contends that, and explores how, 'certain discursive rules enable subjects to produce objects, concepts, statements and strategies . . . ' (Howarth, 2000, pp. 7–8).

References

Alvesson, M. and D. Karreman, 'Varieties of Discourse: On the Study of Organizations Through Discourse Analysis', *Human Relations*, 53 (2000) 1125–1149.

Booth, C., 'The Problems and Possibilities of Reflexive Approaches to Strategy', *Electronic Journal of Radical Organization Theory*, 4, 1 (2003) 1–32.

J. Bracker, 'The Historical Development of the Strategic Management Concept', *Academy of Management Review*, 5 (1980) 219–224.

Daft, R. and V. Buenger, 'Hitching a Ride on the Fast Train to Nowhere'. In J. W. Frederickson (ed.) *Perspectives on Strategic Management* (New York: Harper and Row, 1990).

Foucault, M., *The Archaeology of Knowledge* (London: Tavistock, 1972).

Foucault, M., *Discipline and Punish: The Birth of the Prison* (New York: Vintage Books, 1979).

Foucault, M., 'The Subject and Power'. In H. Dreyfus and P. Rabinow (eds) *Michel Foucault, Beyond Structuralism and Hermeneutics* (Chicago: Chicago University Press, 1982).

Foucault, M., *The History of Sexuality* (London: Allen Lane, 1990).

Hall, W., 'SBUs: Hot, New Topic in the Management of Diversification', *Business Horizons*, 21 (1978) 17–20.

Hambrick, D. C., 'The Adolescence of Strategic Management 1980–1985: Critical Perceptions and Reality'. In J. W. Frederickson (ed.) *Perspectives on Strategic Management* (New York: Harper and Row, 1990).

Hodgkinson, G. P. and G. Johnson, 'Exploring the Mental Models of Competitive Strategists: The Case for a Processual Approach', *Journal of Management Studies*, 31, 4 (1994) 525–551.

Hoskin, K. W., 'Using History to Understand Theory: A Reconsideration of the Historical Genesis of "Strategy"', Paper prepared for *European Institute for Advanced Studies of Management Workshop on Strategy* (Accounting and Control, Venice, October 1990).

Hoskisson, R. E., M. A. Hitt, W. P. Wan and D. Yin, 'Theory and Research in Strategic Management: Swings of a Pendulum', *Journal of Management*, 25, 3 (1999) 417–456.

Howarth, D., *Discourse* (Milton Keynes: Open University, 2000).

Hyman, R., 'Strategy or Structure? Capital, Labor and Control', *Work, Employment and Society*, 1, 1 (1987) 25–55.

Kilduff, P., 'Evolving Strategies, Structures and Relationships in Complex and Turbulent Business Environments: The Textile and Apparel Industries of the New Millennium', *Journal of Textile and Apparel, Technology and Management*, 1, 1 (2000) 1–9.

Knights, D. and G. Morgan, 'Corporate Strategy, Organizations, and Subjectivity: A Critique', *Organization Studies*, 122 (1991) 251–273.

Knights, D. and G. Morgan, 'Strategy Under the Microscope: Strategic Management and IT in Financial Services', *Journal of Management Studies*, 32, 2 (1995) 191–214.

Knights, D. and T. Vurdubakis, 'Foucault, Power, Resistance and All That'. In J. Jermier, D. Knights and W. Nord (eds) Resistance and Power in Organisations (London: Routledge), pp. 167–198.

Levy, D. L., 'Environmental Management as Political Sustainability', *Organization and Environment*, 10, 2 (1997) 126–148.

Levy, D., M. Alvesson and H. C. Willmott, 'Critical Approaches to Strategic Management'. In M. Alvesson and H. Willmott (eds) *Studying Management Critically* (London: Sage, 2003), pp. 92–110.

McKiernan, P. (ed.), *Historical Evolution of Strategic Management* (Aldershot: Dartmouth, 1996).

Mintzberg, H., *The Rise and Fall of Strategic Planning* (New York: Prentice Hall, 1994).

Mintzberg, H., 'Five Ps for Strategy'. In H. Mintzberg, J. B. Quinn and S. Ghoshal (eds) *The Strategy Process*, European edn (London: Prentice Hall, 1995), pp. 13–21.

Mintzberg, H. and J. Quinn, *Strategy Process: Concepts, Context and Cases* (London: Prentice Hall, 1995).

Mintzberg, H. and J. A. Waters, 'Of Strategies, Deliberate and Emergent', *Strategic Management Journal*, 6 (1985) 257–272.

Mintzberg, H., R. E. Quinn and S. Ghosal, *The Strategy Process*, European edn (London: Prentice Hall, 1995).

Mir, R. and A. Watson, 'Strategic Management and the Philosophy of Science: The Case for a Constructivist Methodology', *Strategic Management Journal*, 21 (2000) 941–953.

Nichols, T. and H. Beynon, *Living with Capitalism: Class Relations and the Modern Factory* (London: Routledge and Kegan Paul, 1977).

Pettigrew, A., 'Strategic Management: The Strengths and Limitations of the Field'. In A. Pettigrew, H. Thomas and R. Whittington (eds) *Handbook of Strategy and Management* (London: Sage, 1985), pp. 3–30.

Pettigrew, A., H. Thomas and R. Whittington (eds) *Handbook of Strategy and Management* (London: Sage, 2002).

Porter, M. E., 'How Competitive Forces Shape Strategy', *Harvard Business Review*, March–April (1979) 137–156.

Porter, M. E., *Competitive Strategy: Techniques for Analyzing Industries and Competitors* (New York: Free Press, 1980).

Porter, M. E., *Competitive Advantage: Creating and Sustaining Superior Performance* (New York: Free Press, 1985).

Quinn, J. B., 'Strategies for Change'. In H. Mintzberg, J. B. Quinn and S. Ghoshal (eds) *The Strategy Process*, European edn (London: Prentice Hall, 1995), pp. 5–13.

Shrivastava, P., 'Is Strategic Management Ideological?', *Journal of Management*, 12 (1986) 363–377.

Thomas, P., 'Ideology and the Discourse of Strategic Management: A Critical Research Framework', *Electronic Journal of Radical Organization Theory*, 41 (1998) 1–14.

Whipp, R., 'Creative Deconstruction: Strategy and Organizations'. In S. R. Clegg, C. Hardy and W. Nord (eds) *Managing Organizations, Current Issues* (London: Sage, 1999), pp. 11–25.

Whittington, R., 'Putting Giddens into Action: Social Systems and Managerial Agency', *Journal of Management Studies*, 29, 6 (1992) 493–512.

Whittington, R., *What Is Strategy – And Does It Matter?* (London: Routledge, 1993).

Whittington, R., 'The Work of Strategizing and Organizing: For a Practice Perspective', *Strategic Organization*, 1, 1 (2003) 119–127.

CHAPTER 16

The Theory and Reality of Strategy: How Practitioners and Academics can Form Meaningful Partnerships

Suzanne M. Behr and Margaret A. White

Basic principles

This chapter examines strategic management from the perspective of one practitioner and one academic who have formed a relatively unique cross-profession partnership. While there have been many calls for increased interactions between practicing managers and academics, there are very few examples of such teams researching and writing together. The difficulties caused by the conflicts in perspectives and how to bridge those differences are explored using the case of these two authors. Theoretical rigor and practical relevance are not mutually exclusive, just hard to bridge. However, the effort can be enlightening and fun.

For decades there has been a call for academics and practitioners to interact more than they have in the past and to do a better job of transferring knowledge between the two groups (Hambrick, 1994; Oviatt and Miller, 1989; Starkey and Madan, 2001; Thomas and Tymon, 1982). While academics theorize and study strategic management, practitioners engage in managing, acting upon, and reacting to strategic realities in the workplace. These two groups – academics and practitioners – have different perspectives of strategy which are well understood and documented.

A number of reasons have been given for the separation between the academic theory-building and the practical reality of managers. Among the most common of these are

1. Goal differences in knowledge usage: For academics, the goal is the definition and refinement of theory over time (Ospina and Dodge, 2005; Rynes et al., 2001; Starkey and Madan, 2001). For practicing managers, theory development is not essential – practitioners want to know what techniques will help them achieve performance goals.

2. Differences in language, norms, traditions and interests – basic vocational cultures: Academic–practitioner collaboration has been suggested by a number of researchers, but very view articles have addressed the reason such collaboration is so rare. It is rare in a multitude of fields (not just strategic management). Amabile and colleagues (2001) called such collaboration 'cross-profession' (p. 419). The way academics and practitioners approach problem solving, for example, is fundamentally different. This makes collaboration difficult.

3. Differences in the need for timeliness: For the practicing manager, knowledge is a tool to be used in the environment that is being faced today and the decisions that need to be made now. For the academic, knowledge is to be created and built upon to create a new understanding of phenomena (many practitioners wonder what this means).

4. The difficulty of academics to maintain a foothold in the world of the practicing manager and vice-versa (different types of relevance): Strategic management has been and still claims to be application oriented. All of the management disciplines started as application-oriented fields. However, as strategic management became more defined within academic circles, it has moved more toward the theoretical development model. As a result, the relevance of application has faded. While academics have recognized this and cautioned against losing practical relevance (Aram and Salipante, 2003; Bettis, 1991; Hambrick, 1994; Nicolai, 2004; Thomas and Tymon, 1982), the slide into less applied research has continued.

5. The difficulty of reversing disconnectedness: Because of the first four factors, it is easier for practitioners and academics to become disconnected. For academics, the rewards are tied to 'scholarly' research whether it is useful or not; for practitioners, the rewards are tied to bottom-line success. With such divergent reward systems, it is difficult to reverse the disconnection even though literature is full of calls to do so (all of the previously cited works do so) and cross-profession connections are known to enrich the state of practice and the value of research.

This chapter is about the partnership of one academic and one practitioner – our writing together and our experiences at an academic conference. We will begin with a brief overview of how we began the journey, the ups and downs as we found a common voice, and conclude with reactions to our recent participation at the 2005 Strategic Management Society conference as co-authors and members of a pre-conference panel.

The beginning of our collaboration

Suzanne Behr is a practicing, upper mid-level manager at a telecommunications firm. She has an undergraduate degree in mathematics and chemistry, a master's degree in engineering systems, and an MBA. While pursuing her MBA (after approximately 18 years of work experience as an engineer and manager), she took a class from Dr Margaret White. In the course of the class, Suzanne wrote several position papers and made a presentation about management of technology and innovation which caught the attention of Margaret because of its insightfulness and relevance to her research interests.

How did you get started on the path of collaboration?

MW: I noted the freshness and originality of Suzanne's ideas. One particular position paper about layoffs (at that time, Suzanne had been in organizations that had gone through eight major layoffs) was of particular interest to me since I had co-authored an *Academy of Management Review* piece on downsizing (Fisher and White, 2000). She asked me to review it for comments and thoughts, which I did, taking it a step further by also reformatting it into an article for publication. When Suzanne and I visited, I encouraged her to develop her ideas further and to consider publishing them.

SB: When Margaret returned my layoff essay in the form of an article, I was shocked that she would take the time and energy to reformat it. I used to write a lot of research engineering articles, but had never written a management one. Nor did I have plans on writing one, until Margaret suggested it. I noticed right away that she had a 'knack' for organizing text into a palatable manner for publication in the management field. The style was very different from my research articles. She took my experiences and understanding of this particular layoff series and configured them into neat bullet points and objectives. I was impressed but didn't really know where to go from there. The thoughts were mostly mine, but the structure was much more academic.

What cross-profession (cultural) differences did you notice at first?

MW: The differences in culture appeared relatively early. For example, I began our collaboration with the idea that I would help her get *her* work published. As time went by, I began to feel I deserved co-authorship. We met – me to ask for co-authorship which can be touchy in academic circles and Suzanne, the practitioner, wondering why I was so serious and wanted to meet.

SB: As Margaret said, I wasn't sure why she wanted to meet but she seemed to be a little antsy about it. To be honest, when she first used the term 'practitioner', it took me a while to realize she was referring to me. When I hear the word 'practitioner' I think of doctors as in, 'He's in med school to become a general practitioner.' But in the world of academia there are titles and names and a lingo all its own, like any other field of study or industry.

When she asked me what I thought of the paper, I talked in general terms that I liked it but wasn't sure where to go from here. All along in my mind, she was already a co-author and I was looking to her to do whatever had to be done next: pick a journal or magazine for submittal. However, in her mind, she wasn't sure she was my co-author since I never verbally told her, so she finally asked me awkwardly if I was thinking of publishing it on my own. When I said no, that she deserved to be an author too, she seemed relieved. Authorship was not a matter of large concern to me since I don't get rewarded at my job for writing journal articles, but for Margaret in the academic world the stakes are different. She has a lot of incentive to be an author, I really do not.

MW: I thought Suzanne was a good writing partner, but her approach was very different – while I was pondering and framing, she was wondering why we were not moving faster and making decisions.

The result of the first collaboration was an article in *Executive Excellence* (Behr and White, 2003). While we were both happy with the success, Suzanne could not understand why I was not happier – after all we had gotten published. I tried to explain that this was not an academic piece and I received little reward for such work.

SB: Margaret had only dropped hints now and then regarding the true world of academia. I had heard her frustrations as she explained what type of publication was deemed 'A' quality and which wasn't; and the fact is that collaborating with a 'practitioner' to write articles for practitioner-oriented magazines didn't get her any 'gold stars'.

To me, this response sounded a lot like the story of the famous management expert Peter Drucker, when General Motors asked him to do a study of their company and offer recommendations while he was a professor at Bennington College (Reeves, 2005). Bennington's president warned Drucker, 'You are going to destroy your career in academia forever' (p. A04), because corporations were not a respectable research subject back then. Drucker took the challenge and even persuaded GM to let him write an industrial management book from his detailed series of interviews and data analysis. *The Concept of a Corporation* started him on the road to being called the 'man who invented management'.

Well, apparently things have not changed much over the past 60 years! 'Practitioners' today still are not deemed good writing partners for some inexplicable reason. I guess someone thinks we really do not understand what happens in our own businesses or why; that we don't have the degrees in research and statistics to accurately analyze a situation and problem to reach a valuable conclusion. As I first ran into this sentiment, I found it to be so naturally unbelievable that it was sort of funny in a ridiculous way, but then I realized that this unspoken premise remains a stronghold in many, if not all, academic institutions.

Working on our first academic paper was a real education to me about the world of higher education, but since Margaret indicated she enjoyed our collaboration and wanted to continue it, I was happy to do so. It gave me a way to express my thoughts and feelings as I learned and understood the importance of good strategic decision-making at various departmental levels. Besides that, I also liked the intellectual process.

What have you gotten from the collaboration?

MW: The more I worked with Suzanne, the more I realized that she had insights that I could never gain through my research or experiences as an academic. I learned from her every time we sat down to work on a piece. While the process was slow because of the very different lenses we brought to the process, it was interesting and intellectually stimulating. In addition, I gained a real appreciation for the difference between the academy and practice – while I knew there were differences, seeing them through Suzanne's experiences made me curious. I then began questioning some of the things I did in class and interacting in a different way with the practicing managers in my MBA classes.

We wrote another piece that was published in *Leadership Excellence* (White and Behr, 2005) before delving into a more academic type of collaboration.

What happened when you moved into more academic writing?

MW: This year we submitted an abstract for the 2005 Strategic Management Society (SMS) annual meeting. The article was accepted and we both attended, although Suzanne was the presenter. I'll let Suzanne describe her experiences at the conference, but the differences between academicians and practitioners became quite obvious from the very beginning.

SB: I had attended and presented at many conferences before but they were mostly international oil and gas engineering conferences focused on research and development. All the papers were concentrated on testing, analyzing, modelling, and reporting of results, with emphasis on results. So I was familiar with large meetings, making formal presentations, defending your work, and answering questions, yet this conference was just different.

Everyone was nice enough, but I have to admit, as a 'practitioner,' I felt out of place. And indeed I was. I think I met only one other 'practitioner' during the conference with an attendance of over six hundred people. Although the Strategic Management Society (SMS) was created 25 years ago to 'bring together the worlds of reflective practice and thoughtful scholarship, combining academics with business leaders and consultants – the ABCs' (SMS Conference Program, 2005, p. 6), I hardly heard anyone talk about or introduce themselves as part of the 'B' group – those actively engaged in practicing the art of management. Where were they? If the whole purpose of SMS is to bring the ABCs together to learn from each other's experiences and research, the annual meeting didn't reflect that. If you didn't have a PhD, if you weren't a university professor or a high-powered, reputable consultant from one of the big firms, you felt left out, unimportant, and almost inconsequential. Now they didn't do that on purpose, of course, and I might have felt that way because I was the 'lone' practitioner, but there was definitely an undercurrent of who's in and who's out.

For example, I attended a panel session on 'Dynamic Capabilities' that was well attended with standing room only in a facility that seated probably 300 people. It was the largest meeting I attended while at the conference and you could feel the buzz in the atmosphere. People were still pouring in after the presentation got underway, looking for seating, finding none, and settling for a back wall to lean upon. Everyone seemed keyed up about the topic and the presenters, who were prominent scholars in the field of dynamic capabilities. I was also excited to hear what they had to say because it seemed that this topic, out of all the ones I read in the conference program, had some relevance to my very real world of management. The brief on the session said that 'dynamic capabilities refer to the ability of organizations and their managers/entrepreneurs to build, integrate and reconfigure firm resources and capabilities' (SMS Conference Program, 2005, p. M-34) in order to adapt and succeed in an ever-changing, dynamic industry and market. Well, this certainly described my world of telecommunications over the past 5 years. What I learned from the session, however, was more about the subtleties of word definitions, measurement criteria, conceptual ideas, and statistics than anything that could help a manager, like myself, strategically direct my business and the employees who report to me.

I found the session interesting in a theoretical way, but also frustrating because there was not one thing I could take away from the meeting that would help me become a better manager and user of the resources I had today. I guess they were just teeing up the ball and not really playing the game yet. I, however, was already in the game and have been playing for 20 years. Still the work this team of scholars was discussing could eventually be useful if it was studied through the practitioner's viewfinder. With these thoughts in mind, I left the session thinking: 'Gee, since dynamic capabilities seem to be such a hot topic, maybe a lot of people will show up to my presentation tomorrow since my talk is all about the same thing but in a real-life business setting.'

How wrong could I be! I think there were maybe 10 people at my talk, including the other presenters who would follow me! Where was everybody? Why was no one interested in what a Director of Operations from a very dynamic industry (telecom) had to say about her real-life experience in managing dynamic capabilities? Maybe if I had used the right buzz words, more folks would have come. But that alone is disconcerting. Surely, the academicians could see the parallel between what I did on the job to what they talked about as dynamic capabilities in theory and in the classroom. The consultants (I met a few of them) should also be interested in a successful set of actions. I thought it was a straightforward comparison since my talk was all about how I took a team of employees, redefined their roles using their core competencies or 'capabilities', and restructured their objectives and goals to fit the new and different strategic orientation of our company as it entered and exited bankruptcy. Was this not the perfect follow-up paper to the dynamic capabilities panel session – a real-life example of how a manager adapted to changes in the marketplace and industry through understanding the dynamic capabilities of that team? Apparently not.

MW: I tried to prepare Suzanne for all possibilities – low attendance since our session was at 8:00 in the morning; high attendance because a practitioner was on the program and everything in between. I was disappointed at the attendance, but it also shook me because it was very clear that even when we claim we want to build bridges, we have become academicians not just first and foremost but almost to the exclusion of working with those who practice strategic management. Of all the papers I heard presented, our paper was the only one with implications that were for real managers – maybe because a real manager was presenting the paper. We had gotten kudos for a pre-conference session on crossing boundaries, but the reality hit me squarely that except for top managers making large presentations, for the most part, we were not crossing any boundaries in the field of strategic management or providing any real insight for practicing managers.

In addition, Suzanne presented real results with a set of lessons learned. While they were interesting and everyone acknowledged they were interesting, the main interest was as a case for teaching (a good story to tell), not as a case for enriching our future research on mid-level management of firm capabilities in a dynamic environment (not exactly Suzanne's word, but the academic form of them).

How would you describe the current 'meeting of the minds' between academicians and practicing managers?

SB: Generally speaking, the business and academic realms can be compared to a theatre play where the CEO writes the script, the academicians watch the play and take notes, the academic researchers critique the play and write it up for the Sunday paper, while the employees act out the play in all its glory, passion, and struggles. However, there are some employees who don't want to just be actors in a pre-scripted play, but want to chronicle their own stories by participating in the process of data collection and interpretation. These are the folks that don't want to just be data points, but want to draw the line or curve connecting the dots since those dots could characterize the chart of their lives on the job. And these are the practitioners you should seek after when you are doing your own research.

MW: When I first heard this metaphor used by Suzanne, I flinched. Then I thought there is a place for those who write it up and chronicle the play. There are actors who help with rewrites or who ad lib. They add richness and reality to many productions. Likewise, there is really a lot of interesting stuff to be gleaned from the practitioners who want to build linkages across the perspectives. This is, after all, what got me involved in writing with Suzanne to begin with.

SB: There are many benefits in creating a true partnership between academicians and practitioners. While practitioners bring the depth of their personal experiences in a particular field, academicians bring the depth of their knowledge of how a practitioner's *specific* experience correlates with other practitioners' experiences across broader business sectors. This link allows the development of broader best practices tools and better total solutions.

Why is it so difficult for practitioners and academicians to work together?

SB: If you are reading this story, you are the type of person who is interested in working with practitioners, or at least learning how they think, to create a superior body of data, research, and meaningful conclusions for the business world. In this regard you are the type of person who would rather see practitioners 'as research partners, not just data points', as Margaret would say. In light of this predisposed bent, however, let me burst your bubble by saying that most practitioners aren't too excited about conducting research. And the reason for this attitude is similar to why academicians don't work much with practitioners: they aren't rewarded for it. You won't find 'Work with a local university to discover ways to better manage a team during stressful times' down on anyone's array of annual performance goals. Their goals are focused

Table 16.1 Conflicts in perspectives

Perspectives	Academic	Practitioner
Interest in strategic management	Field of study	Direction of the firm
Starting point	Previous research and 'findings'	Current competitive position
Time orientation	Past actions and activities	Future performance and success
Concerns	Theory development; definition of terms	Decision-making; actions/results
End point: results sought	Conclusions that are 'significant'	Profit, shareholder value
Personal outcomes	Publication; tenure; promotion	Become a better manager; promotion
Broad outcomes	Understanding of a phenomenon	Firm success and growth

more on the bottom line, making money, increasing product quality, opening up new markets, increasing market share, selling above the quota, and so on. And in this vein, it's not their job to perform research with the A's and C's of this world; that is not why they were hired or are getting paid. Even so, there are some practitioners who enjoy research and writing, want to dig deeper, and see the benefit of sharing their own life's experiences from the front row seats of the job amphitheater.

MW: To that end, Suzanne and I have thought about and discussed why this is so difficult. Basically, Table 16.1 summarises our thoughts.

The biggest problems arise from our individual and corporate differences in perspectives. The difficulties enumerated earlier all find their roots in the differences in perspectives. Amabile and colleagues (2001) were right – it is difficult and the reasons it is so difficult can be summarized as follows:

1. Different reasons for interest in the field of strategic management: Strategic management researchers view strategic management as a field of study to be explored. Practicing managers view it as a toolbox for setting direction for the future of the firm or business unit.

2. Different starting points in our approaches: The academicians use previous research and findings to generate ideas for newness in the field. Practitioners use the questions 'where are we now?' and 'where are our competitors?' The starting places are different – in the past for academicians and in the present for practitioners.

3. Different time orientation: The different starting points are reflected in the time orientations. Researchers look at past actions and activities while practicing managers are concerned about pushing to future performance and success. The old adage about those who ignore history are doomed to repeat it has some applicability here. For practitioners often repeat the mistakes of others that researchers have chronicled. However, researchers are not getting the message to practitioners by publishing in purely academic journals.

4. Different concerns and applications of strategic knowledge: Practitioners are interested in making decisions and taking actions that seem appropriate for the environment. Academicians are concerned with theory development, definition of terms, measurement, validity, reliability and so on, that is, sound research with appropriate amounts of rigor.

5. Different results are sought: The academician wants results that reflect a statistically significant conclusion while practitioners look more to the bottom-line—profits, return on investment, and so on.

6. Different personal outcomes are the focus: For the academician, the goal in studying strategic management is to get publications, tenure, and promotion. Likewise, the practicing manager wants promotion, but the other two goals of academicians are irrelevant. The manager wants to understand where his/her work fits into the goals of the firm and how to get better.

7. Different goals for broad outcomes exist: For the practicing manager, firm survival and continuation are keys. The goal for the publicly held firm is to increase shareholder's wealth. While the academicians understand this intellectually, the broad goal for involvement with strategic management is increasing understanding of phenomenon – something practitioners really do not care about.

How can these different perspectives be successfully addressed?

SB: Both groups must be willing to bend the rules. The academic institutions must formally recognize the benefit of joint research with practitioners and reward professors for such. In the business world, executive managers and CEOs must also formally recognize the benefit and reward their staff with career advancement opportunities and monetary increases. People will do things that they are rewarded to do. If sales personnel are provided an incentive to simply sell more, they will – even at a loss! In like fashion, without the proper incentives from higher levels, the call for academicians and practitioners to interact more and do a better job of mutual knowledge transfer will be unheard or unanswered by all but a very few.

MW: Now that we have delineated the differences, it becomes clear we need to reorient the perspective to somewhere in the middle or take the best of both worlds and meld them together. In the end, the goal is to get academicians and practitioners to develop understanding and build knowledge bases that can be practically and aptly used and shared.

To do this the perspectives need to be bridged. Table 16.2 presents an overview of how each of the differences might be bridged.

How would we suggest merging the practitioner's wealth of experiences with the academician's depth of knowledge?

MW: As an academician, much of my research loses touch with the practical question that generated my interest in the first place. To be published in a 'quality' journal, I need lots of rigor. There is nothing wrong with quantitative rigor, but it is not the key to the formation of utilitarian knowledge bases. However, when I look at the research and academic writing that has really impacted the practice of strategic management, it is not in journals–it is in books. For example, Porter's book *Competitive Strategy*, Miles and Snow's *Organizational Strategy, Structure and Process*, and Collins' *Good to Great* are all books that present a framework that informs managers while giving a basis for in-depth study. I believe such results are found in books because the mid-range theories are hard to present in a standard academic article format.

On the other hand, practitioners often make decisions because they seem right. Early in the writing of the SMS article, Suzanne questioned a 'fact' that I wrote. As an academic, I had cited studies, and so on but she found it hard to believe – I sent her copies of several articles to back up my point. What was commonly known from academic research was new information for this practitioner who is trying to connect. So we are not connecting even with information that may have practical implications.

Table 16.2 How to bridge the perspectives

Perspectives	Ideal outcomes
Interest in collaboration	To merge the depth of the practitioner's experiences with the academician's depth of knowledge
Time orientation	To evaluate past activities and their impact to present and future outcomes
Concerns	To develop theories that explain and predict results
Results sought	To create knowledge that leads to actions that optimize shareholder value
Personal outcomes	To receive recognition and reward for the individual; promotion
Broader outcomes	Greater relevant research that leads to significant improvement in strategic management practice

The way for academics to form meaningful partnerships include the following:

1. Develop more organizing frameworks that have an impact on practice – most of our frameworks are about defining terms and developing research questions. The 'rigor' while appropriate in some arenas should not be driving our development of understanding. Relevance is also important.

2. Realize that practitioners are geared toward making decisions to deal with tomorrow's opportunities and threats. Our approach has to inform the future; not just chronicle significance in the past.

3. Make it professionally worthwhile to talk with and learn from practitioners. There are bright, intelligent people who may not have Ph.D.s but they have learned a lot of hard lessons and are very articulate in presenting ideas if we will listen to their stories rather than pontificate about the rigor of our definitions, methods, and our conclusions. After all, interesting, useful research should also be part of our repertoire.

SB: In the end the goal is to get academicians and consultants to partner with practicing managers (and not just with the top-level CEOs and such) to perform research and mutually build solutions. For this to occur, executive management must champion the idea and assign employees as their full-time job to help in this effort, devoted to working with, sharing with, learning from, and strategising and creating solutions together with the academic/consultant team. It's the employees who are usually tasked to implement consultant ideas anyway or to deploy the new concept/process/solution to other parts of the company. Without the support and excitement of the executive team, practitioners will be limited in what they can share and develop simply because their schedules won't allow them the time necessary to truly devote themselves to the rigor of investigative analysis. It is the responsibility of the top-level management team to encourage this type of collaborative research.

It is very possible that CEOs are sceptical about reallocating employees' time to work with academics because they feel they are too ... well, academic. But the structure of the work can certainly be outlined in clear fashion with explicit goals and objectives, constrained by timelines. If these goals are achieved within the allotted timeframe, then the CEO should be happy (and willing to enter into other similar relationships). In fact, this arrangement would be like adding a few additional employees to the staff without having to pay for them. Upper management gains the depth of years of knowledge gathering from the academics in exchange for shifting a few employees' priorities. By crossing employees' more narrow experiences with academicians' broader knowledge base, facts can become truth and great practices can be separated from good ones. Practitioners bring the data, academicians bring the analysis toolkit, and together the pieces of the company puzzle lying on the table can be snapped into place forming the broader and eventual picture which tells the story of how and why the company is the way it is. This powerful combination of practitioner and academician gives the executives a rare opportunity to see themselves, their staff, and their company performance in a very unique way that cannot be achieved without both parties.

What does this all mean?

MW: I do not know, but as an academician I am now trying to think more about what 'results' can occur in the 'real' world of business. What is the takeaway for what I am writing and publishing? I, however, have always liked that. When I perchance find myself presenting to an audience with practitioners, my goal is to give them takeaways that they can try and make a difference with.

Also, what it means, at least to me, that making the extra effort to do cross-profession writing and interaction has been enriching and energizing. Suzanne has given me a perspective and a set of questions to explore that I never would have thought of on my own. While I had read about and written about topics that Suzanne lives with in her work environment (positive and negative), delving into her experiences has given me new perspective. Truly, what I was writing about, while related, was more distantly related than I like admitting.

> *SB*: For me, working with Margaret has been exciting and rewarding because I get to bounce my ideas and theories off on someone who has a deep knowledge in the field of strategic management and who can tell me more about a particular subject. She is a wealth of information that I have never studied or read. For every one of my thoughts she could easily send me dozens of recommended articles or books on the subject. She could also tell me if my concept is a new one – or more likely, an old one with at least a new twist that others would find interesting and worthy of discussion.

Truly, our partnership has been a learning together experience and an exploration of each other's minds and beliefs. Like iron sharpens iron, so have we. I have always felt like I had something to say and insights to give when it came to management, but no real outlet (besides my own confined team!) to properly express them. I felt like I always had a voice, but that it didn't carry very far . . . until Margaret and I teamed up to sing a chorus or two.

Final Advice?

> *SB*: Theory and rigor are great, but so are practicality and experience. These perspectives are not so much opposites as they are different sides of the same coin. The goal is not for one perspective to win, and the other to lose, but to build linkages between the two perspectives that enriches the success of both. There is truly where $1 + 1$ can equal 3 or 4 or more.

As an academician, if you're really interested in making a difference not in the field of strategic management but in the playing field of real businesses, make friends with those in the industry. Ask them questions, test out your theories on them, listen to them tell of their experiences, find out what they think works well and what doesn't and why. And if you're brave enough, ask your business friend to read your proposed paper or article for comments before publishing it!

> *MW*: First, you need to find a practicing manager who is willing to give the time to do so. If you find such a person, hang on – the interaction is sometimes frustrating and trying for both. But the results, at least for this academician and this practitioner, have been intellectually enriching, thought provoking, and satisfying. And dare I say, FUN!

References

Amabile, T., C. Patterson, J. Mueller, T. Wojcid, P. Odomirok, M. Marsh and S. Kramer, 'Academic-Practitioner Collaboration in Management Research: A Case of Cross-Profession Collaboration', *Academy of Management Journal*, 44, 2 (2001) 418–431.

Aram, J. and P. Salipante, 'Bridging Scholarship in Management: Epistemological Reflections', *British Journal of Management*, 14 (2003) 189–205.

Behr, S. M. and M. White, 'Layoff Survivor Sickness', *Executive Excellence*, 20, 11 (2003) 18.

Bettis, R., 'Strategic Management and the Straightjacket: An Editorial Essay', *Organization Science*, 2, 3 (1991) 315–319.

Fisher, S. and M. White, 'Downsizing in a Learning Organization: Are there Hidden Costs?', *Academy of Management Review*, 25, 1 (2000) 244–251.

Hambrick, D., 'What if the Academy Actually Mattered', *Academy of Management Review*, 19, 1 (1994) 11–16.

Nicolai, A., 'The Bridge to the "Real World": Applied Science or a "Schizophrenic Tour De Force?" ' *Journal of Management Studies*, 41, 6 (2004) 951–976.

Ospina, S. and J. Dodge, 'Narrative Inquiry and the Search for Connectedness: Practitioners and Academics Developing Public Administration Scholarship', *Public Administration Review*, 65, 4 (2005) 409–423.

Oviatt, B. and W. Miller, 'Irrelevance, Intransigence, and Business Professors', *Academy of Management Executive*, 3, 4 (1989) 304–312.

Reeves, A., 'Peter Drucker's Keen Insight; Outside the Box: His Ideas and Solutions Revolutionized the Way We Do Business', *Investor's Business Daily*, 28 November 2005, A04.

Rynes, S., J. Bartunek and R. Daft, 'Across the Great Divide: Knowledge Creation and Transfer Between Practitioners and Academics', *Academy of Management Journal*, 44, 2 (2001) 340–355.

Starkey, K. and P. Madan, 'Bridging the Relevance Gap: Aligning Stakeholders in the Future of Management Research', *British Journal of Management*, 12, Special Issue (2001) S3–S26.

Strategic Management Society, 25th Annual International Conference Program, 23–26 October 2005, Orlando, FL.

Thomas, K. and W. Tymon, Jr., 'Necessary Properties of Relevant Research: Lessons from Recent Criticisms of the Organizational Sciences', *Academy of Management Review*, 7, 3 (1982) 345–352.

White, M. and S. Behr, 'The New Employees', *Leadership Excellence*, 22, 4 (2005) 9–10.

CHAPTER 17

Conclusion: Can Multiple Perspectives on Strategic Management Inform Practice?

Véronique Ambrosini and Mark Jenkins

Each perspective covered in *Advanced Strategic Management* focuses on certain aspects of strategy, while none of them can be argued to capture the entirety of the strategy field, despite all their limitations, they all contribute to our understanding of the field. However, there is one question that is worth raising at the end of such a review of theoretical perspectives. This question is about the relevance of such perspectives to the practice of strategic management: Can the perspectives contribute to both the understanding and the practical application of strategic management? More specifically, what can we add to Chapter 16 about the benefits of collaboration between academics and managers?

Most of the contributions in *Advanced Strategic Management* are academic discipline based, research centred, with the focus being on the nature of the type of knowledge and assumptions encompassed in the perspective, that is, knowing what, rather than direct practical application, that is, knowing how. The perspectives provide an understanding of organisations and how they operate. They do not usually deal with the direct, immediate problems that managers may be facing. This does not mean, though, that they are not critical to managerial practice. Without informed research or theory, actions can be taken without clear justification; they can be taken on the basis of anecdotes, taken out of context.

One of the characteristics of much of the work within the field of strategy is that it is typically normative. Strategy is characterised by prescriptions, advice on what managers should do in order for their organisation to outperform competitors. While most of the perspectives covered are about 'knowing what' than about 'knowing how', they do provide useful insights to guide decision-making within organisations. Perhaps one of the most widely used observations relating to the application of theory is Lewin's (1945) quote: 'There is nothing so practical as a good theory.' This does not mean that theory should or can indeed be followed to the letter by practitioners, but it does underline the practical value of well-developed theories because of their rigorous coverage of specific aspects of strategic management. They state clearly what they examine, the elements and variables which are of concern to the theory. They explain what the relationships between the constructs under examination are. Theories also deal with the why, that is, the assumptions, which must be adhered to for the theory to work. Finally, theories indicate when and where they can be applied and to whom they can be applied (Whetten, 1989). This means that theories do not exist in a vacuum; they specify when and where they can be used and as a corollary, when they cannot. This implies that theories need to be well understood to ensure that they are properly applied, that is, applied to the right context, in the right circumstances.

Do theories, though, suggest particular strategies? Do they provide managers with some prescriptions? If you were a manager or a strategy consultant would you have a more insightful understanding of where and with whom you are operating and how to act if you were using the theories rather than remaining theory-free? Some perspectives have suggested particular practical models and tools. Among others we could mention: The Five Forces analysis that helps to understand the competitive

environment in which organisations operate (Chapter 5); the value net which is a way of identifying the players in a game (Chapter 6); or cognitive mapping techniques, which are designed to capture actors' causal belief systems (Chapter 10). The tools that are used in strategy are plentiful and our purpose here is not to review them or explain how to use them (see Ambrosini with Johnson and Scholes [1998] for some practical advice) but just to show that many derive from theory.

Most perspectives also give some guidance about strategising. For instance, the resource-based view of firm suggests that sources of competitive advantage are to be found inside firms and that managers should protect, nurture and leverage these sources. Industrial organisation economics on the other hand suggests that what matters most is the structure of the industry and therefore managers should ensure that they monitor and try to manipulate the structural forces that surrounds or may surround them. Transaction cost economics explains how firms can define and choose an efficient structure that would minimise overall costs. Game theory justifies why it is essential for firms to observe the players in their industry and how they interact in order to achieve the most favourable position. Institutional theory warns that managers need to be aware of the influence of their environment, how it may pressure their organisation to conform to the rules of the game, and therefore managers may not be able to change and create as free of constraints as they may think. The cognition and knowledge chapters highlight that managers' rationality is often limited, that they may rely on simplified representations of the world surrounding them and that managers should be aware of these as how they think and make sense of their world has an effect on the strategic decision they make. The military perspective is maybe the most prescriptive perspective (and is certainly not a theory) as it gives precise guidelines for competing. It suggests that to win organisations need to have clear objectives, strong values and leadership. They also need to assess their competitors' strengths and weaknesses, to attack competitors with speed and surprise trying to stretch their resources without stretching their own.

These few examples highlight that strategic management theories can be used to provide some guidance to managers, and, looking at what strategy consultants typically do confirms this. The consultants' role is characteristically about guiding and facilitating the strategy process; it is to provide managers with some direction and rigour in their decision process. In order to do so, consultants use theoretical frameworks and tools, and one of the roles of consultants is to ensure that these theory-driven frameworks are understood in the context of the daily reality of the business it is going to be applied to.

Obviously, consultants themselves need to understand their 'tool kit'.[1] They need to be able to communicate to the managers they work with and although frameworks and research-driven prescriptions are valuable aids to help make sense of what is going on in their organisation and environment, they are not designed to 'come up with the right answer' or provide some magical solution. They are there primarily to help organise the thinking of individuals. They are valuable as mechanisms to help managerial teams engage in and keep focused on the strategy debate as well as to help them make decisions that would better their organisation's performance. For many managers, strategising or being involved in strategic decision-making for the first time causes them to feel suspicious, nervous or anxious about the potential outcomes. The use of frameworks can allow the debate to proceed in a way which captures the rational objective data as well as the instinctive, subjective nuance. Collecting data in a framework can act as a base point from which the team can move away from their normal or traditional areas of focus and, with confidence, explore more creative ideas and options. They can then come back to the theories and test the strategic fit of these new ideas.

Models facilitate the organising of information and help to make sense of complex issues not easily achieved without any support. Frameworks are dynamic tools. Theories and frameworks can be imagined to be rather like the pieces of a jigsaw. To begin with, there is a box full of bits and the strategy team needs to be helped to understand how to create the picture which will become the finished jigsaw, that is, the strategy. The frameworks are used rather like the interlocking jigsaw pieces to demonstrate the relationship between one part of the strategy and another. The only difference

with a jigsaw is that there is no unique picture that can be built; the picture keeps evolving. The frameworks are very much part of the building process and help to test the validity of the data and their influence on the finished picture. The important thing about frameworks is how they link together and relate to each other in order to build up the complete picture. Sometimes it is necessary to select a technique to get a particular response.

Theories can help the team reframe how the organisation behaves and its ability to adapt to change. It may provide insights into how and why things are always done in one way inside the organisation. Because organisations are 'living, emotional' organisms functioning in a complex, diverse and volatile environment, it is often difficult for managers to deal with a strategic issue without any help from theories. Dealing with strategic issues can be 'messy' and 'fuzzy'. Using frameworks may help in coping with this extreme uncertainty. They help in bringing some discipline and understanding. For instance, they help revealing taken-for-granted assumptions, exploring relationships between different areas of the organisations, types of resources, surfacing paradoxes in the environment and managers' behaviours and so on. Tools are useful as long as they are used critically and in the right context.

So as a conclusion one can assert that what matters most for managers are not theories per se but how they are used. It is by their judgement and interpretation of the theory and the data they collect that managers can add value to the strategy process. Theories cannot give solutions or definitive answers but they will inform management judgement and decision-making. They help managers think, and applying different theories to a situation or problem broadens and further informs this thinking.

Note

1. We would like to thank Simon Carter Managing Director of Transition Strategies Ltd and an Associate of Cranfield's Centre for Customised Executive Development, for his contribution to this section of the conclusion.

References

Ambrosini, V., with G. Johnson and K. Scholes, *Exploring Techniques of Analysis and Evaluation in Strategic Management* (London: Prentice Hall, 1998).

Lewin, K., 'The Research Center for Group Dynamics at Massachusetts Institute of Technology', *Sociometry*, 8 (1945) 126–136.

Whetten, D. A., 'What Constitutes a Theoretical Contribution?', *Academy of Management Review*, 14, 4 (1989) 490–495.

CHAPTER 18

Case Study: Cosworth Engineering

Within each chapter we have included a series of short cases that explore some of the issues relating to each particular perspective. However, the real power of these differing views on strategy is when they are used together in order to create a richer picture of a set of strategic issues. In order to facilitate this process we have included a case study Cosworth Engineering: which can be explored from a number of different perspectives. We also suggest a number of case questions that can be used to support this process. We have used the four parts of the book to group the questions.

1. Institutionalist perspectives:

   a. What were the major events in the development of Cosworth Engineering?
   b. Do you see any evidence of isomorphism in the industry? And if so what are the implications of this?
   c. What end-state does Cosworth wish to achieve and what are its strategies and tactics for accomplishing this?
   d. What were the strengths and weaknesses of Cosworth's various locations during its history?

2. Economic perspectives:

   a. What is the competitive nature of the industry in which Cosworth operates?
   b. How was Cosworth able to use the competitive forces of the industry to create a competitive advantage?
   c. Are there examples of where Cosworth both competes and co-operates with rivals? What is your explanation for why this happens?
   d. How do you explain both Cosworth's and Ford's strategies to the motor racing industry from a transaction cost perspective?
   e. Does Cosworth have any VRIN resources? If so what are they and what should be done to protect them?
   f. What do you think were the implications of the changes to Cosworth's ownership from an agency theory perspective?

3. Behaviouralist perspectives:

   a. How would you describe Keith Duckworth's cognitive map for running Cosworth? What threats and opportunities may go unnoticed from this perspective?

b. How does Cosworth gather knowledge about its situation?

c. What levels of awareness do you suppose there are concerning the knowledge held across various departments?

d. How does Cosworth use the organisations it has relationships with, and their resources, to create new value?

4. Emergent and integrating perspectives:

a. How is strategy 'done' in Cosworth and what are the implications of this?

b. What are the implications of taking a critical perspective to look at the strategy of Cosworth?

c. What role do you think diversity and interconnectivity have played in the development of Cosworth, and how may this be appropriate moving forward?

d. Would Cosworth benefit from a partnership with an academic institution?

Cosworth Engineering

In August 2006 Autosport.com announced that specialist racing engine manufacturer Cosworth would be making redundant around 40 per cent of its 375 employees in the United Kingdom at the end of the year. The main reasons were a change to the regulations in Formula 1 (F1), which meant that engine design would be frozen for 2007, and that one of Cosworth's two customers for the 2006 season, Williams F1, would be switching to using Toyota F1 engines in 2007, making it likely that Cosworth would be, at best, supplying only 1 of the 11 teams expected to compete in 2007. The 50 plus staff at the company's US operation in Torrance, California, which supplies engines for the entire Champ Car grid, as well as teams competing in other series such as NASCAR would be unaffected.

Cosworth Engineering Ltd was incorporated on 30 September 1958 by Mike Costin and Keith Duckworth (hence Cos . . . worth). Mike Costin was born in 1929 and started his career as an apprentice engineer working for the de Havilland Aircraft Co. He was a motor racing enthusiast and participated both as an accomplished race driver and as an experienced race mechanic. Costin's involvement with motor racing had enabled him to build up a strong network of contacts in the racing world, which led him to move to racing car manufacturer Lotus in 1953, where his all-round engineering skills resulted in his being promoted to Technical Director in 1956. Keith Duckworth was born in 1933. After graduating in mechanical engineering from Imperial College London, Duckworth took on the job of 'transmission development engineer' with Lotus.

It was at Lotus that Duckworth and Costin first met and decided to establish Cosworth. According to Duckworth their aims and ambitions were pretty straightforward: 'We thought it must be possible to make an interesting living, messing about with racing cars and engines. That was the total objective behind the formation of Cosworth Engineering.' However, their first problem was that Mike Costin had recently entered into a 3-year service agreement with Lotus, which meant that he could not work for Cosworth until the agreement had expired. It was therefore left to Keith Duckworth to start their fledgling business on his own, using his own funds, with some 'unofficial' help from Costin.

Cosworth's first premises were rented and located in Shaftsbury Mews, London W8, not far from Kensington High Street. Yet, as far as Duckworth was concerned these premises were temporary, as he needed to find somewhere to install a dynamometer (or dyno), a device used to run and analyse engines while they were out of the car. Duckworth saw this as an essential investment for the future of Cosworth: 'As far as I could see none of the other tuning firms were using a dyno which was incredible. At least if we used a dyno we could prove we were getting somewhere.' The problem was that due to the noise and exhaust fumes created by testing an engine, a dynamometer required its own specialist facility. Duckworth eventually found the ideal spot: some old coaching stables in Friern Barnet, North London.

However, there was a problem with getting a dynamometer from the supplier: 'I had £1,000 of my own earmarked for a dyno, but it only cost £600 [note: £1000 in 1958 would be worth approximately £16,000 in 2006]. The wonderful situation was that the supplier was worried about my creditworthiness. . . . They put some credit inspectors on to the job to find out if I was credit worthy – and then they went and asked Mike [Costin – still officially at Lotus], and Mike kindly said that I was!'

Customers at the time ranged from wealthy individuals, who wanted their racing cars prepared, to manufacturers such as Lotus who required engines to be built and fitted as original equipment in their racing cars, such as the Lotus Elite which was built in Kenningdale Road, Edmonton, 4 miles east of Friern Barnet, a facility which would eventually become Cosworth's third location in 1961 following a tip-off from Mike Costin.

In 1959 interest was growing across Europe in a new racing formula 'Formula Junior'. Formula Junior was designed to be a nursery for budding racing drivers who could compete in relatively low-cost machinery, before progressing to the more expensive series, such as F1. The idea behind Formula Junior was that the cars required modified mass-production engines. This was clearly an opportunity for Cosworth and after an initial attempt to develop a modified version of the Fiat 1100cc Millecento engine, it was suggested to Duckworth, by a former fellow student and now customer, that he should look at a new engine developed by Ford for its new Anglia model, the 105E engine. Cosworth then secured a contract with Lotus to provide modified 105E engines for their Lotus 18 Formula Junior car. However, this was not a straightforward project and Duckworth experienced many technical challenges to get the engine to perform, including a total redesign of the camshaft to work at racing speeds. This almost bankrupted Cosworth at the end of 1959, as it had to carry all the development costs before it could deliver the engines to Lotus.

In 1960 the Cosworth-modified Ford 105E engine proved to be the most successful engine in Formula Junior, and during the first 10 months of the year they supplied 125 Formula Junior engines to Lotus alone. In this arrangement Lotus would buy the engines from Ford, send them to Cosworth who would strip them down and modify them and then return them to Lotus for a fixed fee. Cosworth also made their specially modified parts (such as the camshaft) available for other engine builders to use. 'Everyone was trying to tune 105E's at the time, but our A2 camshaft was the only one that would work for years afterwards. We used to sell it to our rivals for the outrageous sum of £17.50 to allow them to keep going.'

Cosworth used the services of a wide range of suppliers from distributors of basic components, such as bolts, washers and nuts, to specialist suppliers such as Heenan and Froude who produced dynamometers. Duckworth had a particular philosophy when dealing with suppliers and getting money from competitors which he described as follows: 'You extract your money promptly from customers, ensure that you pay up promptly, so that at any time the money in the bank represents your position, and you don't have to do much paperwork.' One of Cosworth's suppliers was specialist machine shop owner Ben Rood. Ben employed three people at his small workshop in Walthamstow and was rather taken aback by Keith Duckworth's approach to supplier relations: 'The important thing, the unbelievable thing, is that he used to pay me – without being asked. Everyone else was hanging fire and taking as long to pay as possible. But Keith would actually corner me and say "we owe you some money" and write a cheque.' This approach was matched by a similarly straightforward approach to managing cash flow:

'We never had an overdraft during the years that I owned Cosworth, or if we did, it was for purely technical purposes, just for a week or so. I managed to buy all our equipment on a totally self-financing basis. . . . When we had enough money, I used to go out and buy some machinery. I wouldn't buy anything until we had the money to pay for it, that's a good North Country habit'.

In 1962 Costin was released from his obligations at Lotus and was able to join Cosworth as a director. At that time Cosworth had around 22 employees and was a successful small business. However, as Cosworth grew they started to think about how they were going to develop the company:

'We used to spend the first week of our annual holiday shut-down having a running board meeting to work out what the strategy should be for the next year. We'd already had to change our views about 'making an interesting living, messing about ...'. Every year we had to sit down and think 'What on earth are we going to do next?' We'd all been so busy running our various departments throughout the year, that the only time there was any peace and quiet was when everyone else went on holiday for two weeks'.

Four individuals made up the senior management team, Keith Duckworth who focused on engine design, and was described by Costin as 'the guv'nor'; Costin, who concentrated more on development and getting the designs to work in practice; Ben Rood who looked after the production side (he had joined Cosworth after closing down his own machine shop business); and Bill Brown who ran the administration side. In 1963 they had 28 employees and were still based in Edmonton. They were now generating enough cash to make the notion of buying their next premises feasible and in 1964 they moved out of London to Northampton (50 miles north of London). By the end of the year they employed 50 people with a turnover of £160,000.

In 1965 the owner and CEO of Lotus, Colin Chapman, approached Keith Duckworth to explore whether Cosworth could build an F1 engine for Lotus. The problem that Chapman faced was that in 1963 motor racing's regulatory body had stipulated that from 1 January 1966 F1 engines could be either 3000cc normally aspirated or 1500cc turbo-charged. At that time Lotus had been successfully using 1500cc normally aspirated Coventry Climax F1 engines; however, in early 1965 Coventry Climax announced that it would not incur the costs of developing a brand new 3000cc engine and would withdraw from F1. Chapman therefore needed to find a new engine supplier, and ideally one that would help Lotus to win Grand Prix and World Championships. A natural place to start was with his two former employees. After discussing the idea with Chapman, Duckworth estimated that the entire design and development project would cost approximately £100,000. There was no detailed analysis, this was simply his ballpark estimate of how much it would cost.

Chapman then visited Walter Hayes of Ford. Hayes, who was keen to increase Ford's profile in F1, put the proposal to the board of Ford, again using the ballpark figure of £100,000, and secured their agreement to proceed. In fact, the agreement was not to produce one but two engines: a four-cylinder Formula 2 engine, known as the FVA, which when doubled up in a 'V' formation created the eight-cylinder F1 engine, the DFV.

The engine was developed in 1966 along with a new Lotus F1 car, the Lotus 49. The Lotus 49 had been specifically designed around the Cosworth DFV (publicly known as a Ford DFV engine), with the engine forming an integral part of the structure of the car. The car engine package had its first competitive appearance at the Dutch Grand Prix at Zandvoort on 4 June 1967 and convincingly won its first race. While Ford was delighted with the success of the project, Hayes had some misgivings regarding the potential dominance of the Lotus–Cosworth package: 'Almost at once I began to think that we might destroy the sport. I realised that we had to widen the market for the DFV engine, so that other teams could have access to it.'

In 1968, Ford took the decision to make the DFV available to other F1 teams; Cosworth's first customer was Tyrrell Racing's Ken Tyrrell:

'This meant that anyone with enough money, and in the first year it was only £7,500, went to Cosworth, you bought the engine and you came away with an engine that was capable of winning the next race and that went on for many years. This is the reason why there are so many British Formula 1 teams – because that engine was available'.

The Cosworth DFV changed the balance of power away from the vertically integrated teams who built their own engines, such as Ferrari, BRM and Honda, to those who concentrated on building the chassis and bought in the engines from Cosworth; these included teams such as Lotus, Tyrrell, McLaren, Brabham and Williams. These organisations focused on designing car chassis, suspensions systems, aerodynamics and other aspects of handling performance, safe in the knowledge that if they had the DFV engine they would be highly competitive.

In 1971 and 1973 every Grand Prix in the World Championship series was won by a car fitted with the Cosworth DFV engine. Initially Ford had vetted the potential customers for the DFV, but in the early 1970s Cosworth was free to sell engines to whomever it wanted. For Hayes this was about strengthening the capabilities at Cosworth rather than about making money for Ford:

'I thought it important that Keith should price the engine, and then he should sell them all. He would keep all the money he made – none would come to us – he would sell all the spare parts, and he would keep all the money he made from servicing and rebuilds. I hoped, I sincerely hoped, that this would make him rich enough to invest in a much more comprehensive facility to go on to do even greater things. I wanted to make Cosworth bigger, more powerful, and I wanted it to have more resources'.

The success of the DFV in F1 created a situation during the 1970s where Cosworth had far more customers than it could satisfy, and although there was some prioritisation, it was an important principle in Cosworth that every DFV should perform as well as the next, and that parts be standardised as much as possible. The success of the DFV 8-cylinder engine led a number of competitors to move to potentially more powerful 12-cylinder engines such as the V12 Eagle Weslake which was tried by Brabham and BRM. However, this engine was unsuccessful and the project was abandoned in 1974 having cost £150,000 to design and develop. Ferrari proved to have a more effective concept with the 'Flat 12' boxer engine, which demonstrated a potential performance advantage in the mid-1970s, as described by Brabham designer Gordon Murray, who was, in 1975, using Cosworth engines: '[H]alf way through that year it was pretty obvious that a twelve cylinder engine was going to end the reign of the DFV, because Ferrari didn't have any other magic at that time, they just powered away on all the quick circuits.' This led Brabham to explore other potential engine suppliers such as Porsche and they eventually contracted with Alfa Romeo to supply them with a 12-cylinder engine similar to that of Ferrari. For other F1 constructors, such as Lotus, their approach was to retain the DFV but to seek performance advantage through improved road-holding by innovative aerodynamics using what became known as 'ground effect'. Ground effect used the shape of the Cosworth DFV to allow two venturi or tunnels to create a low-pressure area under the car, thereby significantly increasing cornering speeds. The success of ground effect led to a resurgence in demand for the DFV in the late 1970s and early 1980s.

However, the early 1980s saw the introduction of a new technology in F1 engines – turbo-charging. Since 1966 the regulations had stated that an engine could either be 3000cc normally aspirated or 1500cc turbo-charged. The technology in 1966 was such that a 1500cc turbo engine would be totally uncompetitive. However, in 1977 Renault entered F1 with their own car and by using a 1500cc turbo-charged engine, they were able to demonstrate the potential of turbo-charging and firms such as Ferrari, Porsche and Honda quickly followed with their own versions, generating power levels far in excess of the normally aspirated DFV. Cosworth had also developed a turbo-charged version of the DFV, the DFX, which was targeted at the US open-wheel Indy car racing series and launched in 1975. The engine was successful and led to Cosworth establishing a new company, Cosworth Engineering Inc., at Torrance in California, to build, service and rebuild Indy car engines.

During the 1970s Cosworth had also begun to branch into other areas, producing a successful rally engine, the BDA, which was used in the world beating Ford Escort rally cars. They also produced high-performance road-worthy engines that were used in a number of Ford cars, General Motors'

Vauxhall Chevette HSR, and a high-performance version of the Mercedes Benz 190E. However, not all their innovations were successful: in 1969 they had tested their first (and last) attempt to build a racing car, the four-wheel drive Cosworth F1 car, which was shelved before it could be raced; a foray into motorcycle engines and F1 automatic transmissions were also aborted.

Cosworth's success during the 1970s led to its acquisition in 1980 by United Engineering Industries (UEI) Group, and its establishment as a separate division. In 1988 UEI was taken over by Carlton Communications, and Cosworth was then sold in 1990 to Vickers plc for £163.5 million. Vickers, a defence-based conglomerate, also owned Rolls-Royce Motor Cars, and in 1998 after experiencing difficulties in the core business sold both Rolls-Royce and Cosworth to VW. The VW subsidiary, the Audi Group, purchased Cosworth for £120 million and then sold the racing side of Cosworth Engineering to Ford, whom many considered to be Cosworth's rightful owner, and had certainly been its biggest customer, spending £50 million in 1999. Neil Ressler, Ford's Vice-President for Research and Vehicle Technology, became the new chairman of Cosworth and Dick Scammell, a Cosworth man from the DFV heyday, was brought out of retirement to become temporary Managing Director. Cosworth Racing was incorporated into Ford's Premier Performance division, and former Jaguar Cars executive Trevor Crisp became Managing Director and CEO. Crisp was close to retirement and in November 2001 was replaced by Brendan Connor as CEO and MD, with Nick Hayes being promoted to Engineering MD, to concentrate on the technical side of the business. However, changes in the Ford hierarchy led to Connor being replaced by Tim Routsis, the former MD of Ford's specialist electronics arm Pi Research, in October 2003. Hayes also stepped down from his MD role to become Technical Director. Ford then divested themselves of Cosworth in September 2004, selling it to owners of the US Champ Car series Gerard Forsythe and Kevin Karlkhoven.

References

This case study has been compiled using published sources and interviews. The following publications were particularly helpful:

Jenkins, M., K. Pasternak and R. West, *Performance at the Limit: Business Lessons from Formula 1 Motor Racing* (Cambridge: Cambridge University Press, 2005).
Robson, G., *Cosworth: The Search for Power* (Yeovil: Haynes Publishing, 1999).

Index